TOMARE!

[STOP!]

You are going the wrong way!

Manga is a completely different type of reading experience.

To start at the *beginning,* go to the *end*!

That's right! Authentic manga is read the traditional Japanese way— from right to left, exactly the opposite of how American books are read. It's easy to follow: Just go to the other end of the book, and read each page—and each panel—from the right side to the left side, starting at the top right. Now you're experiencing manga as it was meant to be.

-chan: This is used to express endearment, mostly toward girls. It is also used for little boys, pets, and even among lovers. It gives a sense of childish cuteness.

Bozu: This is an informal way to refer to a boy, similar to the English terms "kid" and "squirt."

Sempai/Senpai: This title suggests that the addressee is one's senior in a group or organization. It is most often used in a school setting, where underclassmen refer to their upperclassmen as "sempai." It can also be used in the workplace, such as when a newer employee addresses an employee who has seniority in the company.

Kohai: This is the opposite of "sempai" and is used toward underclassmen in school or newcomers in the workplace. It connotes that the addressee is of a lower station.

Sensei: Literally meaning "one who has come before," this title is used for teachers, doctors, or masters of any profession or art.

-[blank]: This is usually forgotten in these lists, but it is perhaps the most significant difference between Japanese and English. The lack of honorific means that the speaker has permission to address the person in a very intimate way. Usually, only family, spouses, or very close friends have this kind of permission. Known as yobisute, it can be gratifying when someone who has earned the intimacy starts to call one by one's name without an honorific. But when that intimacy hasn't been earned, it can be very insulting.

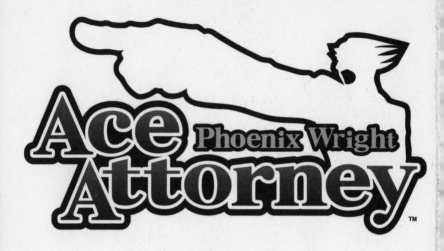

Ace Phoenix Wright Attorney™

VOLUME FOUR

Story by Kenji Kuroda
Art by Kazuo Maekawa
Supervised by CAPCOM

Translated and adapted by Alethea Nibley and Athena Nibley

Lettered by Karl Felton

KC
KODANSHA
COMICS

This book is a faithful translation of the book
released in Japan on July 4, 2008.

A Kodansha Comics Trade Paperback Original.

Phoenix Wright: Ace Attorney™ volume 4 copyright © 2008 CAPCOM/Kenji Kuroda/Kazuo Maekawa
English translation copyright © 2011 CAPCOM/Kenji Kuroda/Kazuo Maekawa

Published in the United States by Kodansha Comics, an imprint of Kodansha USA Publishing, LLC., New York.

Publication rights for this English edition arranged through Kodansha Ltd., Tokyo.

First published in Japan in 2008 by Kodansha Ltd., Tokyo.

ISBN 978-1-935-42972-2
Printed in the United States of America.

www.kodanshacomics.com

2 3 4 5 6 7 8 9

Translators: Alethea Nibley and Athena Nibley
Lettering: Karl Felton

CONTENTS

Honorifics Explained

Throughout the Kodansha Comics books, you will find Japanese honorifics left intact in the translations. For those not familiar with how the Japanese use honorifics and, more important, how they differ from American honorifics, we present this brief overview.

Politeness has always been a critical facet of Japanese culture. Ever since the feudal era, when Japan was a highly stratified society, use of honorifics—which can be defined as polite speech that indicates relationship or status—has played an essential role in the Japanese language. When addressing someone in Japanese, an honorific usually takes the form of a suffix attached to one's name (example: "Asuna-san"), is used as a title at the end of one's name, or appears in place of the name itself (example: "Negi-sensei," or simply "Sensei!").

Honorifics can be expressions of respect or endearment. In the context of manga and anime, honorifics give insight into the nature of the relationship between characters. Many English translations leave out these important honorifics and therefore distort the feel of the original Japanese. Because Japanese honorifics contain nuances that English honorifics lack, it is our policy at Kodansha Comics not to translate them. Here, instead, is a guide to some of the honorifics you may encounter in Kodansha Comics books.

-san: This is the most common honorific and is equivalent to Mr., Miss, Ms., or Mrs. It is the all-purpose honorific and can be used in any situation where politeness is required.

-sama: This is one level higher than "-san" and is used to confer great respect.

-dono: This comes from the word "tono," which means "lord." It is an even higher level than "-sama" and confers utmost respect.

-kun: This suffix is used at the end of boys' names to express familiarity or endearment. It is also sometimes used by men among friends, or when addressing someone younger or of a lower station.

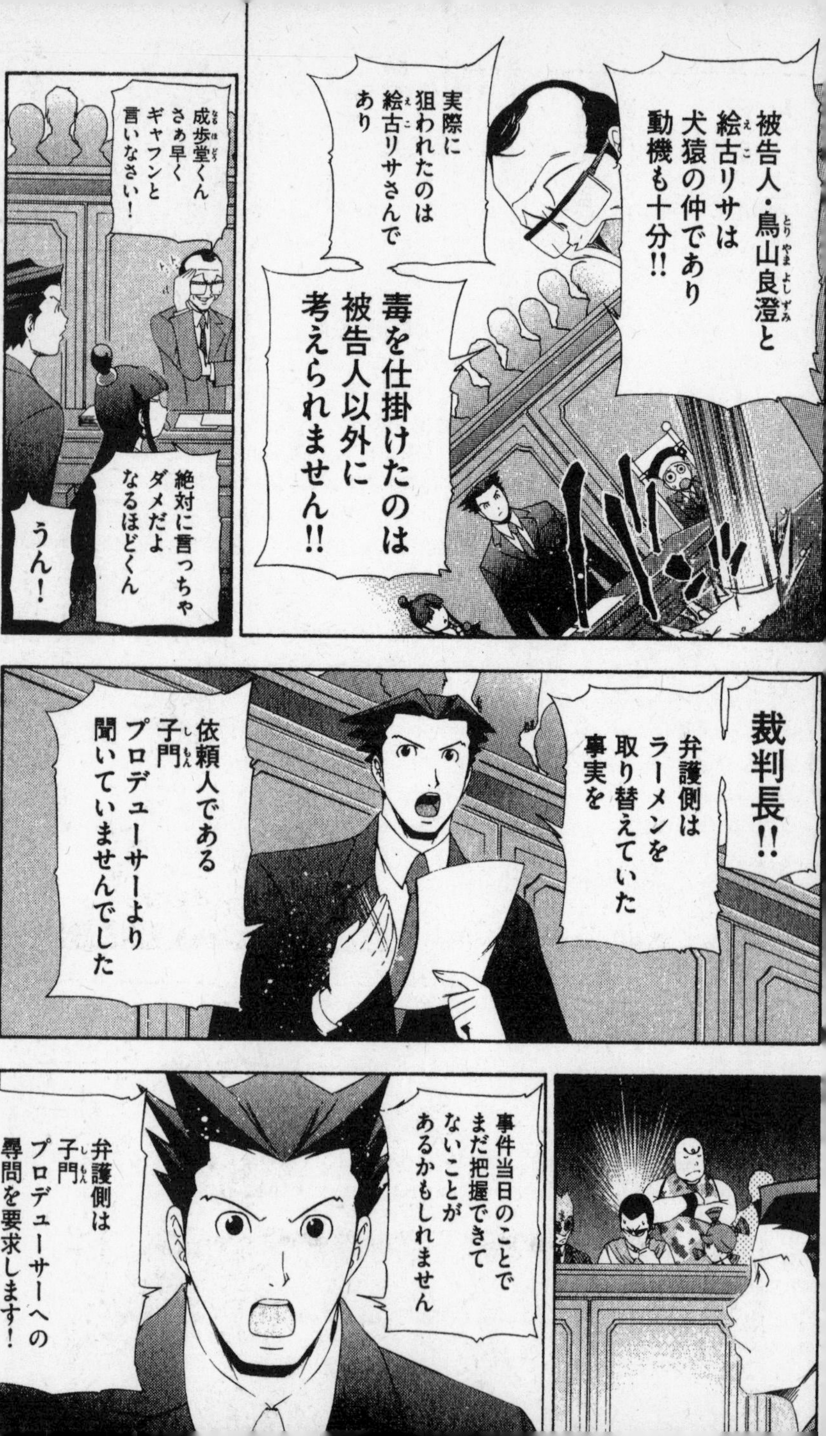
被告人・鳥山良澄と絵古リサは犬猿の仲であり動機も十分!!
実際に狙われたのは絵古リサさんであり
毒を仕掛けたのは被告人以外に考えられません!!
成歩堂くんさぁ早くギャフンと言いなさい!
絶対に言っちゃダメだよなるほどくん
うん!
裁判長!!
弁護側はラーメンを取り替えていた事実を
依頼人である子門プロデューサーより聞いていませんでした
事件当日のことでまだ把握できてないことがあるかもしれません
弁護側は子門プロデューサーへの尋問を要求します!

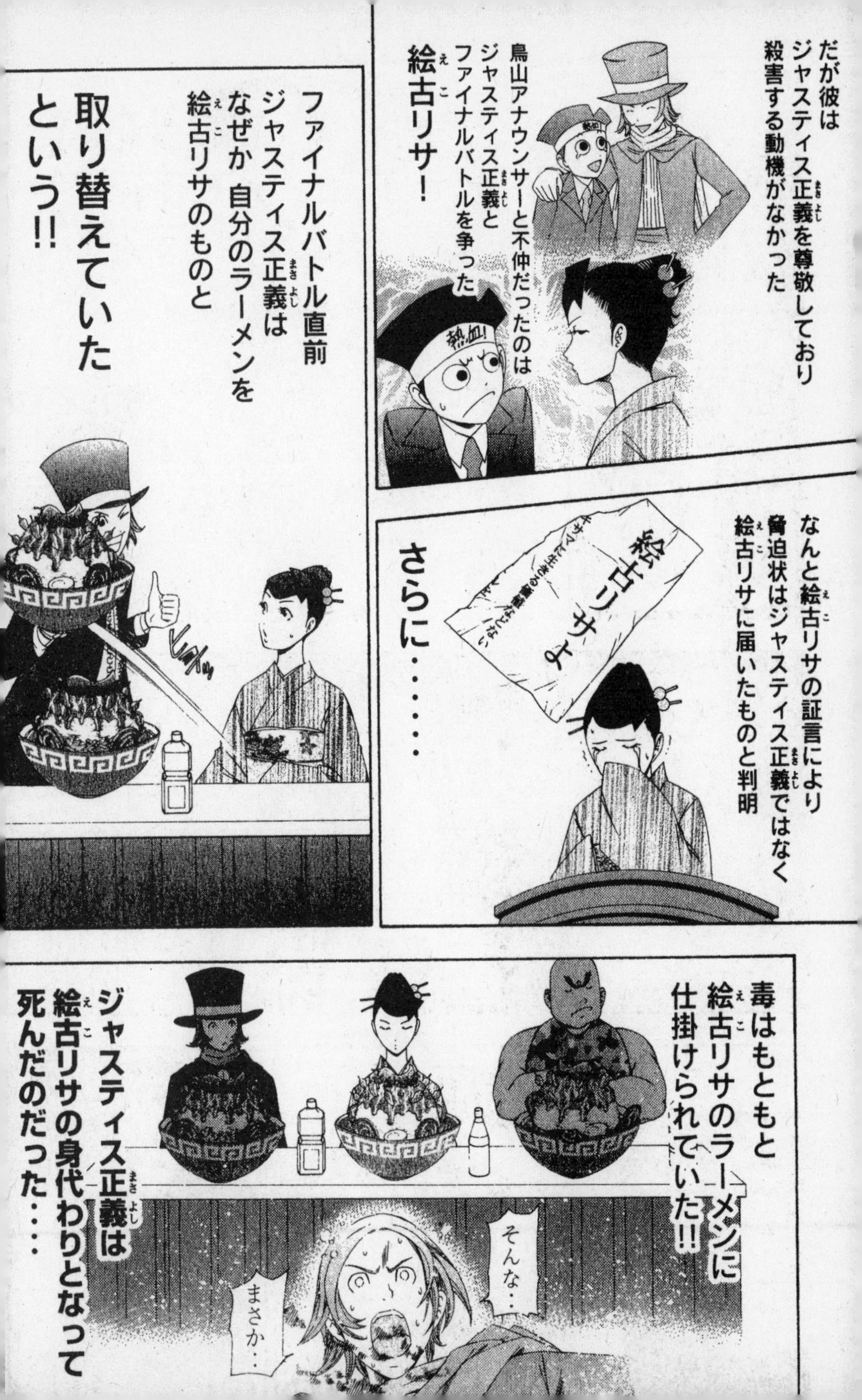

だが彼は
ジャスティス正義を尊敬しており
殺害する動機がなかった
鳥山アナウンサーと不仲だったのは
ジャスティス正義と
ファイナルバトルを争った
絵古リサ！
なんと絵古リサの証言により
脅迫状はジャスティス正義ではなく
絵古リサに届いたものと判明
絵古リサよ
さらに・・・・・・
ファイナルバトル直前
ジャスティス正義は
なぜか 自分のラーメンを
絵古リサのものと
取り替えていた
という!!
毒はもともと
絵古リサのラーメンに
仕掛けられていた!!
ジャスティス正義は
絵古リサの身代わりとなって
死んだのだった・・・
そんな・・・
まさか・・・

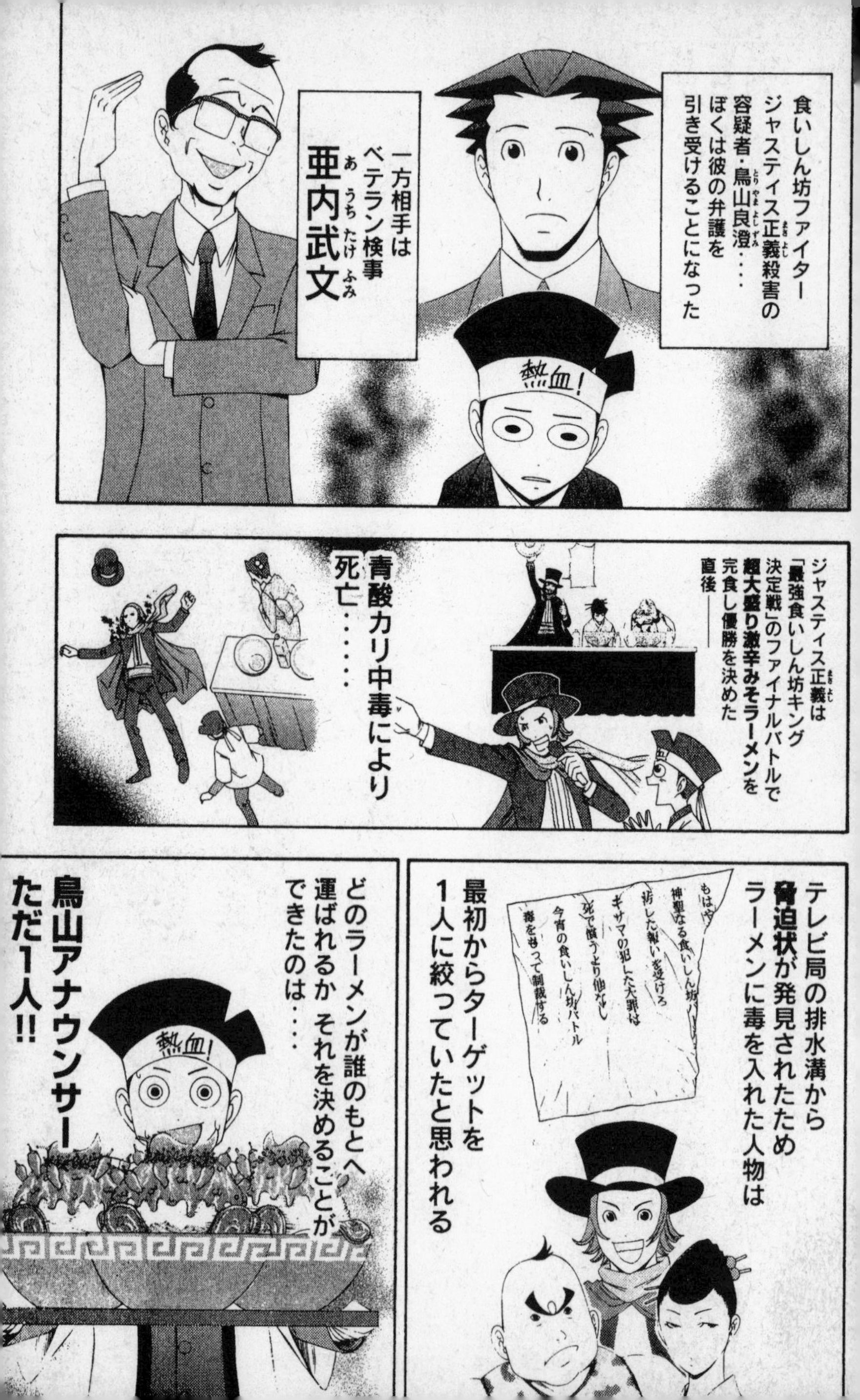
食いしん坊ファイター
ジャスティス正義殺害の
容疑者・鳥山良澄・・・・
ぼくは彼の弁護を
引き受けることになった
一方相手は
ベテラン検事
亜内武文
熱血!
ジャスティス正義は「最強食いしん坊キング決定戦」のファイナルバトルで超大盛り激辛みそラーメンを完食し優勝を決めた直後——
青酸カリ中毒により死亡……
テレビ局の排水溝から脅迫状が発見されたため
ラーメンに毒を入れた人物は
もはや
神聖なる食いしん坊
汚した報いを受けろ
キサマの犯した大罪は
死で償うより他なし
今宵の食いしん坊バトル
毒をもって制裁する
最初からターゲットを1人に絞っていたと思われる
どのラーメンが誰のもとへ運ばれるか それを決めることができたのは・・・・
熱血!
鳥山アナウンサーただ1人!!

第13話
逆転食いしん坊《後編》

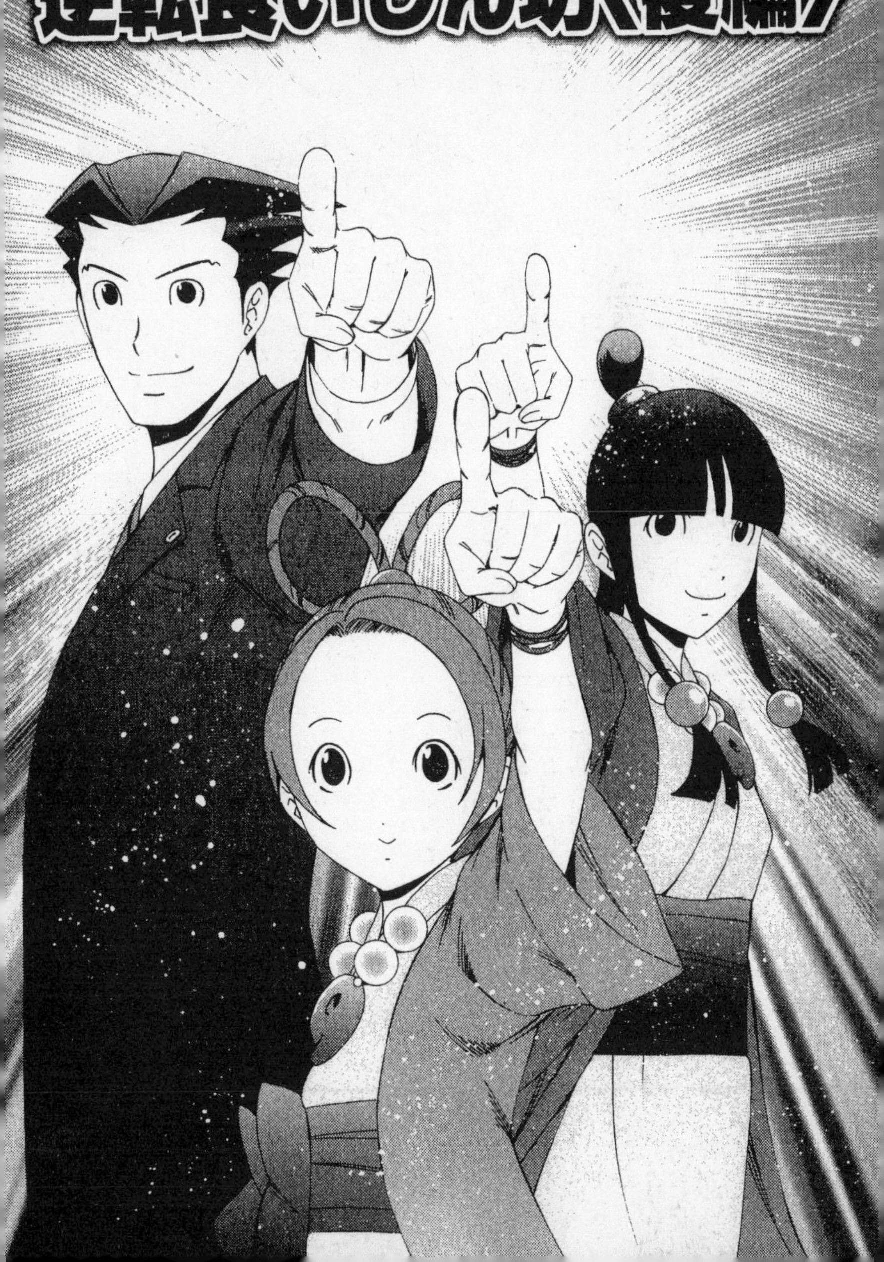

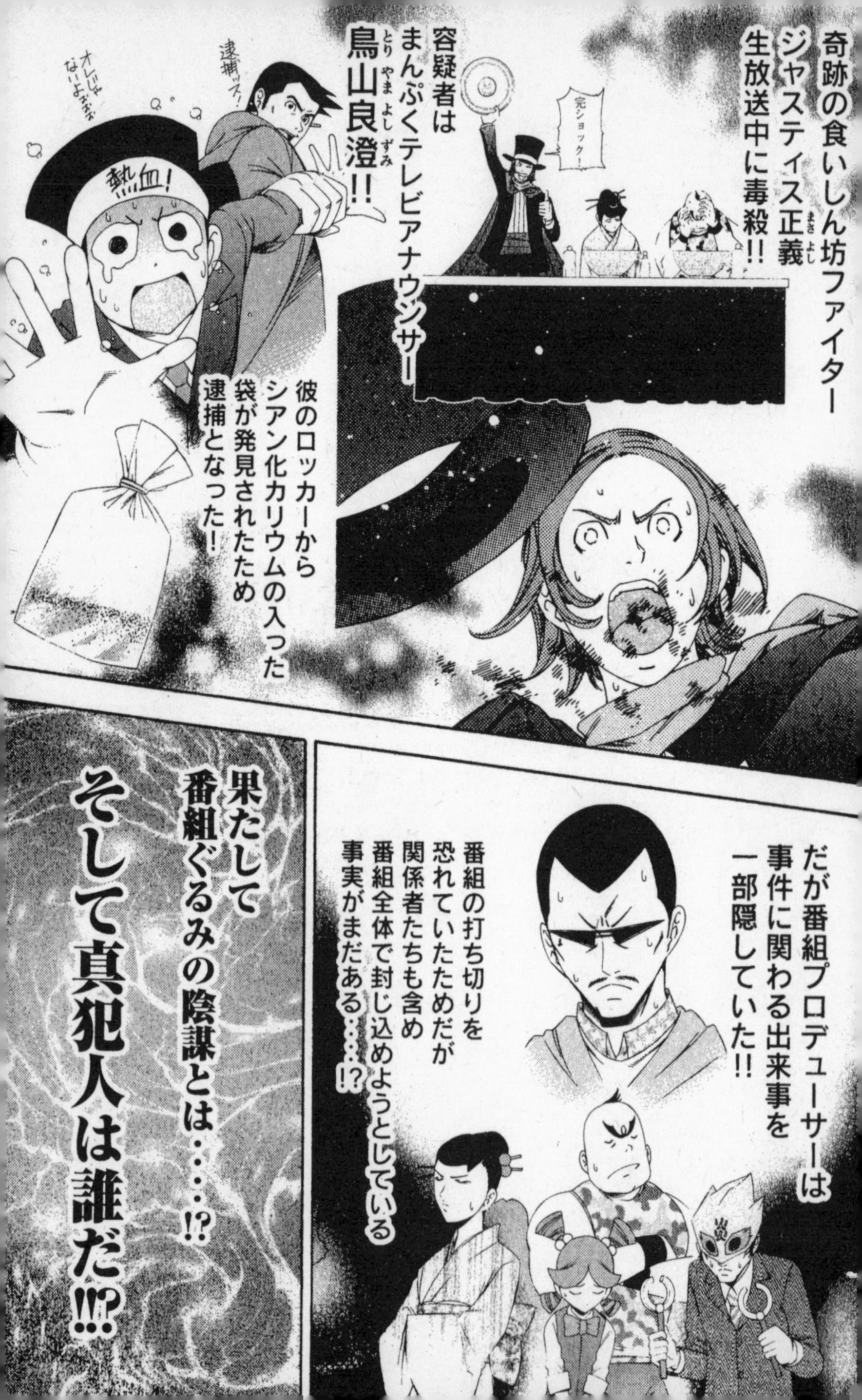

奇跡の食いしん坊ファイター
ジャスティス正義
生放送中に毒殺!!
完ショック!
容疑者は
まんぷくテレビアナウンサー
鳥山良澄!!
逮捕ッス!
オレじゃないよぉぉぉ
熱血!
彼のロッカーから
シアン化カリウムの入った
袋が発見されたため
逮捕となった!
だが番組プロデューサーは
事件に関わる出来事を
一部隠していた!!
番組の打ち切りを
恐れていたためだが
関係者たちも含め
番組全体で封じ込めようとしている
事実がまだある・・・・!?
果たして
番組ぐるみの陰謀とは・・・・!?
そして真犯人は誰だ!!?

Preview of

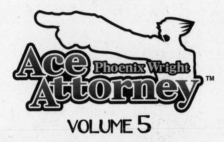

Ace Attorney
Phoenix Wright
VOLUME 5

We're pleased to present you a preview from
Phoenix Wright: Ace Attorney™, volume 5.
Please check our website
(www.kodanshacomics.com) to see when this
volume will be available in English. For now you'll
have to make do with Japanese!

Michizane Shimon, Carl Caesar
A shimon'ya is someone who would go through the streets (michi) selling cheap food. This made us think of fast food, so we named him Carl after Carl's Jr., and Caesar after Little Caesar's. We thought of a few other names like Carl Rubio and Carl LaRosa, but we thought Rubio and LaRosa might be too local, and not very widely familiar.

Ran Tatsumaki, Gale Cyclone
This character is named after her tornado of mayonnaise, and her tornado hair. Ran means "storm" and tatsumaki means "tornado." Hence, Gale Cyclone.

Kaen Homura, Caliente del Fuego
Kaen and homura both mean "flame," so we wanted to give him a name that was "hot."

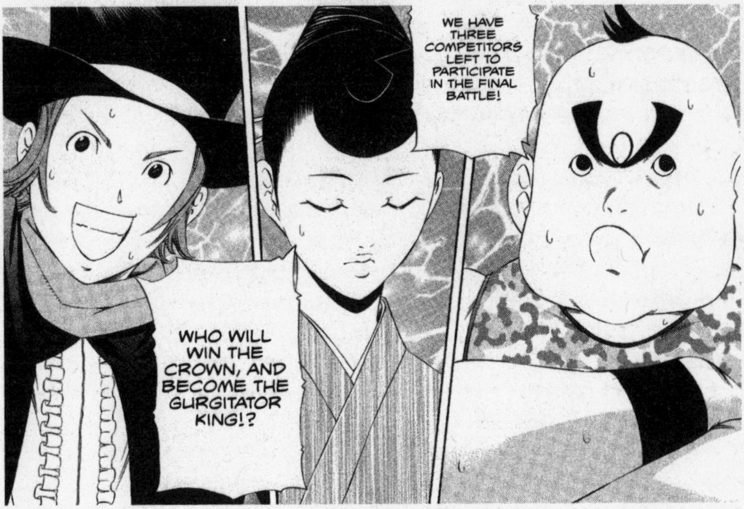
WE HAVE THREE COMPETITORS LEFT TO PARTICIPATE IN THE FINAL BATTLE!
WHO WILL WIN THE CROWN, AND BECOME THE GURGITATOR KING!?

Muscle Taketora, Arnold "Muscles" Balboa

The Gormand Fighters use stage names. His is Muscle Taketora. Muscle is pretty obvious, and Taketora means "strong tiger," being a reference to his muscliness. We kept the name "Muscles" as a nickname (making it plural, because that's how we do that in the States) and gave him a couple of really strong sounding names: Arnold from Arnold Schwarzenegger and Balboa as in Rocky Balboa.

Risa Eko, Risa Iko

The important thing in Risa Eko (or Eko Lisa, as it would be pronounced in the original Japanese) is the pun on ecology. Because her character design is very Japanese, we wanted to give her Japanese names, but we changed Eko to Iko, to make the name sound a little like "recycle."

Justice Masayoshi, Milo "Fairplay" Kent

Masayoshi, like Justice, means "justice." Thanks to Apollo Justice, we can't use this name. Instead, we gave him the nickname Fairplay, because he always plays fair, and the last name Kent, after Superman's alterego. We gave him the first name Milo, because it means "merciful," and because we wanted to keep the alliteration with his magician name, Magical Masayoshi (Magical Milo).

Manpüku, El Breakfast Nook
Manpüku is the Japanese word for "full stomach (manpuku)" with an American accent. Since they serve omelets, we called it a breakfast nook, and for the faux ethnic feel, we stuck an "el" at the beginning of it.

Umasoba Ichiban, Top Kitty Noodles
Ichiban is part of a brand name of soba noodles in Japan, and Top Ramen is part of a brand of ramen in the States. Since there's a cat on the packaging, we thought it would be safe to call it Top Kitty (but not Top Cat, because that's a copyrighted cartoon character). Umasoba Ichiban means "yummy soba number one."

Turnabout Gurgitation

Yoshizumi Toriyama, Kevin Hattori
Yoshizumi is the name of an announcer in Japan. We couldn't quite figure out what Toriyama is a reference to, but it means "bird mountain," and can refer to the giant gatherings of birds over parts of the ocean where the most fish can be found. For now, we've decided to go with Kevin Hattori, after Yukio Hattori (a commentator on "Iron Chef") and Kevin Brauch (an announcer on "Iron Chef: America").

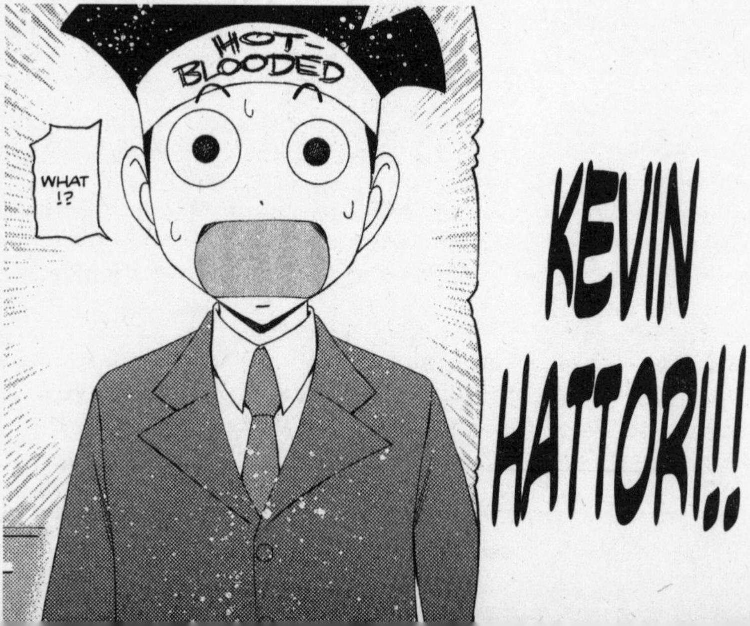
KEVIN HATTORI!!
HOT-BLOODED
WHAT !?

Yumeko Aizawa, Dreama Love
Pretty straightforward. Dreama comes from the yume (dream) in Yumeko, and Love comes from the ai (love) in Aizawa.

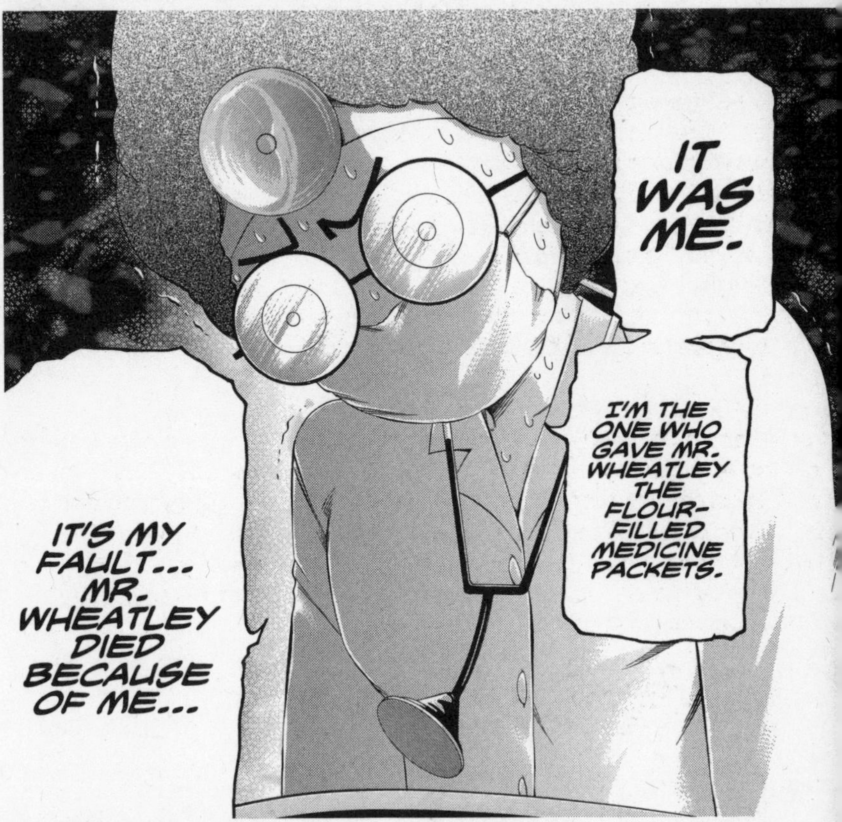
IT WAS ME.
I'M THE ONE WHO GAVE MR. WHEATLEY THE FLOUR-FILLED MEDICINE PACKETS.
IT'S MY FAULT... MR. WHEATLEY DIED BECAUSE OF ME...

Morie Kidai, Alice Butler
Kidai is a very polite term to refer to someone's house, and morie comes from moru, to serve (as in food). We named her Alice after the housekeeper in *"The Brady Bunch,"* and Butler because she's a housekeeper.

Dream Clinic, Sogni d'Oro Clinic
We thought "Dream Clinic" would be too close to the name "Dreama," so we changed her clinic's name to the Italian for sweet dreams, Sogni d'Oro (literally "golden dreams").

Tsukimi Kanenari, Diana Wheatley
Tsukimi means "beauty of the moon," so we named her Diana after the Roman goddess.

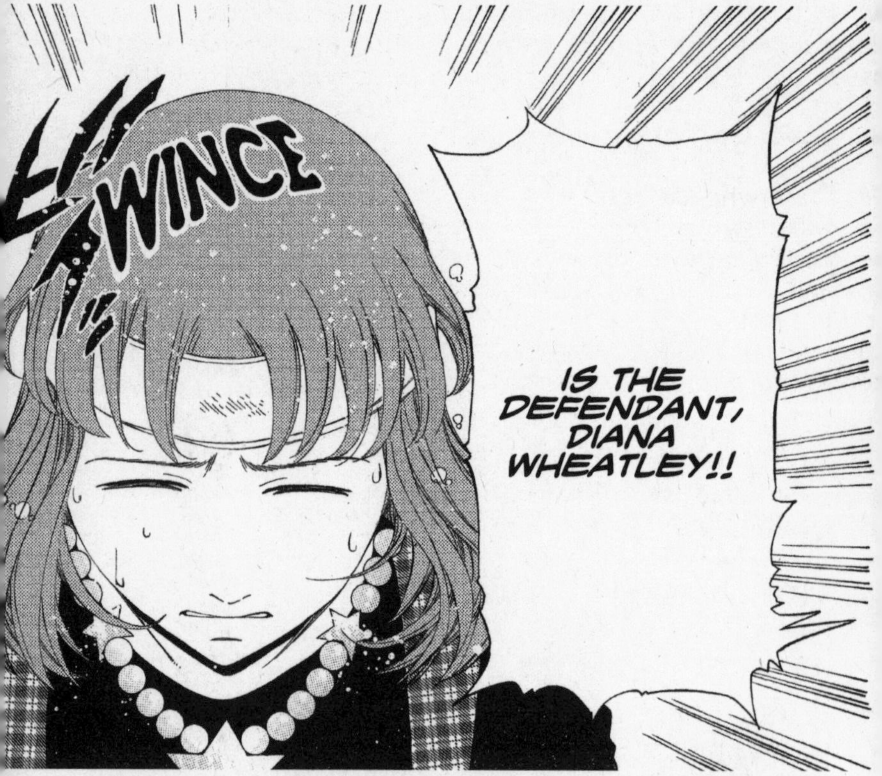
WINCE
IS THE DEFENDANT, DIANA WHEATLEY!!

Kasumi Kanenari, Vale Wheatley,
Kasumi means mist, but the obvious English version of that name, Misty, is already the name of a prominent character in the Ace Attorney series. We took the "mist" to be a reference to the haziness of Tsukimi's memories, and called Kasumi "Vale," as a play on "veil."

TRANSLATION NOTES

Japanese is a tricky language for most Westerners, and translation is often more art than science. For your edification and reading pleasure, here are notes on some of the places where we could have gone in a different direction with our translation of the work, or where a Japanese cultural reference is used.

Beetroots and betrothal, page 18

For those who are interested, the pun in the Japanese version was based on kon'yaku (betrothal) and konnyaku, or konjac, a kind of plant used to make jellies, and as an ingredient in all kinds of things. The foods Maya lists are konnyaku salad, shirataki soup (shirataki are noodles made from konnyaku), ito-konnyaku spaghetti (ito-konnyaku is another kind of noodle made from konnyaku), and of course, red konnyaku steak.

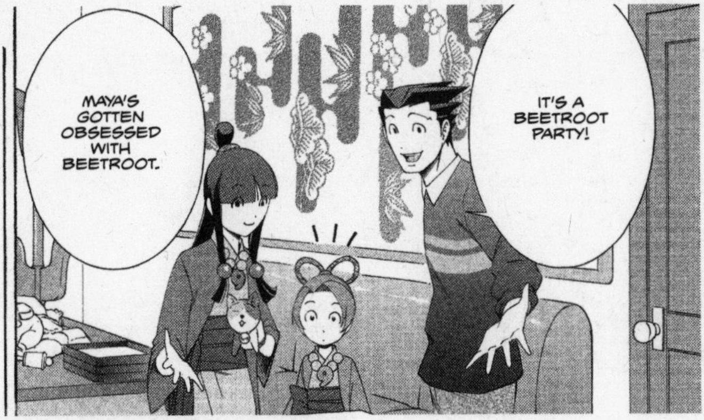
IT'S A BEETROOT PARTY!
MAYA'S GOTTEN OBSESSED WITH BEETROOT.

Gyakuten Saiban name notes

Turnabout from Heaven

Nihachi Kanenari, Buck Wheatley
Nihachi-soba (or two-eight soba) is a reference to a kind of soba, which is two parts udon flour and eight parts soba (buckwheat) flour. Kanenari is a reference to money, and how wealthy he is. We called him Buck Wheatley, relying mostly on the pun, but also on the fact that "buck" is slang for money.

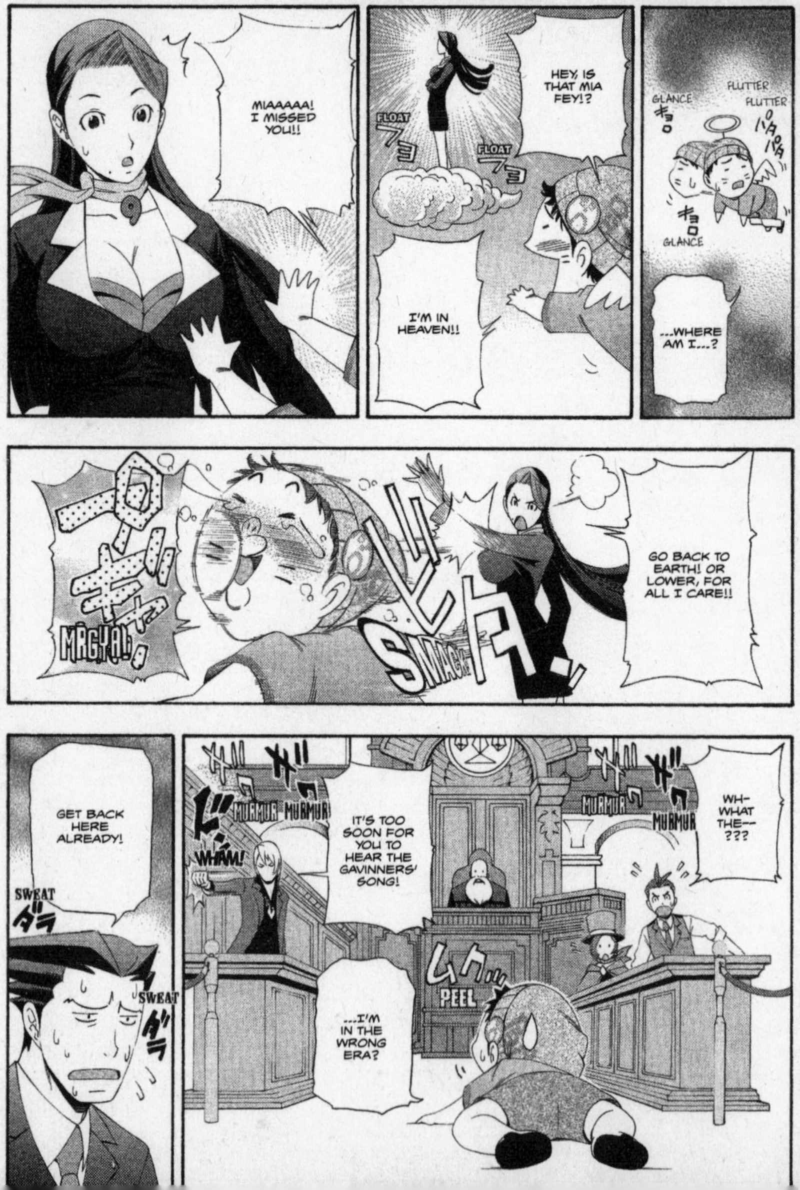

GLANCE
FLUTTER
FLUTTER
GLANCE
...WHERE AM I...?
HEY, IS THAT MIA FEY!?
FLOAT
FLOAT
I'M IN HEAVEN!!
MIAAAAA! I MISSED YOU!!
GO BACK TO EARTH! OR LOWER, FOR ALL I CARE!!
SMACK
MRGYAH!
WH- WHAT THE--???
MURMUR
MURMUR
IT'S TOO SOON FOR YOU TO HEAR THE GAVINNERS' SONG!
MURMUR
MURMUR
WHAM!
PEEL
...I'M IN THE WRONG ERA?
GET BACK HERE ALREADY!
SWEAT
SWEAT

JULY 20, 10:17 AM
LORDLY TAILOR MAIN EXHIBITION HALL

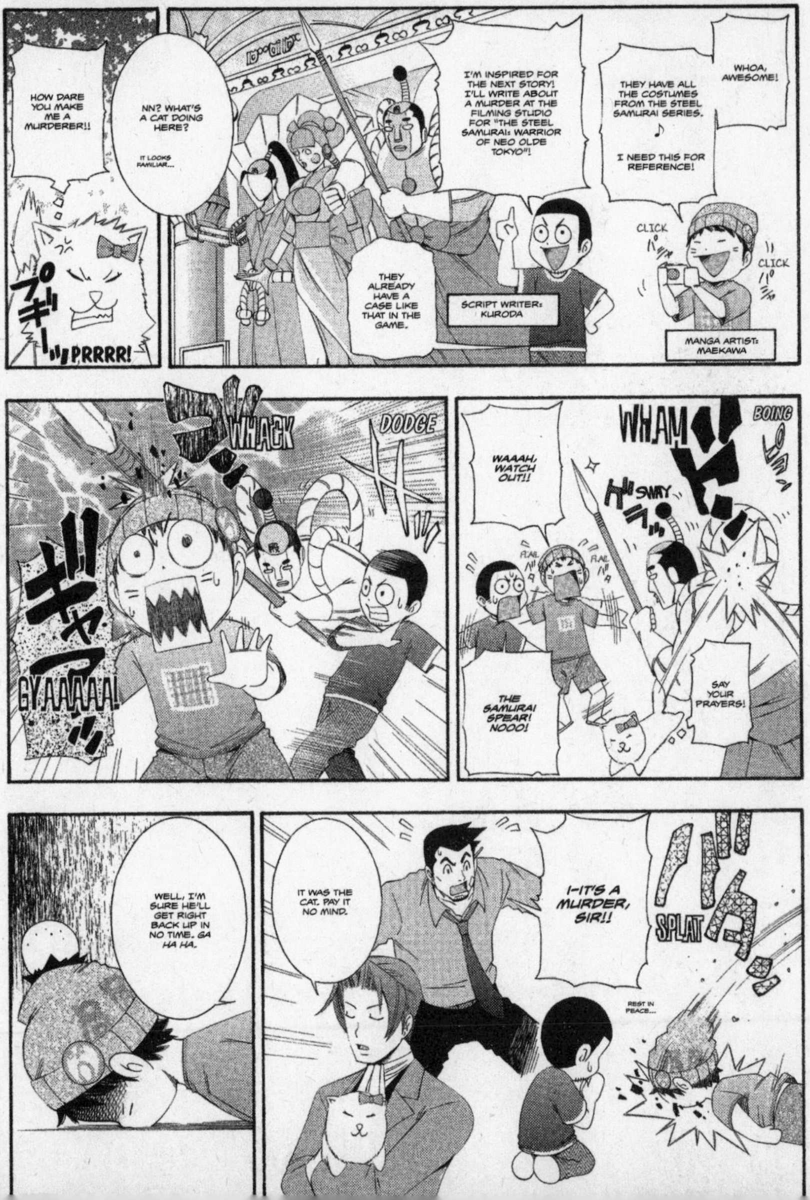
WHOA, AWESOME!
THEY HAVE ALL THE COSTUMES FROM THE STEEL SAMURAI SERIES. ♪
I NEED THIS FOR REFERENCE!
CLICK
CLICK
I'M INSPIRED FOR THE NEXT STORY! I'LL WRITE ABOUT A MURDER AT THE FILMING STUDIO FOR "THE STEEL SAMURAI: WARRIOR OF NEO OLDE TOKYO"!
MANGA ARTIST: MAEKAWA
SCRIPT WRITER: KURODA
THEY ALREADY HAVE A CASE LIKE THAT IN THE GAME.
NN? WHAT'S A CAT DOING HERE?
IT LOOKS FAMILIAR...
HOW DARE YOU MAKE ME A MURDERER!!
PRRRR!
BOING
WHAM
WAAAH, WATCH OUT!!
SWAY
FLAIL
FLAIL
SAY YOUR PRAYERS!
THE SAMURAI SPEAR! NOOO!
DODGE
WHACK
GYAAAAA!
SPLAT
I-IT'S A MURDER, SIR!!
IT WAS THE CAT. PAY IT NO MIND.
REST IN PEACE...
WELL, I'M SURE HE'LL GET RIGHT BACK UP IN NO TIME. GA HA HA.

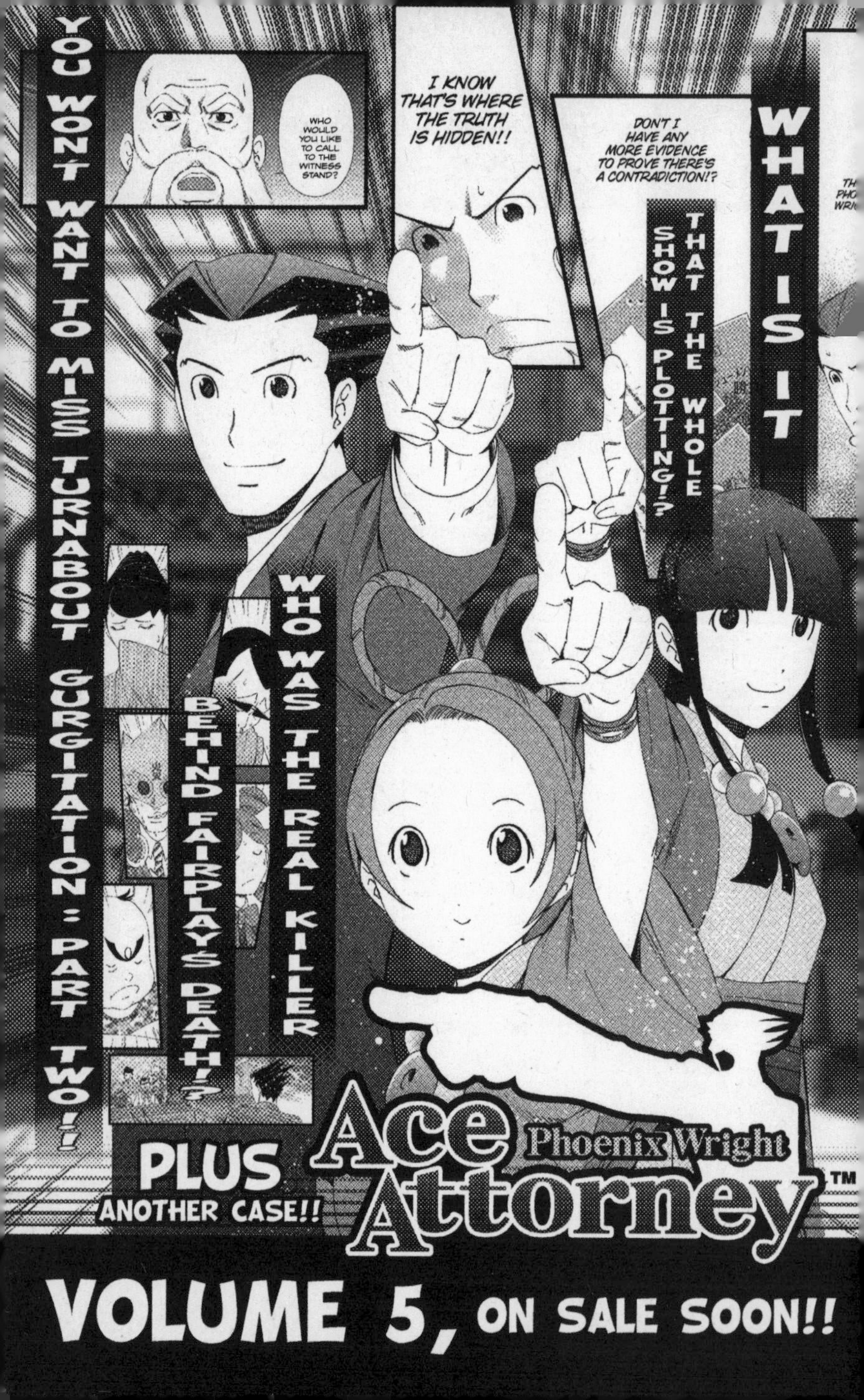
WHAT IS IT
THAT THE WHOLE SHOW IS PLOTTING!?
DON'T I HAVE ANY MORE EVIDENCE TO PROVE THERE'S A CONTRADICTION!?
I KNOW THAT'S WHERE THE TRUTH IS HIDDEN!!
WHO WOULD YOU LIKE TO CALL TO THE WITNESS STAND?
YOU WON'T WANT TO MISS TURNABOUT GURGITATION : PART TWO!!
WHO WAS THE REAL KILLER
BEHIND FAIRPLAY'S DEATH!?
PLUS ANOTHER CASE!!
Phoenix Wright Ace Attorney™
VOLUME 5, ON SALE SOON!!

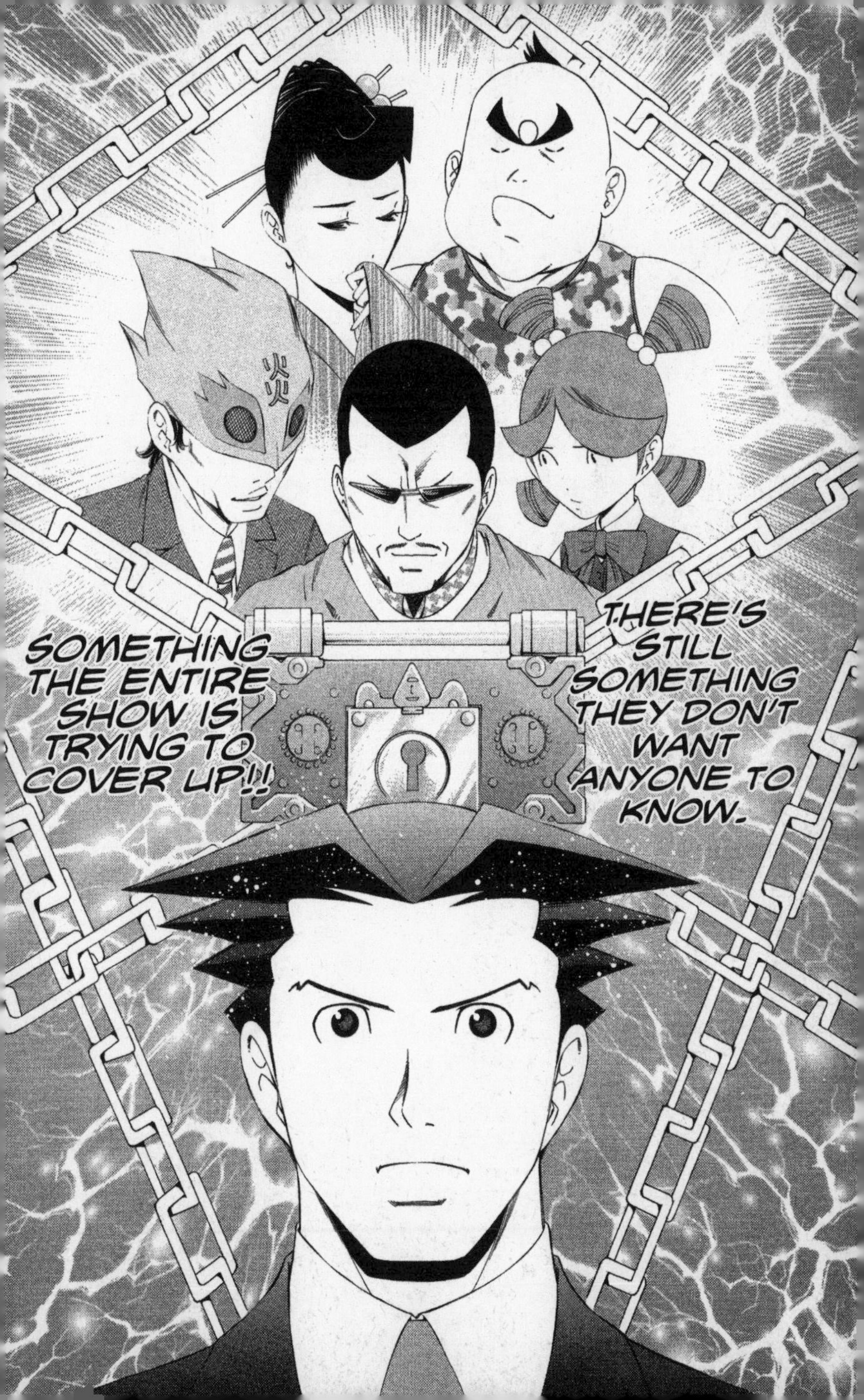
THERE'S STILL SOMETHING THEY DON'T WANT ANYONE TO KNOW.
SOMETHING THE ENTIRE SHOW IS TRYING TO COVER UP!!

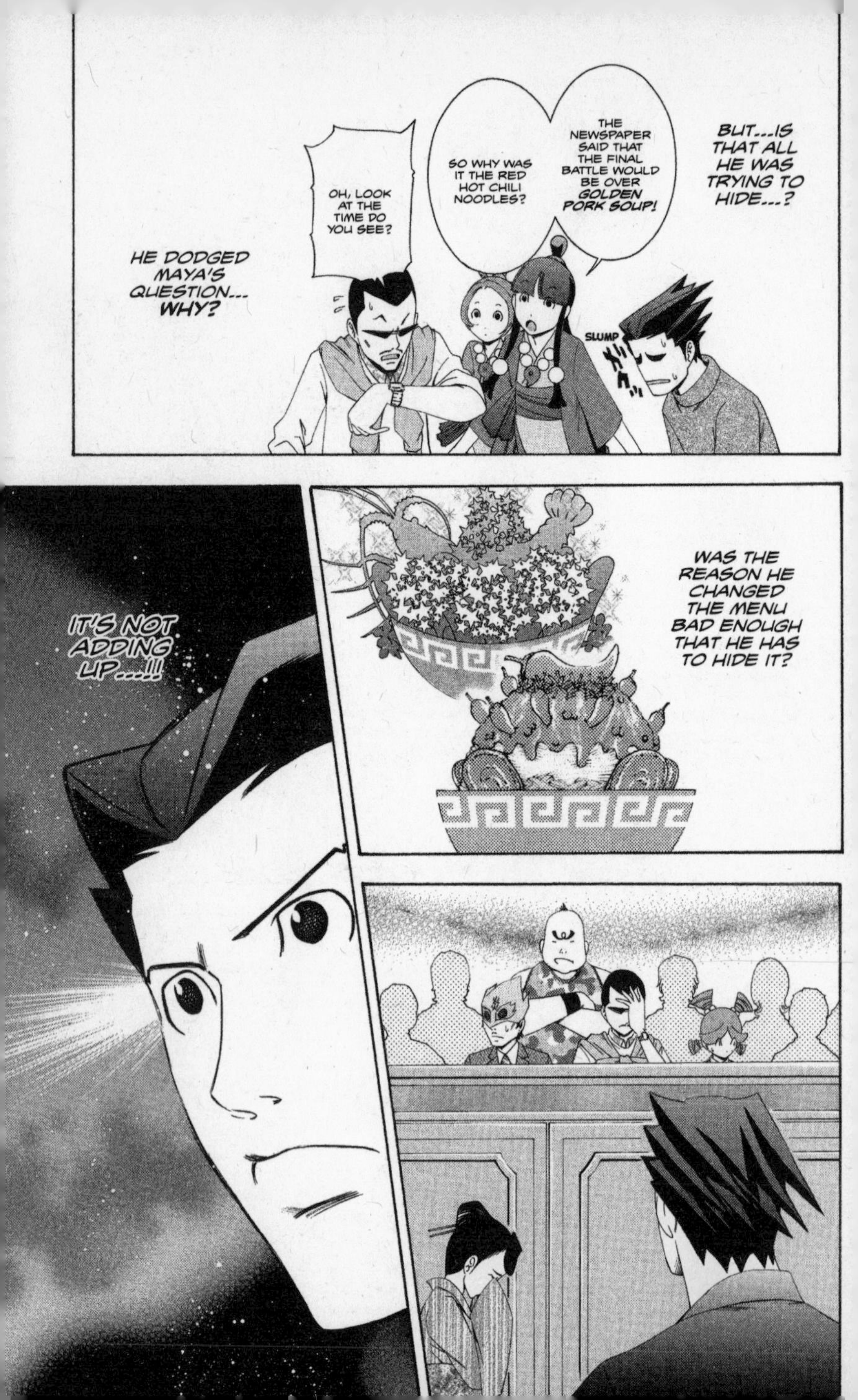
BUT...IS THAT ALL HE WAS TRYING TO HIDE...?
THE NEWSPAPER SAID THAT THE FINAL BATTLE WOULD BE OVER GOLDEN PORK SOUP!
SO WHY WAS IT THE RED HOT CHILI NOODLES?
OH, LOOK AT THE TIME DO YOU SEE?
SLUMP
HE DODGED MAYA'S QUESTION... WHY?
WAS THE REASON HE CHANGED THE MENU BAD ENOUGH THAT HE HAS TO HIDE IT?
IT'S NOT ADDING UP...!!!

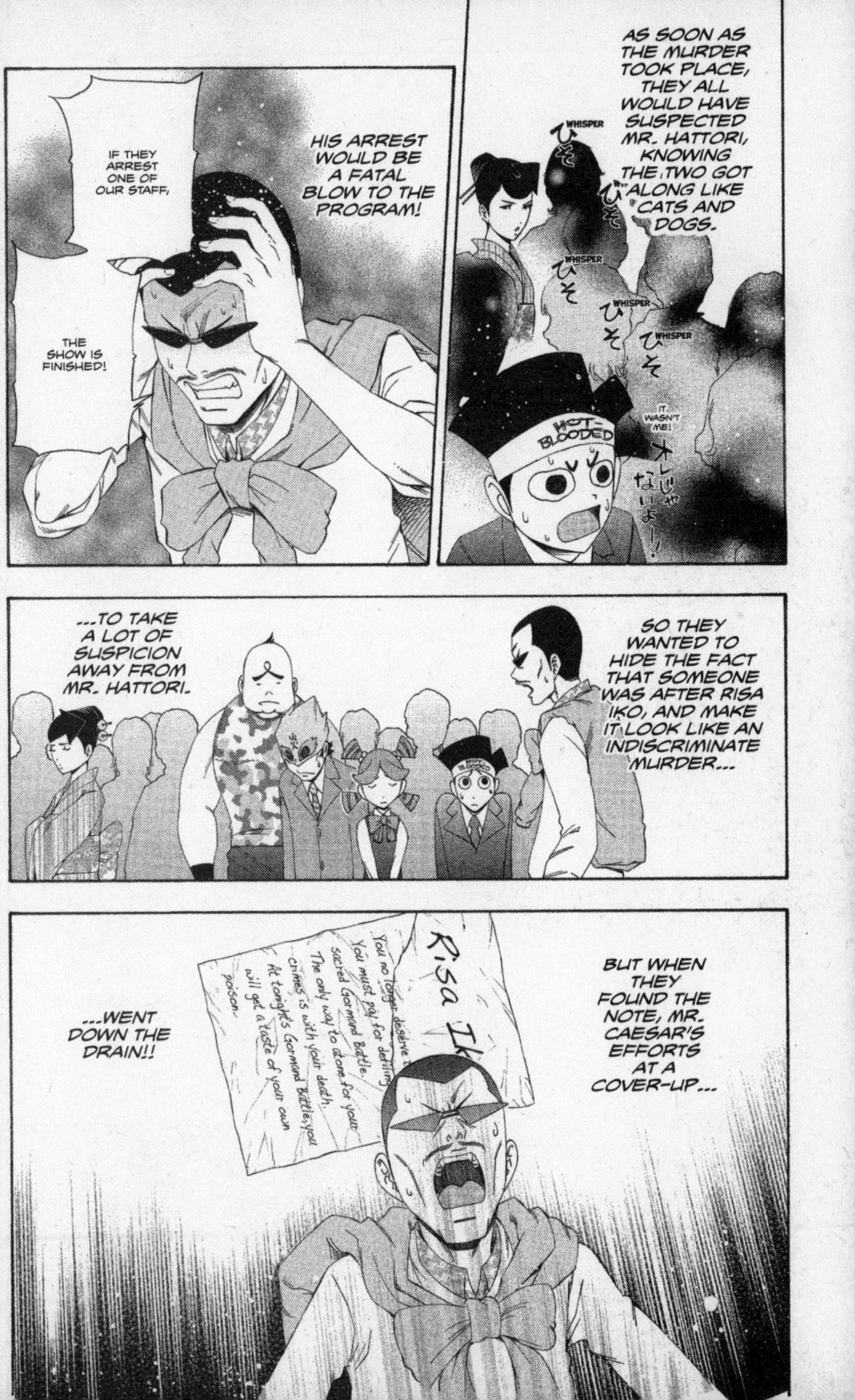
AS SOON AS THE MURDER TOOK PLACE, THEY ALL WOULD HAVE SUSPECTED MR. HATTORI, KNOWING THE TWO GOT ALONG LIKE CATS AND DOGS.
WHISPER
ひそ
WHISPER
ひそ
WHISPER
ひそ
WHISPER
ひそ
HOT-BLOODED
IT WASN'T ME!
オレじゃないよー!!
HIS ARREST WOULD BE A FATAL BLOW TO THE PROGRAM!
IF THEY ARREST ONE OF OUR STAFF,
THE SHOW IS FINISHED!
SO THEY WANTED TO HIDE THE FACT THAT SOMEONE WAS AFTER RISA IKO, AND MAKE IT LOOK LIKE AN INDISCRIMINATE MURDER...
...TO TAKE A LOT OF SUSPICION AWAY FROM MR. HATTORI.
BUT WHEN THEY FOUND THE NOTE, MR. CAESAR'S EFFORTS AT A COVER-UP...
Risa Ik
You no longer deserve
You must pay for defiling
sacred Gormond Battle.
The only way to atone for your
crimes is with your death.
At tonight's Gormond Battle, you
will get a taste of your own
poison.
...WENT DOWN THE DRAIN!!

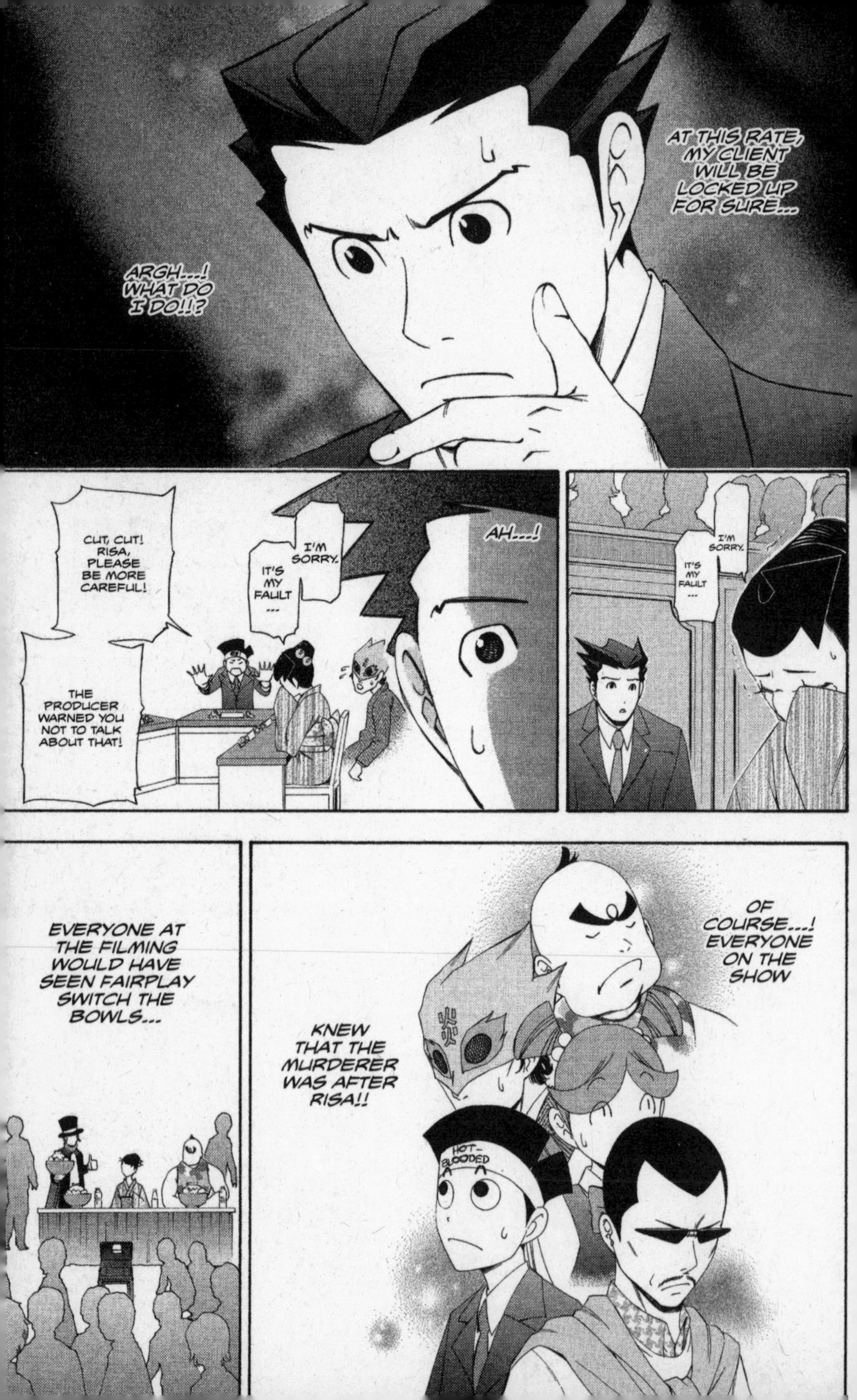
AT THIS RATE, MY CLIENT WILL BE LOCKED UP FOR SURE...
ARGH...! WHAT DO I DO!!?
I'M SORRY.
IT'S MY FAULT...
AH...!
I'M SORRY.
IT'S MY FAULT...
CUT, CUT! RISA, PLEASE BE MORE CAREFUL!
THE PRODUCER WARNED YOU NOT TO TALK ABOUT THAT!
OF COURSE...! EVERYONE ON THE SHOW
KNEW THAT THE MURDERER WAS AFTER RISA!!
HOT-BLOODED
EVERYONE AT THE FILMING WOULD HAVE SEEN FAIRPLAY SWITCH THE BOWLS...

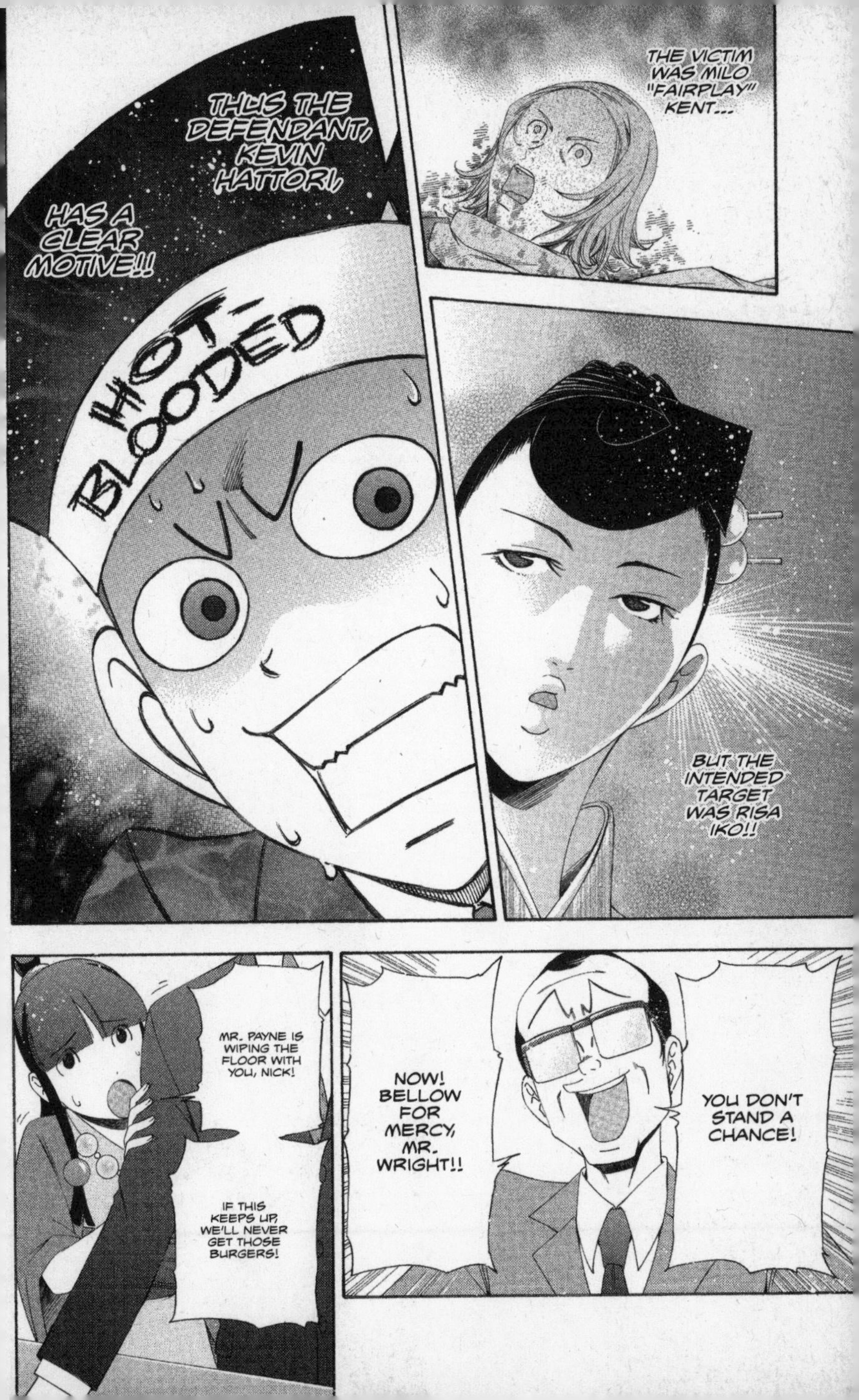
THE VICTIM WAS MILO "FAIRPLAY" KENT...
BUT THE INTENDED TARGET WAS RISA IKO!!
THUS THE DEFENDANT, KEVIN HATTORI,
HAS A CLEAR MOTIVE!!
HOT-BLOODED
YOU DON'T STAND A CHANCE!
NOW! BELLOW FOR MERCY, MR. WRIGHT!!
MR. PAYNE IS WIPING THE FLOOR WITH YOU, NICK!
IF THIS KEEPS UP, WE'LL NEVER GET THOSE BURGERS!

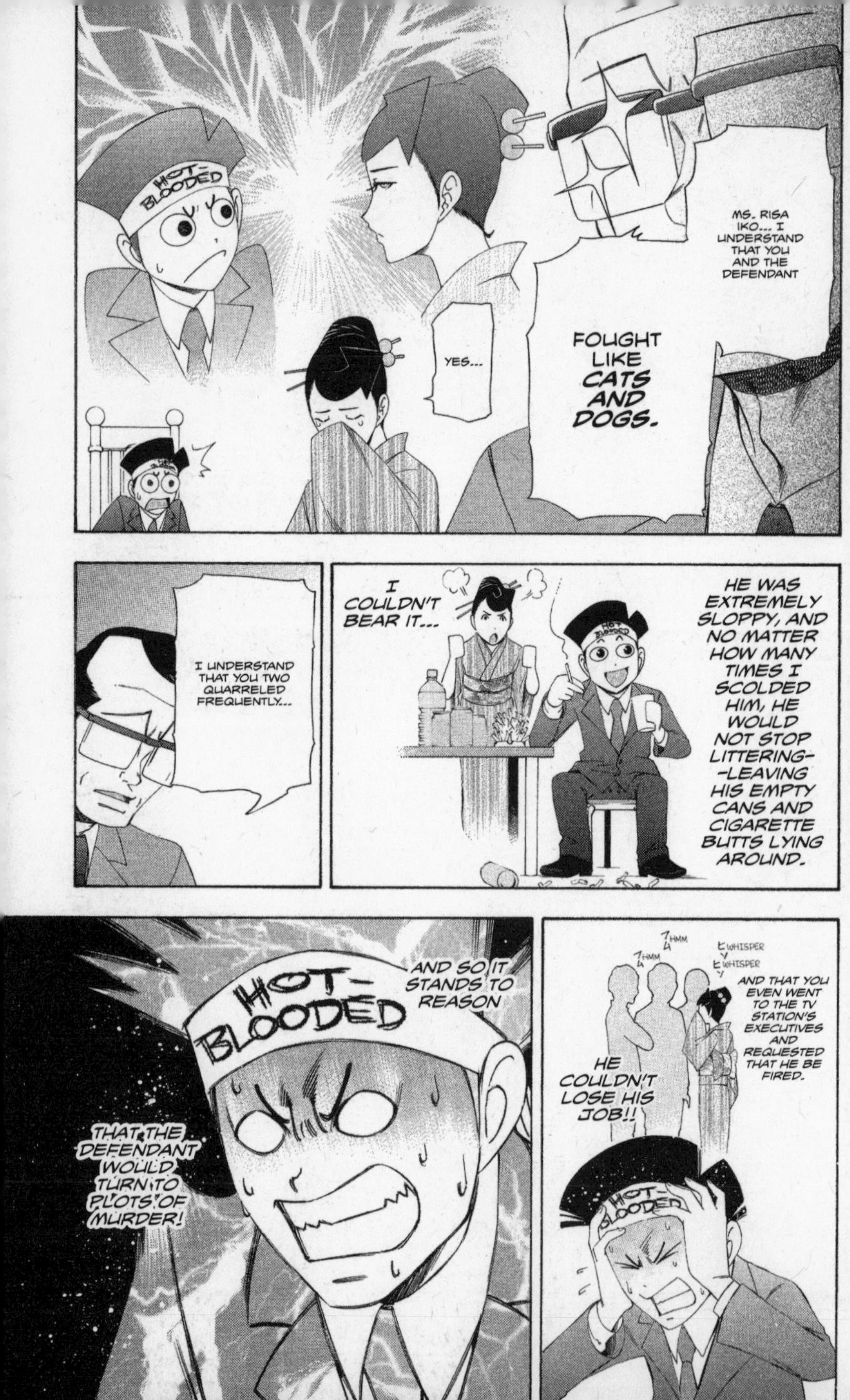
MS. RISA IKO... I UNDERSTAND THAT YOU AND THE DEFENDANT
FOUGHT LIKE CATS AND DOGS.
HOT-BLOODED
YES...
HOT-BLOODED
HE WAS EXTREMELY SLOPPY, AND NO MATTER HOW MANY TIMES I SCOLDED HIM, HE WOULD NOT STOP LITTERING--LEAVING HIS EMPTY CANS AND CIGARETTE BUTTS LYING AROUND.
I COULDN'T BEAR IT...
HOT-BLOODED
I UNDERSTAND THAT YOU TWO QUARRELED FREQUENTLY...
WHISPER
WHISPER
HMM
HMM
AND THAT YOU EVEN WENT TO THE TV STATION'S EXECUTIVES AND REQUESTED THAT HE BE FIRED.
HE COULDN'T LOSE HIS JOB!!
HOT-BLOODED
AND SO IT STANDS TO REASON
HOT-BLOODED
THAT THE DEFENDANT WOULD TURN TO PLOTS OF MURDER!

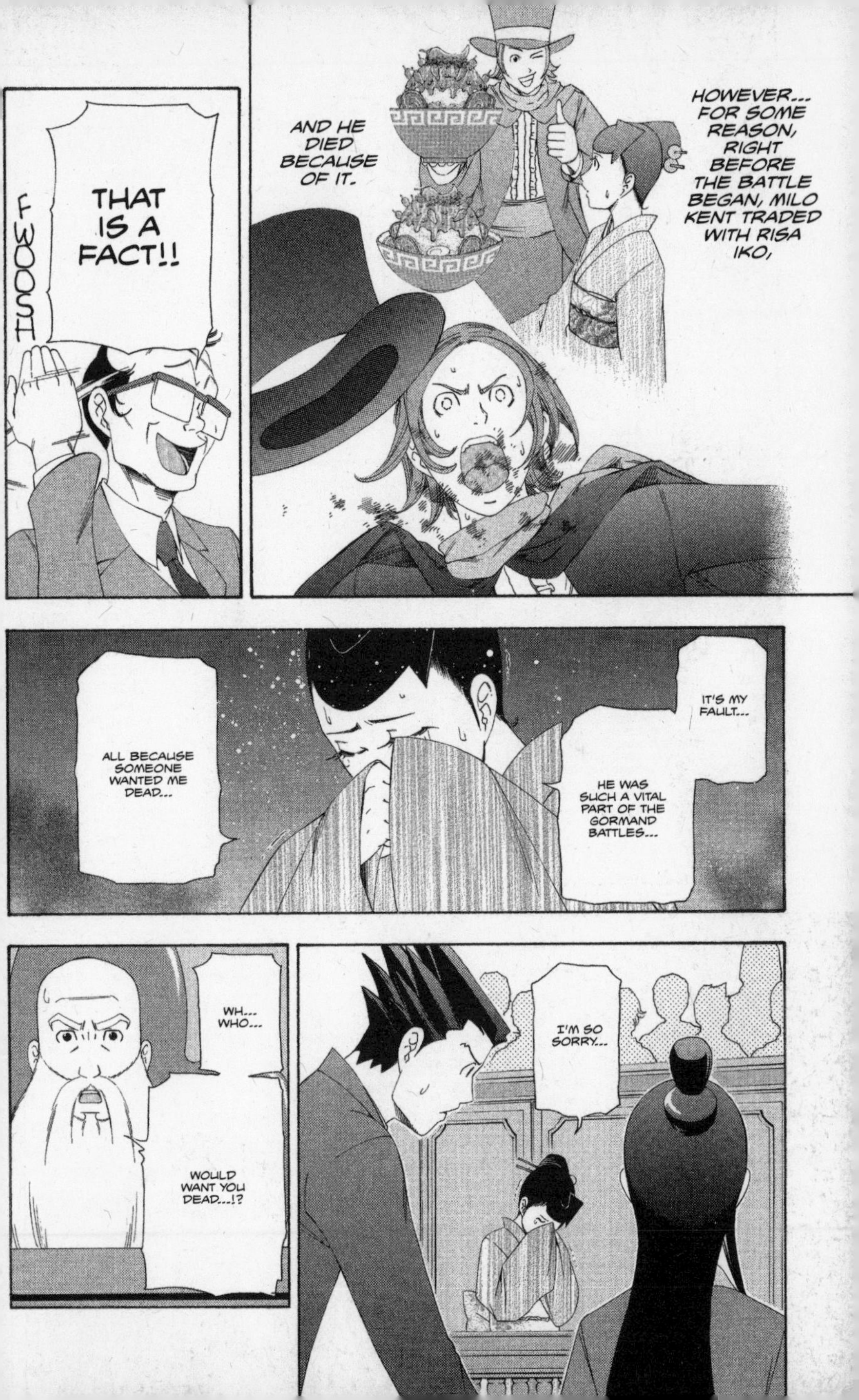
HOWEVER... FOR SOME REASON, RIGHT BEFORE THE BATTLE BEGAN, MILO KENT TRADED WITH RISA IKO,
AND HE DIED BECAUSE OF IT.
THAT IS A FACT!!
FWOOSH
IT'S MY FAULT...
HE WAS SUCH A VITAL PART OF THE GORMAND BATTLES...
ALL BECAUSE SOMEONE WANTED ME DEAD...
I'M SO SORRY...
WH... WHO...
WOULD WANT YOU DEAD...!?

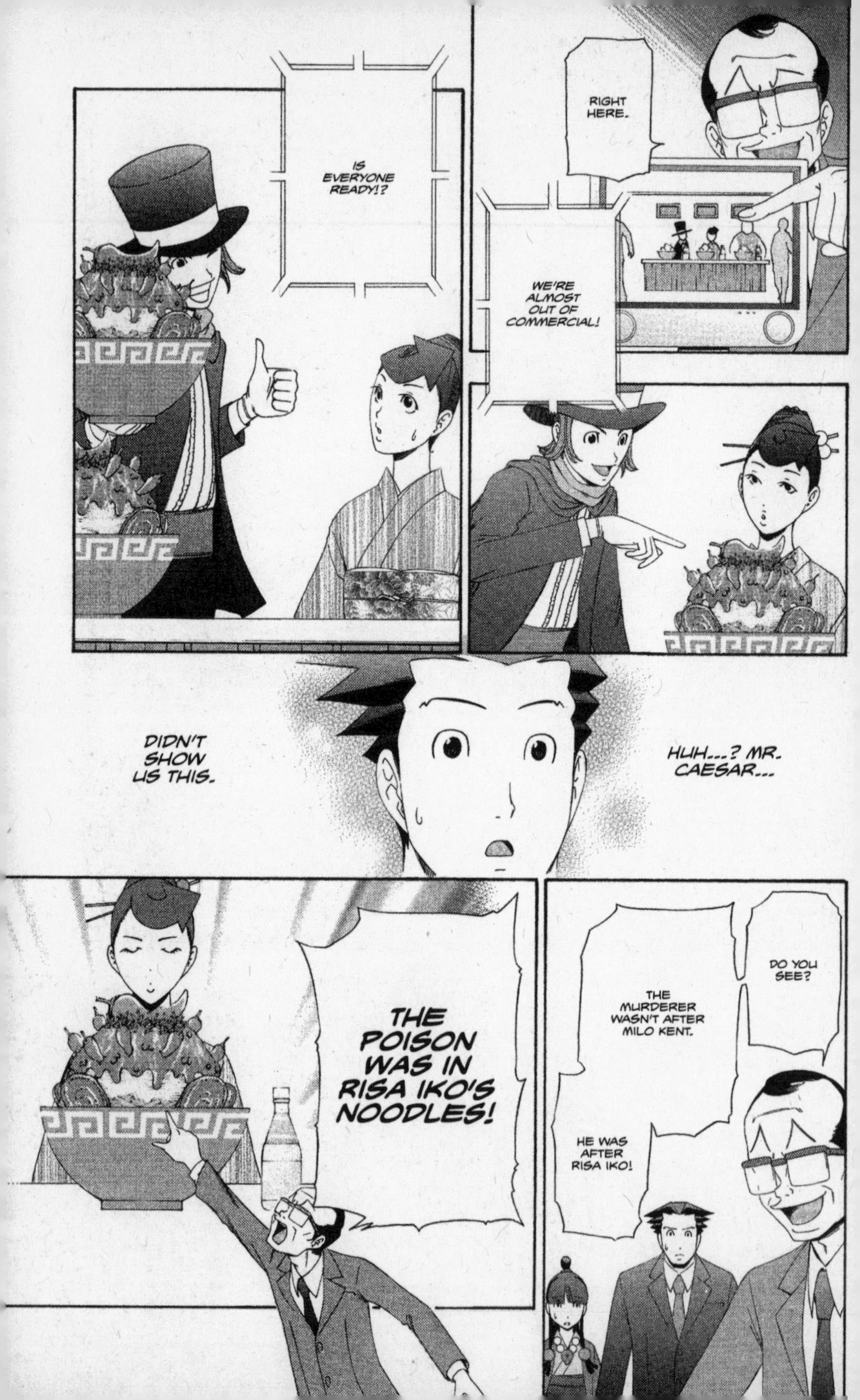
RIGHT HERE.
WE'RE ALMOST OUT OF COMMERCIAL!
IS EVERYONE READY!?
HUH...? MR. CAESAR...
DIDN'T SHOW US THIS.
DO YOU SEE?
THE MURDERER WASN'T AFTER MILO KENT.
HE WAS AFTER RISA IKO!
THE POISON WAS IN RISA IKO'S NOODLES!

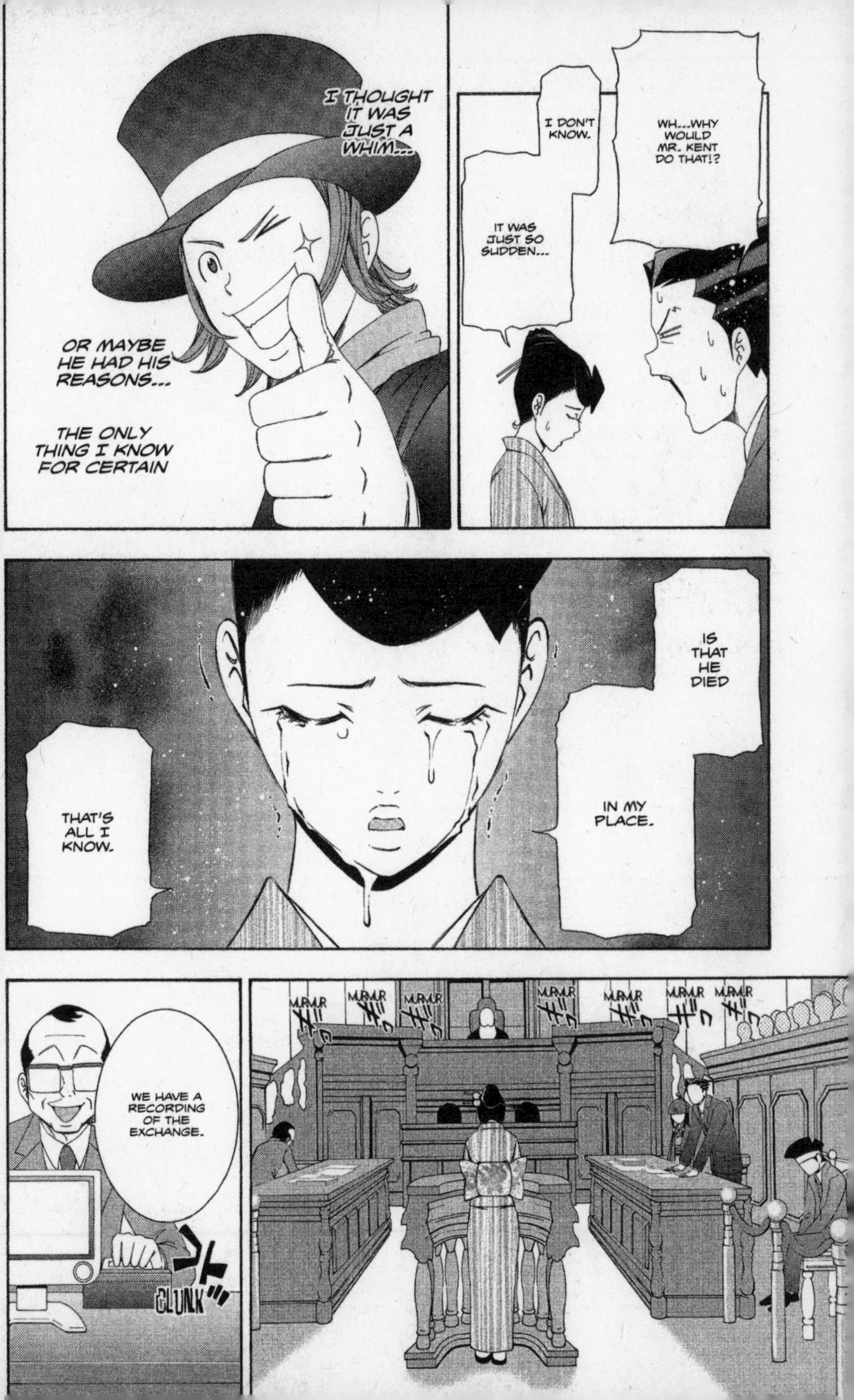
WH...WHY WOULD MR. KENT DO THAT!?
I DON'T KNOW.
IT WAS JUST SO SUDDEN...
I THOUGHT IT WAS JUST A WHIM...
OR MAYBE HE HAD HIS REASONS...
THE ONLY THING I KNOW FOR CERTAIN
IS THAT HE DIED
IN MY PLACE.
THAT'S ALL I KNOW.
MURMUR
MURMUR
MURMUR
MURMUR
MURMUR
MURMUR
MURMUR
WE HAVE A RECORDING OF THE EXCHANGE.
CLUNK

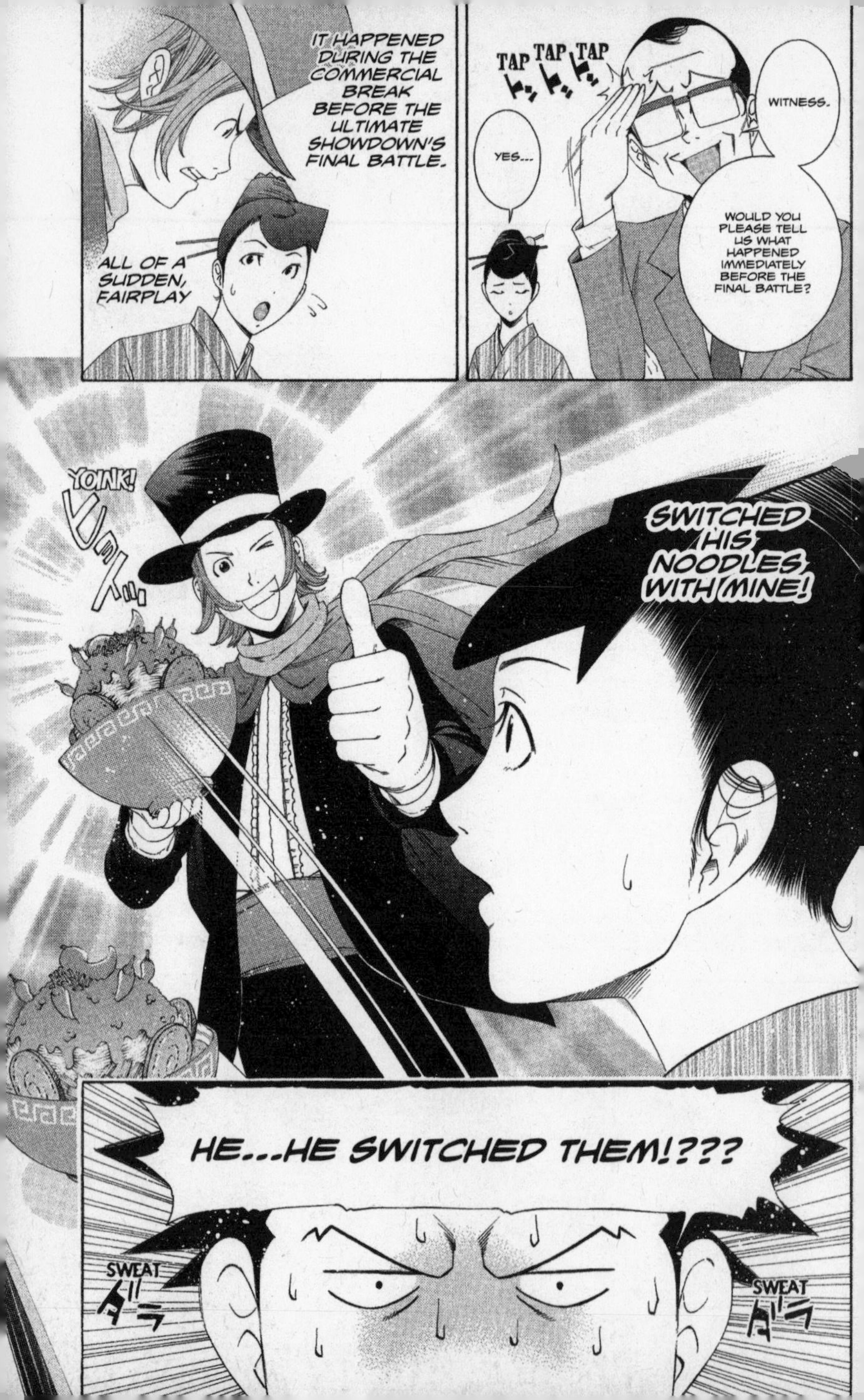

WITNESS.
WOULD YOU PLEASE TELL US WHAT HAPPENED IMMEDIATELY BEFORE THE FINAL BATTLE?
TAP TAP TAP
YES...
IT HAPPENED DURING THE COMMERCIAL BREAK BEFORE THE ULTIMATE SHOWDOWN'S FINAL BATTLE.
ALL OF A SUDDEN, FAIRPLAY
SWITCHED HIS NOODLES WITH MINE!
YOINK!
HE...HE SWITCHED THEM!???
SWEAT
SWEAT

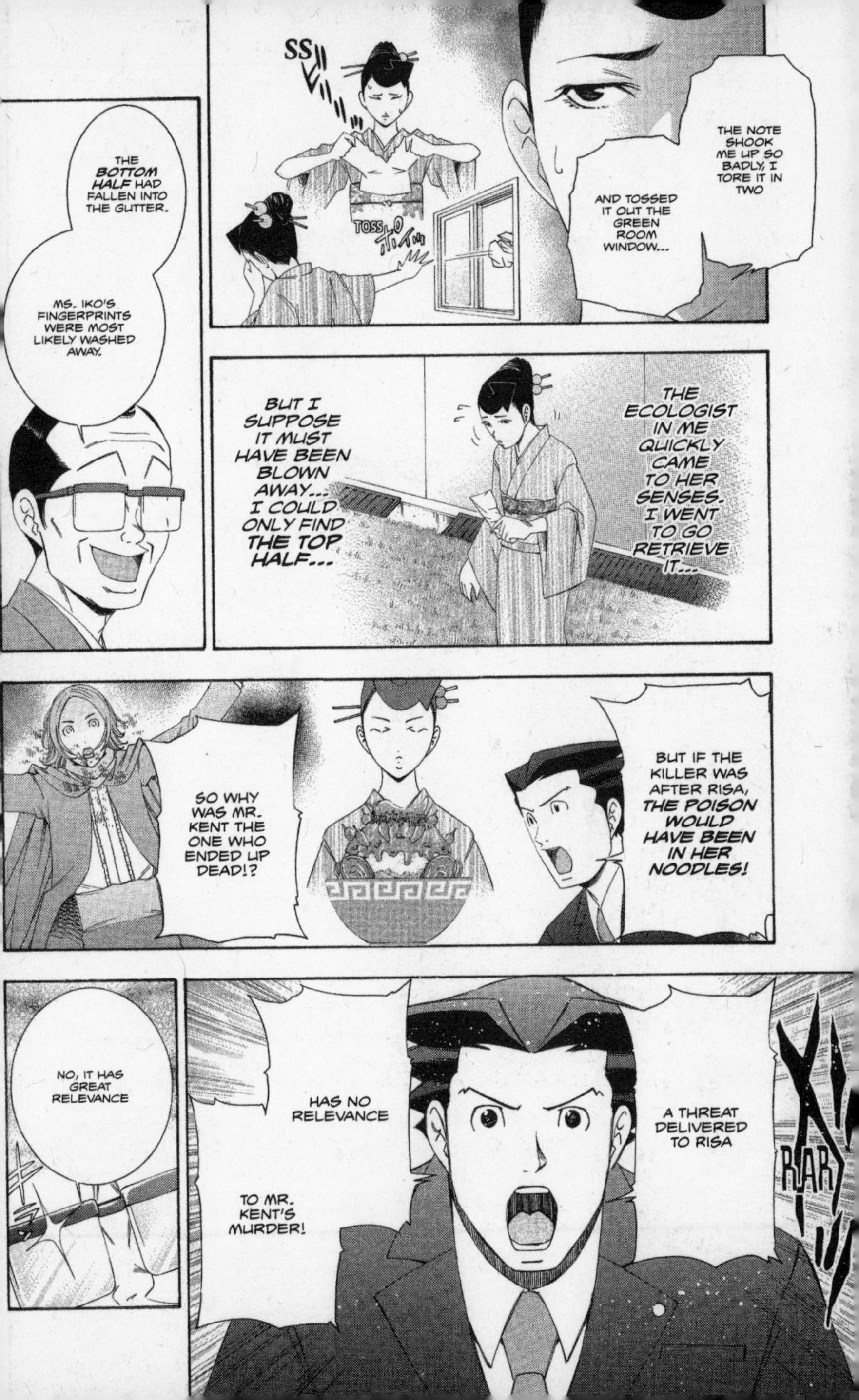
THE NOTE SHOOK ME UP SO BADLY, I TORE IT IN TWO
AND TOSSED IT OUT THE GREEN ROOM WINDOW...
SS
TOSS
THE ECOLOGIST IN ME QUICKLY CAME TO HER SENSES. I WENT TO GO RETRIEVE IT...
BUT I SUPPOSE IT MUST HAVE BEEN BLOWN AWAY... I COULD ONLY FIND **THE TOP HALF...**
THE ***BOTTOM HALF*** HAD FALLEN INTO THE GUTTER.
MS. IKO'S FINGERPRINTS WERE MOST LIKELY WASHED AWAY.
BUT IF THE KILLER WAS AFTER RISA, ***THE POISON WOULD HAVE BEEN IN HER NOODLES!***
SO WHY WAS MR. KENT THE ONE WHO ENDED UP DEAD!?
RAR
A THREAT DELIVERED TO RISA
HAS NO RELEVANCE
TO MR. KENT'S MURDER!
NO, IT HAS GREAT RELEVANCE

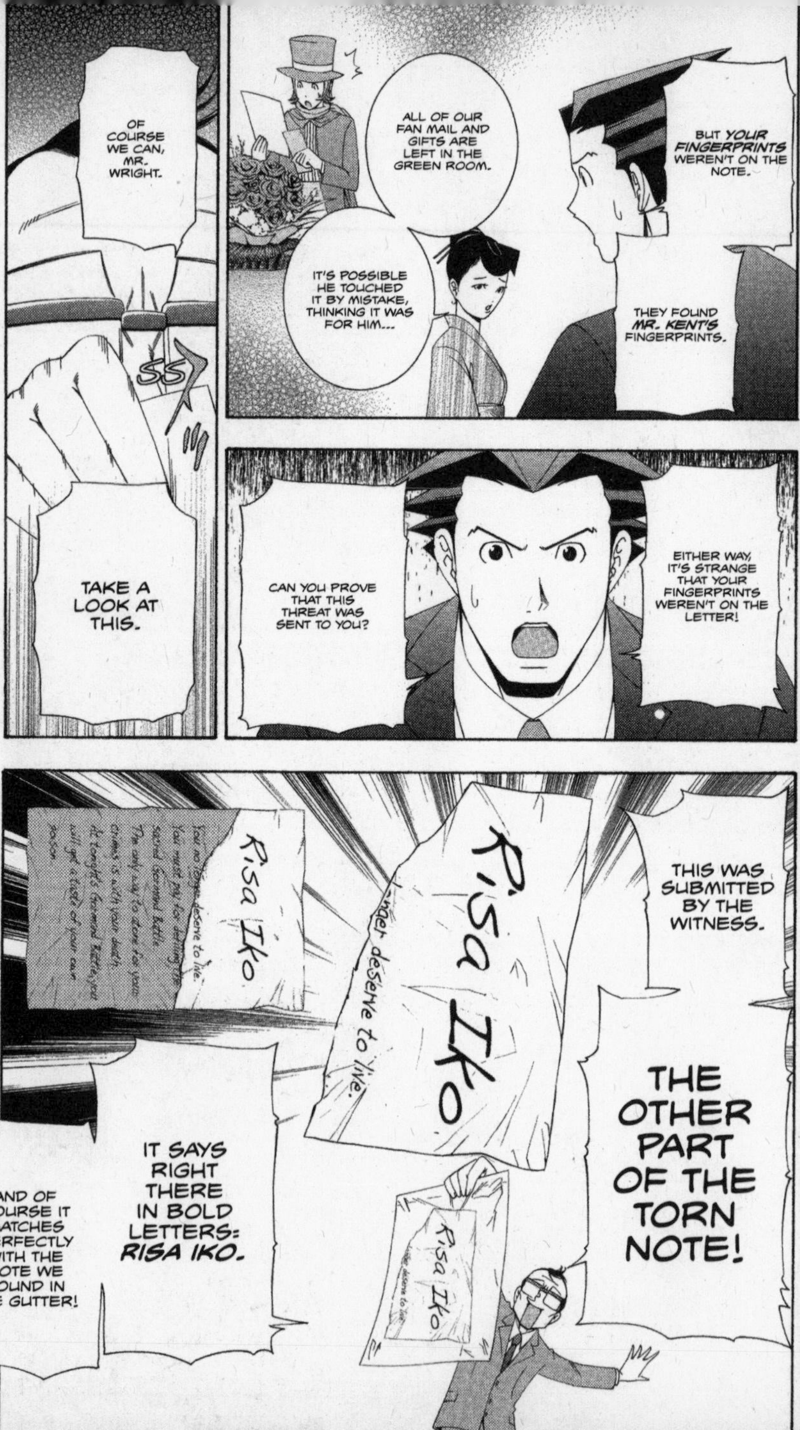
BUT YOUR FINGERPRINTS WEREN'T ON THE NOTE.
THEY FOUND MR. KENT'S FINGERPRINTS.
ALL OF OUR FAN MAIL AND GIFTS ARE LEFT IN THE GREEN ROOM.
IT'S POSSIBLE HE TOUCHED IT BY MISTAKE, THINKING IT WAS FOR HIM...
EITHER WAY, IT'S STRANGE THAT YOUR FINGERPRINTS WEREN'T ON THE LETTER!
CAN YOU PROVE THAT THIS THREAT WAS SENT TO YOU?
OF COURSE WE CAN, MR. WRIGHT.
SS
TAKE A LOOK AT THIS.
THIS WAS SUBMITTED BY THE WITNESS.
THE OTHER PART OF THE TORN NOTE!
Risa Iko
nger deserve to live.
Risa Iko
IT SAYS RIGHT THERE IN BOLD LETTERS: RISA IKO.
AND OF COURSE IT MATCHES PERFECTLY WITH THE NOTE WE FOUND IN THE GUTTER!

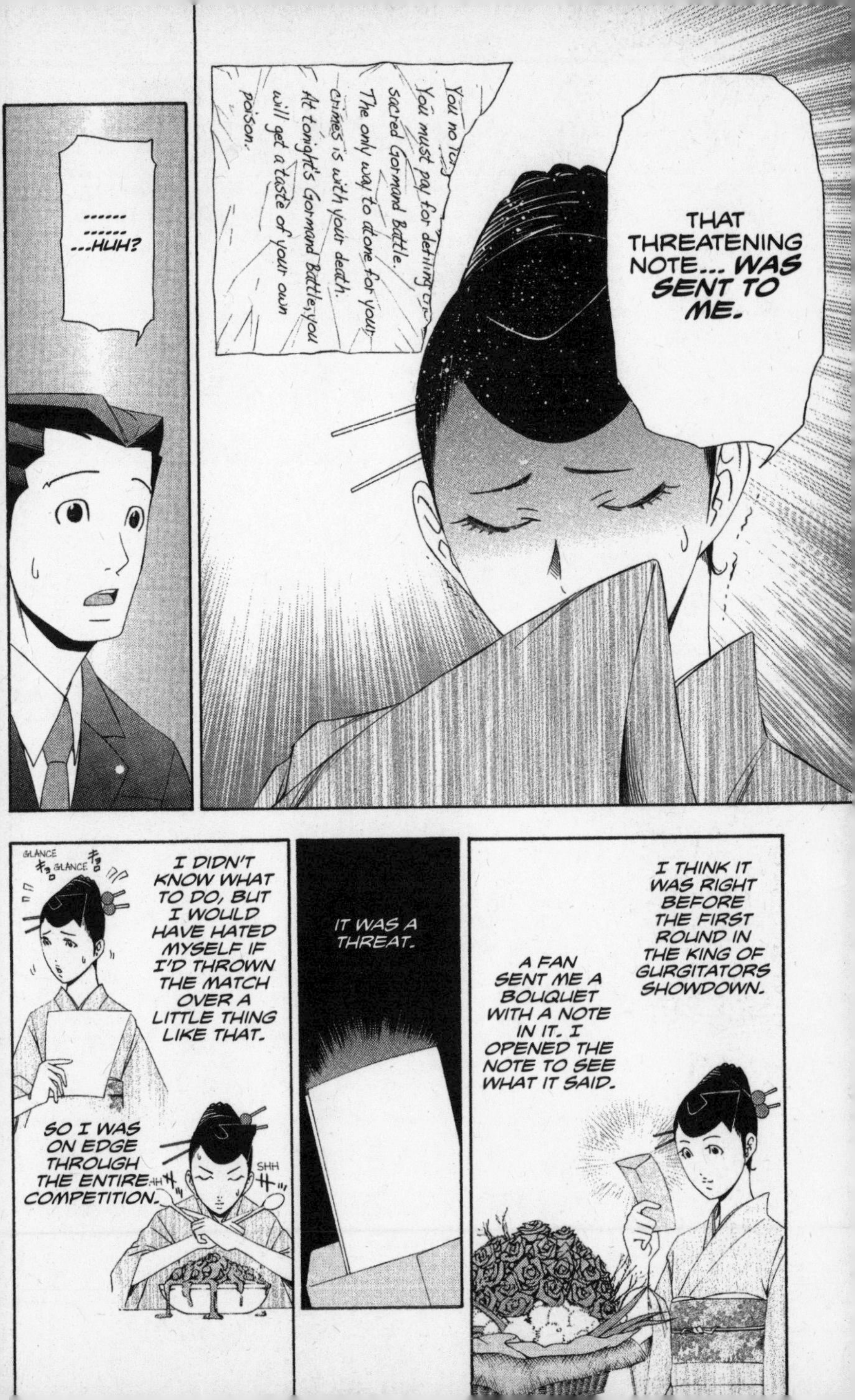
THAT THREATENING NOTE... WAS SENT TO ME.
You no lo
You must pay for defiling th
Sacred Gormand Battle.
The only way to atone for your
crimes is with your death.
At tonight's Gormand Battle, you
will get a taste of your own
poison.

---HUH?
I THINK IT WAS RIGHT BEFORE THE FIRST ROUND IN THE KING OF GURGITATORS SHOWDOWN.
A FAN SENT ME A BOUQUET WITH A NOTE IN IT. I OPENED THE NOTE TO SEE WHAT IT SAID.
IT WAS A THREAT.
GLANCE
GLANCE
I DIDN'T KNOW WHAT TO DO, BUT I WOULD HAVE HATED MYSELF IF I'D THROWN THE MATCH OVER A LITTLE THING LIKE THAT.
SO I WAS ON EDGE THROUGH THE ENTIRE COMPETITION.
SHH

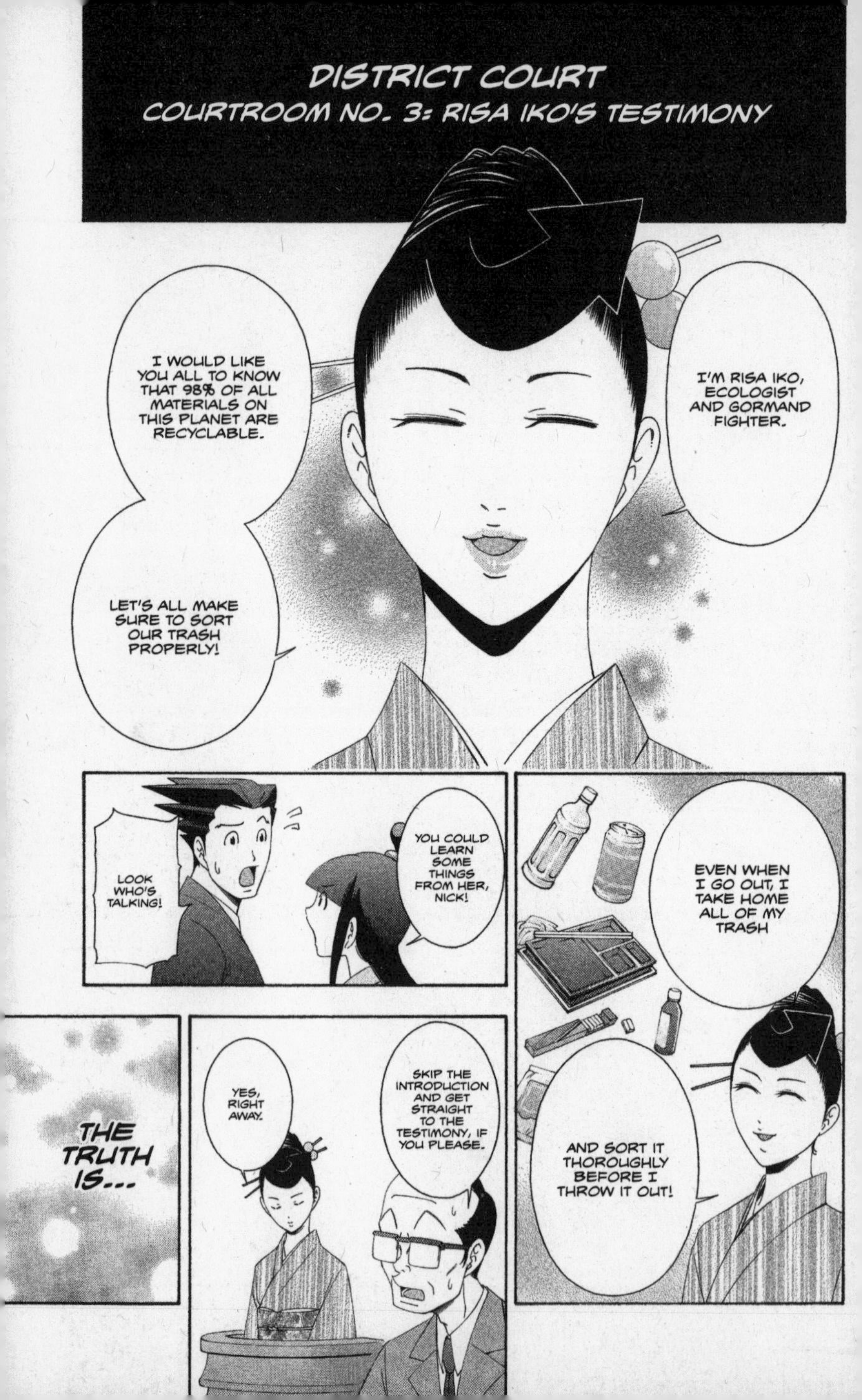
DISTRICT COURT
COURTROOM NO. 3: RISA IKO'S TESTIMONY
I'M RISA IKO, ECOLOGIST AND GORMAND FIGHTER.
I WOULD LIKE YOU ALL TO KNOW THAT 98% OF ALL MATERIALS ON THIS PLANET ARE RECYCLABLE.
LET'S ALL MAKE SURE TO SORT OUR TRASH PROPERLY!
EVEN WHEN I GO OUT, I TAKE HOME ALL OF MY TRASH
AND SORT IT THOROUGHLY BEFORE I THROW IT OUT!
YOU COULD LEARN SOME THINGS FROM HER, NICK!
LOOK WHO'S TALKING!
SKIP THE INTRODUCTION AND GET STRAIGHT TO THE TESTIMONY, IF YOU PLEASE.
YES, RIGHT AWAY.
THE TRUTH IS...

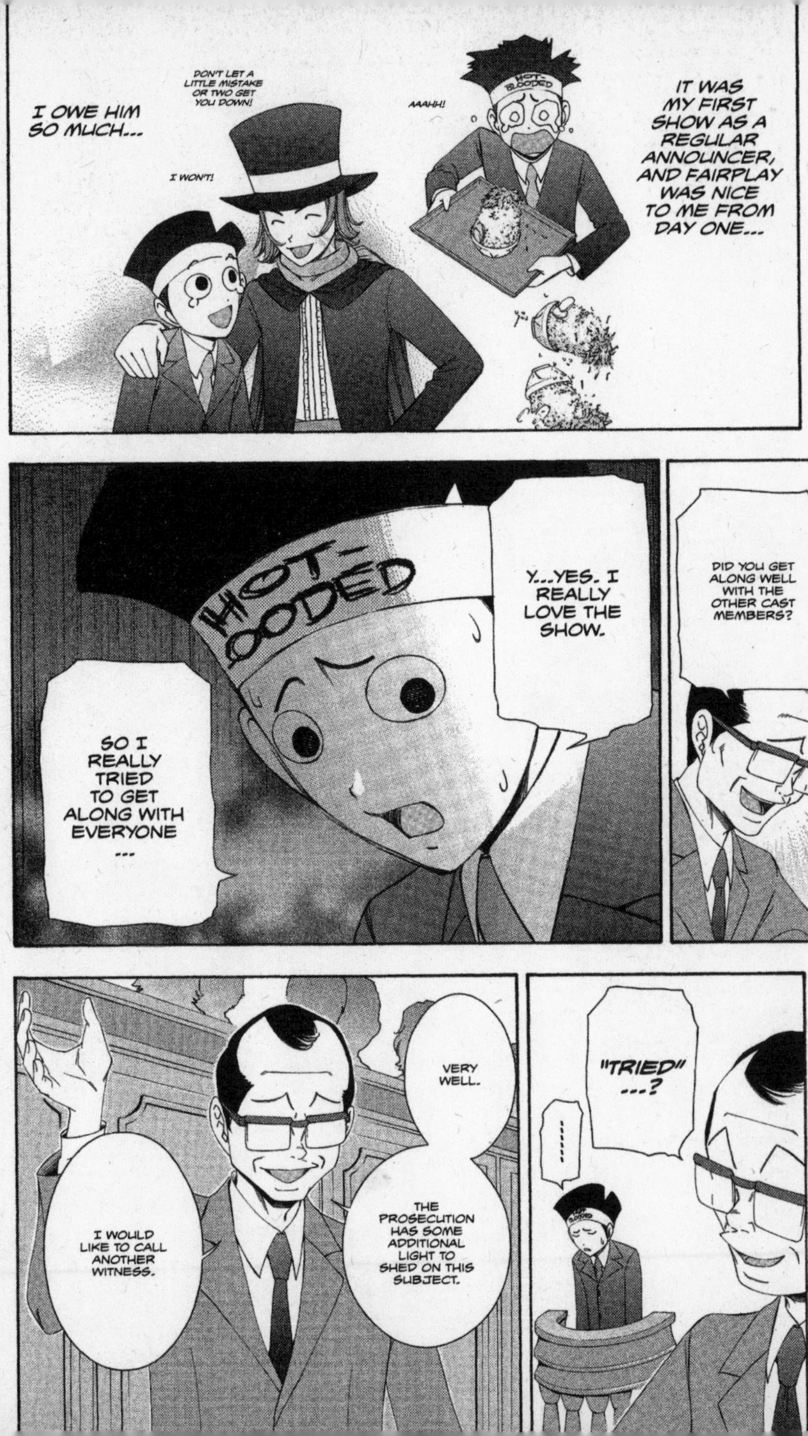
IT WAS MY FIRST SHOW AS A REGULAR ANNOUNCER, AND FAIRPLAY WAS NICE TO ME FROM DAY ONE...
AAAHH!
DON'T LET A LITTLE MISTAKE OR TWO GET YOU DOWN!
I OWE HIM SO MUCH...
I WON'T!
DID YOU GET ALONG WELL WITH THE OTHER CAST MEMBERS?
Y...YES. I REALLY LOVE THE SHOW.
SO I REALLY TRIED TO GET ALONG WITH EVERYONE...
"TRIED"...?
......
VERY WELL.
THE PROSECUTION HAS SOME ADDITIONAL LIGHT TO SHED ON THIS SUBJECT.
I WOULD LIKE TO CALL ANOTHER WITNESS.

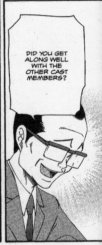

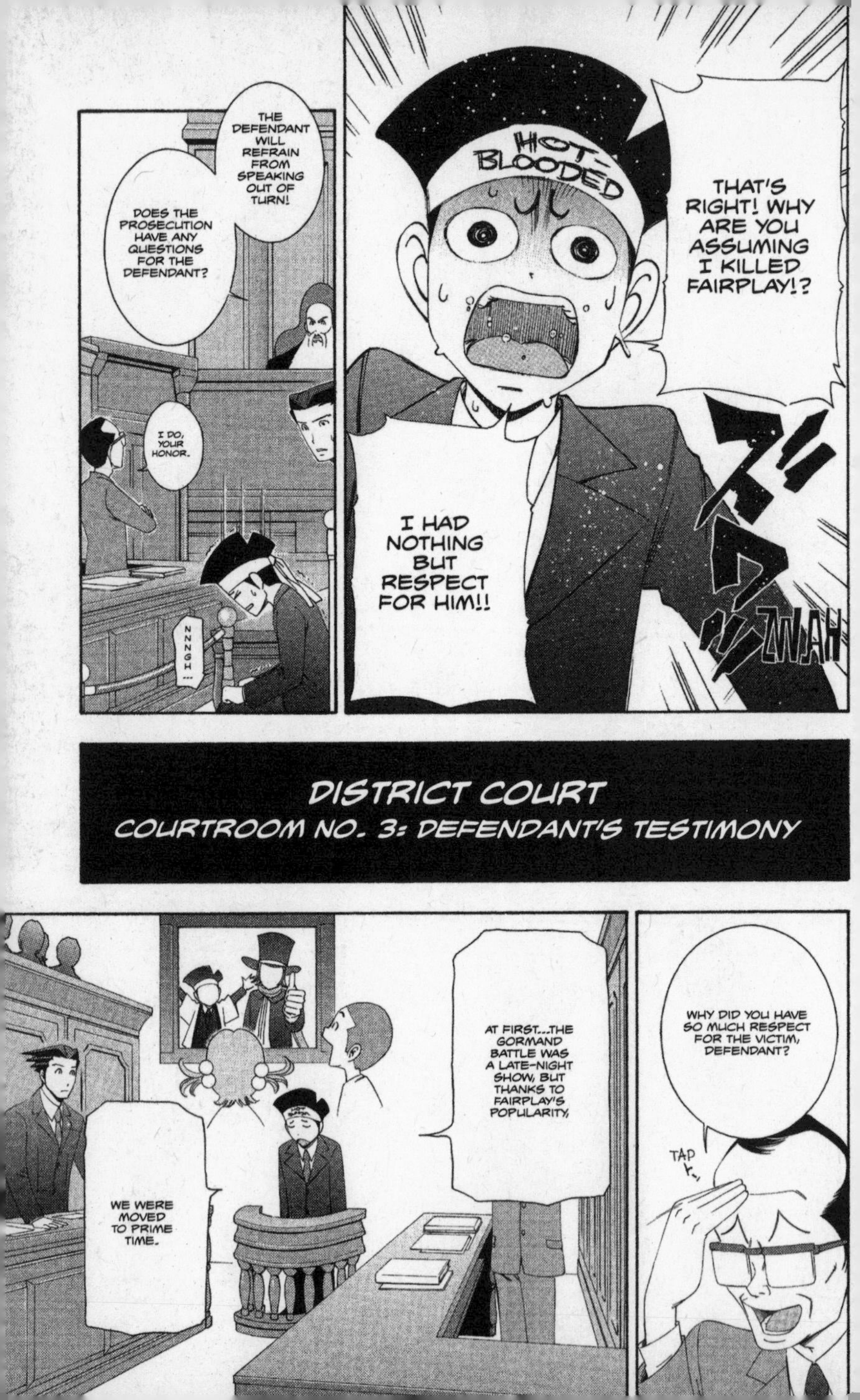
HOT-BLOODED
THAT'S RIGHT! WHY ARE YOU ASSUMING I KILLED FAIRPLAY!?
I HAD NOTHING BUT RESPECT FOR HIM!!
ZWAH
THE DEFENDANT WILL REFRAIN FROM SPEAKING OUT OF TURN!
DOES THE PROSECUTION HAVE ANY QUESTIONS FOR THE DEFENDANT?
I DO, YOUR HONOR.
NNNGH...
DISTRICT COURT
COURTROOM NO. 3: DEFENDANT'S TESTIMONY
WHY DID YOU HAVE SO MUCH RESPECT FOR THE VICTIM, DEFENDANT?
TAP
AT FIRST...THE GORMAND BATTLE WAS A LATE-NIGHT SHOW, BUT THANKS TO FAIRPLAY'S POPULARITY,
WE WERE MOVED TO PRIME TIME.

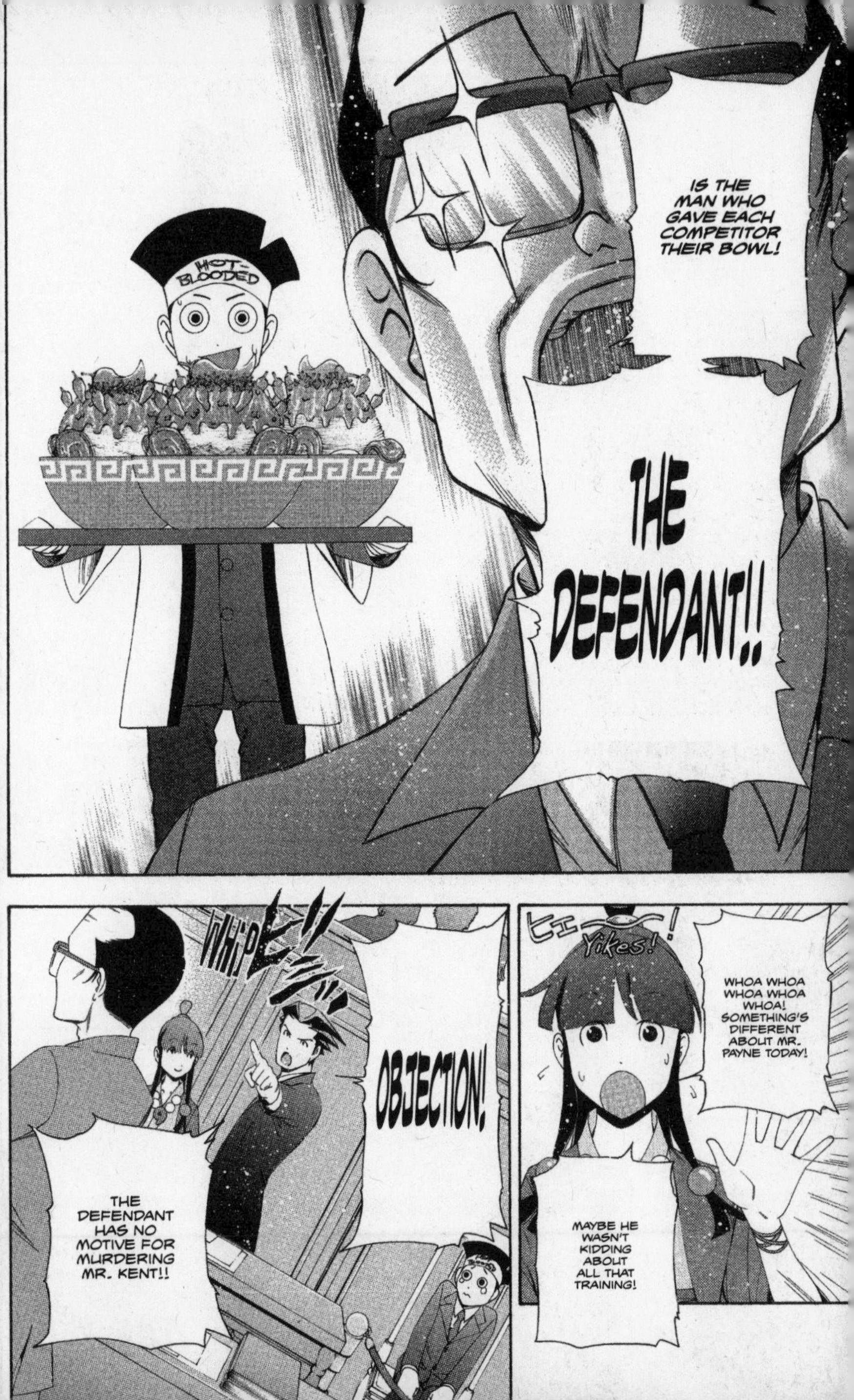
IS THE MAN WHO GAVE EACH COMPETITOR THEIR BOWL!
THE DEFENDANT!!
HOT-BLOODED
Yikes!
WHOA WHOA WHOA WHOA WHOA! SOMETHING'S DIFFERENT ABOUT MR. PAYNE TODAY!
MAYBE HE WASN'T KIDDING ABOUT ALL THAT TRAINING!
WHIP
OBJECTION!
THE DEFENDANT HAS NO MOTIVE FOR MURDERING MR. KENT!!

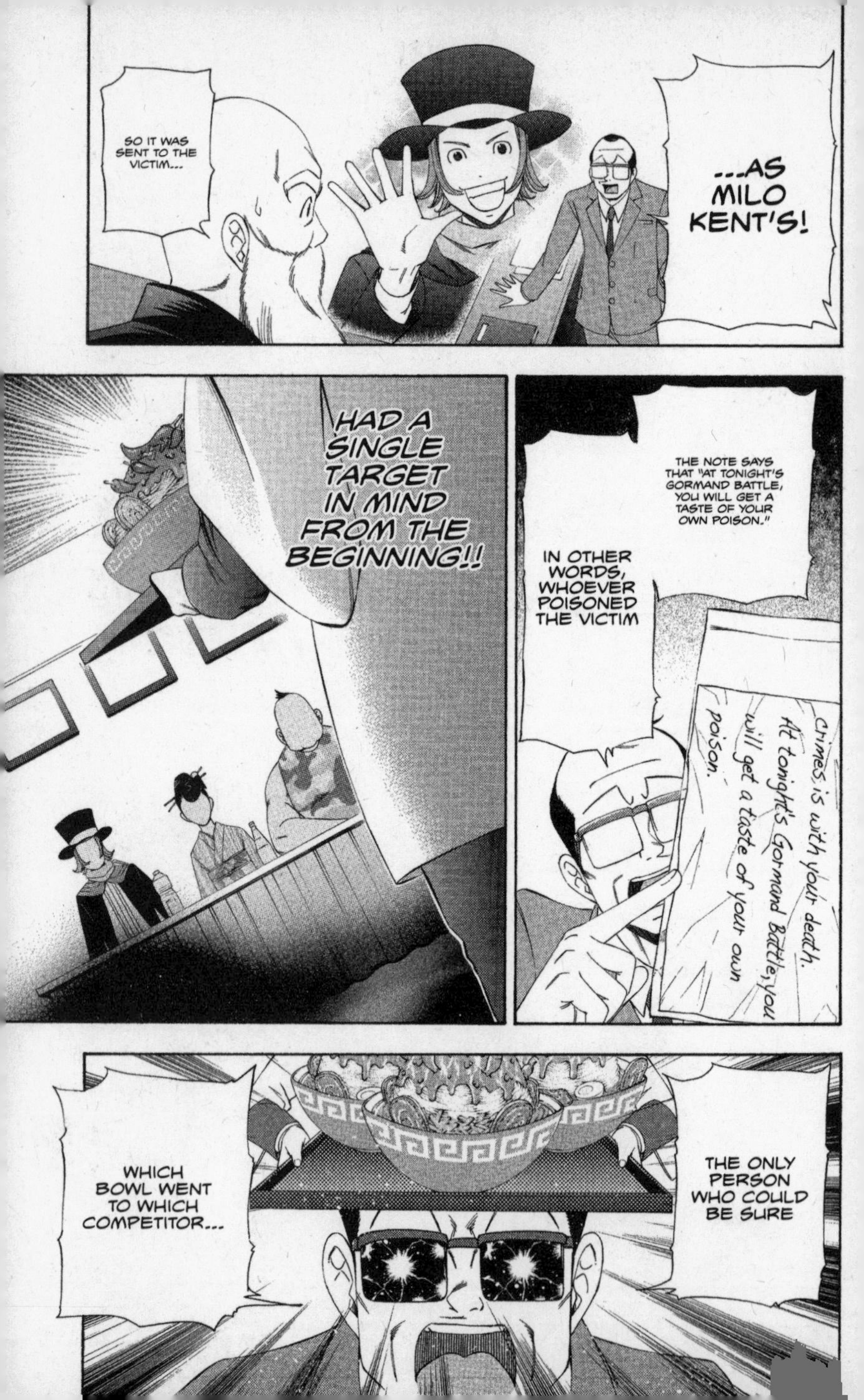
SO IT WAS SENT TO THE VICTIM...
...AS MILO KENT'S!
THE NOTE SAYS THAT "AT TONIGHT'S GORMAND BATTLE, YOU WILL GET A TASTE OF YOUR OWN POISON."
IN OTHER WORDS, WHOEVER POISONED THE VICTIM
crimes is with your death. At tonight's Gormand Battle, you will get a taste of your own poison.
HAD A SINGLE TARGET IN MIND FROM THE BEGINNING!!
THE ONLY PERSON WHO COULD BE SURE
WHICH BOWL WENT TO WHICH COMPETITOR...

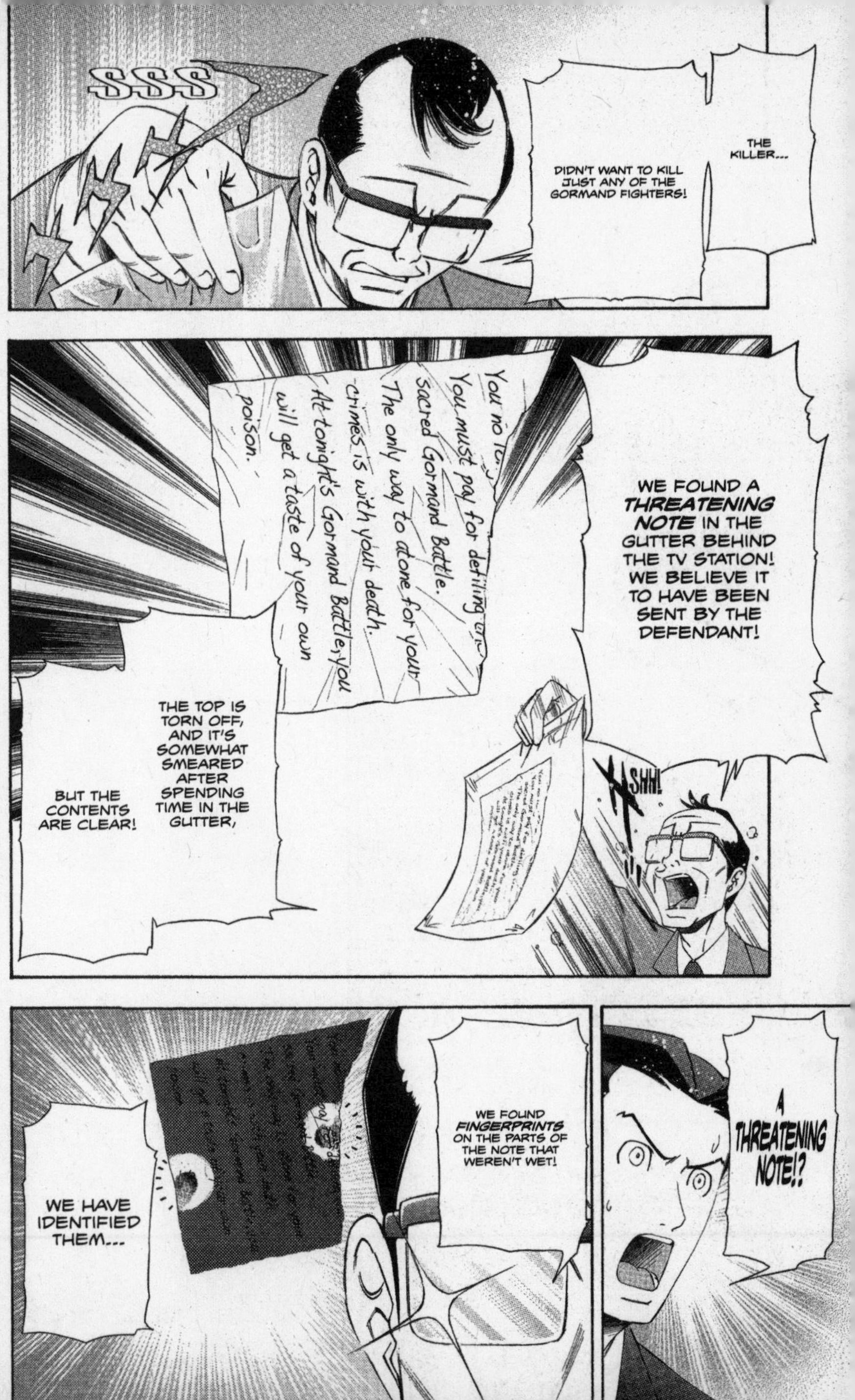
THE KILLER...
DIDN'T WANT TO KILL JUST ANY OF THE GORMAND FIGHTERS!
SSS
WE FOUND A THREATENING NOTE IN THE GUTTER BEHIND THE TV STATION! WE BELIEVE IT TO HAVE BEEN SENT BY THE DEFENDANT!
You must pay for defiling
Sacred Gormand Battle.
The only way to atone for your crimes is with your death.
At tonight's Gormand Battle, you will get a taste of your own poison.
SHH!
THE TOP IS TORN OFF, AND IT'S SOMEWHAT SMEARED AFTER SPENDING TIME IN THE GUTTER,
BUT THE CONTENTS ARE CLEAR!
A THREATENING NOTE!?
WE FOUND FINGERPRINTS ON THE PARTS OF THE NOTE THAT WEREN'T WET!
WE HAVE IDENTIFIED THEM...

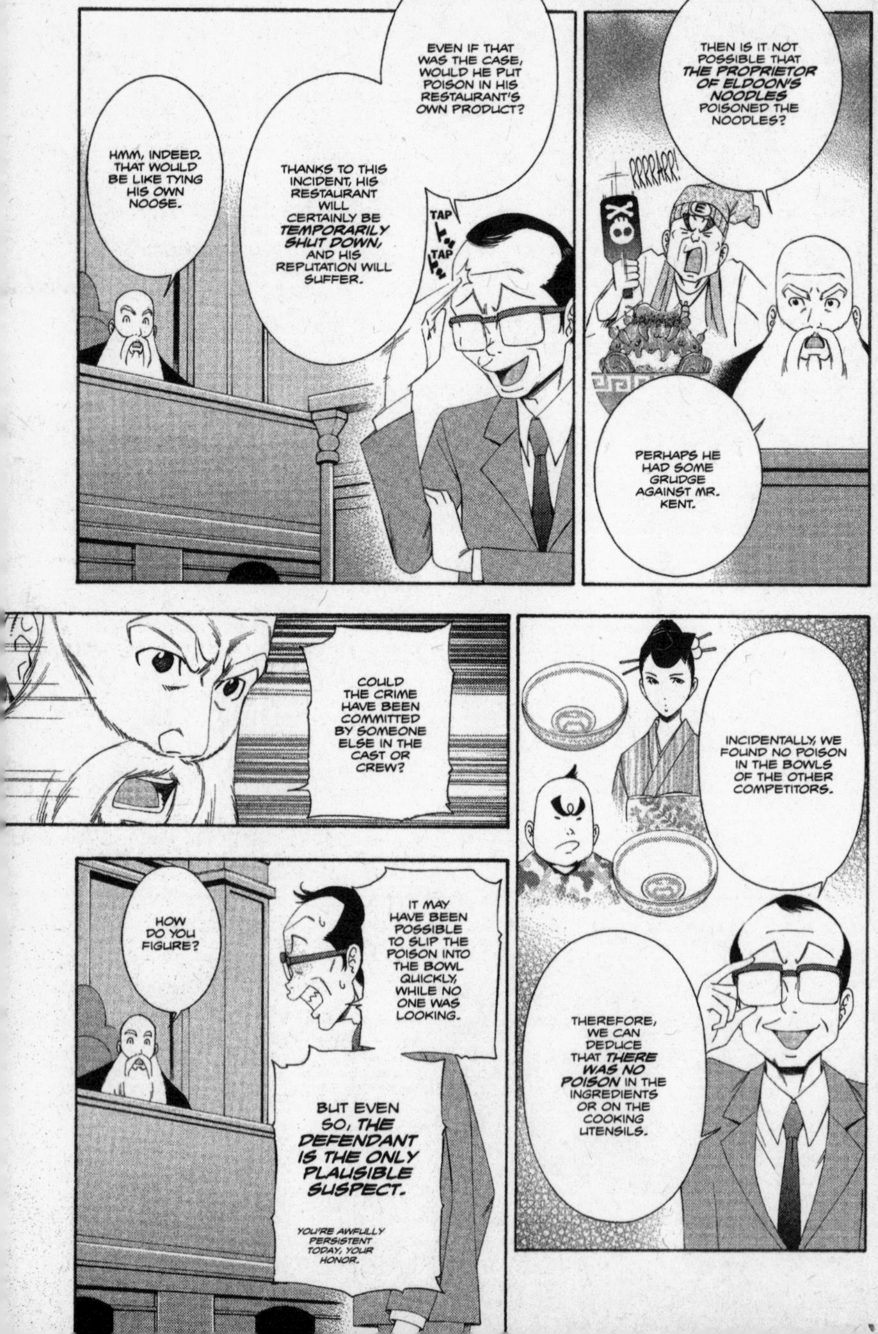
THEN IS IT NOT POSSIBLE THAT THE PROPRIETOR OF ELDOON'S NOODLES POISONED THE NOODLES?
RRRRARR!
PERHAPS HE HAD SOME GRUDGE AGAINST MR. KENT.
EVEN IF THAT WAS THE CASE, WOULD HE PUT POISON IN HIS RESTAURANT'S OWN PRODUCT?
THANKS TO THIS INCIDENT, HIS RESTAURANT WILL CERTAINLY BE TEMPORARILY SHUT DOWN, AND HIS REPUTATION WILL SUFFER.
TAP TAP
HMM, INDEED. THAT WOULD BE LIKE TYING HIS OWN NOOSE.
INCIDENTALLY, WE FOUND NO POISON IN THE BOWLS OF THE OTHER COMPETITORS.
THEREFORE, WE CAN DEDUCE THAT THERE WAS NO POISON IN THE INGREDIENTS OR ON THE COOKING UTENSILS.
COULD THE CRIME HAVE BEEN COMMITTED BY SOMEONE ELSE IN THE CAST OR CREW?
IT MAY HAVE BEEN POSSIBLE TO SLIP THE POISON INTO THE BOWL QUICKLY, WHILE NO ONE WAS LOOKING.
HOW DO YOU FIGURE?
BUT EVEN SO, THE DEFENDANT IS THE ONLY PLAUSIBLE SUSPECT.
YOU'RE AWFULLY PERSISTENT TODAY, YOUR HONOR.

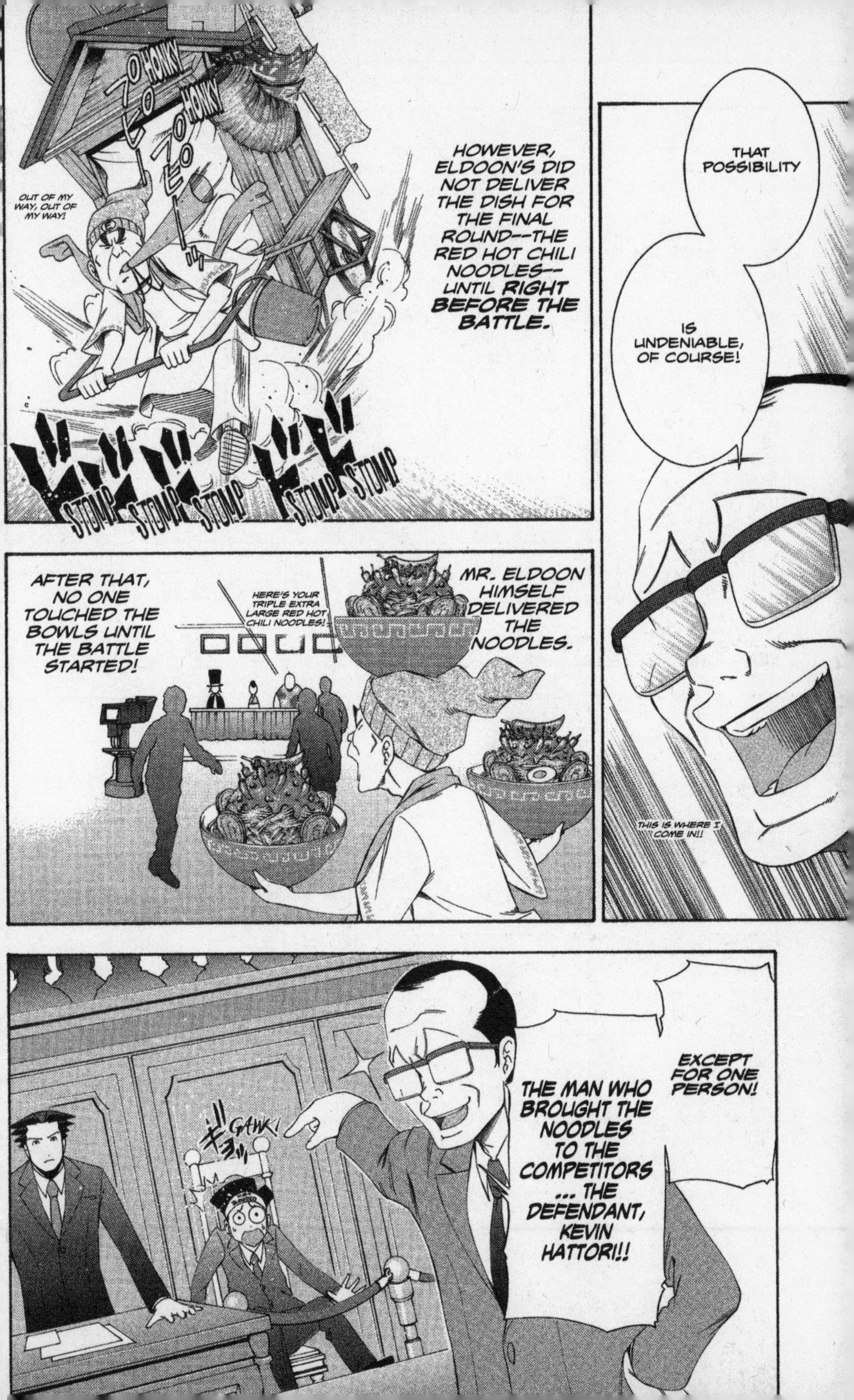
THAT POSSIBILITY
IS UNDENIABLE, OF COURSE!
THIS IS WHERE I COME IN!!
HOWEVER, ELDOON'S DID NOT DELIVER THE DISH FOR THE FINAL ROUND--THE RED HOT CHILI NOODLES--UNTIL RIGHT BEFORE THE BATTLE.
HONKY
HONKY
OUT OF MY WAY, OUT OF MY WAY!
STOMP
STOMP
STOMP
STOMP
STOMP
MR. ELDOON HIMSELF DELIVERED THE NOODLES.
HERE'S YOUR TRIPLE EXTRA LARGE RED HOT CHILI NOODLES!
AFTER THAT, NO ONE TOUCHED THE BOWLS UNTIL THE BATTLE STARTED!
EXCEPT FOR ONE PERSON!
THE MAN WHO BROUGHT THE NOODLES TO THE COMPETITORS ... THE DEFENDANT, KEVIN HATTORI!!
GAWK!

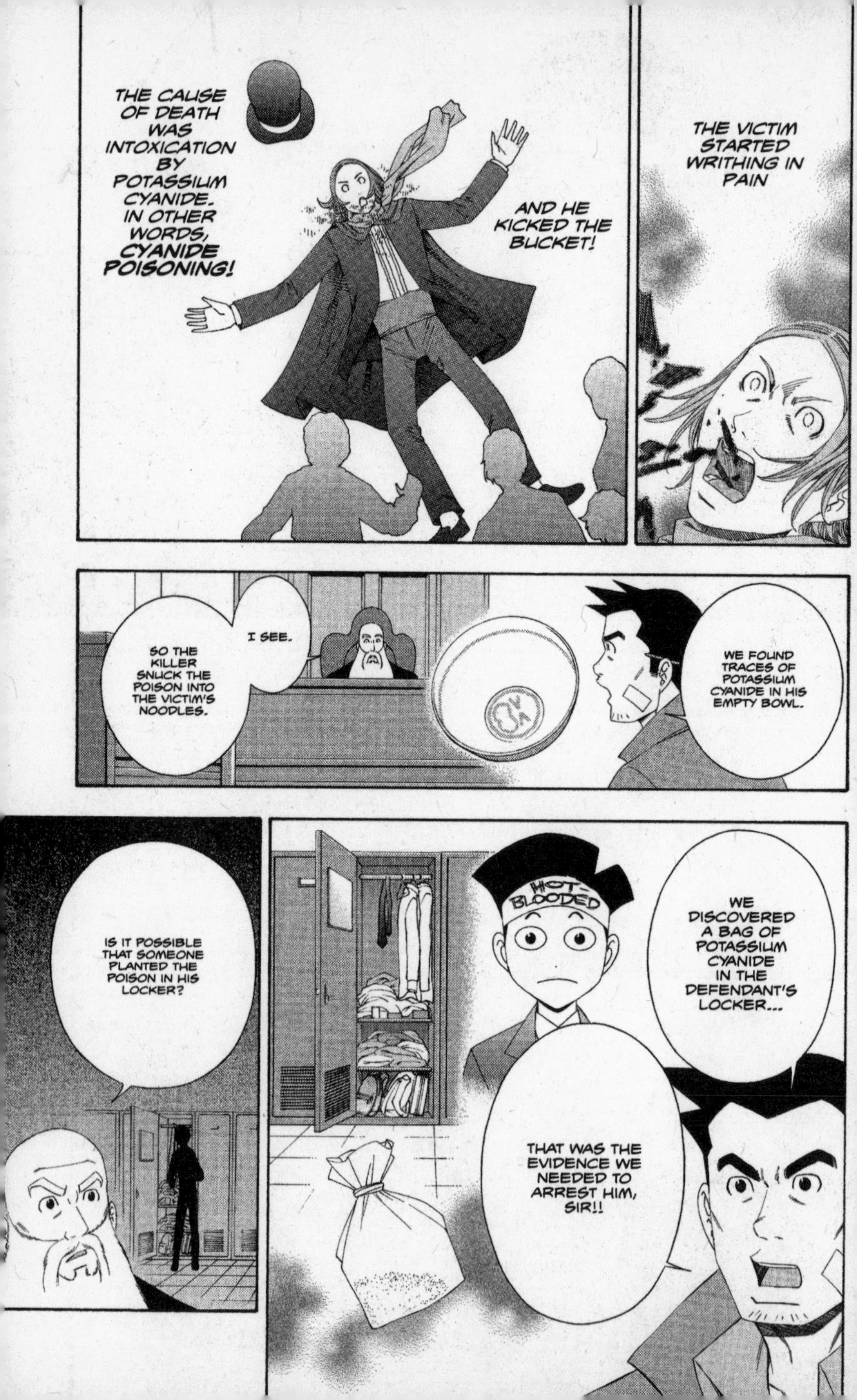
THE VICTIM STARTED WRITHING IN PAIN
AND HE KICKED THE BUCKET!
THE CAUSE OF DEATH WAS INTOXICATION BY POTASSIUM CYANIDE. IN OTHER WORDS, CYANIDE POISONING!
WE FOUND TRACES OF POTASSIUM CYANIDE IN HIS EMPTY BOWL.
I SEE.
SO THE KILLER SNUCK THE POISON INTO THE VICTIM'S NOODLES.
WE DISCOVERED A BAG OF POTASSIUM CYANIDE IN THE DEFENDANT'S LOCKER...
HOT-BLOODED
THAT WAS THE EVIDENCE WE NEEDED TO ARREST HIM, SIR!!
IS IT POSSIBLE THAT SOMEONE PLANTED THE POISON IN HIS LOCKER?

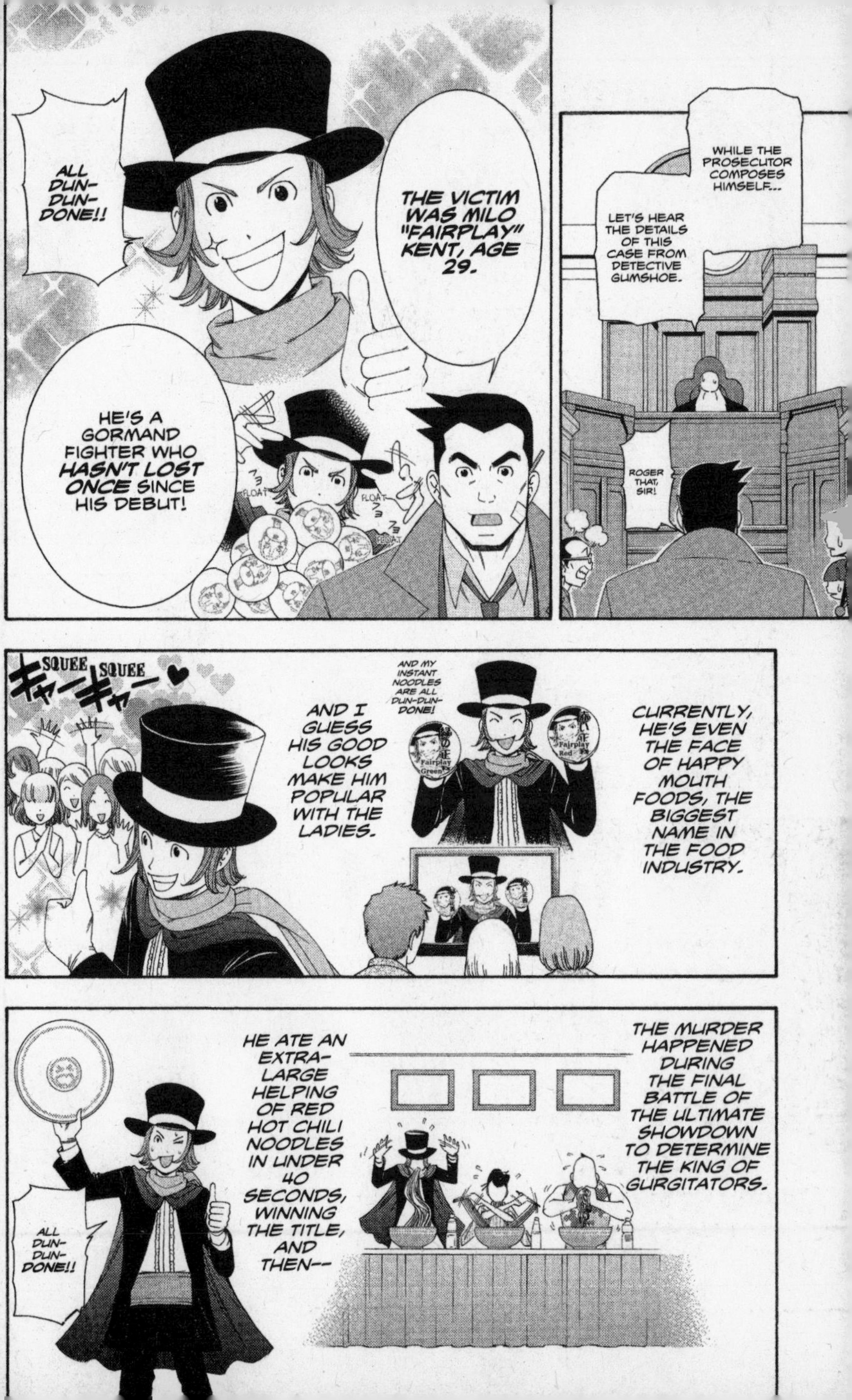
WHILE THE PROSECUTOR COMPOSES HIMSELF...
LET'S HEAR THE DETAILS OF THIS CASE FROM DETECTIVE GUMSHOE.
ROGER THAT, SIR!
THE VICTIM WAS MILO "FAIRPLAY" KENT, AGE 29.
ALL DUN-DUN-DONE!!
HE'S A GORMAND FIGHTER WHO HASN'T LOST ONCE SINCE HIS DEBUT!
FLOAT
FLOAT
FLOAT
CURRENTLY, HE'S EVEN THE FACE OF HAPPY MOUTH FOODS, THE BIGGEST NAME IN THE FOOD INDUSTRY.
AND MY INSTANT NOODLES ARE ALL DUN-DUN-DONE!
Fairplay Red
Fairplay Green
AND I GUESS HIS GOOD LOOKS MAKE HIM POPULAR WITH THE LADIES.
SQUEE SQUEE
キャーキャー
THE MURDER HAPPENED DURING THE FINAL BATTLE OF THE ULTIMATE SHOWDOWN TO DETERMINE THE KING OF GURGITATORS.
HE ATE AN EXTRA-LARGE HELPING OF RED HOT CHILI NOODLES IN UNDER 40 SECONDS, WINNING THE TITLE, AND THEN--
ALL DUN-DUN-DONE!!

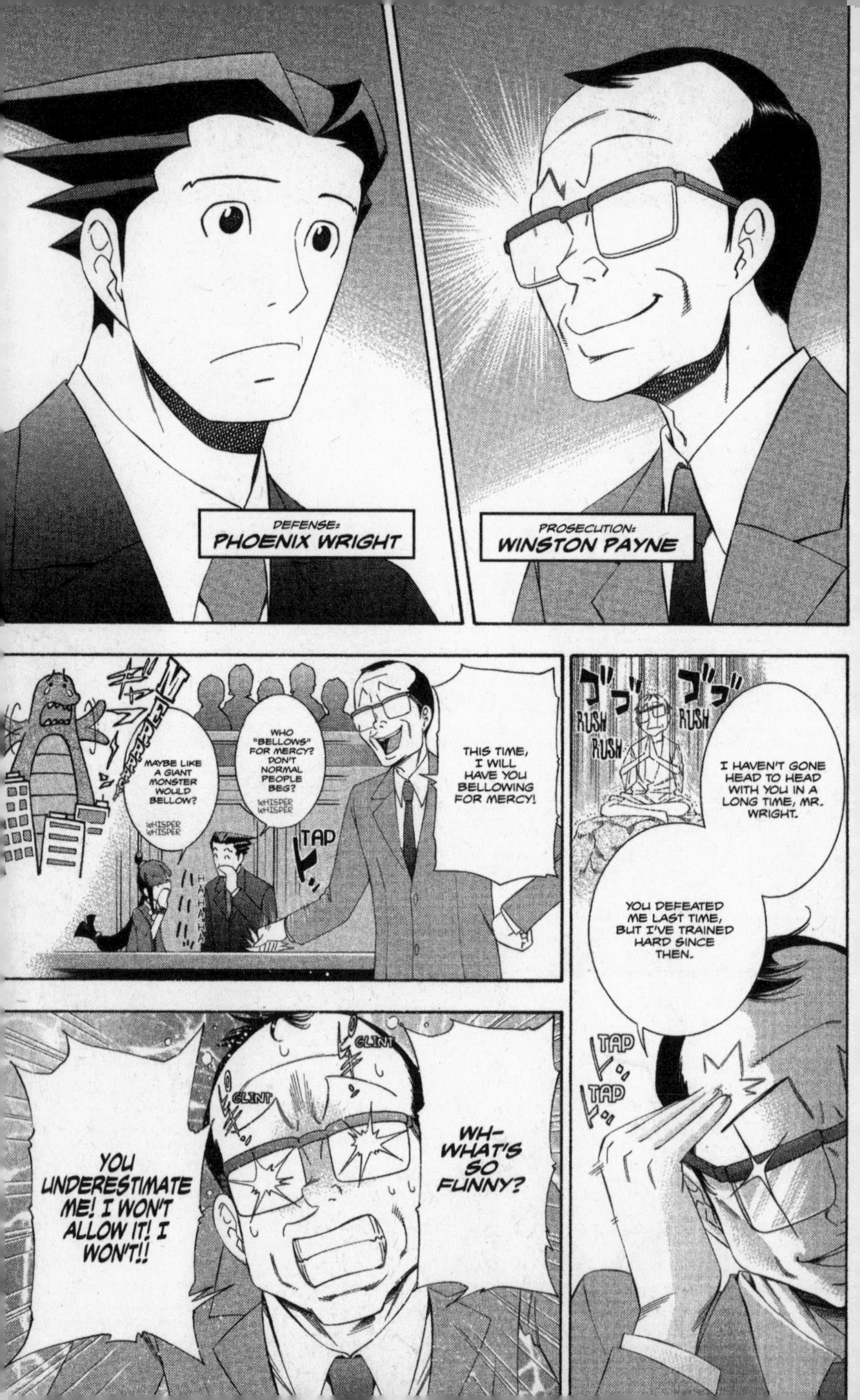
PROSECUTION: WINSTON PAYNE
DEFENSE: PHOENIX WRIGHT
RUSH RUSH RUSH
I HAVEN'T GONE HEAD TO HEAD WITH YOU IN A LONG TIME, MR. WRIGHT.
YOU DEFEATED ME LAST TIME, BUT I'VE TRAINED HARD SINCE THEN.
TAP TAP
THIS TIME, I WILL HAVE YOU BELLOWING FOR MERCY!
TAP
WHO "BELLOWS" FOR MERCY? DON'T NORMAL PEOPLE BEG?
WHISPER WHISPER
MAYBE LIKE A GIANT MONSTER WOULD BELLOW?
WHISPER WHISPER
HAHAHA
WH- WHAT'S SO FUNNY?
GLINT
GLINT
YOU UNDERESTIMATE ME! I WON'T ALLOW IT! I WON'T!!

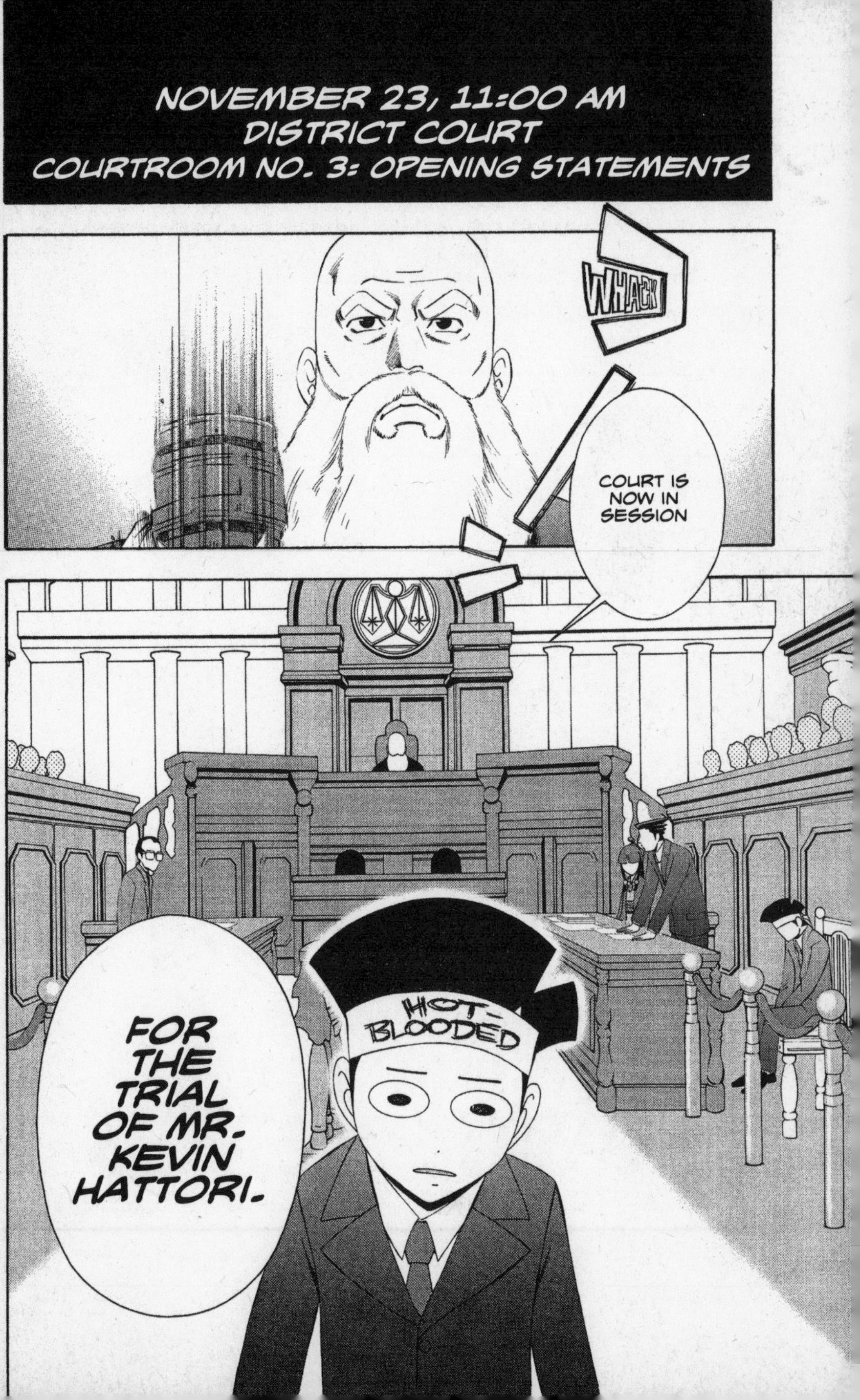
NOVEMBER 23, 11:00 AM
DISTRICT COURT
COURTROOM NO. 3: OPENING STATEMENTS
WHACK
COURT IS NOW IN SESSION
FOR THE TRIAL OF MR. KEVIN HATTORI.
HOT-BLOODED

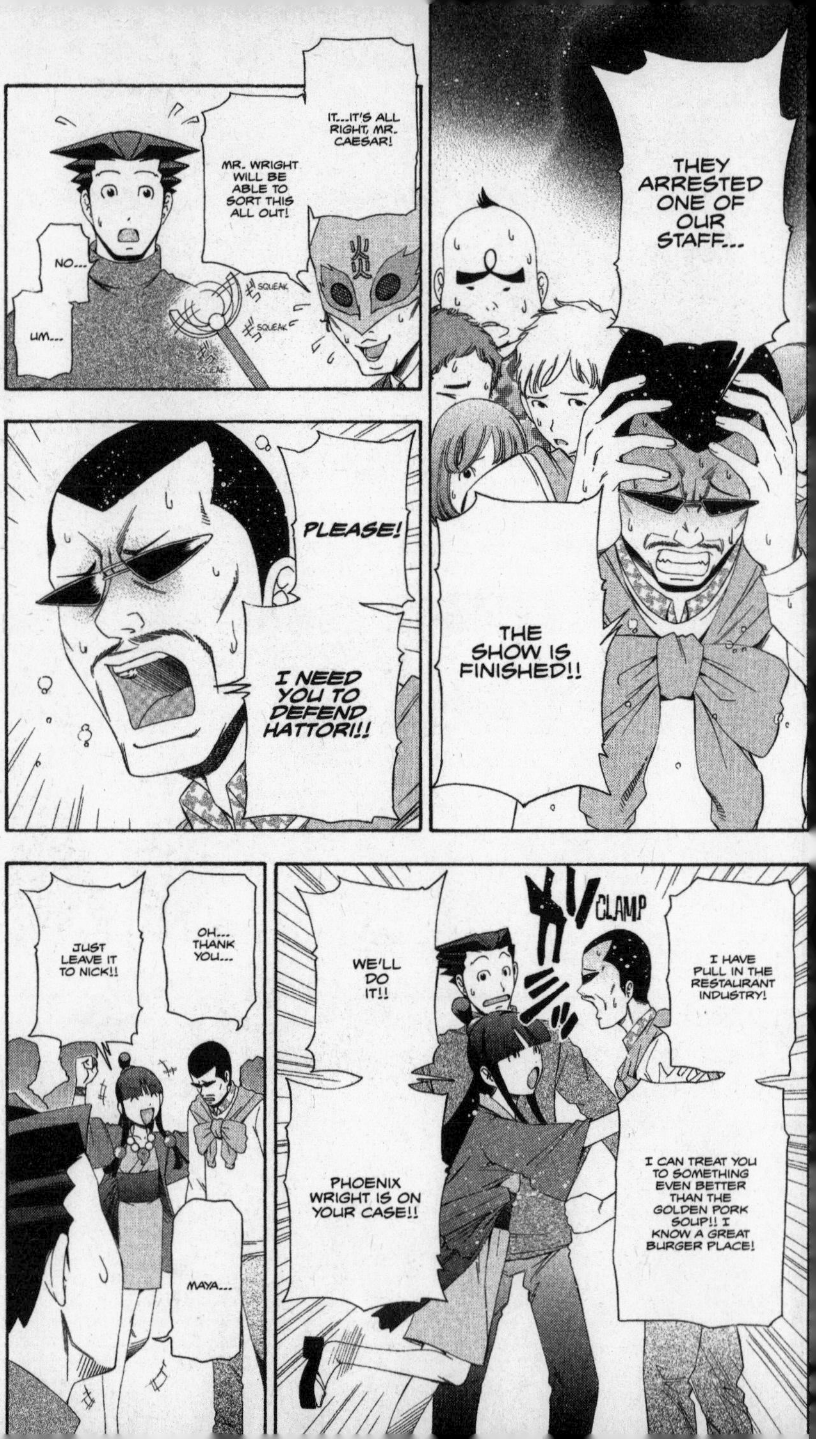
THEY ARRESTED ONE OF OUR STAFF...
THE SHOW IS FINISHED!!
IT...IT'S ALL RIGHT, MR. CAESAR!
MR. WRIGHT WILL BE ABLE TO SORT THIS ALL OUT!
SQUEAK
SQUEAK
SQUEAK
NO...
UM...
PLEASE!
I NEED YOU TO DEFEND HATTORI!!
I HAVE PULL IN THE RESTAURANT INDUSTRY!
CLAMP
WE'LL DO IT!!
I CAN TREAT YOU TO SOMETHING EVEN BETTER THAN THE GOLDEN PORK SOUP!! I KNOW A GREAT BURGER PLACE!
PHOENIX WRIGHT IS ON YOUR CASE!!
OH... THANK YOU...
JUST LEAVE IT TO NICK!!
MAYA...

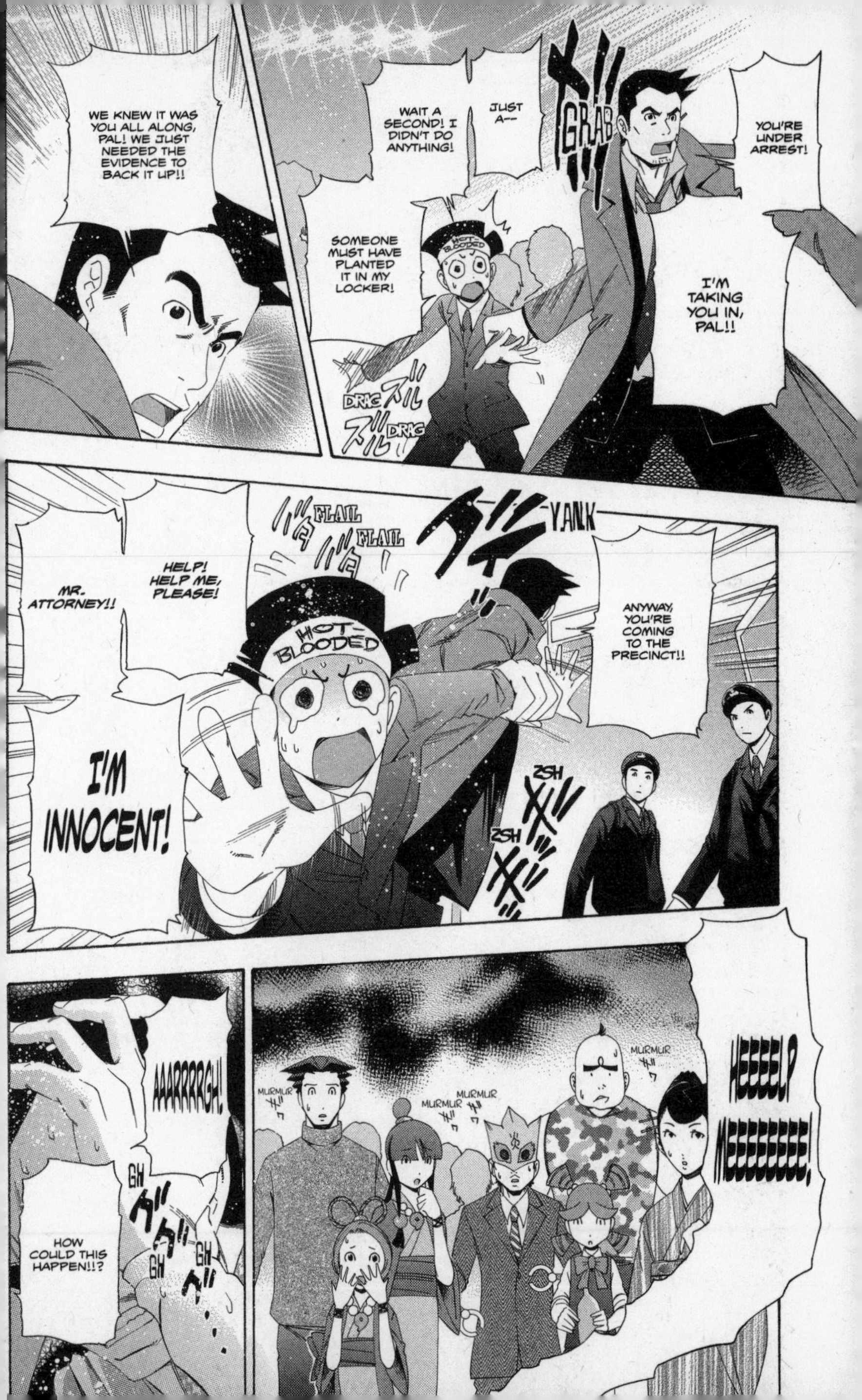
YOU'RE UNDER ARREST!
GRAB
JUST A--
WAIT A SECOND! I DIDN'T DO ANYTHING!
I'M TAKING YOU IN, PAL!!
SOMEONE MUST HAVE PLANTED IT IN MY LOCKER!
DRAG
DRAG
WE KNEW IT WAS YOU ALL ALONG, PAL! WE JUST NEEDED THE EVIDENCE TO BACK IT UP!!
YANK
ANYWAY, YOU'RE COMING TO THE PRECINCT!!
FLAIL
FLAIL
HELP! HELP ME, PLEASE!
MR. ATTORNEY!!
I'M INNOCENT!
ZSH
ZSH
HEEEEELP MEEEEEEEEE!
MURMUR
MURMUR
MURMUR
MURMUR
AAARRRRGH!
GH
GH
GH
HOW COULD THIS HAPPEN!!?

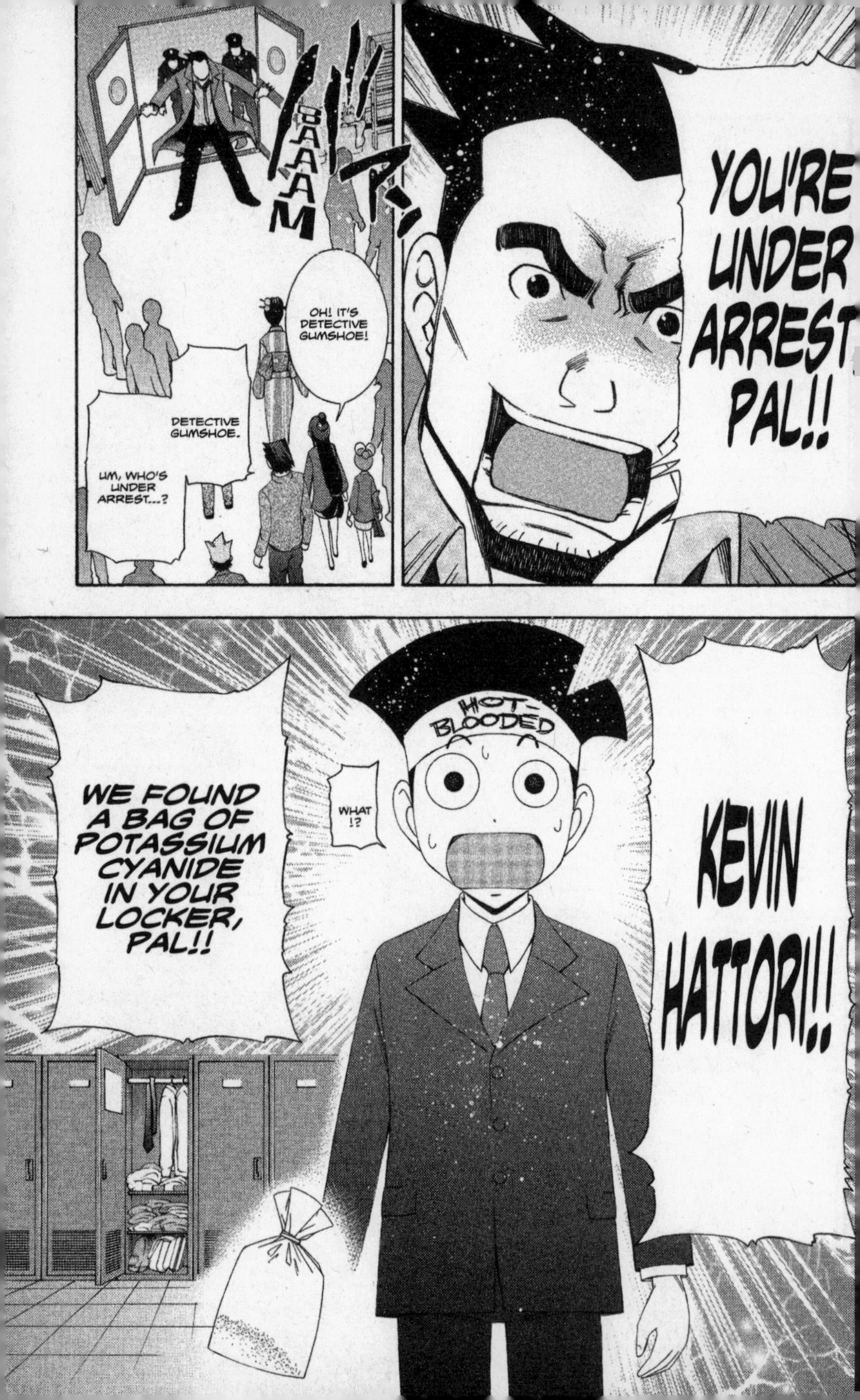
YOU'RE UNDER ARREST, PAL!!
BAAAAM
OH! IT'S DETECTIVE GUMSHOE!
DETECTIVE GUMSHOE.
UM, WHO'S UNDER ARREST...?
KEVIN HATTORI!!!
HOT-BLOODED
WHAT!?
WE FOUND A BAG OF POTASSIUM CYANIDE IN YOUR LOCKER, PAL!!

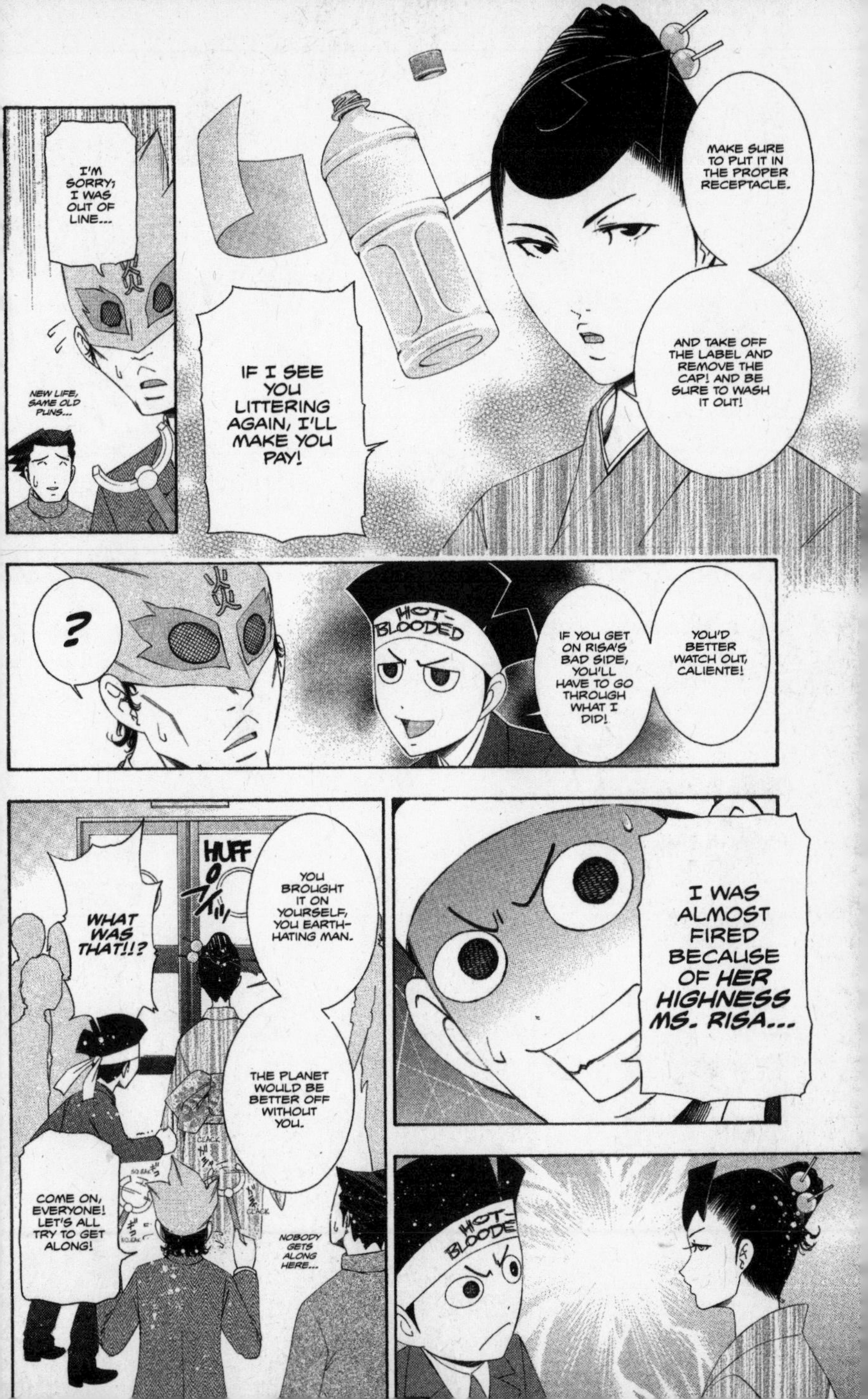
MAKE SURE TO PUT IT IN THE PROPER RECEPTACLE.
AND TAKE OFF THE LABEL AND REMOVE THE CAP! AND BE SURE TO WASH IT OUT!
IF I SEE YOU LITTERING AGAIN, I'LL MAKE YOU PAY!
I'M SORRY; I WAS OUT OF LINE...
NEW LIFE, SAME OLD PUNS...
YOU'D BETTER WATCH OUT, CALIENTE!
IF YOU GET ON RISA'S BAD SIDE, YOU'LL HAVE TO GO THROUGH WHAT I DID!
HOT-BLOODED
?
I WAS ALMOST FIRED BECAUSE OF HER HIGHNESS MS. RISA...
HUFF
YOU BROUGHT IT ON YOURSELF, YOU EARTH-HATING MAN.
WHAT WAS THAT!!?
THE PLANET WOULD BE BETTER OFF WITHOUT YOU.
COME ON, EVERYONE! LET'S ALL TRY TO GET ALONG!
NOBODY GETS ALONG HERE...

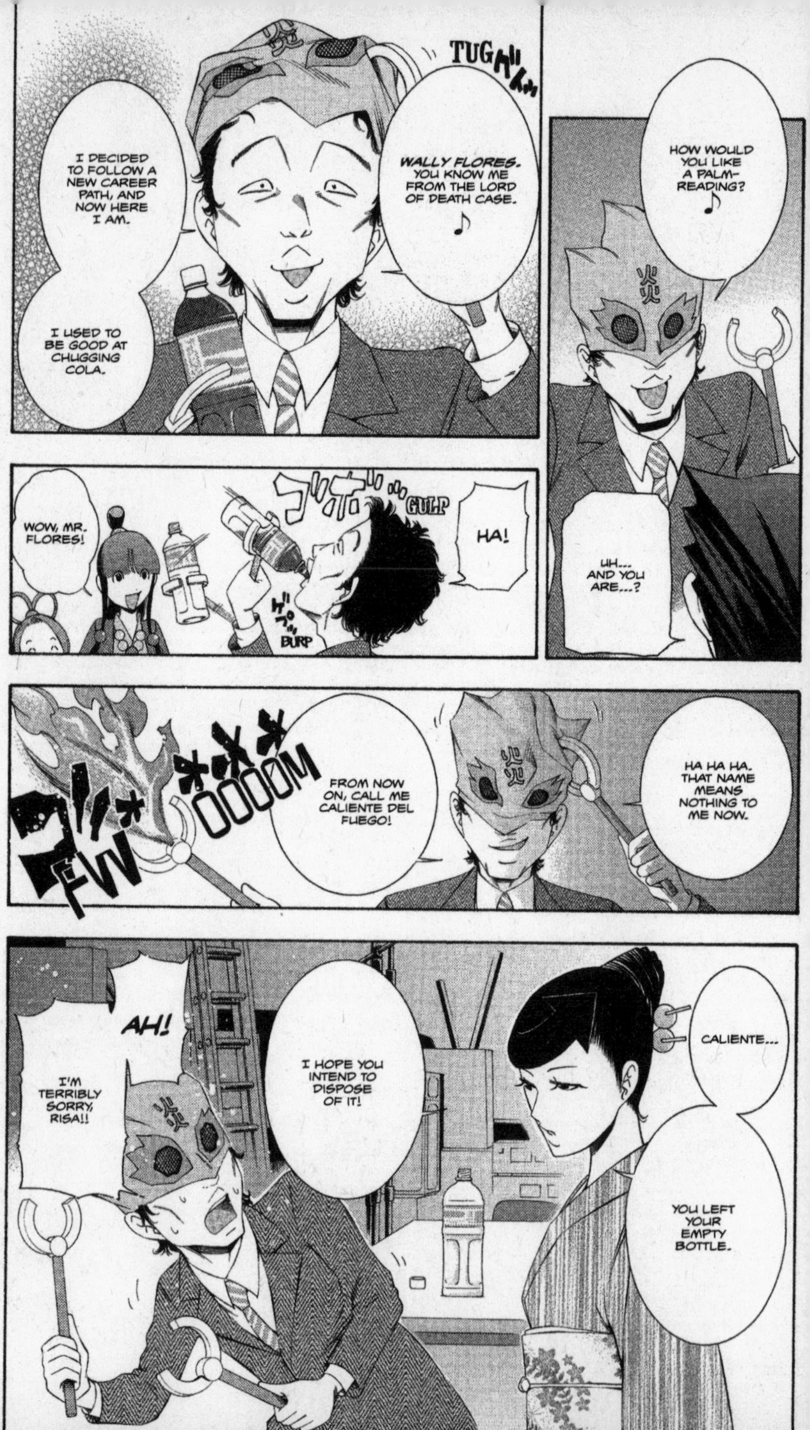
HOW WOULD YOU LIKE A PALM-READING? ♪
UH... AND YOU ARE...?
TUG
WALLY FLORES. YOU KNOW ME FROM THE LORD OF DEATH CASE. ♪
I DECIDED TO FOLLOW A NEW CAREER PATH, AND NOW HERE I AM.
I USED TO BE GOOD AT CHUGGING COLA.
HA!
GULP
BURP
WOW, MR. FLORES!
HA HA HA. THAT NAME MEANS NOTHING TO ME NOW.
FROM NOW ON, CALL ME CALIENTE DEL FUEGO!
FWOOOOOM
CALIENTE...
YOU LEFT YOUR EMPTY BOTTLE.
I HOPE YOU INTEND TO DISPOSE OF IT!
AH!
I'M TERRIBLY SORRY, RISA!!

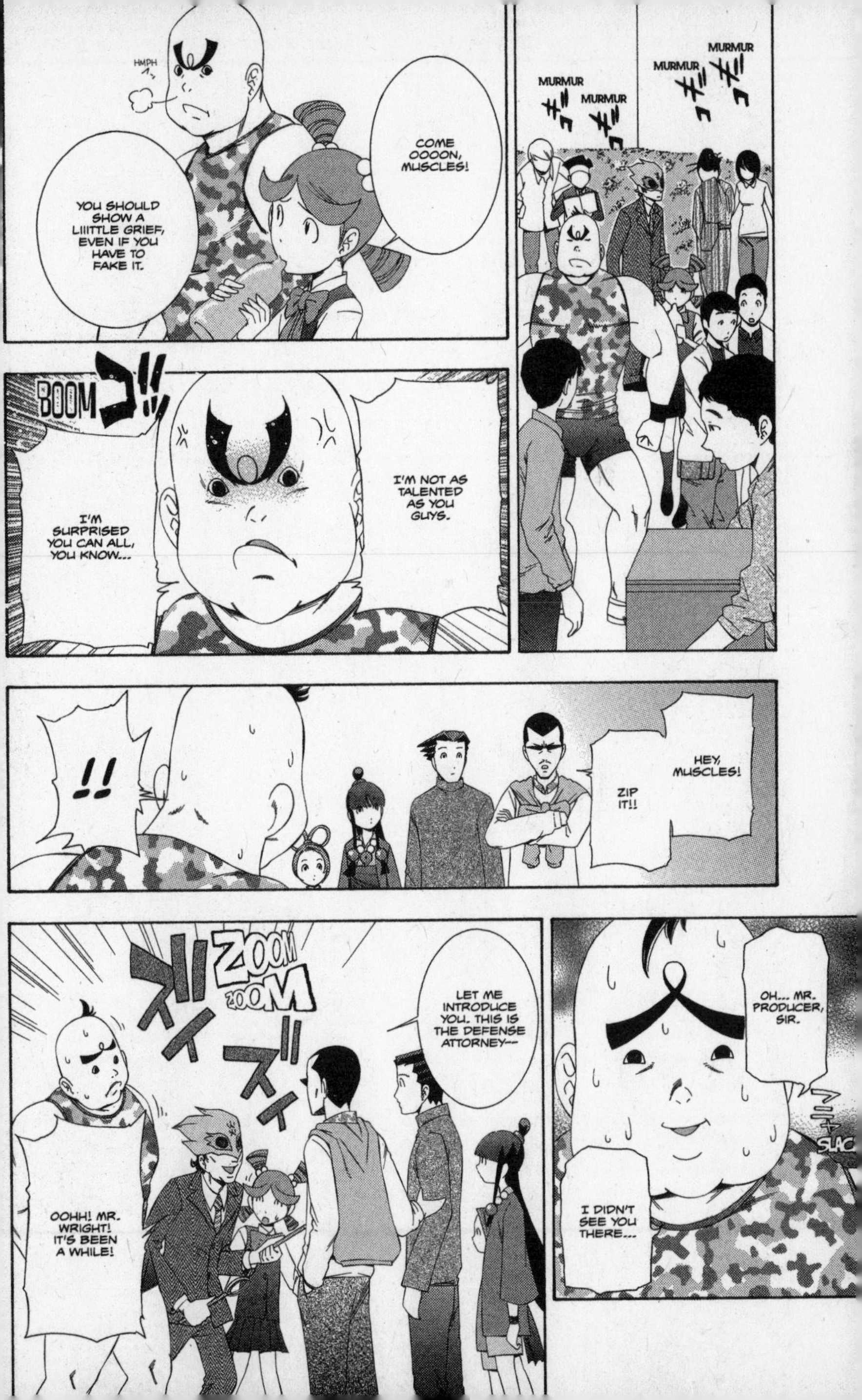
MURMUR
MURMUR
MURMUR
MURMUR
COME OOOON, MUSCLES!
HMPH
YOU SHOULD SHOW A LIIITTLE GRIEF, EVEN IF YOU HAVE TO FAKE IT.
I'M NOT AS TALENTED AS YOU GUYS.
BOOM
I'M SURPRISED YOU CAN ALL, YOU KNOW...
HEY, MUSCLES!
ZIP IT!!
!!
OH... MR. PRODUCER, SIR.
SLAC
I DIDN'T SEE YOU THERE...
LET ME INTRODUCE YOU. THIS IS THE DEFENSE ATTORNEY--
ZOOM
ZOOM
OOHH! MR. WRIGHT! IT'S BEEN A WHILE!

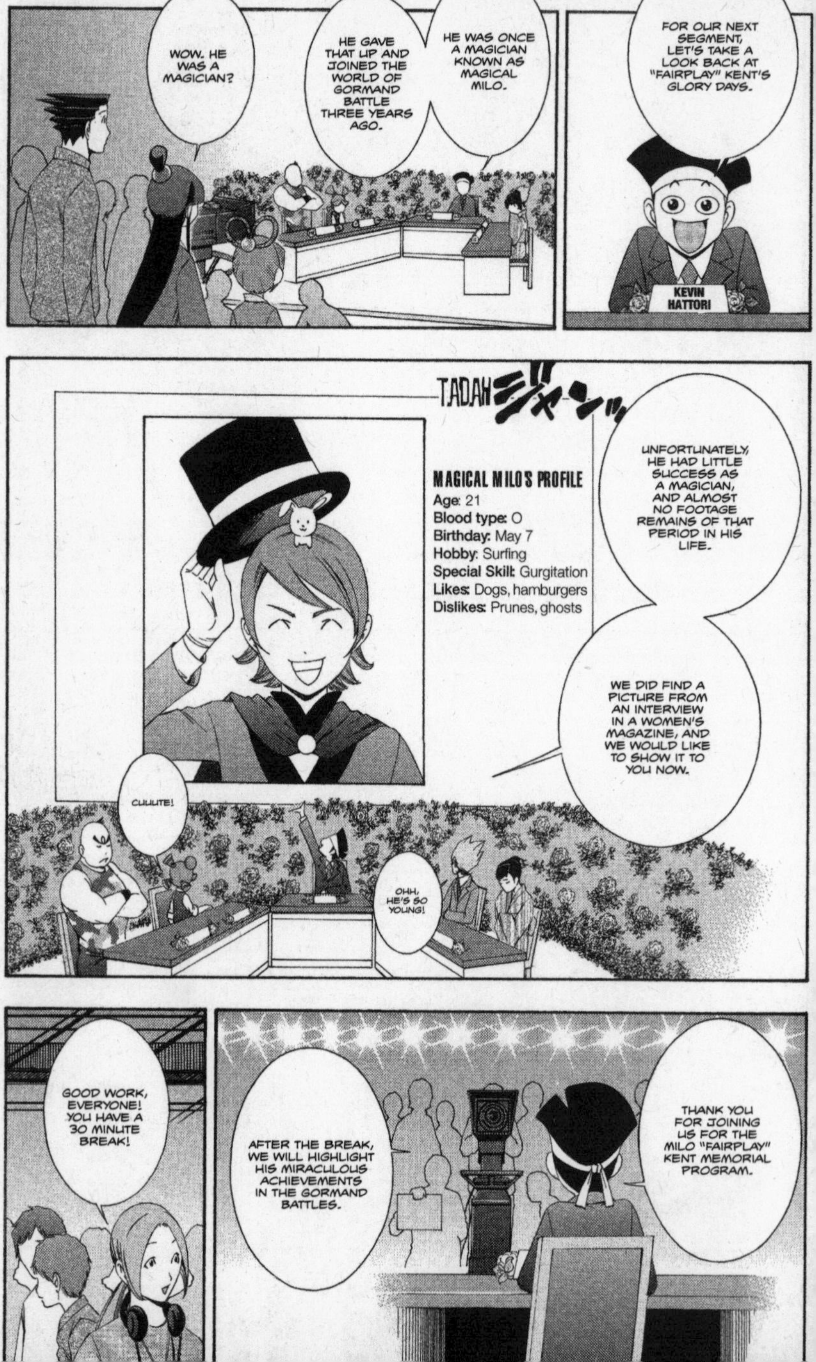
FOR OUR NEXT SEGMENT, LET'S TAKE A LOOK BACK AT "FAIRPLAY" KENT'S GLORY DAYS.
KEVIN HATTORI
HE WAS ONCE A MAGICIAN KNOWN AS MAGICAL MILO.
HE GAVE THAT UP AND JOINED THE WORLD OF GORMAND BATTLE THREE YEARS AGO.
WOW. HE WAS A MAGICIAN?
TADAH
MAGICAL MILO'S PROFILE
Age: 21
Blood type: O
Birthday: May 7
Hobby: Surfing
Special Skill: Gurgitation
Likes: Dogs, hamburgers
Dislikes: Prunes, ghosts
UNFORTUNATELY, HE HAD LITTLE SUCCESS AS A MAGICIAN, AND ALMOST NO FOOTAGE REMAINS OF THAT PERIOD IN HIS LIFE.
WE DID FIND A PICTURE FROM AN INTERVIEW IN A WOMEN'S MAGAZINE, AND WE WOULD LIKE TO SHOW IT TO YOU NOW.
OHH, HE'S SO YOUNG!
CUUUTE!
THANK YOU FOR JOINING US FOR THE MILO "FAIRPLAY" KENT MEMORIAL PROGRAM.
AFTER THE BREAK, WE WILL HIGHLIGHT HIS MIRACULOUS ACHIEVEMENTS IN THE GORMAND BATTLES.
GOOD WORK, EVERYONE! YOU HAVE A 30 MINUTE BREAK!

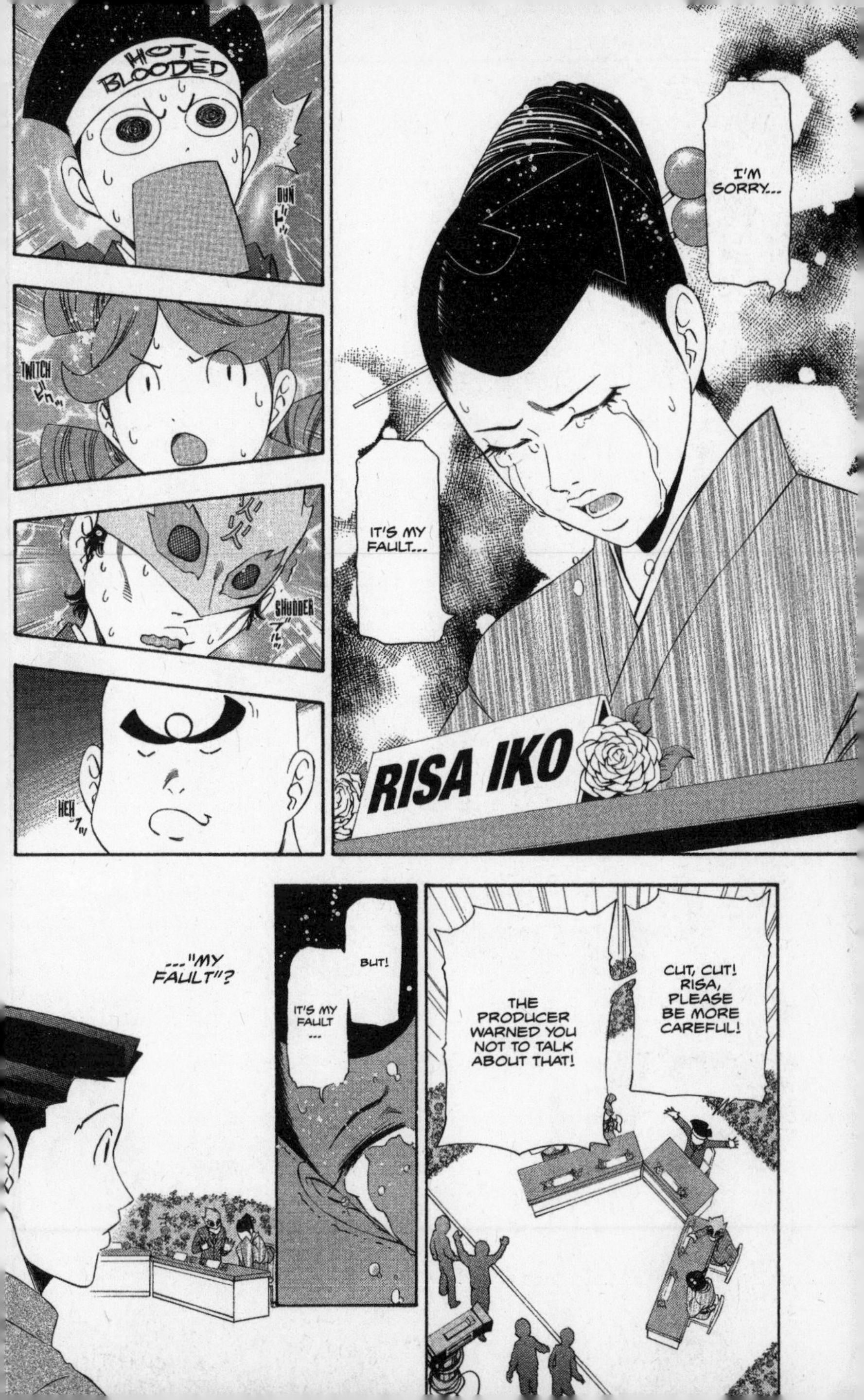
I'M SORRY...
IT'S MY FAULT...
RISA IKO
HOT-BLOODED
DUN
TWITCH
SHUDDER
HEH
CUT, CUT! RISA, PLEASE BE MORE CAREFUL!
THE PRODUCER WARNED YOU NOT TO TALK ABOUT THAT!
BUT!
IT'S MY FAULT...
..."MY FAULT"?

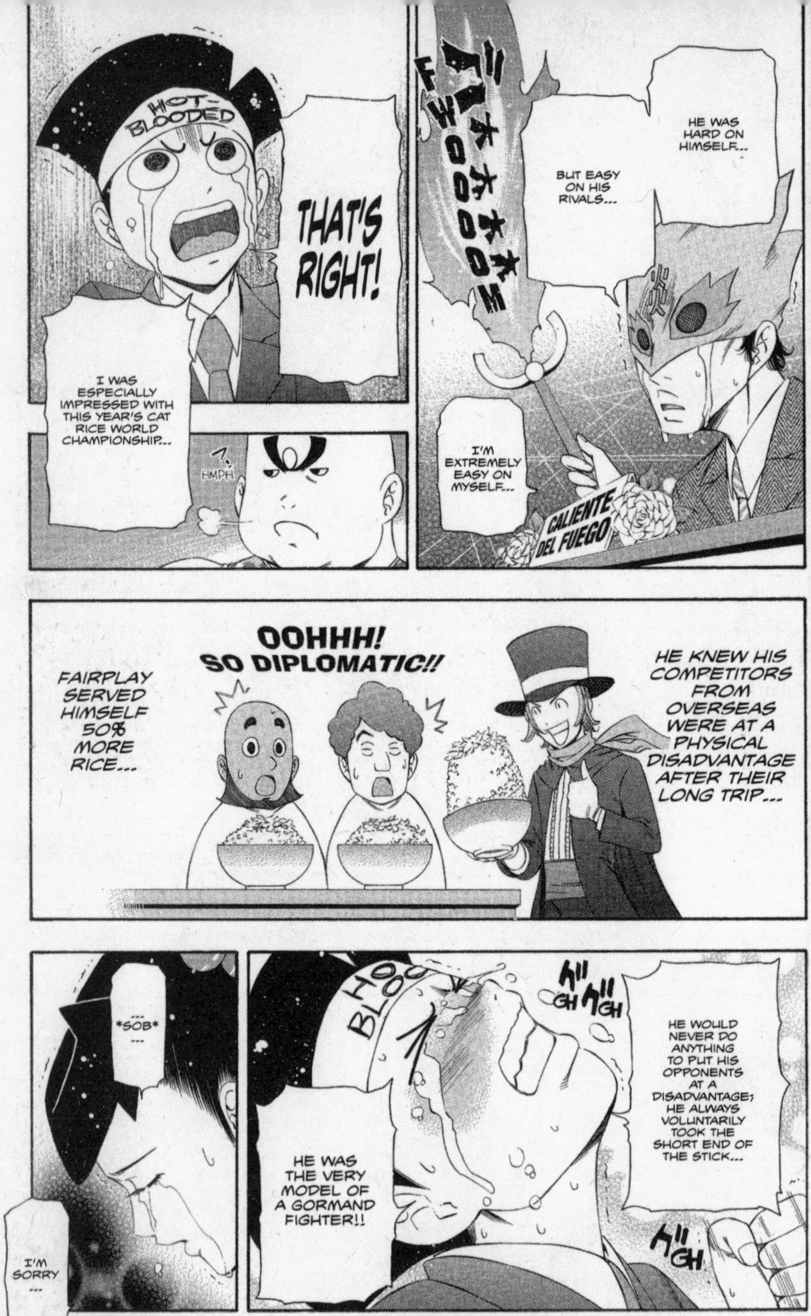
HE WAS HARD ON HIMSELF...
BUT EASY ON HIS RIVALS...
FWOOOOOM
I'M EXTREMELY EASY ON MYSELF...
CALIENTE DEL FUEGO
HOT-BLOODED
THAT'S RIGHT!
I WAS ESPECIALLY IMPRESSED WITH THIS YEAR'S CAT RICE WORLD CHAMPIONSHIP...
HMPH
HE KNEW HIS COMPETITORS FROM OVERSEAS WERE AT A PHYSICAL DISADVANTAGE AFTER THEIR LONG TRIP...
OOHHH! SO DIPLOMATIC!!
FAIRPLAY SERVED HIMSELF 50% MORE RICE...
GH GH
HE WOULD NEVER DO ANYTHING TO PUT HIS OPPONENTS AT A DISADVANTAGE; HE ALWAYS VOLUNTARILY TOOK THE SHORT END OF THE STICK...
HE WAS THE VERY MODEL OF A GORMAND FIGHTER!!
GH
... *SOB* ...
I'M SORRY ...

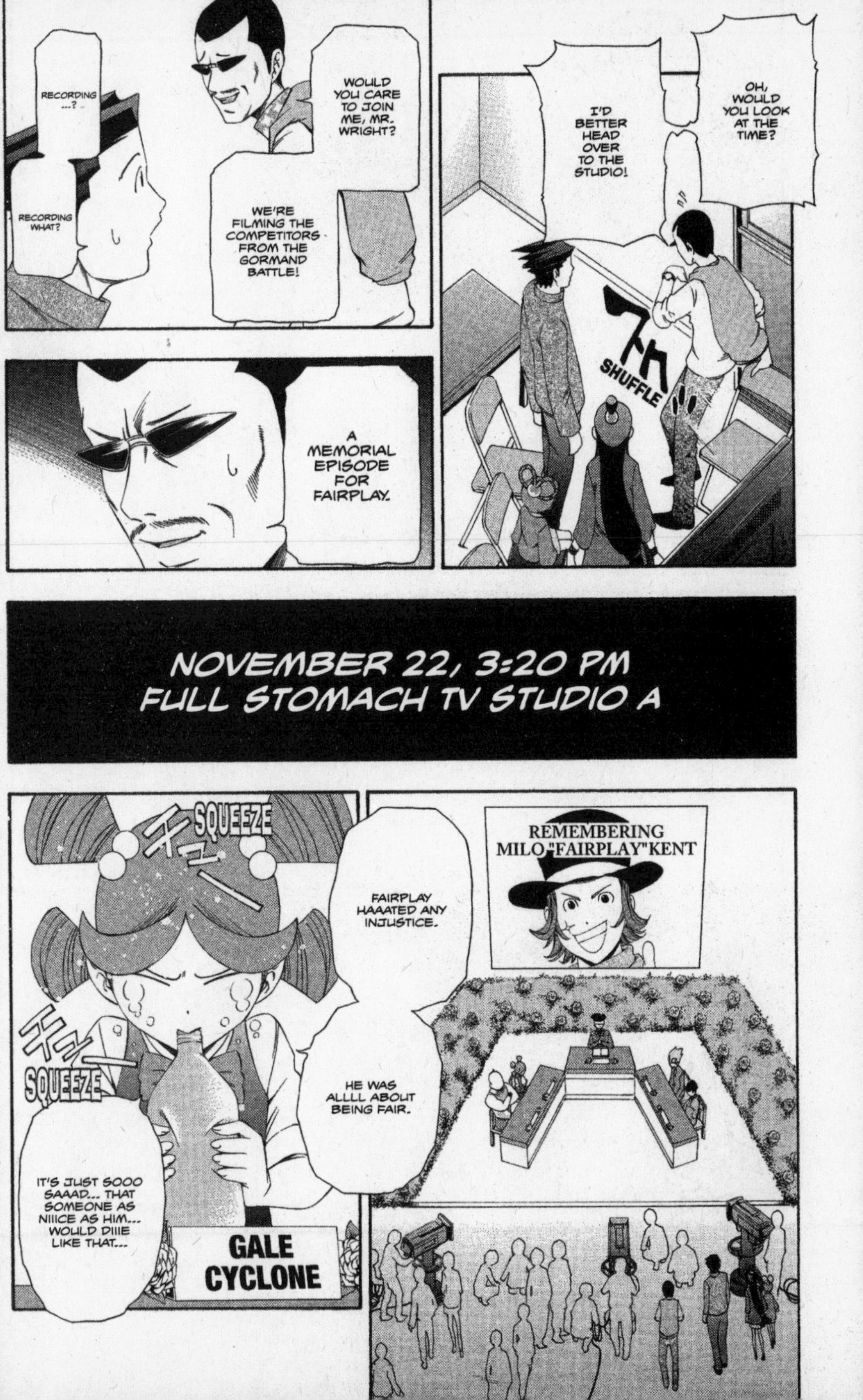
OH, WOULD YOU LOOK AT THE TIME?
I'D BETTER HEAD OVER TO THE STUDIO!
SHUFFLE
WOULD YOU CARE TO JOIN ME, MR. WRIGHT?
RECORDING ...?
WE'RE FILMING THE COMPETITORS FROM THE GORMAND BATTLE!
RECORDING WHAT?
A MEMORIAL EPISODE FOR FAIRPLAY.
NOVEMBER 22, 3:20 PM
FULL STOMACH TV STUDIO A
REMEMBERING MILO "FAIRPLAY" KENT
FAIRPLAY HAAATED ANY INJUSTICE.
HE WAS ALLLL ABOUT BEING FAIR.
SQUEEZE
SQUEEZE
IT'S JUST SOOO SAAAD... THAT SOMEONE AS NIIICE AS HIM... WOULD DIIIE LIKE THAT...
GALE CYCLONE

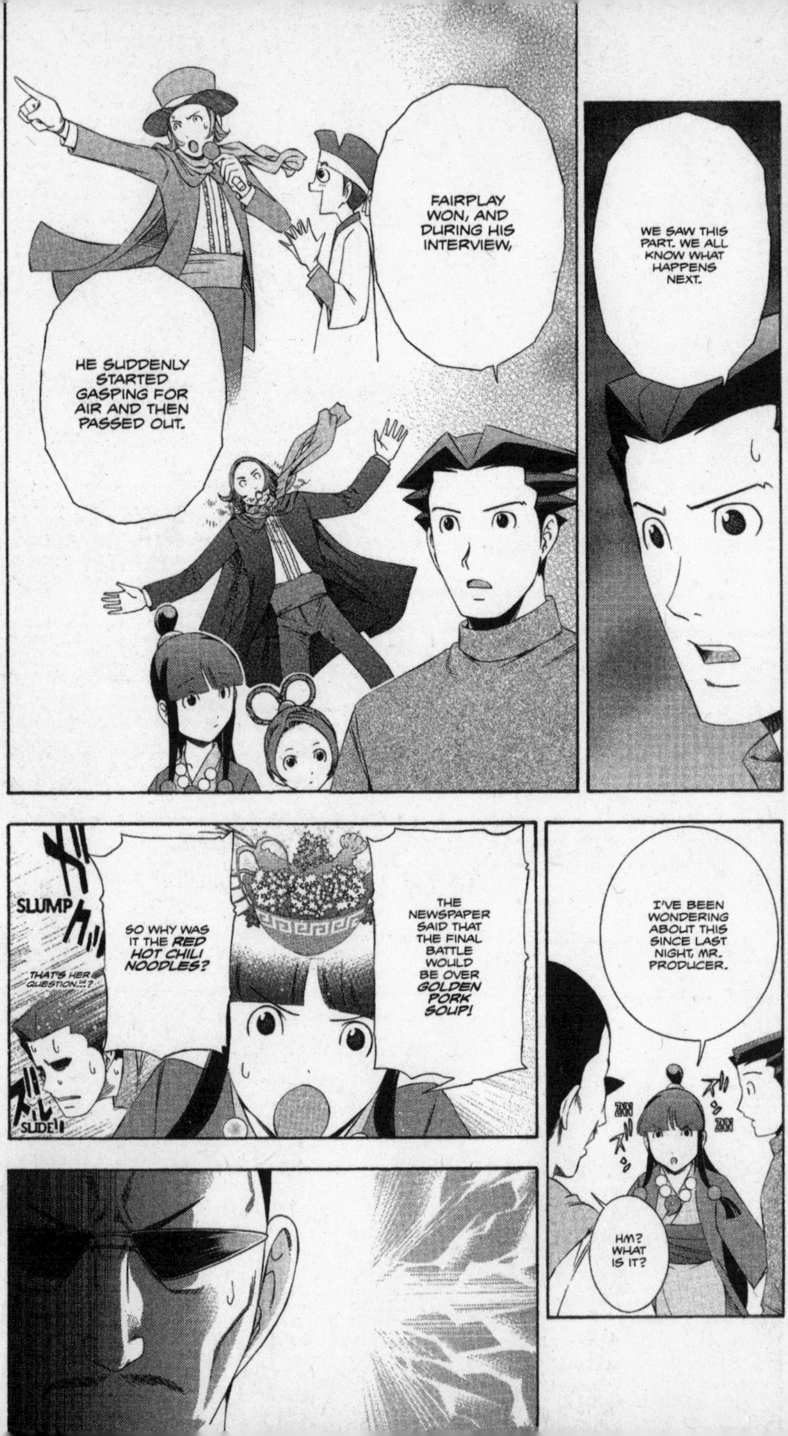
WE SAW THIS PART. WE ALL KNOW WHAT HAPPENS NEXT.
FAIRPLAY WON, AND DURING HIS INTERVIEW,
HE SUDDENLY STARTED GASPING FOR AIR AND THEN PASSED OUT.
I'VE BEEN WONDERING ABOUT THIS SINCE LAST NIGHT, MR. PRODUCER.
ZNN
ZNN
HM? WHAT IS IT?
THE NEWSPAPER SAID THAT THE FINAL BATTLE WOULD BE OVER *GOLDEN PORK SOUP!*
SO WHY WAS IT THE *RED HOT CHILI NOODLES?*
SLUMP
THAT'S HER QUESTION...?
SLIDE!!

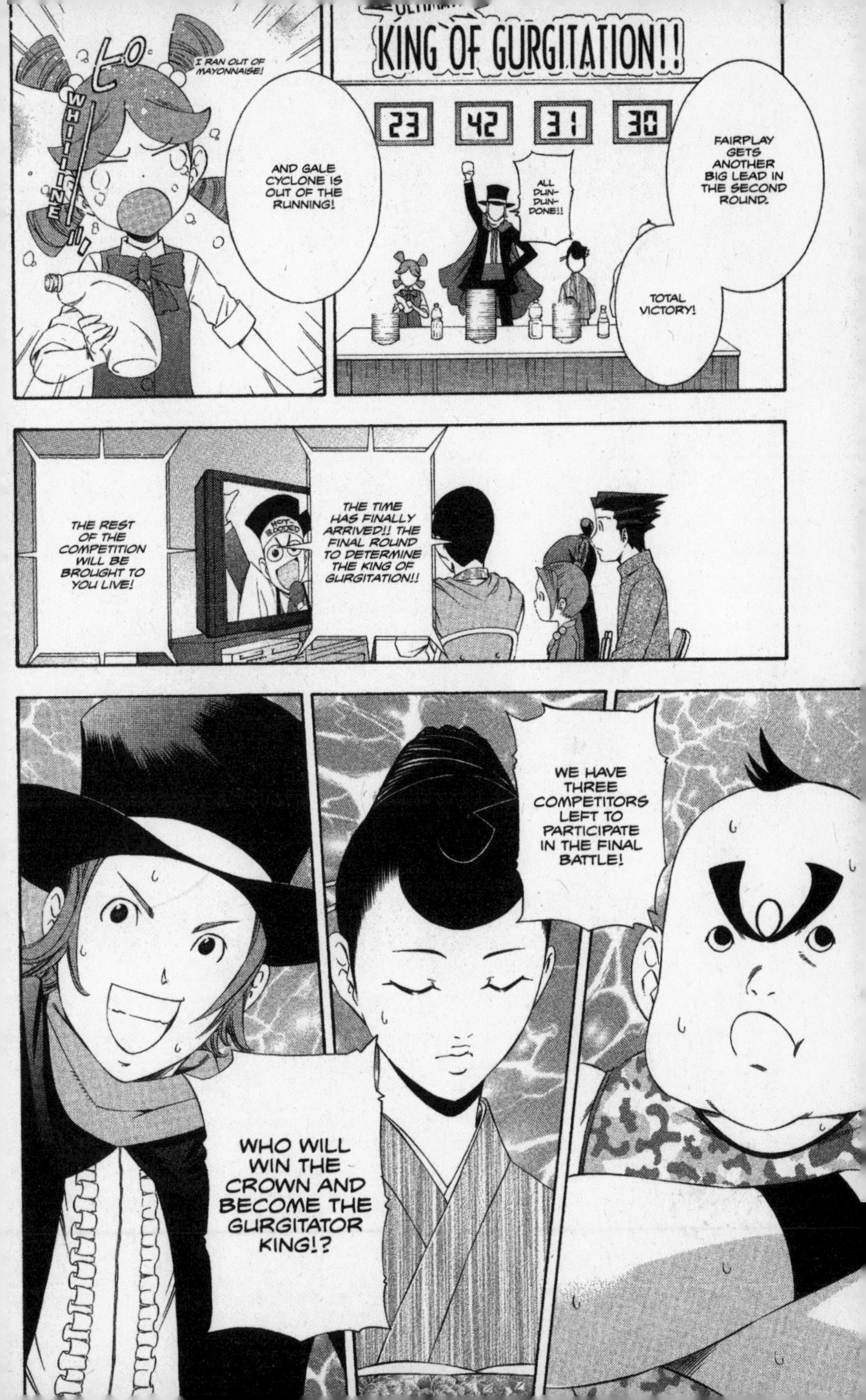
KING OF GURGITATION!!
23 42 31 30
FAIRPLAY GETS ANOTHER BIG LEAD IN THE SECOND ROUND.
ALL DUN-DUN-DONE!!
TOTAL VICTORY!
AND GALE CYCLONE IS OUT OF THE RUNNING!
I RAN OUT OF MAYONNAISE!
WHIIIINE
THE TIME HAS FINALLY ARRIVED!! THE FINAL ROUND TO DETERMINE THE KING OF GURGITATION!!
THE REST OF THE COMPETITION WILL BE BROUGHT TO YOU LIVE!
WE HAVE THREE COMPETITORS LEFT TO PARTICIPATE IN THE FINAL BATTLE!
WHO WILL WIN THE CROWN AND BECOME THE GURGITATOR KING!?

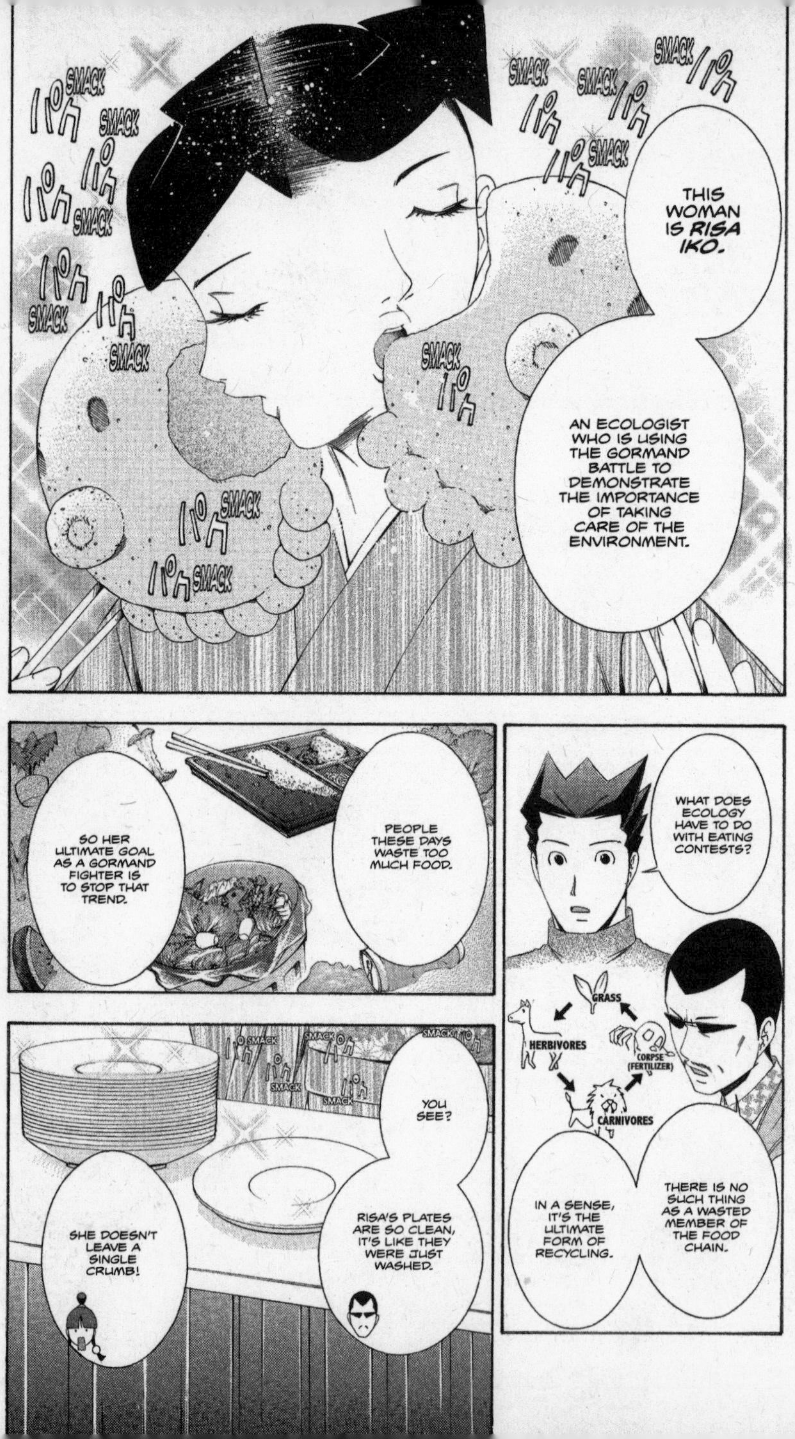
SMACK パク
SMACK パク
SMACK パク
SMACK パク
THIS WOMAN IS RISA IKO.
AN ECOLOGIST WHO IS USING THE GORMAND BATTLE TO DEMONSTRATE THE IMPORTANCE OF TAKING CARE OF THE ENVIRONMENT.
SMACK パク
SMACK パク
SMACK パク
SMACK パク
SMACK パク
SMACK パク
SMACK パク
WHAT DOES ECOLOGY HAVE TO DO WITH EATING CONTESTS?
GRASS
HERBIVORES
CARNIVORES
CORPSE (FERTILIZER)
THERE IS NO SUCH THING AS A WASTED MEMBER OF THE FOOD CHAIN.
IN A SENSE, IT'S THE ULTIMATE FORM OF RECYCLING.
PEOPLE THESE DAYS WASTE TOO MUCH FOOD.
SO HER ULTIMATE GOAL AS A GORMAND FIGHTER IS TO STOP THAT TREND.
SMACK
SMACK
SMACK
SMACK
SMACK
YOU SEE?
RISA'S PLATES ARE SO CLEAN, IT'S LIKE THEY WERE JUST WASHED.
SHE DOESN'T LEAVE A SINGLE CRUMB!

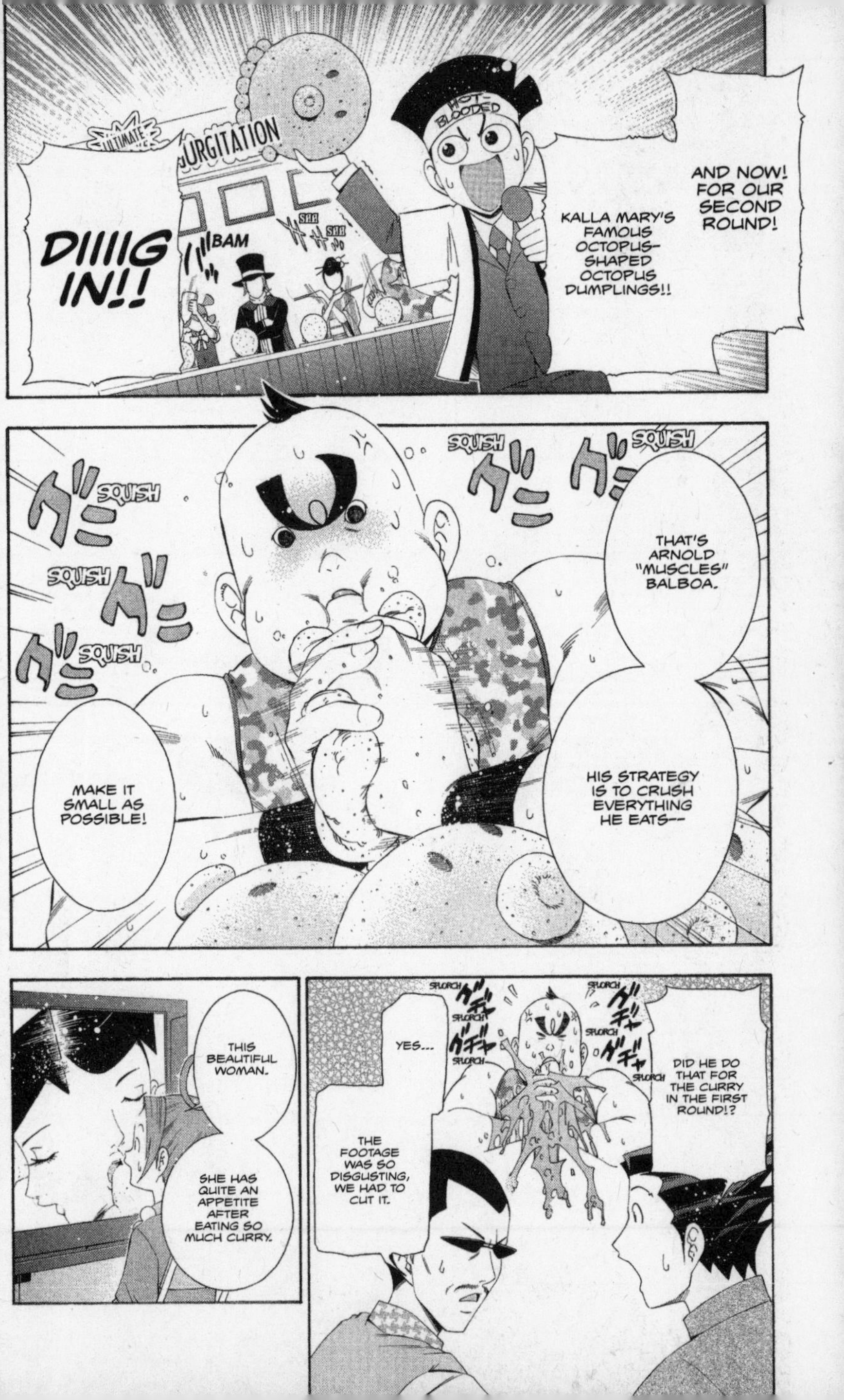
AND NOW! FOR OUR SECOND ROUND!
KALLA MARY'S FAMOUS OCTOPUS-SHAPED OCTOPUS DUMPLINGS!!
HOT-BLOODED
ULTIMATE
BAM
DIIIIG IN!!
SQUISH
SQUISH
THAT'S ARNOLD "MUSCLES" BALBOA.
HIS STRATEGY IS TO CRUSH EVERYTHING HE EATS--
SQUISH
SQUISH
SQUISH
MAKE IT SMALL AS POSSIBLE!
SPLORCH
SPLORCH
DID HE DO THAT FOR THE CURRY IN THE FIRST ROUND!?
YES...
THE FOOTAGE WAS SO DISGUSTING, WE HAD TO CUT IT.
THIS BEAUTIFUL WOMAN.
SHE HAS QUITE AN APPETITE AFTER EATING SO MUCH CURRY.

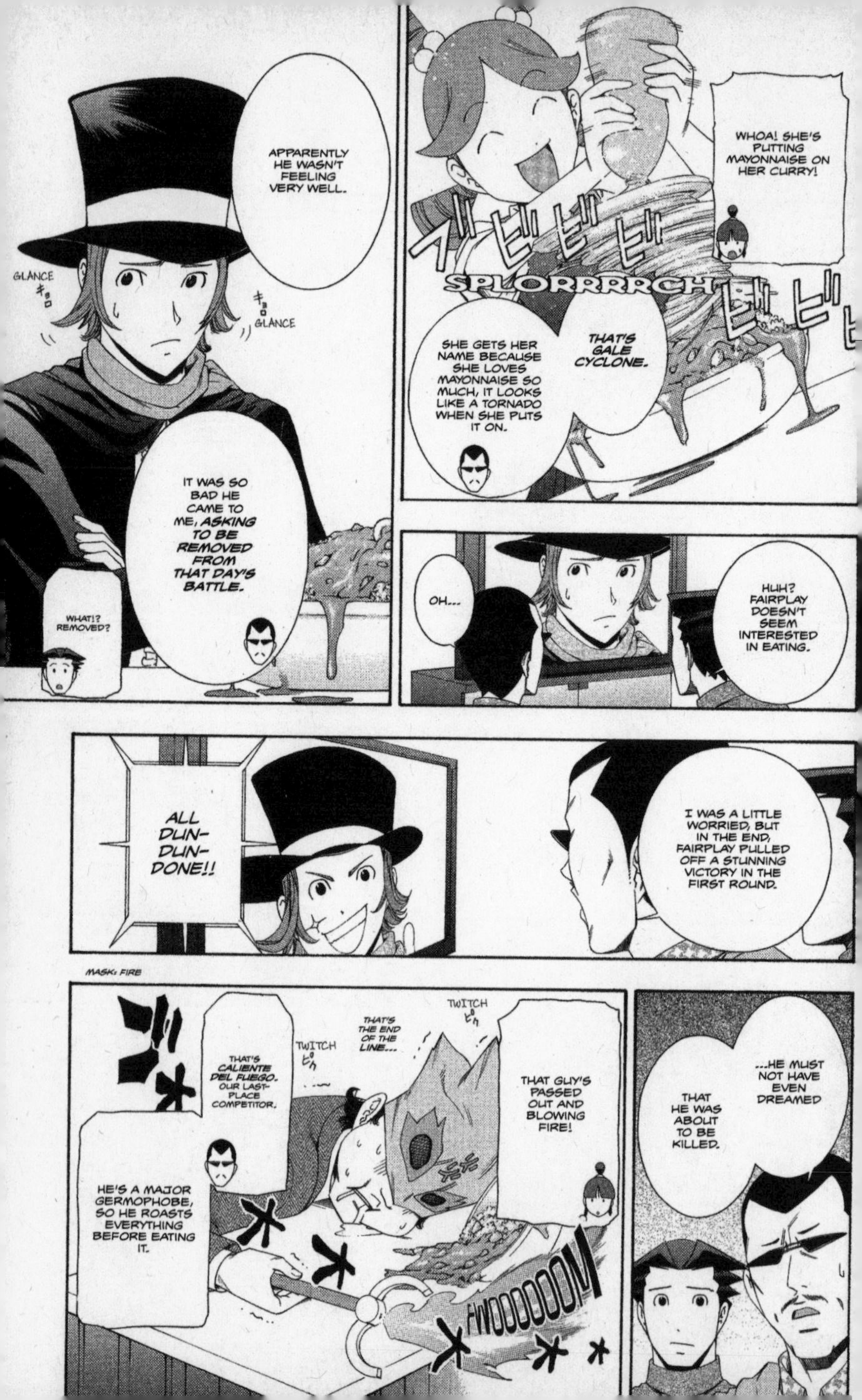
WHOA! SHE'S PUTTING MAYONNAISE ON HER CURRY!
SPLORRRRCH
THAT'S GALE CYCLONE.
SHE GETS HER NAME BECAUSE SHE LOVES MAYONNAISE SO MUCH, IT LOOKS LIKE A TORNADO WHEN SHE PUTS IT ON.
HUH? FAIRPLAY DOESN'T SEEM INTERESTED IN EATING.
OH...
APPARENTLY HE WASN'T FEELING VERY WELL.
GLANCE
GLANCE
IT WAS SO BAD HE CAME TO ME, ASKING TO BE REMOVED FROM THAT DAY'S BATTLE.
WHAT!? REMOVED?
I WAS A LITTLE WORRIED, BUT IN THE END, FAIRPLAY PULLED OFF A STUNNING VICTORY IN THE FIRST ROUND.
ALL DUN-DUN-DONE!!
MASK: FIRE
...HE MUST NOT HAVE EVEN DREAMED
THAT HE WAS ABOUT TO BE KILLED.
TWITCH
THAT GUY'S PASSED OUT AND BLOWING FIRE!
THAT'S THE END OF THE LINE...
TWITCH
THAT'S CALIENTE DEL FUEGO. OUR LAST-PLACE COMPETITOR.
HE'S A MAJOR GERMOPHOBE, SO HE ROASTS EVERYTHING BEFORE EATING IT.
FWOOOOOOM

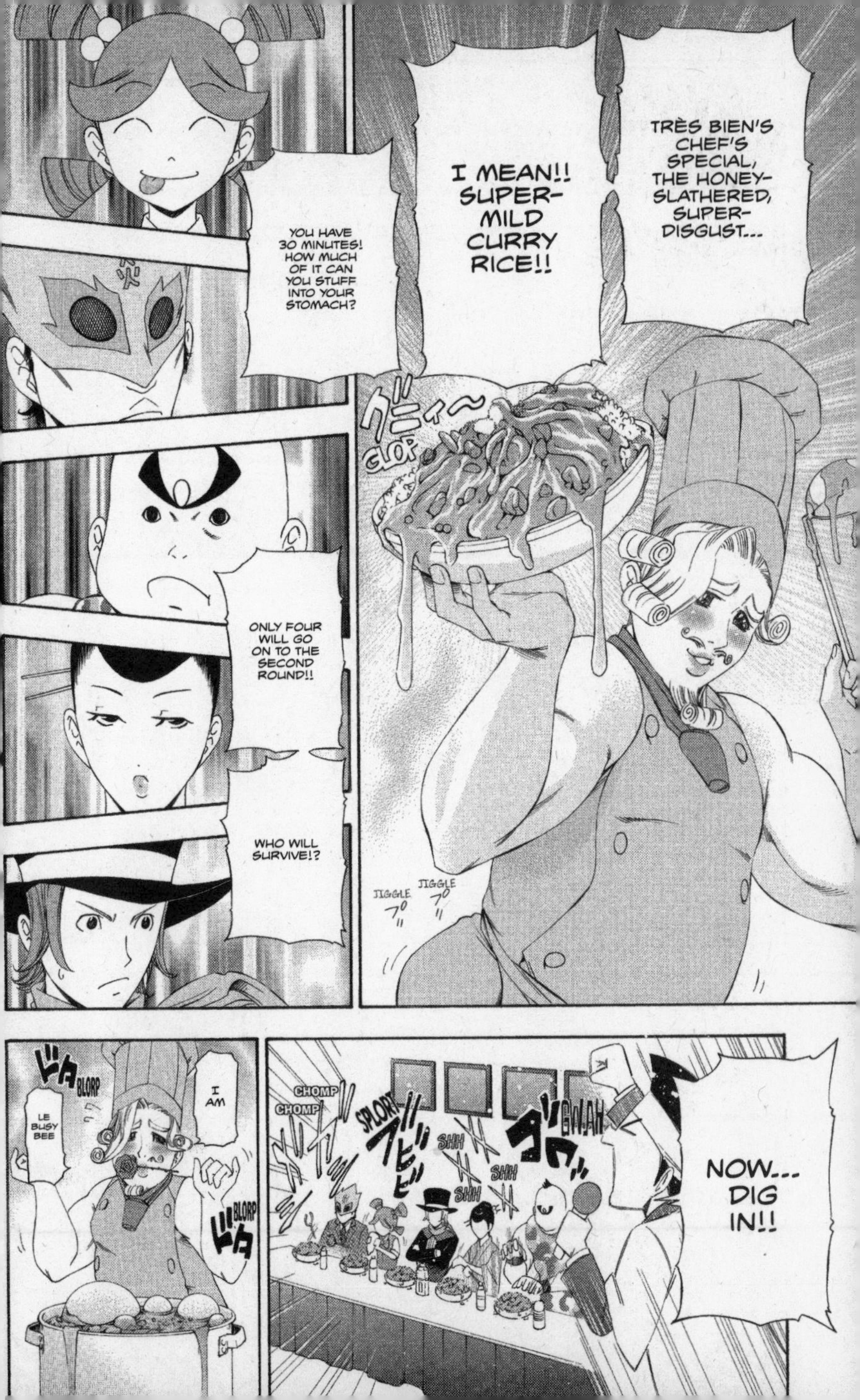
TRÈS BIEN'S CHEF'S SPECIAL, THE HONEY-SLATHERED, SUPER-DISGUST...
I MEAN!! SUPER-MILD CURRY RICE!!
GLOP
JIGGLE
JIGGLE
YOU HAVE 30 MINUTES! HOW MUCH OF IT CAN YOU STUFF INTO YOUR STOMACH?
ONLY FOUR WILL GO ON TO THE SECOND ROUND!!
WHO WILL SURVIVE!?
NOW... DIG IN!!
GWAH
SPLORT
CHOMP
CHOMP
SHH
SHH
SHH
I AM
LE BUSY BEE
BLORP
BLORP

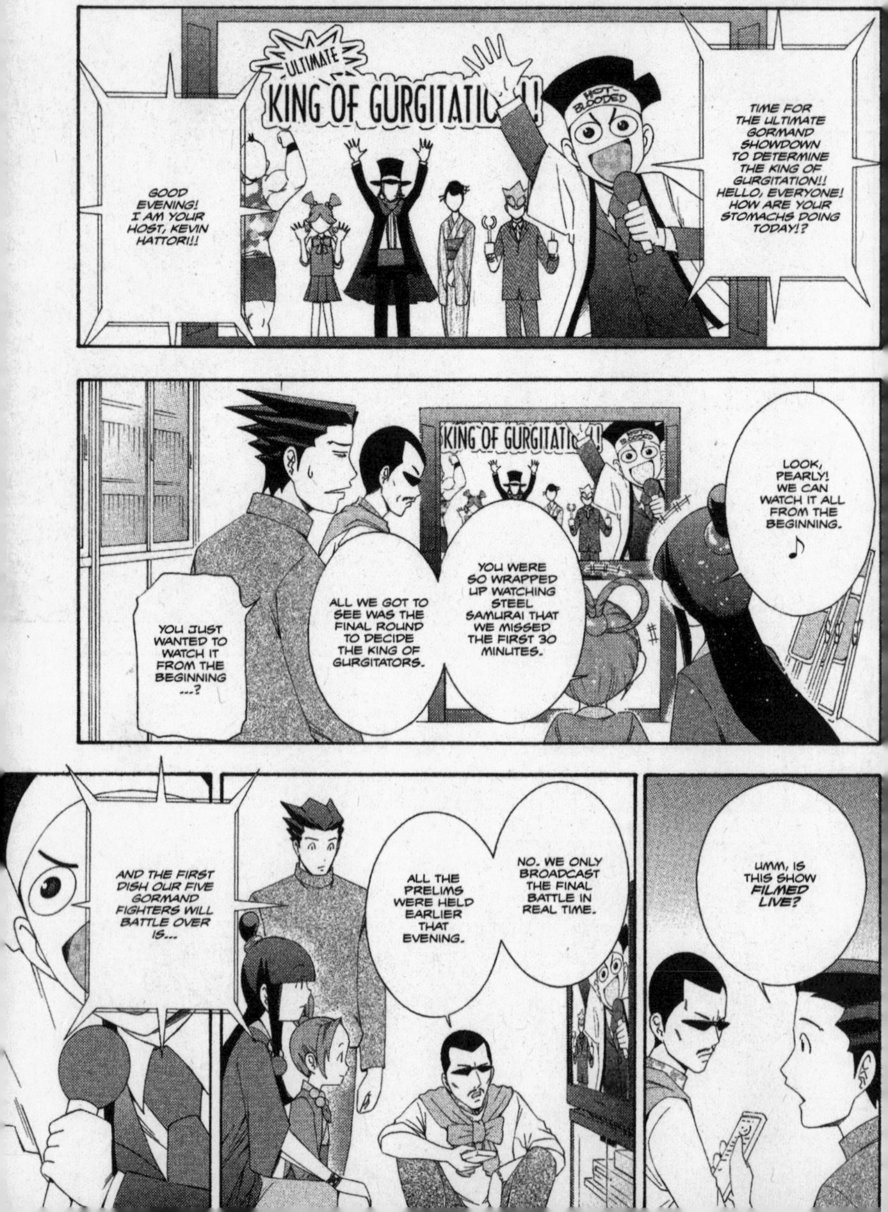
ULTIMATE
KING OF GURGITATIO
HOT-BLOODED
TIME FOR THE ULTIMATE GORMAND SHOWDOWN TO DETERMINE THE KING OF GURGITATION!! HELLO, EVERYONE! HOW ARE YOUR STOMACHS DOING TODAY!?
GOOD EVENING! I AM YOUR HOST, KEVIN HATTORI!!
LOOK, PEARLY! WE CAN WATCH IT ALL FROM THE BEGINNING. ♪
YOU WERE SO WRAPPED UP WATCHING STEEL SAMURAI THAT WE MISSED THE FIRST 30 MINUTES.
ALL WE GOT TO SEE WAS THE FINAL ROUND TO DECIDE THE KING OF GURGITATORS.
YOU JUST WANTED TO WATCH IT FROM THE BEGINNING ...?
UMM, IS THIS SHOW *FILMED LIVE?*
NO. WE ONLY BROADCAST THE FINAL BATTLE IN REAL TIME.
ALL THE PRELIMS WERE HELD EARLIER THAT EVENING.
AND THE FIRST DISH OUR FIVE GORMAND FIGHTERS WILL BATTLE OVER IS...

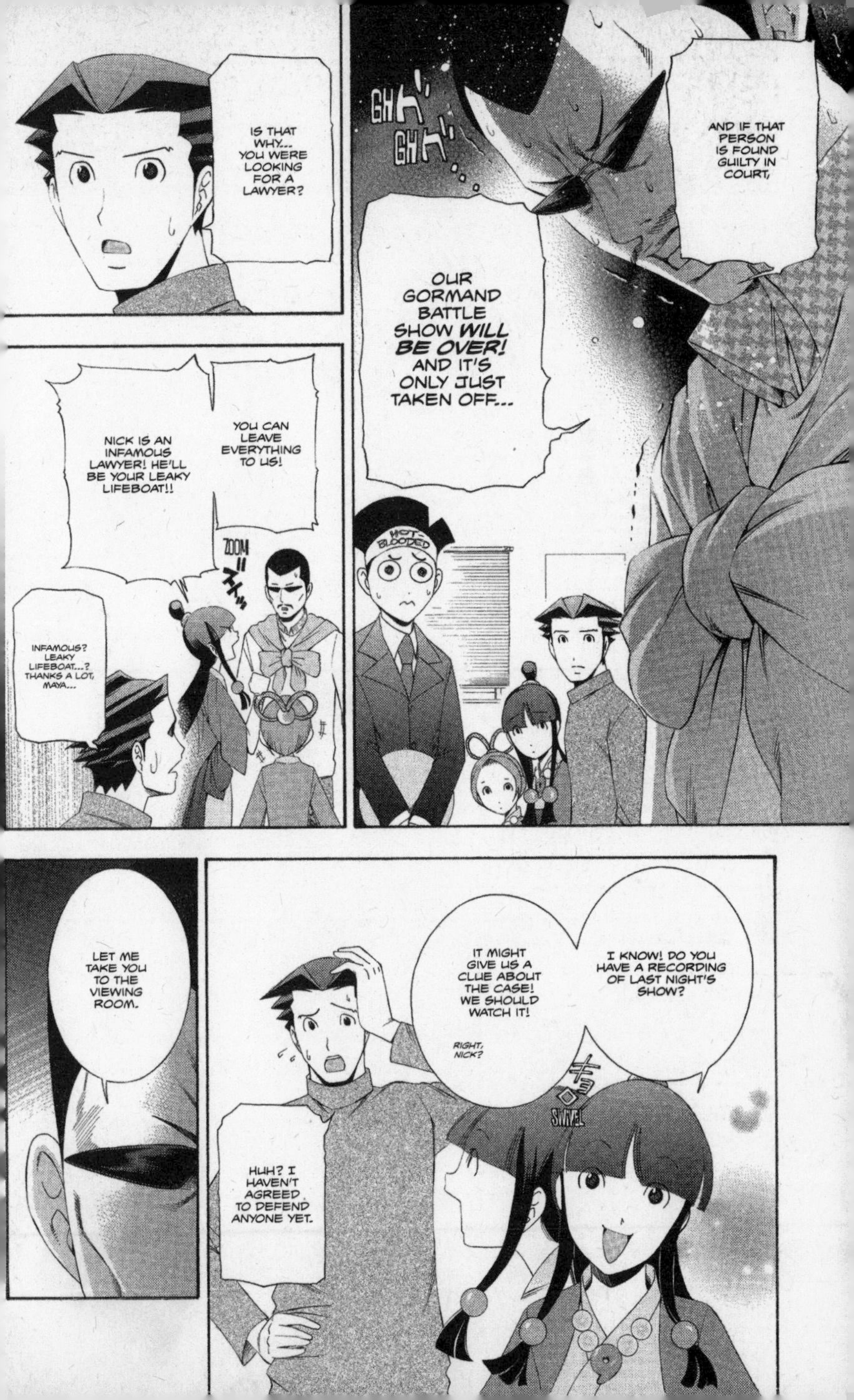

AND IF THAT PERSON IS FOUND GUILTY IN COURT,
GH GH...
OUR GORMAND BATTLE SHOW ***WILL BE OVER!*** AND IT'S ONLY JUST TAKEN OFF...
HOT-BLOODED
IS THAT WHY... YOU WERE LOOKING FOR A LAWYER?
YOU CAN LEAVE EVERYTHING TO US!
NICK IS AN INFAMOUS LAWYER! HE'LL BE YOUR LEAKY LIFEBOAT!!
ZOOM
INFAMOUS? LEAKY LIFEBOAT...? THANKS A LOT, MAYA...
I KNOW! DO YOU HAVE A RECORDING OF LAST NIGHT'S SHOW?
IT MIGHT GIVE US A CLUE ABOUT THE CASE! WE SHOULD WATCH IT!
RIGHT, NICK?
SWIVEL
HUH? I HAVEN'T AGREED TO DEFEND ANYONE YET.
LET ME TAKE YOU TO THE VIEWING ROOM.

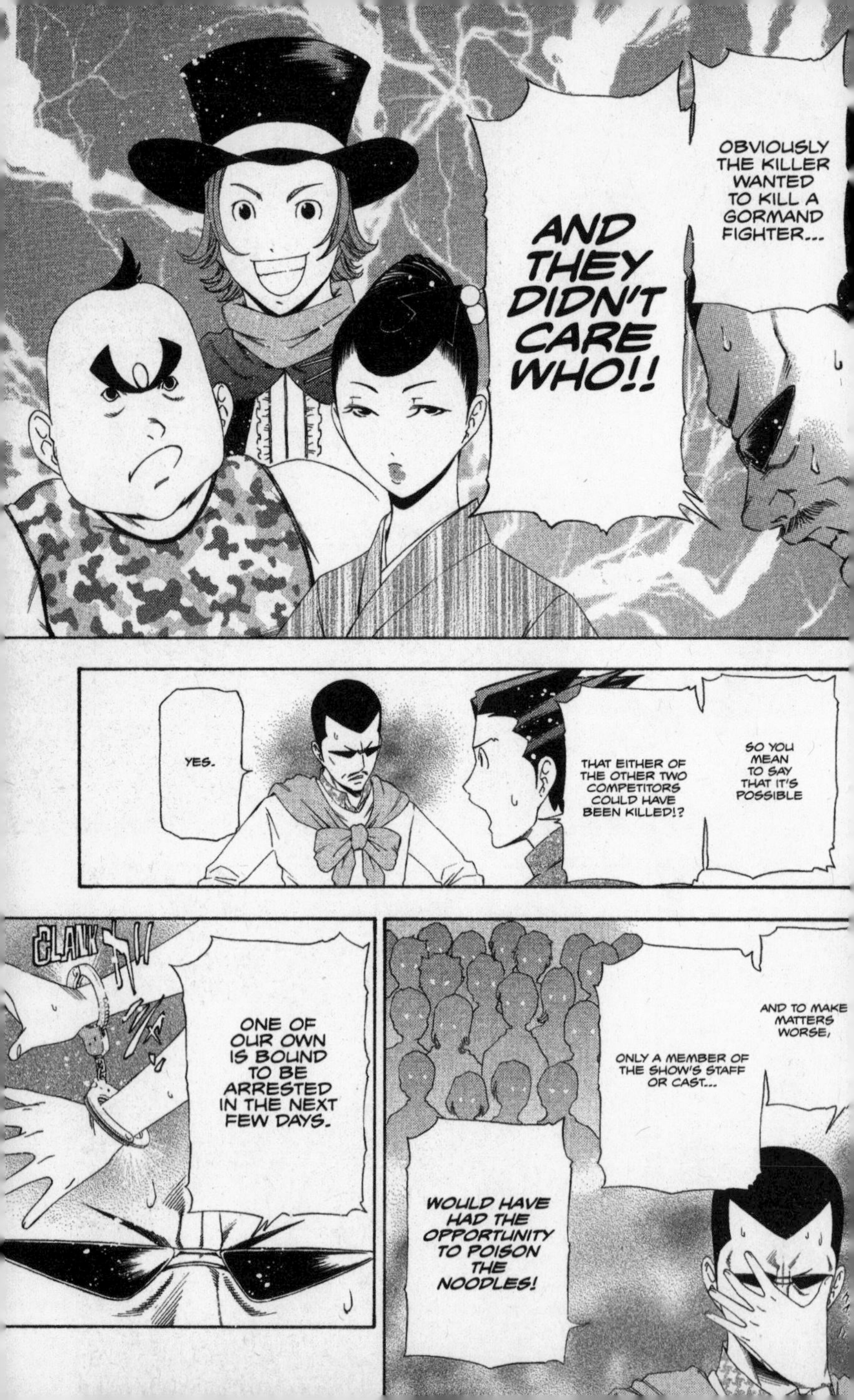
OBVIOUSLY THE KILLER WANTED TO KILL A GORMAND FIGHTER...
AND THEY DIDN'T CARE WHO!!
SO YOU MEAN TO SAY THAT IT'S POSSIBLE
THAT EITHER OF THE OTHER TWO COMPETITORS COULD HAVE BEEN KILLED!?
YES.
AND TO MAKE MATTERS WORSE,
ONLY A MEMBER OF THE SHOW'S STAFF OR CAST...
WOULD HAVE HAD THE OPPORTUNITY TO POISON THE NOODLES!
CLANK
ONE OF OUR OWN IS BOUND TO BE ARRESTED IN THE NEXT FEW DAYS.

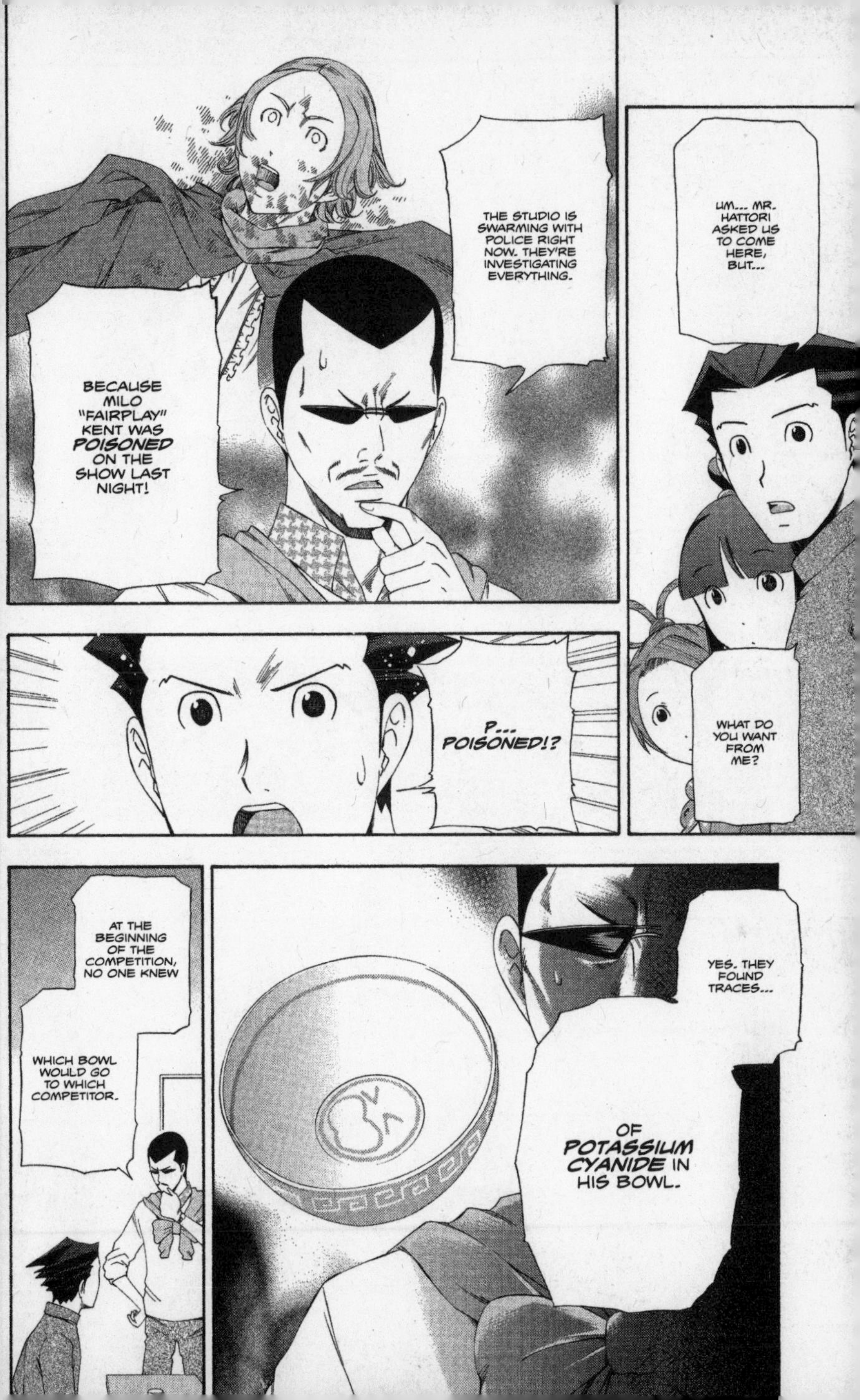
UM... MR. HATTORI ASKED US TO COME HERE, BUT...
WHAT DO YOU WANT FROM ME?
THE STUDIO IS SWARMING WITH POLICE RIGHT NOW. THEY'RE INVESTIGATING EVERYTHING.
BECAUSE MILO "FAIRPLAY" KENT WAS *POISONED* ON THE SHOW LAST NIGHT!
P... *POISONED!?*
YES. THEY FOUND TRACES...
OF *POTASSIUM CYANIDE* IN HIS BOWL.
AT THE BEGINNING OF THE COMPETITION, NO ONE KNEW
WHICH BOWL WOULD GO TO WHICH COMPETITOR.

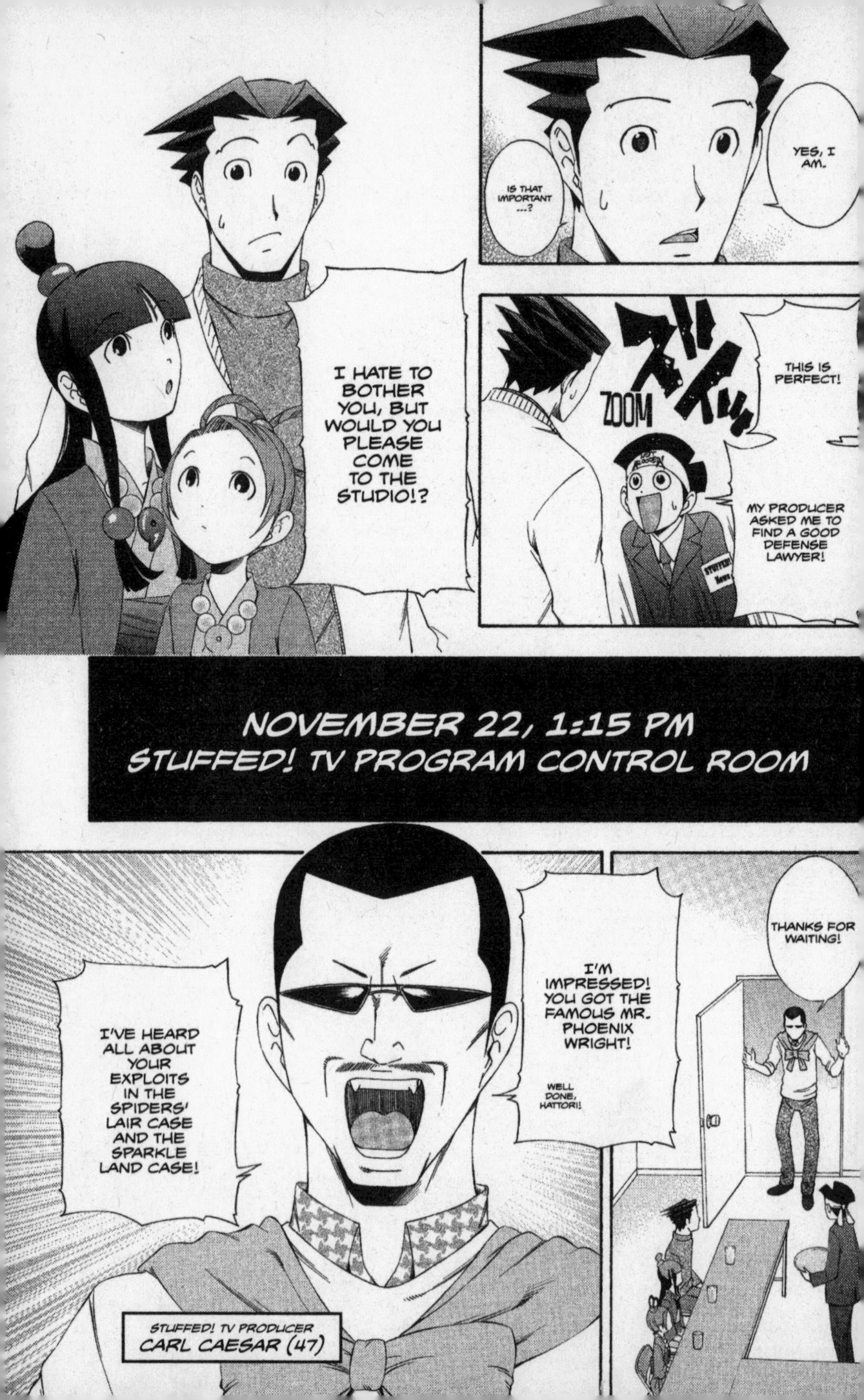
YES, I AM.
IS THAT IMPORTANT ...?
THIS IS PERFECT!
ZOOM
MY PRODUCER ASKED ME TO FIND A GOOD DEFENSE LAWYER!
I HATE TO BOTHER YOU, BUT WOULD YOU PLEASE COME TO THE STUDIO!?
NOVEMBER 22, 1:15 PM
STUFFED! TV PROGRAM CONTROL ROOM
THANKS FOR WAITING!
I'M IMPRESSED! YOU GOT THE FAMOUS MR. PHOENIX WRIGHT!
WELL DONE, HATTORI!
I'VE HEARD ALL ABOUT YOUR EXPLOITS IN THE SPIDERS' LAIR CASE AND THE SPARKLE LAND CASE!
STUFFED! TV PRODUCER
CARL CAESAR (47)

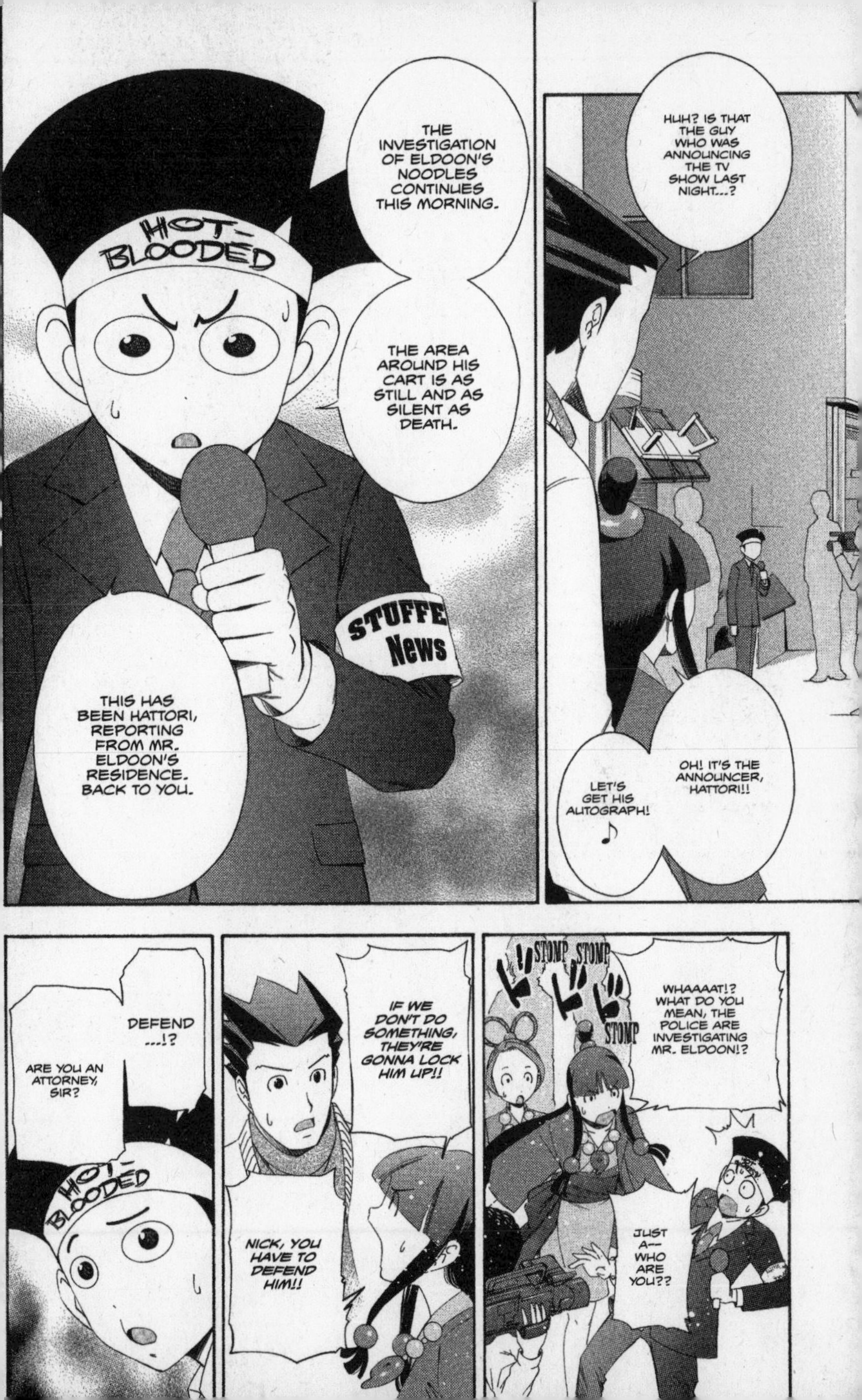
HUH? IS THAT THE GUY WHO WAS ANNOUNCING THE TV SHOW LAST NIGHT...?
OH! IT'S THE ANNOUNCER, HATTORI!!
LET'S GET HIS AUTOGRAPH! ♪
THE INVESTIGATION OF ELDOON'S NOODLES CONTINUES THIS MORNING.
HOT-BLOODED
THE AREA AROUND HIS CART IS AS STILL AND AS SILENT AS DEATH.
STUFFE News
THIS HAS BEEN HATTORI, REPORTING FROM MR. ELDOON'S RESIDENCE. BACK TO YOU.
STOMP STOMP
STOMP
WHAAAAT!? WHAT DO YOU MEAN, THE POLICE ARE INVESTIGATING MR. ELDOON!?
JUST A-- WHO ARE YOU??
IF WE DON'T DO SOMETHING, THEY'RE GONNA LOCK HIM UP!!
NICK, YOU HAVE TO DEFEND HIM!!
DEFEND ...!?
ARE YOU AN ATTORNEY, SIR?
HOT-BLOODED

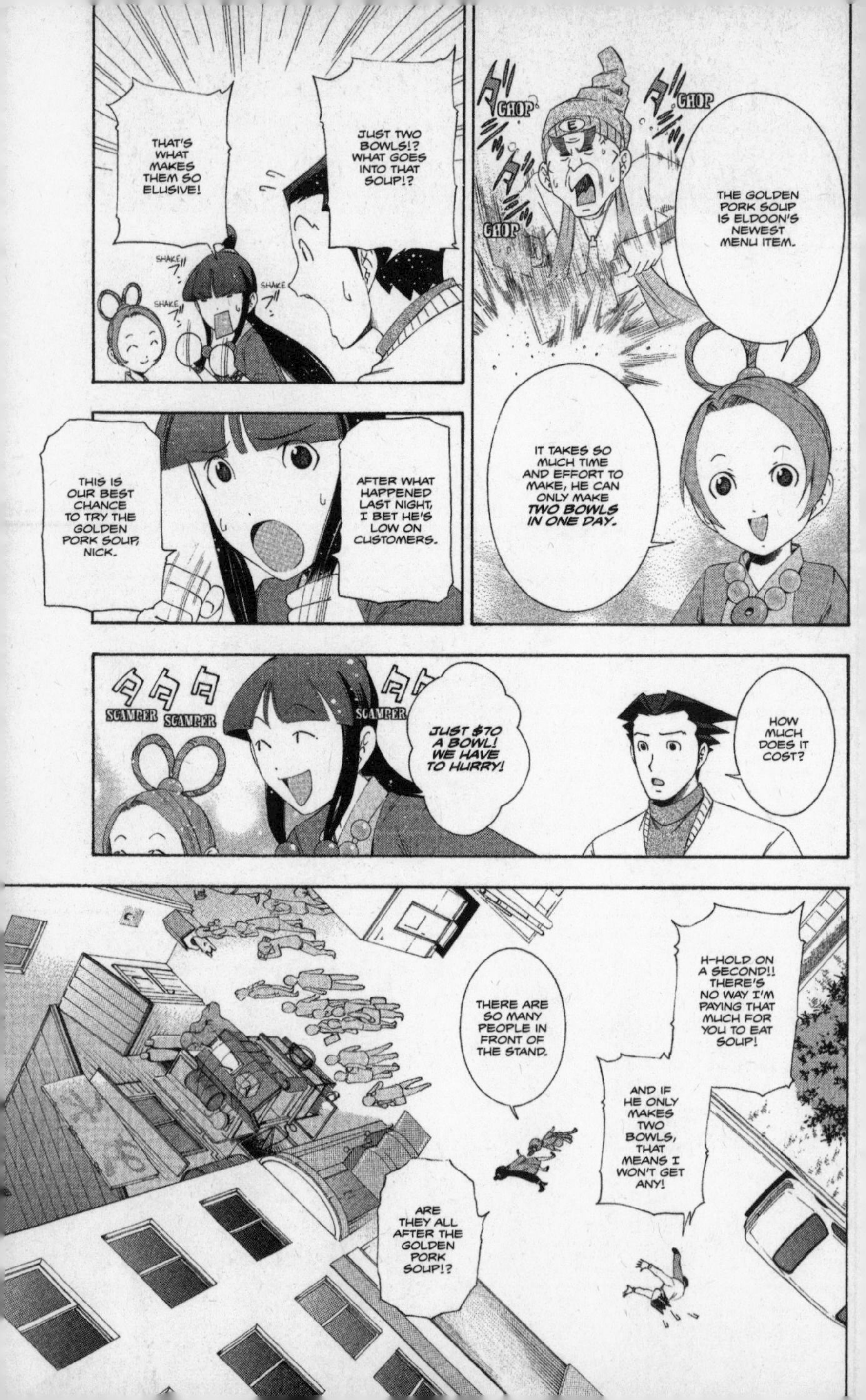
GHOP
GHOP
GHOP
THE GOLDEN PORK SOUP IS ELDOON'S NEWEST MENU ITEM.
IT TAKES SO MUCH TIME AND EFFORT TO MAKE, HE CAN ONLY MAKE *TWO BOWLS IN ONE DAY.*
JUST TWO BOWLS!? WHAT GOES INTO THAT SOUP!?
THAT'S WHAT MAKES THEM SO ELUSIVE!
SHAKE
SHAKE
SHAKE
AFTER WHAT HAPPENED LAST NIGHT, I BET HE'S LOW ON CUSTOMERS.
THIS IS OUR BEST CHANCE TO TRY THE GOLDEN PORK SOUP, NICK.
HOW MUCH DOES IT COST?
JUST $70 A BOWL! WE HAVE TO HURRY!
SCAMPER
SCAMPER
SCAMPER
H-HOLD ON A SECOND!! THERE'S NO WAY I'M PAYING THAT MUCH FOR YOU TO EAT SOUP!
AND IF HE ONLY MAKES TWO BOWLS, THAT MEANS I WON'T GET ANY!
THERE ARE SO MANY PEOPLE IN FRONT OF THE STAND.
ARE THEY ALL AFTER THE GOLDEN PORK SOUP!?

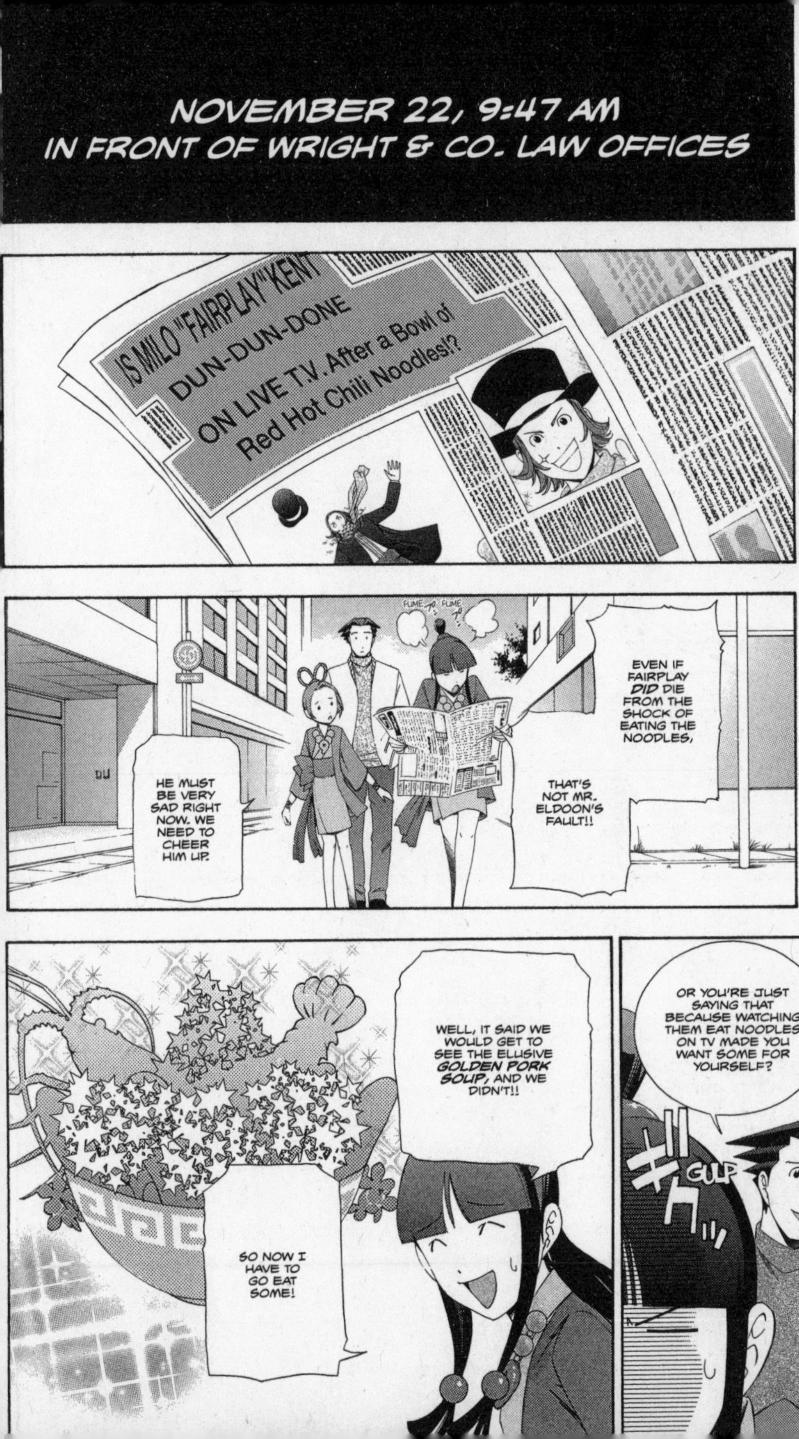
NOVEMBER 22, 9:47 AM
IN FRONT OF WRIGHT & CO. LAW OFFICES
IS MILO "FAIRPLAY" KENT DUN-DUN-DONE ON LIVE T.V. After a Bowl of Red Hot Chili Noodles!?
FUME FUME
EVEN IF FAIRPLAY *DID* DIE FROM THE SHOCK OF EATING THE NOODLES,
THAT'S NOT MR. ELDOON'S FAULT!!
HE MUST BE VERY SAD RIGHT NOW. WE NEED TO CHEER HIM UP.
OR YOU'RE JUST SAYING THAT BECAUSE WATCHING THEM EAT NOODLES ON TV MADE YOU WANT SOME FOR YOURSELF?
GULP
WELL, IT SAID WE WOULD GET TO SEE THE ELUSIVE *GOLDEN PORK SOUP*, AND WE DIDN'T!!
SO NOW I HAVE TO GO EAT SOME!

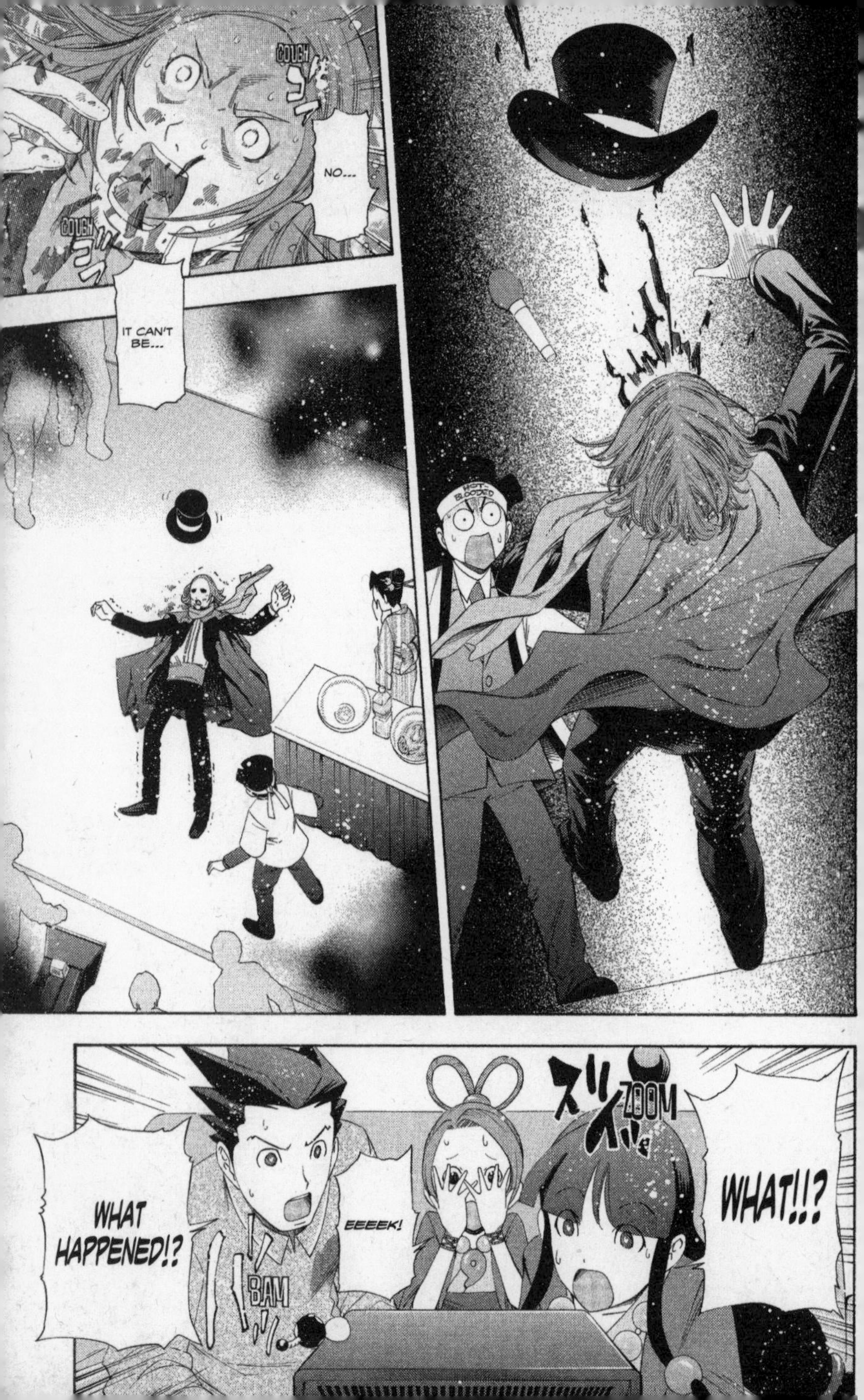
HOT-BLOODED
COUGH
NO...
COUGH
IT CAN'T BE...
WHAT!!?
ZOOM
EEEEK!
BAM
WHAT HAPPENED!?

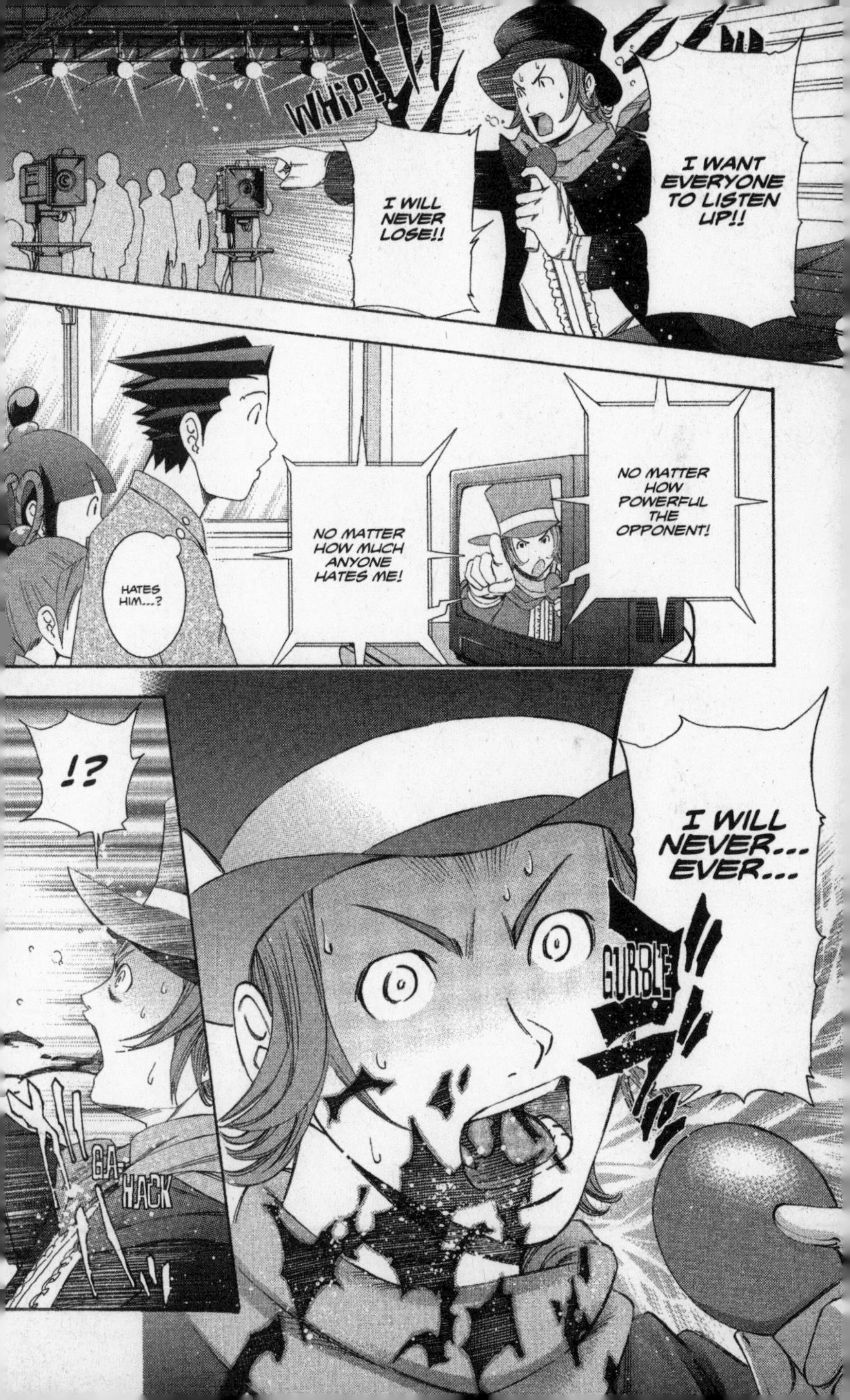
I WANT EVERYONE TO LISTEN UP!!
WHIP!
I WILL NEVER LOSE!!
NO MATTER HOW POWERFUL THE OPPONENT!
NO MATTER HOW MUCH ANYONE HATES ME!
HATES HIM...?
I WILL NEVER... EVER...
GURBLE
!?
GA-HACK

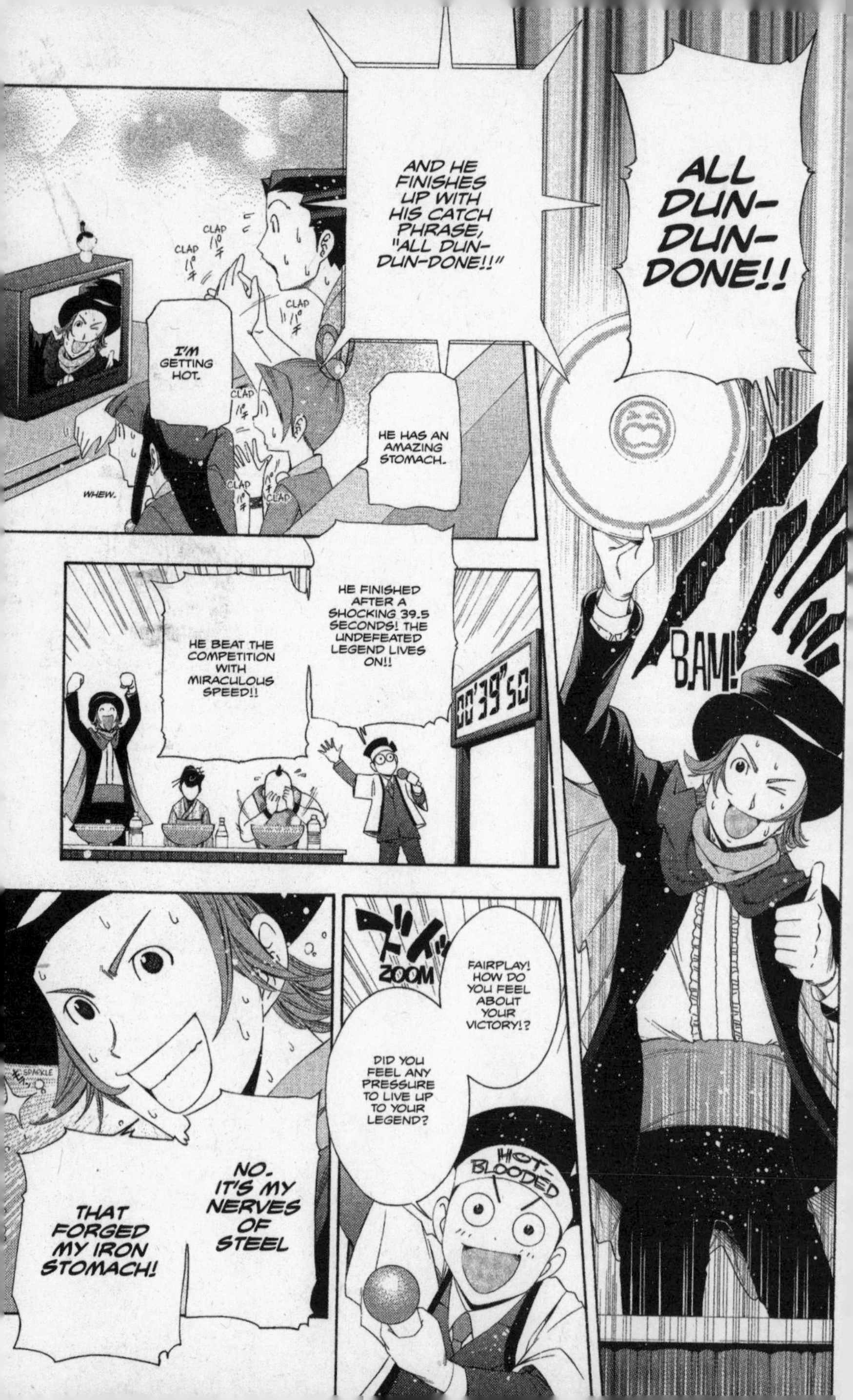

AND HE FINISHES UP WITH HIS CATCH PHRASE, "ALL DUN-DUN-DONE!!"
ALL DUN-DUN-DONE!!
BAM!
CLAP
CLAP
CLAP
I'M GETTING HOT.
HE HAS AN AMAZING STOMACH.
CLAP
CLAP
CLAP
WHEW.
HE FINISHED AFTER A SHOCKING 39.5 SECONDS! THE UNDEFEATED LEGEND LIVES ON!!
HE BEAT THE COMPETITION WITH MIRACULOUS SPEED!!
00'39"50
ZOOM
FAIRPLAY! HOW DO YOU FEEL ABOUT YOUR VICTORY!?
DID YOU FEEL ANY PRESSURE TO LIVE UP TO YOUR LEGEND?
HOT-BLOODED
NO. IT'S MY NERVES OF STEEL
THAT FORGED MY IRON STOMACH!
SPARKLE

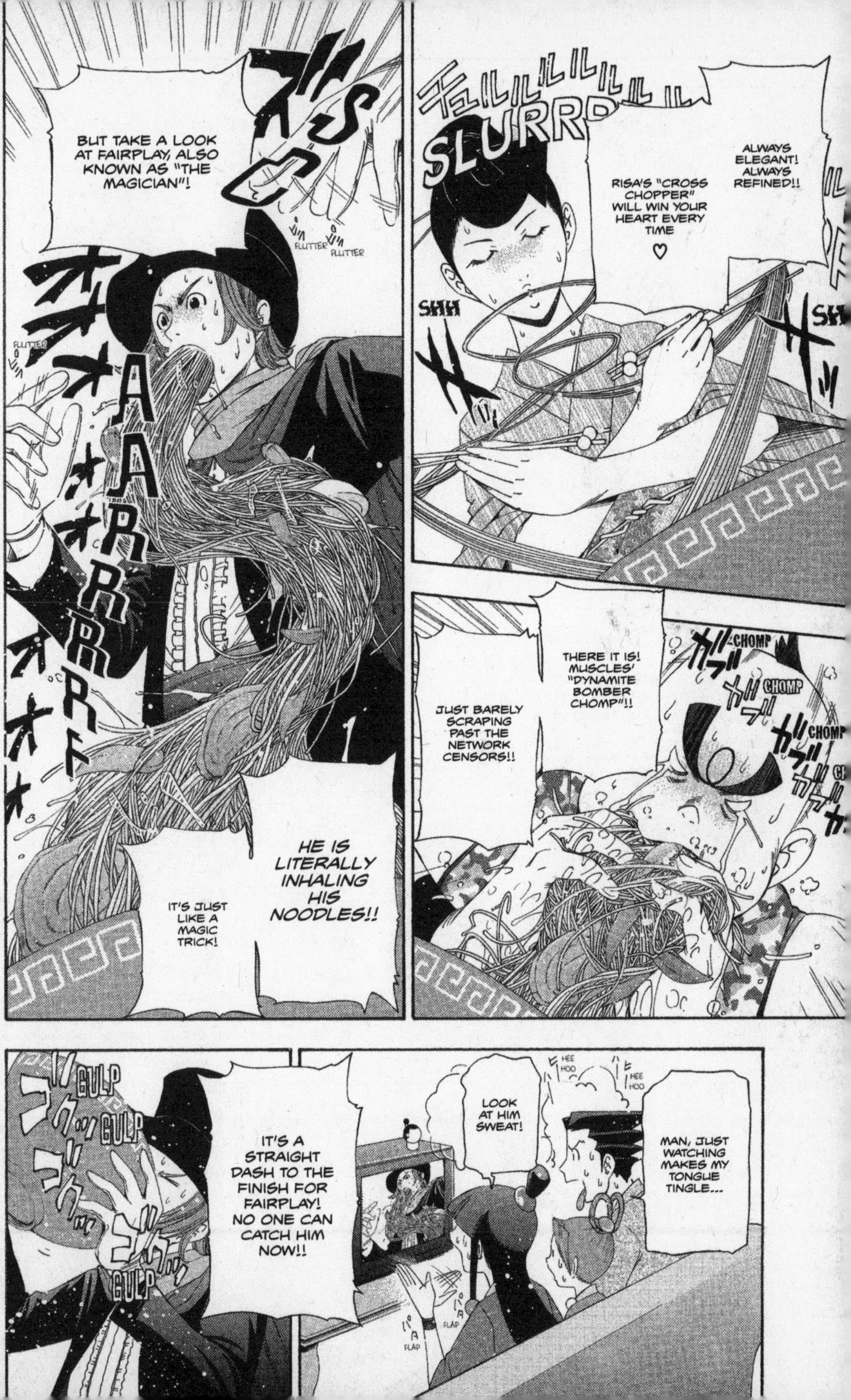

SLURRP
ALWAYS ELEGANT! ALWAYS REFINED!!
RISA'S "CROSS CHOPPER" WILL WIN YOUR HEART EVERY TIME ♡
SHH
SHH
CHOMP
CHOMP
CHOMP
THERE IT IS! MUSCLES' "DYNAMITE BOMBER CHOMP"!!
JUST BARELY SCRAPING PAST THE NETWORK CENSORS!!
BUT TAKE A LOOK AT FAIRPLAY, ALSO KNOWN AS "THE MAGICIAN"!
FLUTTER FLUTTER
FLUTTER
AARRRRT
HE IS LITERALLY INHALING HIS NOODLES!!
IT'S JUST LIKE A MAGIC TRICK!
HEE HOO
HEE HOO
MAN, JUST WATCHING MAKES MY TONGUE TINGLE...
LOOK AT HIM SWEAT!
FLAP
FLAP
IT'S A STRAIGHT DASH TO THE FINISH FOR FAIRPLAY! NO ONE CAN CATCH HIM NOW!!
GULP
GULP
GULP

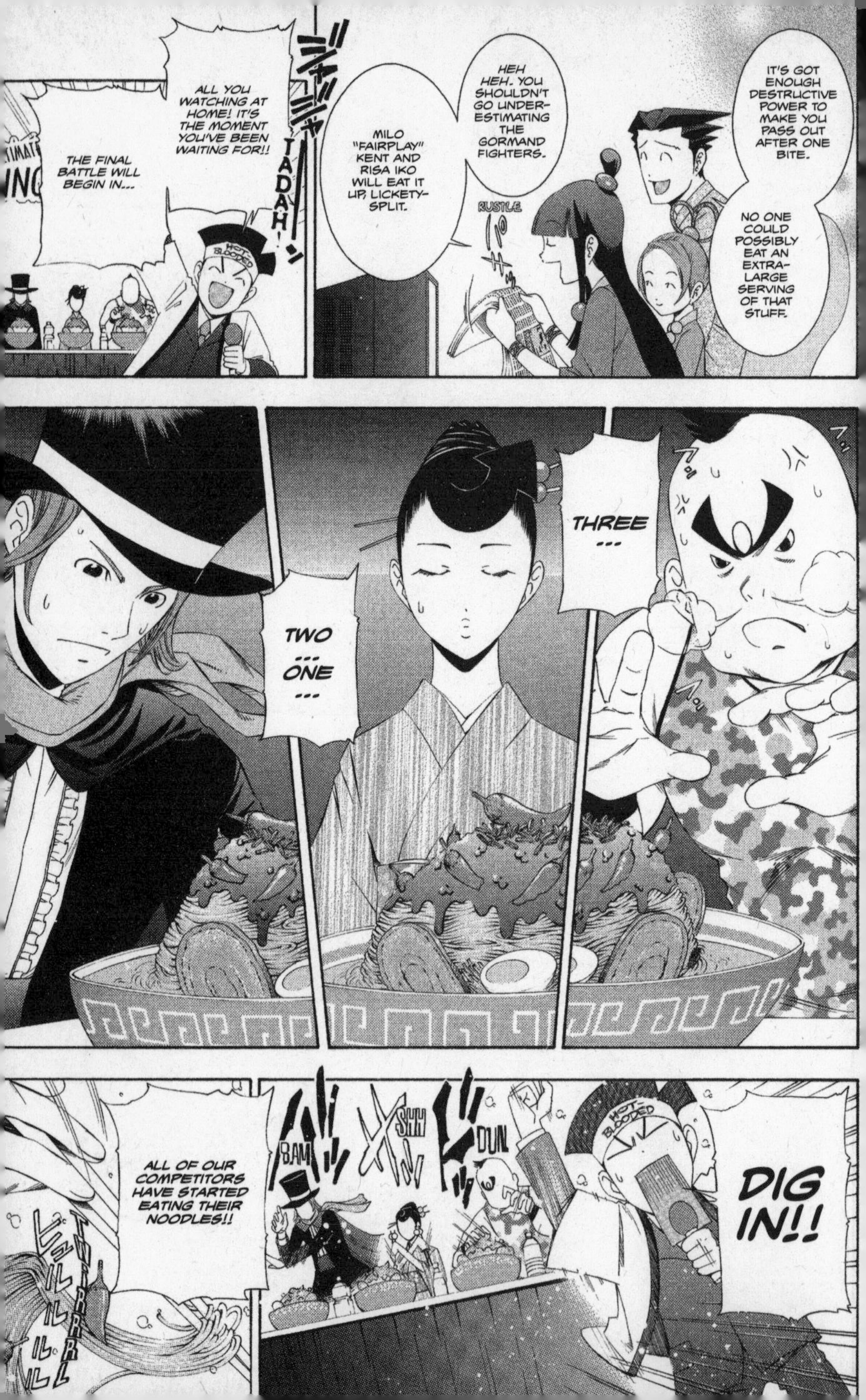
IT'S GOT ENOUGH DESTRUCTIVE POWER TO MAKE YOU PASS OUT AFTER ONE BITE.
NO ONE COULD POSSIBLY EAT AN EXTRA-LARGE SERVING OF THAT STUFF.
HEH HEH. YOU SHOULDN'T GO UNDER-ESTIMATING THE GORMAND FIGHTERS.
RUSTLE
MILO "FAIRPLAY" KENT AND RISA IKO WILL EAT IT UP, LICKETY-SPLIT.
TADAH!
HOT-BLOODED
ALL YOU WATCHING AT HOME! IT'S THE MOMENT YOU'VE BEEN WAITING FOR!!
THE FINAL BATTLE WILL BEGIN IN...
THREE...
TWO... ONE...
DIG IN!!
HOT-BLOODED
DUN
SHH
BAM
ALL OF OUR COMPETITORS HAVE STARTED EATING THEIR NOODLES!!
TWIRRRL

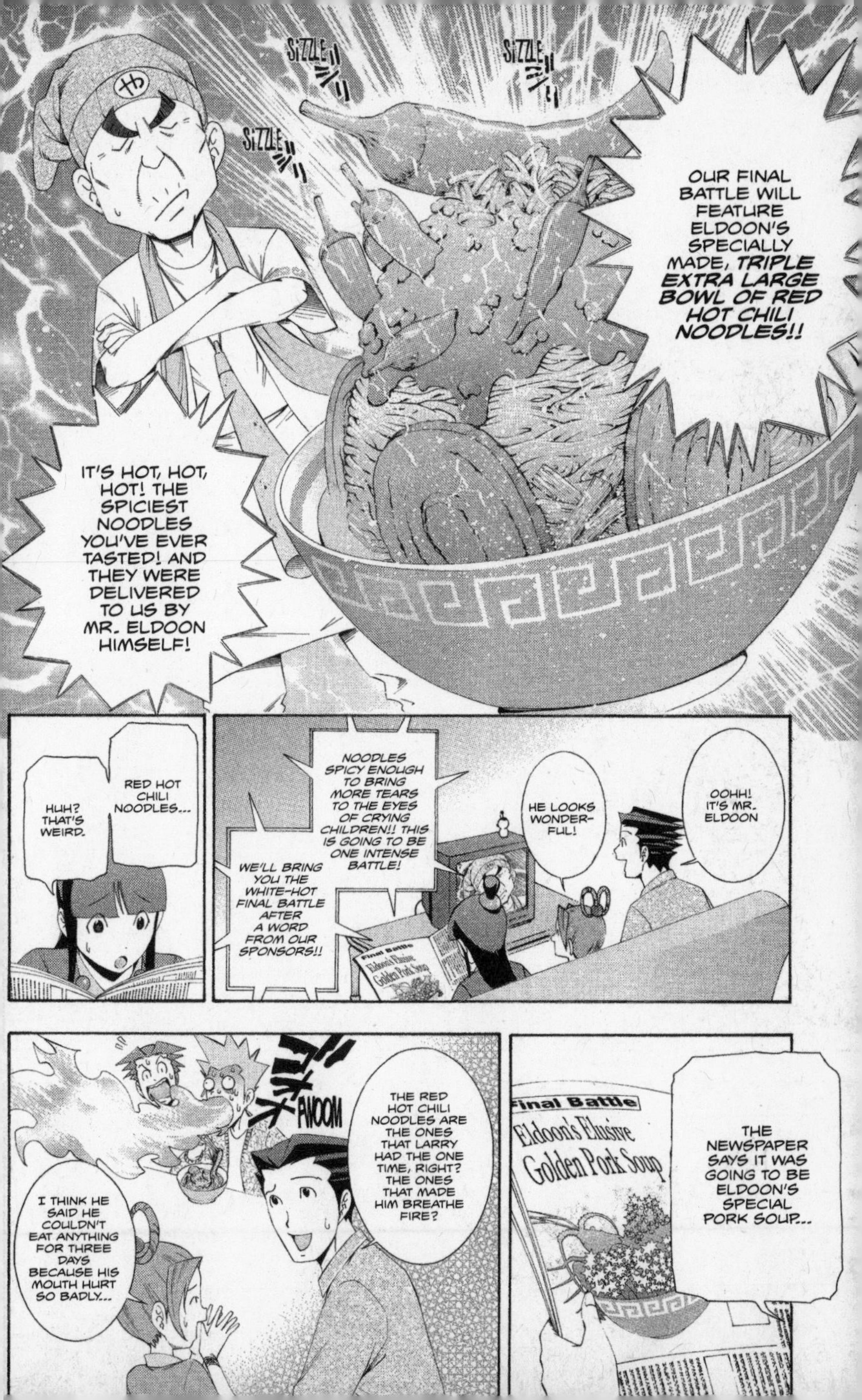
SIZZLE
SIZZLE
SIZZLE
OUR FINAL BATTLE WILL FEATURE ELDOON'S SPECIALLY MADE, TRIPLE EXTRA LARGE BOWL OF RED HOT CHILI NOODLES!!
IT'S HOT, HOT, HOT! THE SPICIEST NOODLES YOU'VE EVER TASTED! AND THEY WERE DELIVERED TO US BY MR. ELDOON HIMSELF!
OOHH! IT'S MR. ELDOON
HE LOOKS WONDERFUL!
NOODLES SPICY ENOUGH TO BRING MORE TEARS TO THE EYES OF CRYING CHILDREN!! THIS IS GOING TO BE ONE INTENSE BATTLE!
WE'LL BRING YOU THE WHITE-HOT FINAL BATTLE AFTER A WORD FROM OUR SPONSORS!!
Final Battle
Eldoon's Elusive Golden Pork Soup
RED HOT CHILI NOODLES...
HUH? THAT'S WEIRD.
Final Battle
Eldoon's Elusive Golden Pork Soup
THE NEWSPAPER SAYS IT WAS GOING TO BE ELDOON'S SPECIAL PORK SOUP...
THE RED HOT CHILI NOODLES ARE THE ONES THAT LARRY HAD THE ONE TIME, RIGHT? THE ONES THAT MADE HIM BREATHE FIRE?
FWOOM
I THINK HE SAID HE COULDN'T EAT ANYTHING FOR THREE DAYS BECAUSE HIS MOUTH HURT SO BADLY...

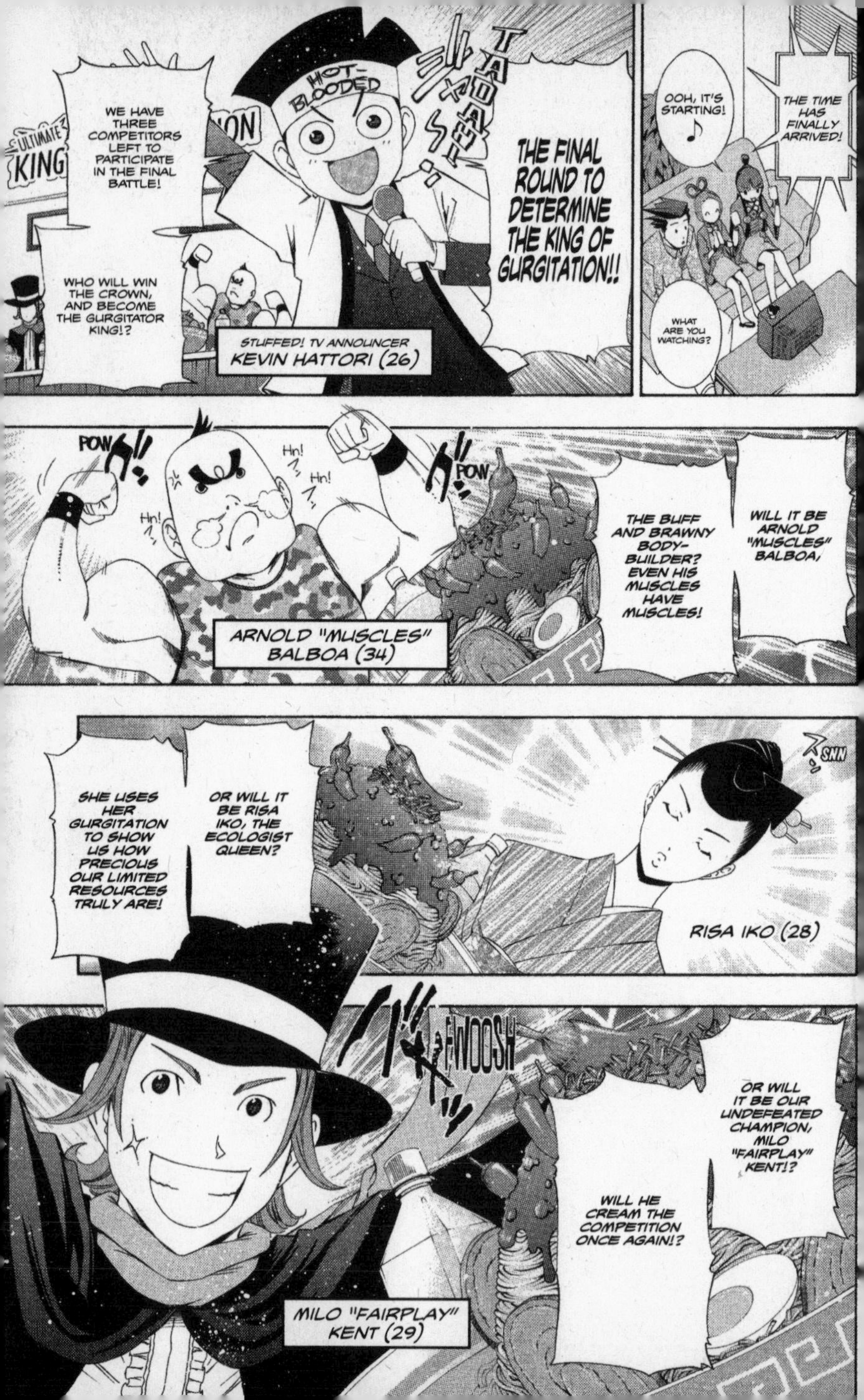
THE TIME HAS FINALLY ARRIVED!
OOH, IT'S STARTING! ♪
WHAT ARE YOU WATCHING?
TADAAH
HOT-BLOODED
THE FINAL ROUND TO DETERMINE THE KING OF GURGITATION!!
WE HAVE THREE COMPETITORS LEFT TO PARTICIPATE IN THE FINAL BATTLE!
ULTIMATE KING
ION
WHO WILL WIN THE CROWN, AND BECOME THE GURGITATOR KING!?
STUFFED! TV ANNOUNCER
KEVIN HATTORI (26)
WILL IT BE ARNOLD "MUSCLES" BALBOA,
THE BUFF AND BRAWNY BODY-BUILDER? EVEN HIS MUSCLES HAVE MUSCLES!
POW
Hn!
Hn!
Hn!
POW
ARNOLD "MUSCLES" BALBOA (34)
SNN
RISA IKO (28)
OR WILL IT BE RISA IKO, THE ECOLOGIST QUEEN?
SHE USES HER GURGITATION TO SHOW US HOW PRECIOUS OUR LIMITED RESOURCES TRULY ARE!
OR WILL IT BE OUR UNDEFEATED CHAMPION, MILO "FAIRPLAY" KENT!?
WILL HE CREAM THE COMPETITION ONCE AGAIN!?
FWOOSH
MILO "FAIRPLAY" KENT (29)

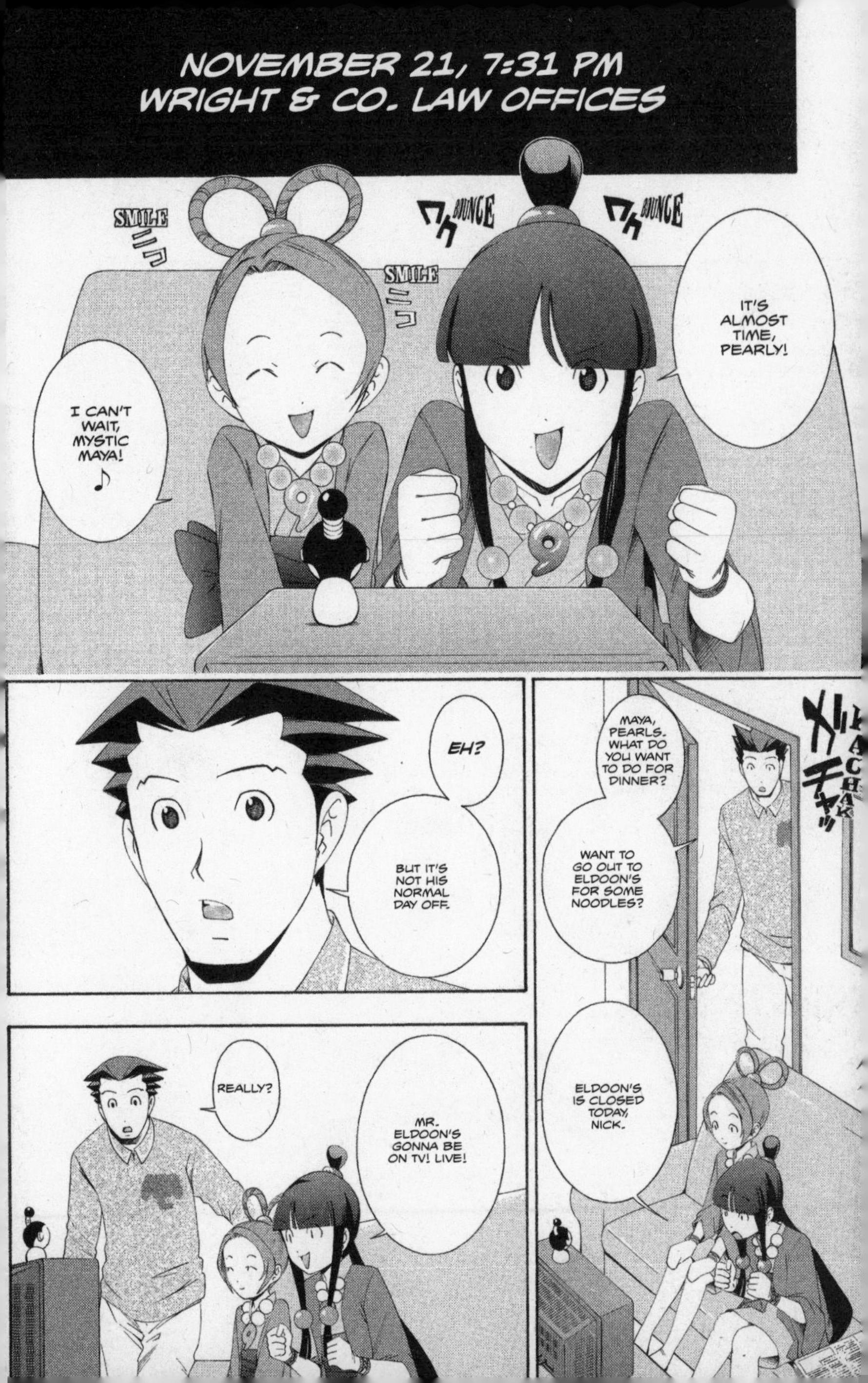
NOVEMBER 21, 7:31 PM
WRIGHT & CO. LAW OFFICES
BOUNCE
BOUNCE
IT'S ALMOST TIME, PEARLY!
SMILE
SMILE
I CAN'T WAIT, MYSTIC MAYA! ♪
KACHAK
MAYA, PEARLS. WHAT DO YOU WANT TO DO FOR DINNER?
WANT TO GO OUT TO ELDOON'S FOR SOME NOODLES?
ELDOON'S IS CLOSED TODAY, NICK.
EH?
BUT IT'S NOT HIS NORMAL DAY OFF.
MR. ELDOON'S GONNA BE ON TV! LIVE!
REALLY?

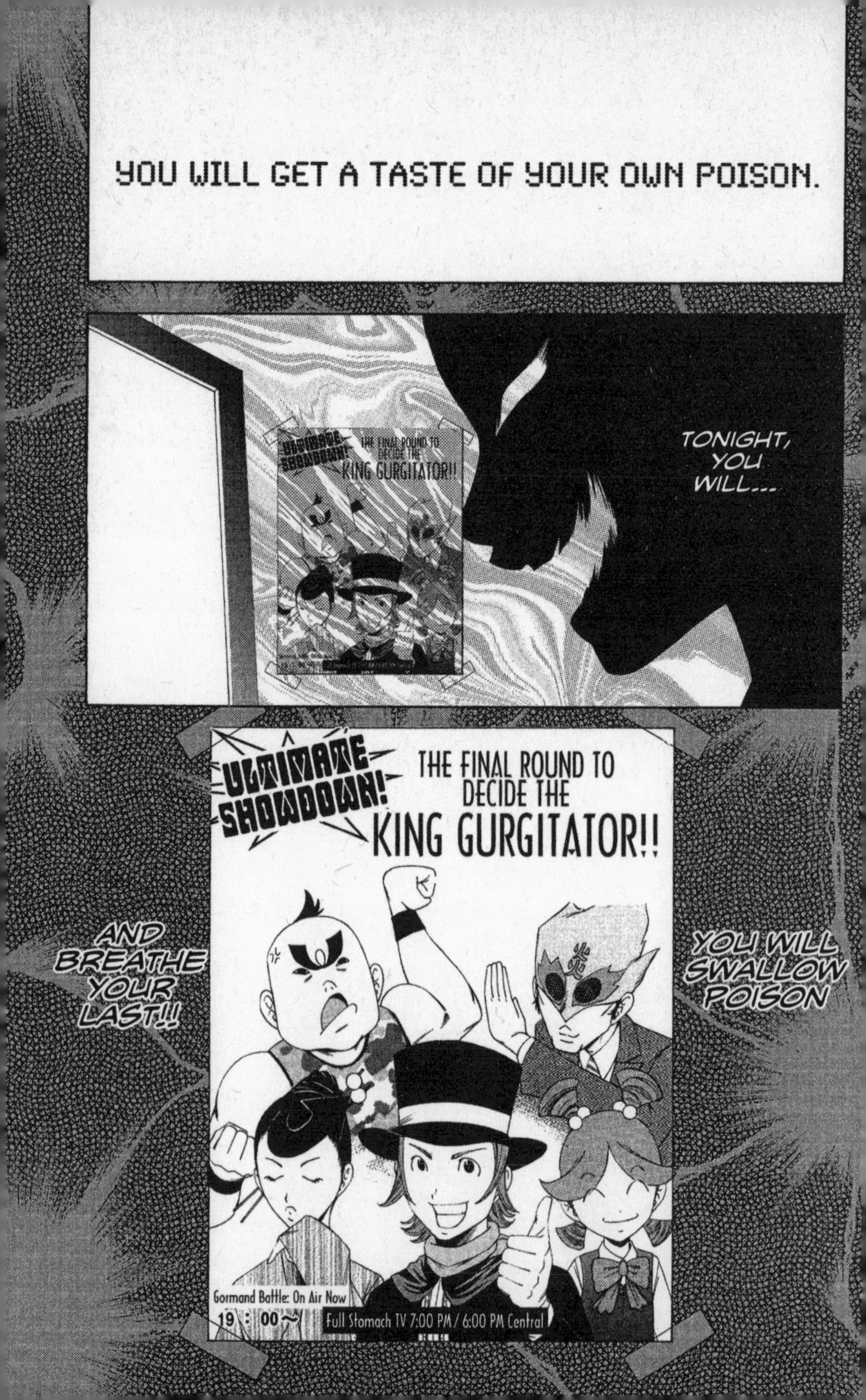
YOU WILL GET A TASTE OF YOUR OWN POISON.
TONIGHT, YOU WILL...
YOU WILL SWALLOW POISON
ULTIMATE SHOWDOWN!
THE FINAL ROUND TO DECIDE THE KING GURGITATOR!!
Gormand Battle: On Air Now
19 : 00~
Full Stomach TV 7:00 PM / 6:00 PM Central
AND BREATHE YOUR LAST!!

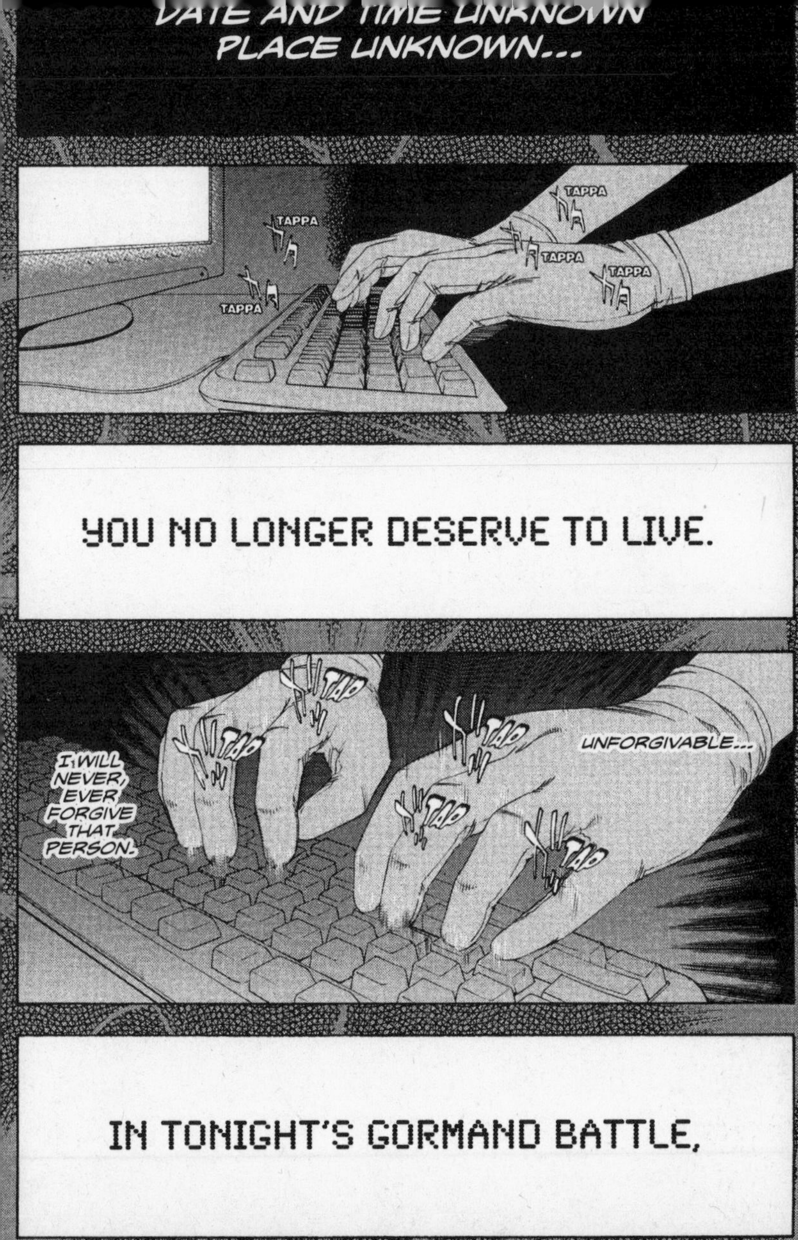
DATE AND TIME UNKNOWN
PLACE UNKNOWN...
TAPPA
TAPPA
TAPPA
TAPPA
TAPPA
YOU NO LONGER DESERVE TO LIVE.
UNFORGIVABLE...
I WILL NEVER, EVER FORGIVE THAT PERSON.
TAP
TAP
TAP
TAP
TAP
IN TONIGHT'S GORMAND BATTLE,

TURNABOUT GURGITATION
(PART ONE)

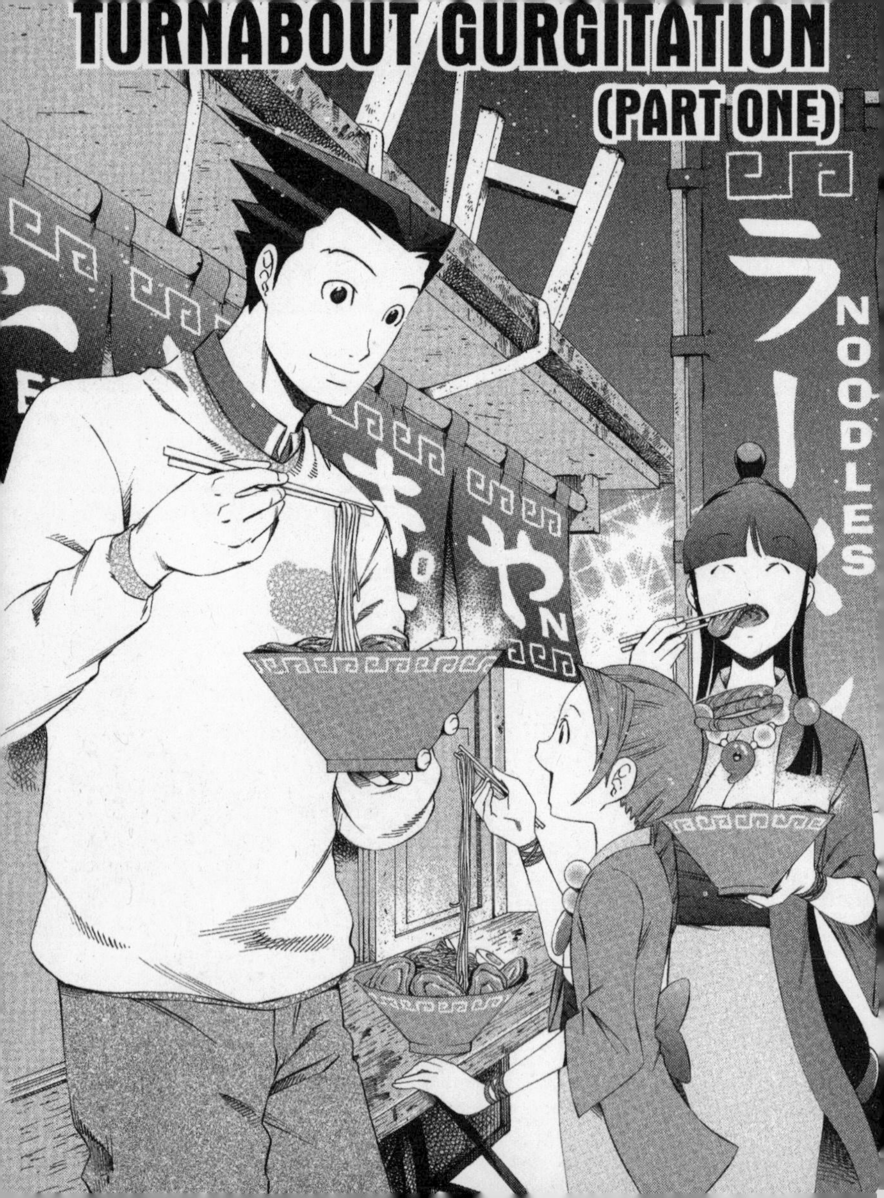

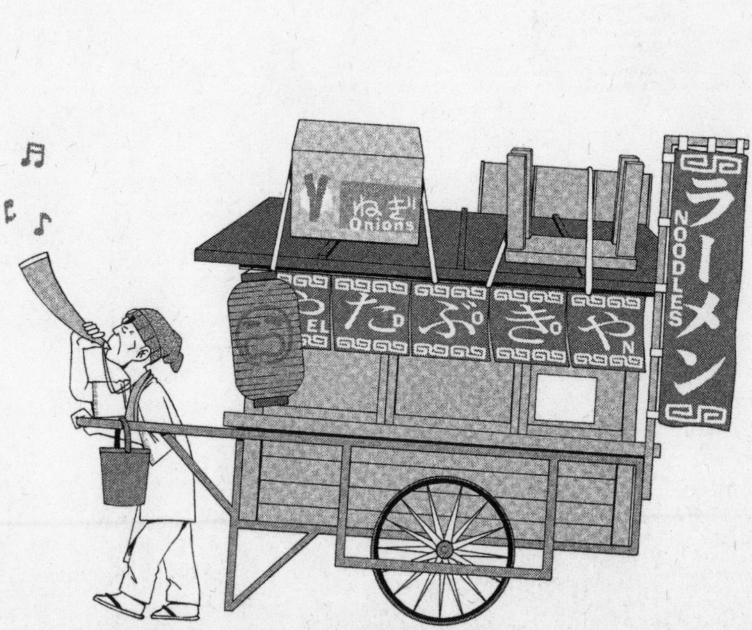
ねぎ
Onions
ラーメン
NOODLES

Ace Attorney

Phoenix Wright

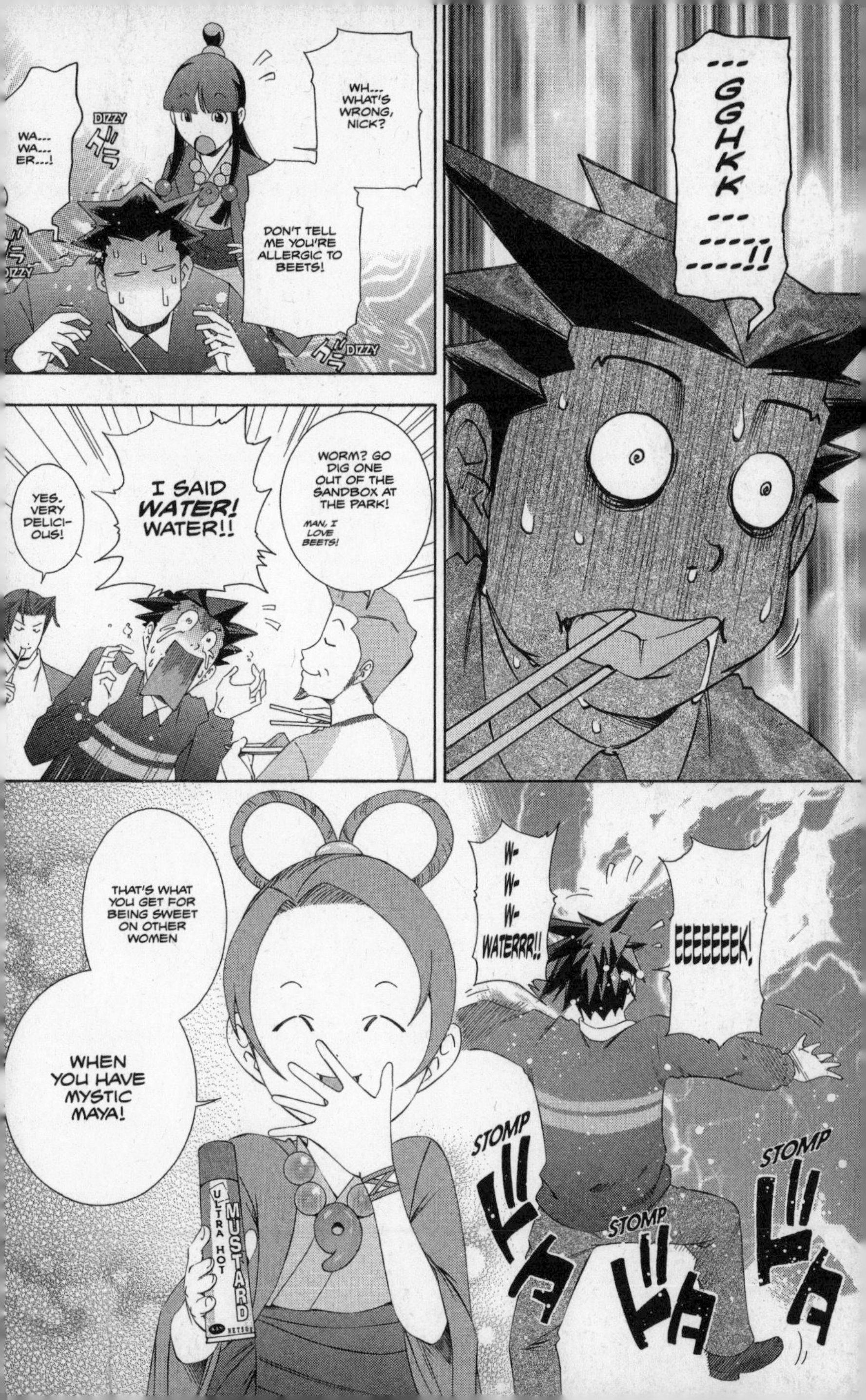
...GGHKK...-----!!
WH... WHAT'S WRONG, NICK?
DON'T TELL ME YOU'RE ALLERGIC TO BEETS!
DIZZY
WA... WA... ER...!
DIZZY
DIZZY
WORM? GO DIG ONE OUT OF THE SANDBOX AT THE PARK!
MAN, I LOVE BEETS!
I SAID *WATER!* WATER!!
YES. VERY DELICI-OUS!
EEEEEEEEK!
W-W-W-WATERRR!!
STOMP
STOMP
STOMP
THAT'S WHAT YOU GET FOR BEING SWEET ON OTHER WOMEN
WHEN YOU HAVE MYSTIC MAYA!
ULTRA HOT MUSTARD

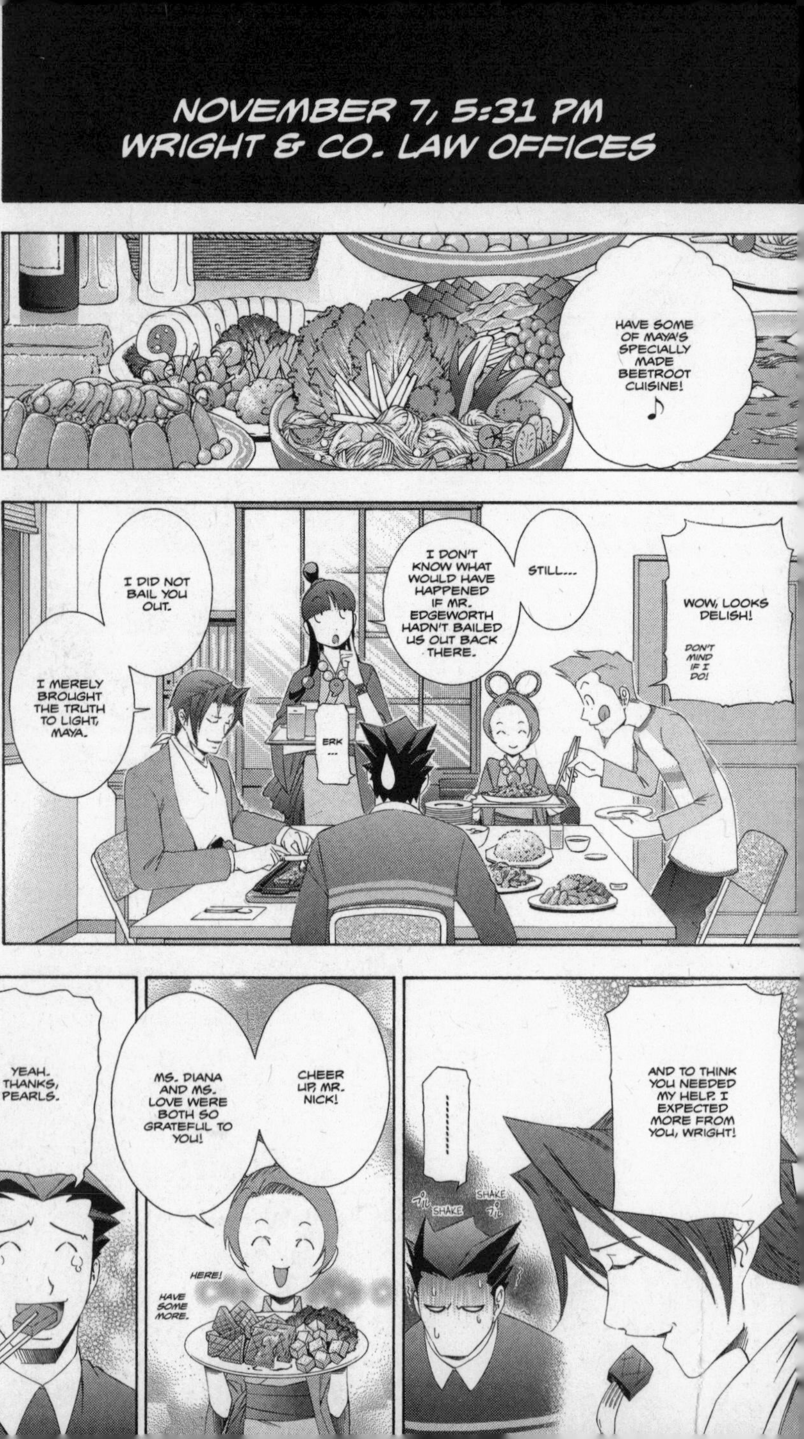
NOVEMBER 7, 5:31 PM
WRIGHT & CO. LAW OFFICES
HAVE SOME OF MAYA'S SPECIALLY MADE BEETROOT CUISINE! ♪
WOW, LOOKS DELISH!
DON'T MIND IF I DO!
STILL...
I DON'T KNOW WHAT WOULD HAVE HAPPENED IF MR. EDGEWORTH HADN'T BAILED US OUT BACK THERE.
I DID NOT BAIL YOU OUT.
I MERELY BROUGHT THE TRUTH TO LIGHT, MAYA.
ERK...
AND TO THINK YOU NEEDED MY HELP. I EXPECTED MORE FROM YOU, WRIGHT!
SHAKE
SHAKE
....
CHEER UP, MR. NICK!
MS. DIANA AND MS. LOVE WERE BOTH SO GRATEFUL TO YOU!
HERE!
HAVE SOME MORE.
YEAH. THANKS, PEARLS.

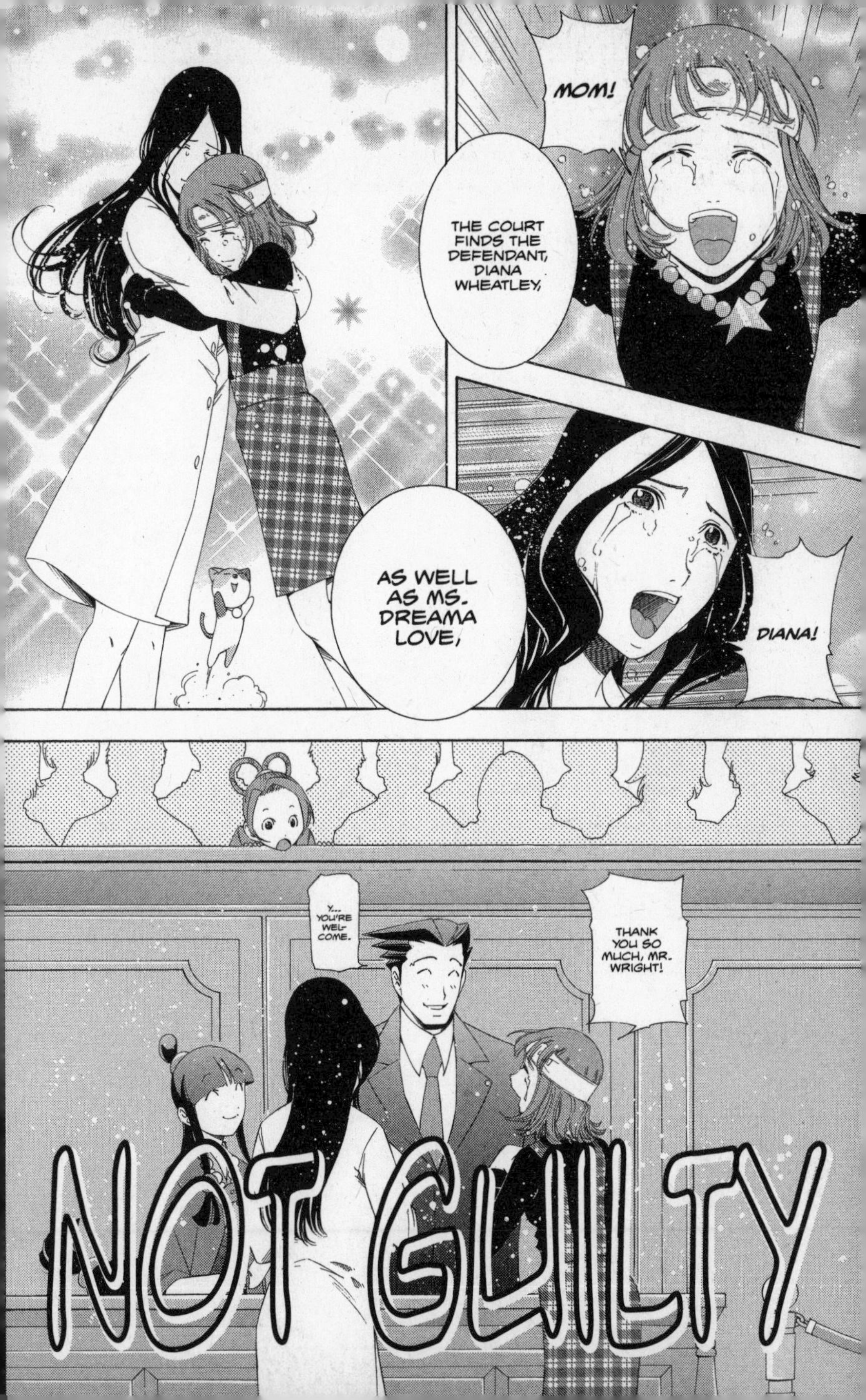
MOM!
THE COURT FINDS THE DEFENDANT, DIANA WHEATLEY,
DIANA!
AS WELL AS MS. DREAMA LOVE,
THANK YOU SO MUCH, MR. WRIGHT!
Y... YOU'RE WEL-COME.
NOT GUILTY

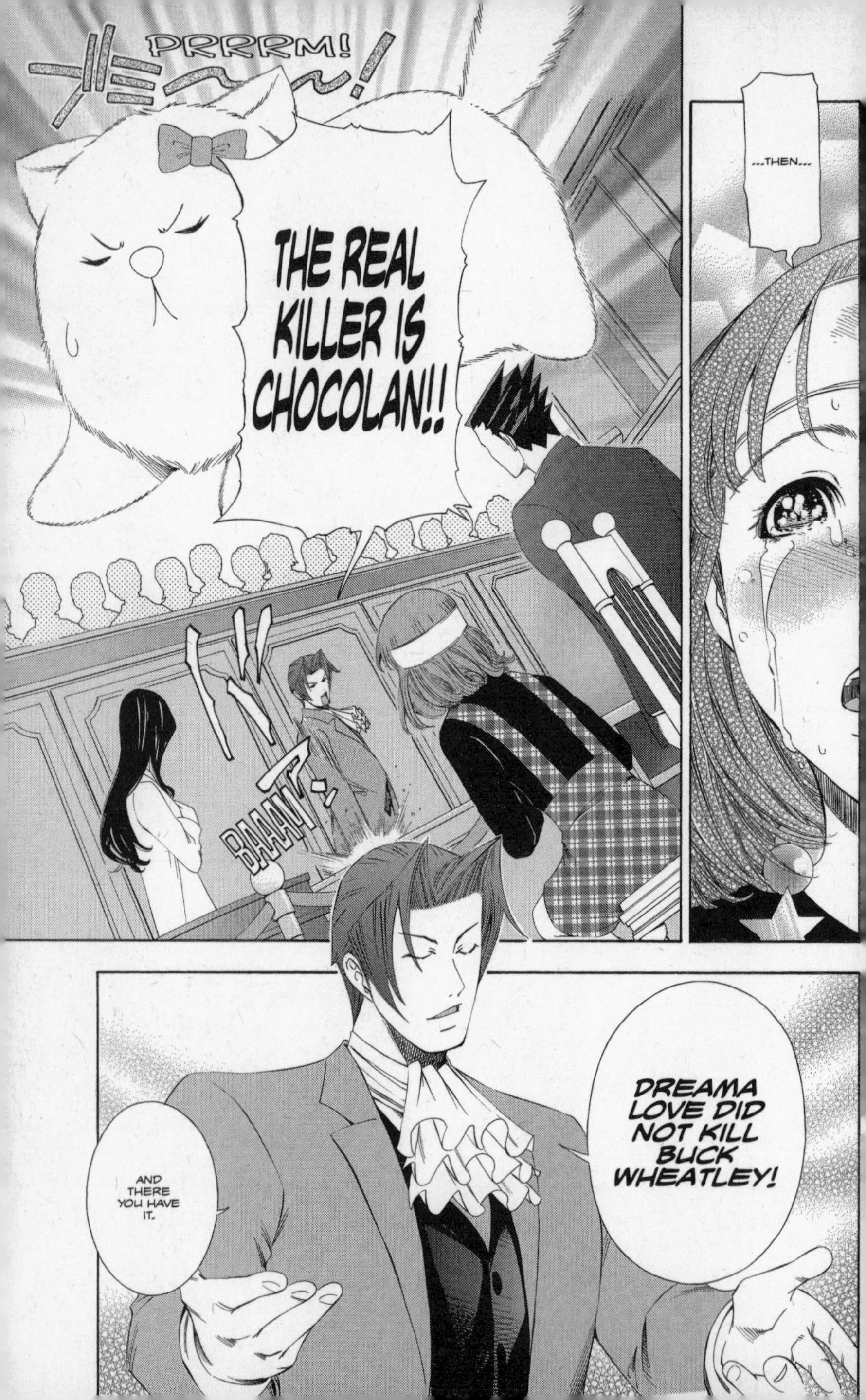
...THEN...
PRRRM!
THE REAL KILLER IS CHOCOLAN!!
BAAAM!
DREAMA LOVE DID NOT KILL BUCK WHEATLEY!
AND THERE YOU HAVE IT.

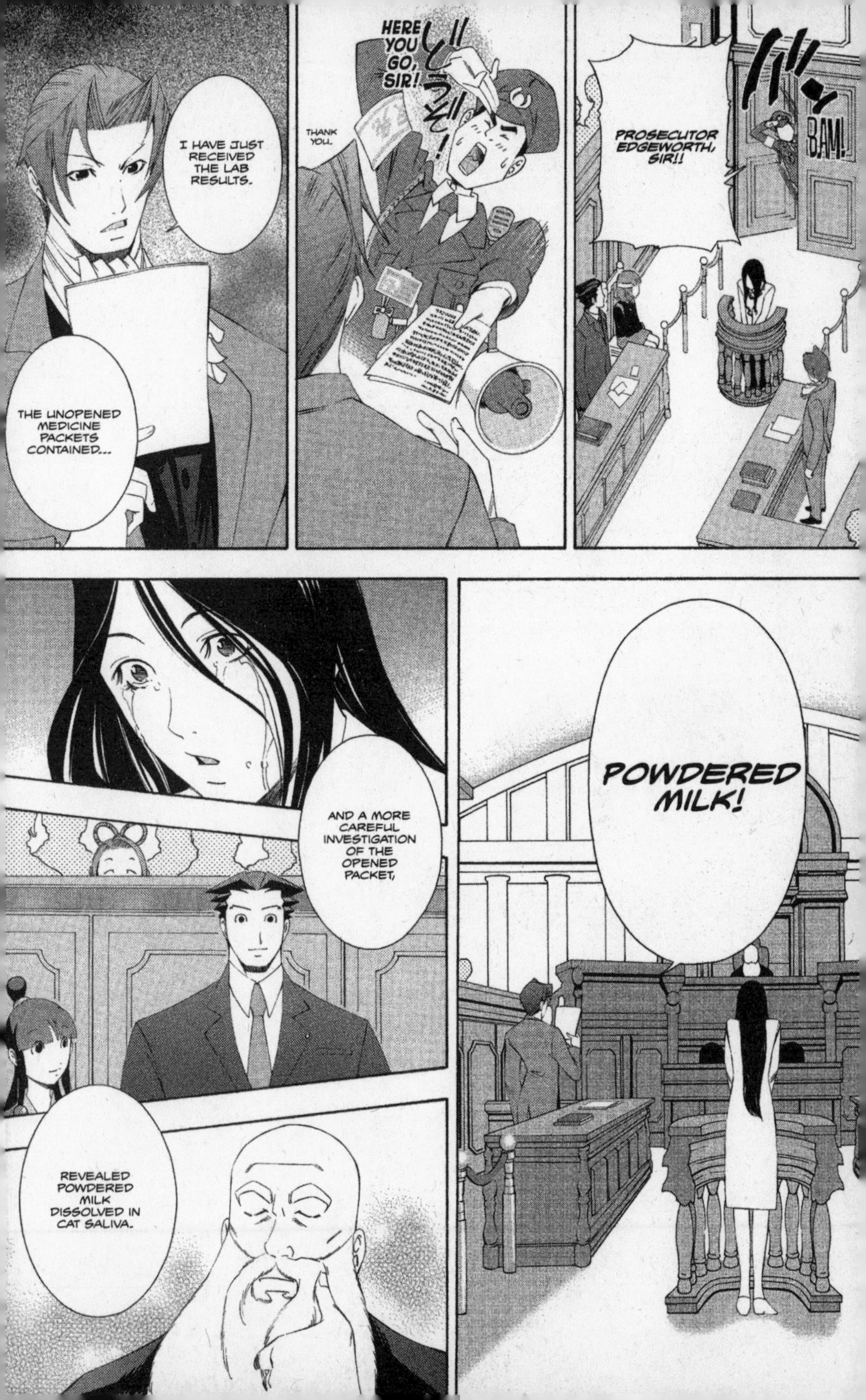
BAM!
PROSECUTOR EDGEWORTH, SIR!!
HERE YOU GO, SIR!
THANK YOU.
I HAVE JUST RECEIVED THE LAB RESULTS.
THE UNOPENED MEDICINE PACKETS CONTAINED...
POWDERED MILK!
AND A MORE CAREFUL INVESTIGATION OF THE OPENED PACKET,
REVEALED POWDERED MILK DISSOLVED IN CAT SALIVA.

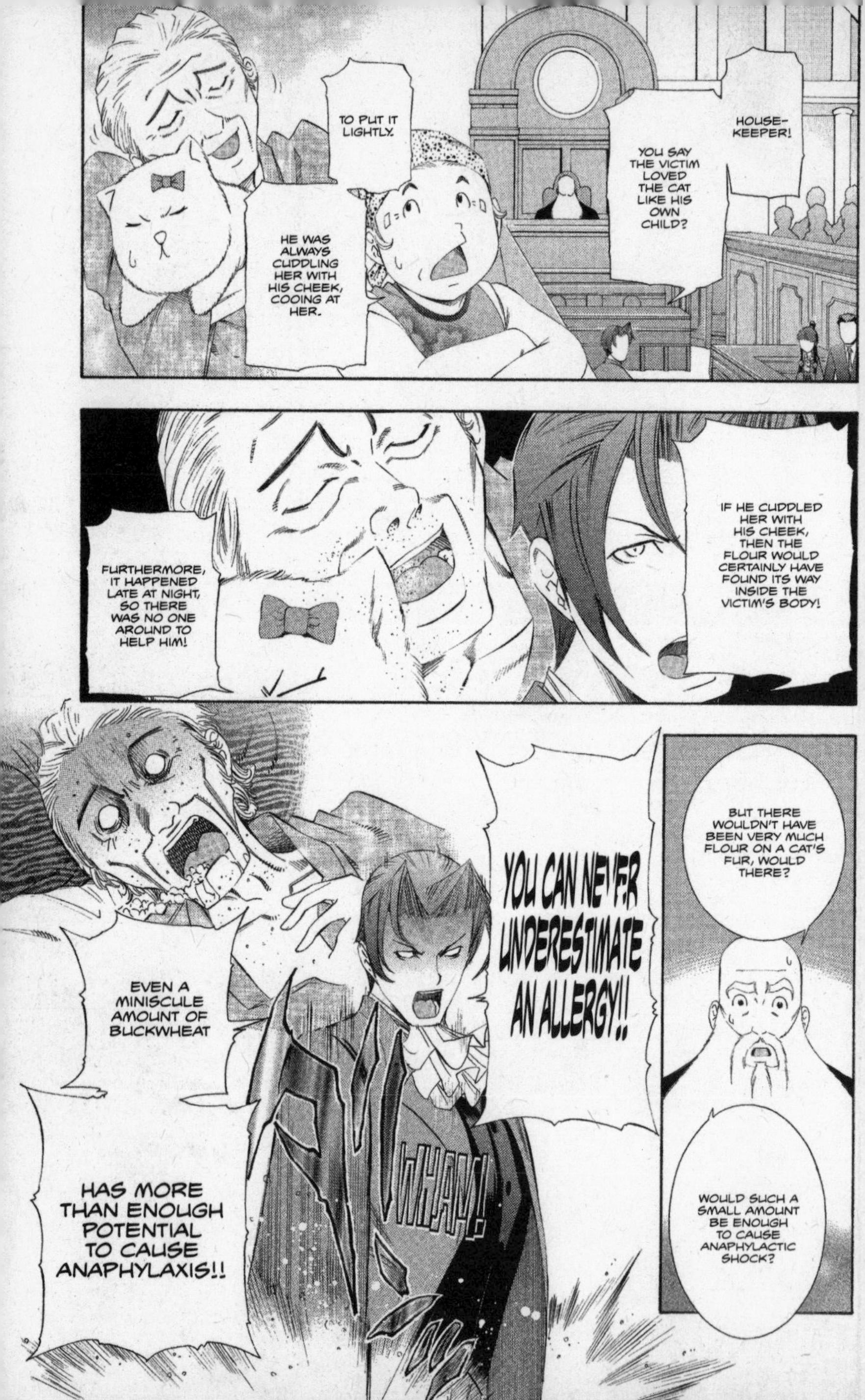
HOUSE-KEEPER!
YOU SAY THE VICTIM LOVED THE CAT LIKE HIS OWN CHILD?
TO PUT IT LIGHTLY.
HE WAS ALWAYS CUDDLING HER WITH HIS CHEEK, COOING AT HER.
IF HE CUDDLED HER WITH HIS CHEEK, THEN THE FLOUR WOULD CERTAINLY HAVE FOUND ITS WAY INSIDE THE VICTIM'S BODY!
FURTHERMORE, IT HAPPENED LATE AT NIGHT, SO THERE WAS NO ONE AROUND TO HELP HIM!
BUT THERE WOULDN'T HAVE BEEN VERY MUCH FLOUR ON A CAT'S FUR, WOULD THERE?
WOULD SUCH A SMALL AMOUNT BE ENOUGH TO CAUSE ANAPHYLACTIC SHOCK?
YOU CAN NEVER UNDERESTIMATE AN ALLERGY!!
WHAM!
EVEN A MINISCULE AMOUNT OF BUCKWHEAT
HAS MORE THAN ENOUGH POTENTIAL TO CAUSE ANAPHYLAXIS!!

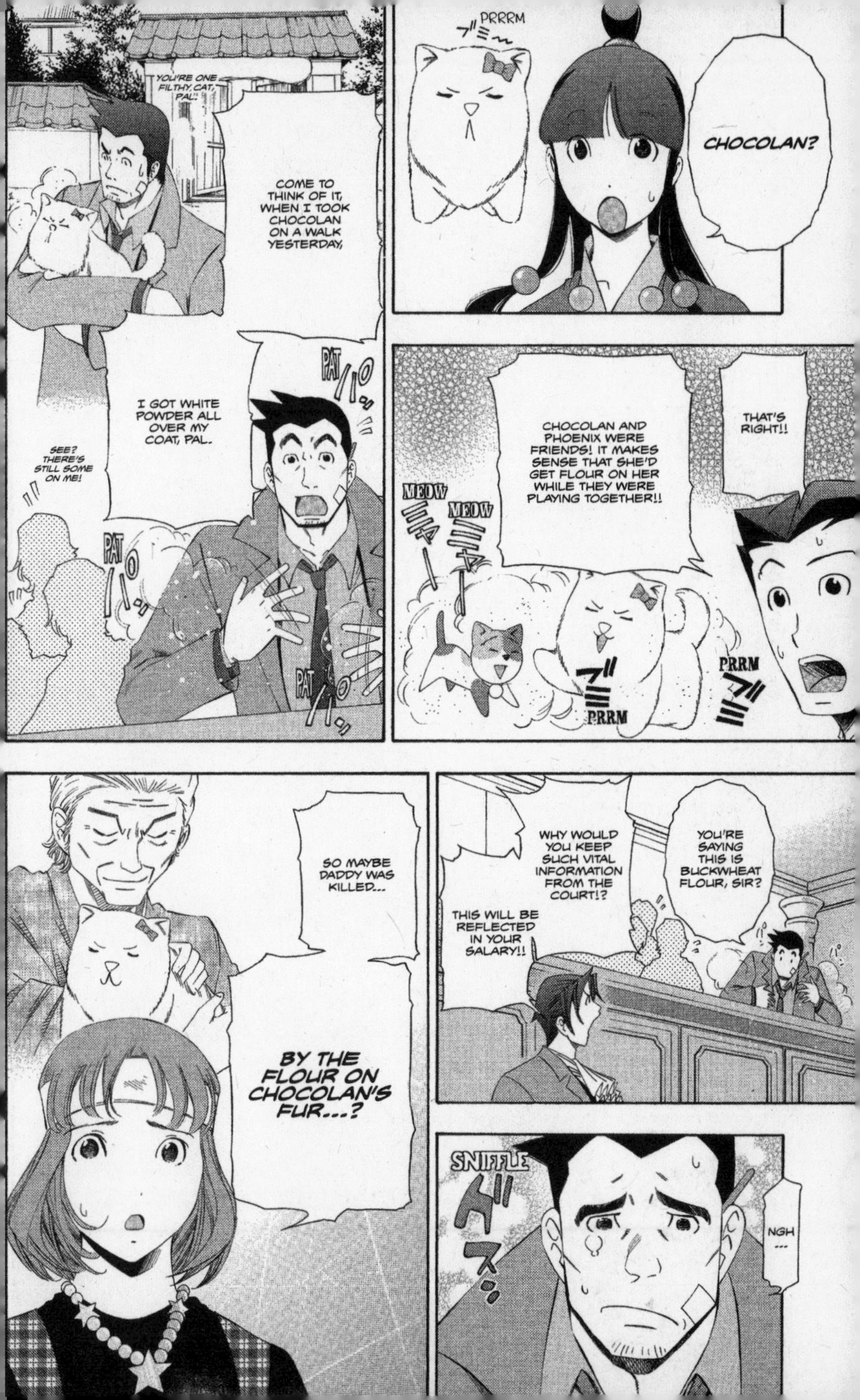
PRRRM
CHOCOLAN?
THAT'S RIGHT!!
CHOCOLAN AND PHOENIX WERE FRIENDS! IT MAKES SENSE THAT SHE'D GET FLOUR ON HER WHILE THEY WERE PLAYING TOGETHER!!
MEOW
MEOW
PRRM
PRRM
YOU'RE ONE FILTHY CAT, PAL...
COME TO THINK OF IT, WHEN I TOOK CHOCOLAN ON A WALK YESTERDAY,
PAT
I GOT WHITE POWDER ALL OVER MY COAT, PAL.
SEE? THERE'S STILL SOME ON ME!
PAT
PAT
YOU'RE SAYING THIS IS BUCKWHEAT FLOUR, SIR?
WHY WOULD YOU KEEP SUCH VITAL INFORMATION FROM THE COURT!?
THIS WILL BE REFLECTED IN YOUR SALARY!!
SNIFFLE
NGH...
SO MAYBE DADDY WAS KILLED...
BY THE FLOUR ON CHOCOLAN'S FUR...?

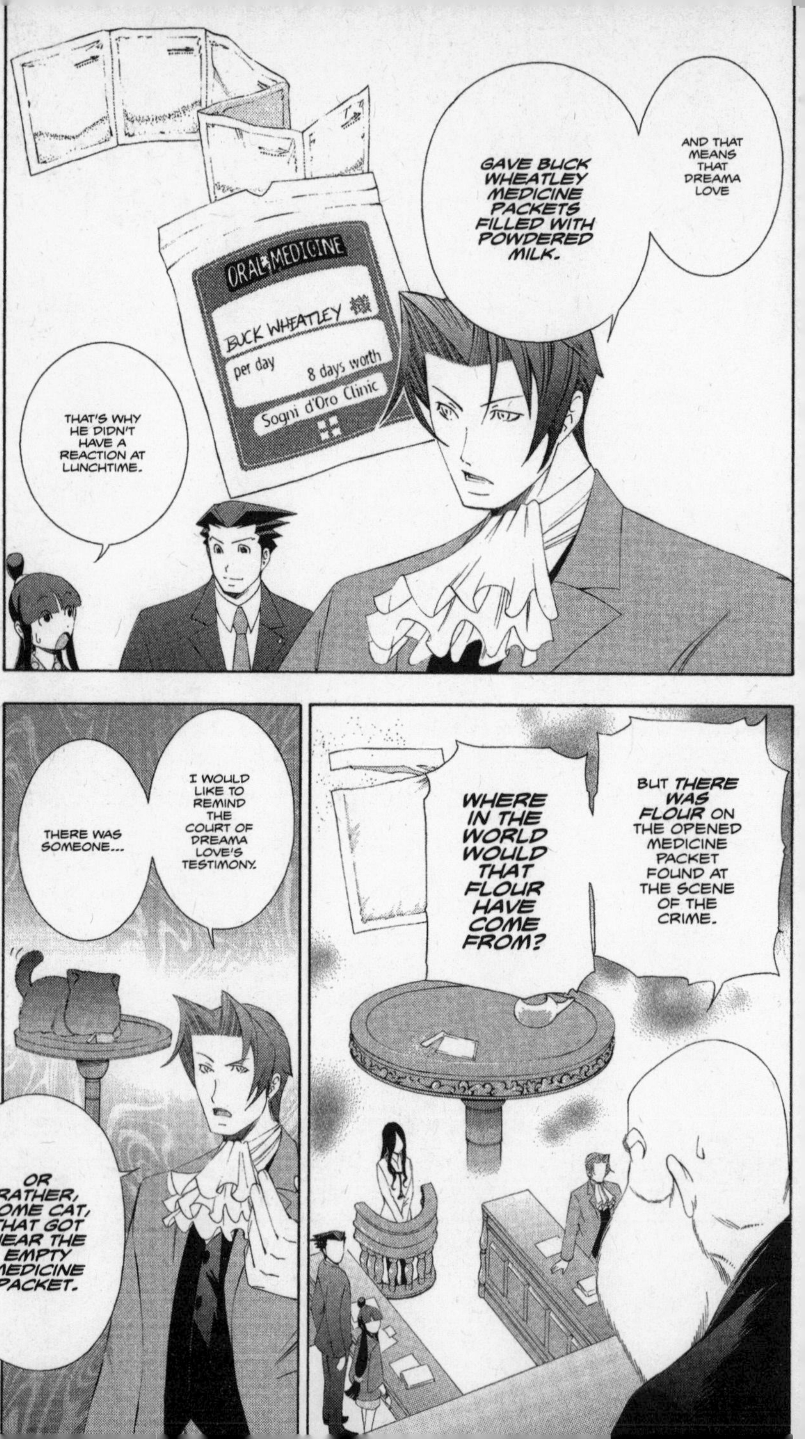
AND THAT MEANS THAT DREAMA LOVE
GAVE BUCK WHEATLEY MEDICINE PACKETS FILLED WITH POWDERED MILK.
ORAL MEDICINE
BUCK WHEATLEY 様
per day
8 days worth
Sogni d'Oro Clinic
THAT'S WHY HE DIDN'T HAVE A REACTION AT LUNCHTIME.
BUT THERE WAS FLOUR ON THE OPENED MEDICINE PACKET FOUND AT THE SCENE OF THE CRIME.
WHERE IN THE WORLD WOULD THAT FLOUR HAVE COME FROM?
I WOULD LIKE TO REMIND THE COURT OF DREAMA LOVE'S TESTIMONY.
THERE WAS SOMEONE...
OR RATHER, SOME CAT, THAT GOT NEAR THE EMPTY MEDICINE PACKET.

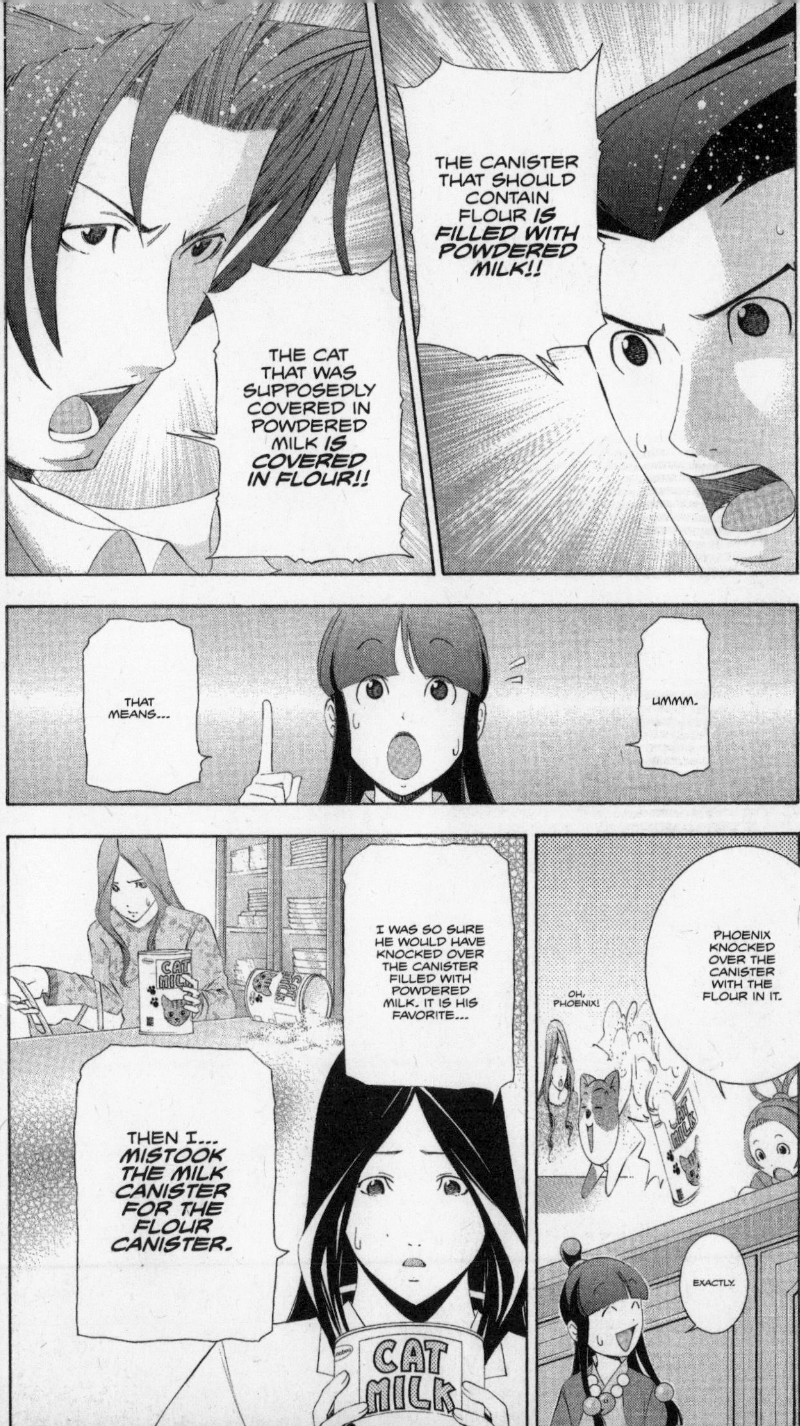
THE CANISTER THAT SHOULD CONTAIN FLOUR IS FILLED WITH POWDERED MILK!!
THE CAT THAT WAS SUPPOSEDLY COVERED IN POWDERED MILK IS COVERED IN FLOUR!!
UMMM.
THAT MEANS...
PHOENIX KNOCKED OVER THE CANISTER WITH THE FLOUR IN IT.
OH, PHOENIX!
CAT MILK
EXACTLY.
I WAS SO SURE HE WOULD HAVE KNOCKED OVER THE CANISTER FILLED WITH POWDERED MILK. IT IS HIS FAVORITE...
CAT MILK
THEN I... MISTOOK THE MILK CANISTER FOR THE FLOUR CANISTER.
CAT MILK

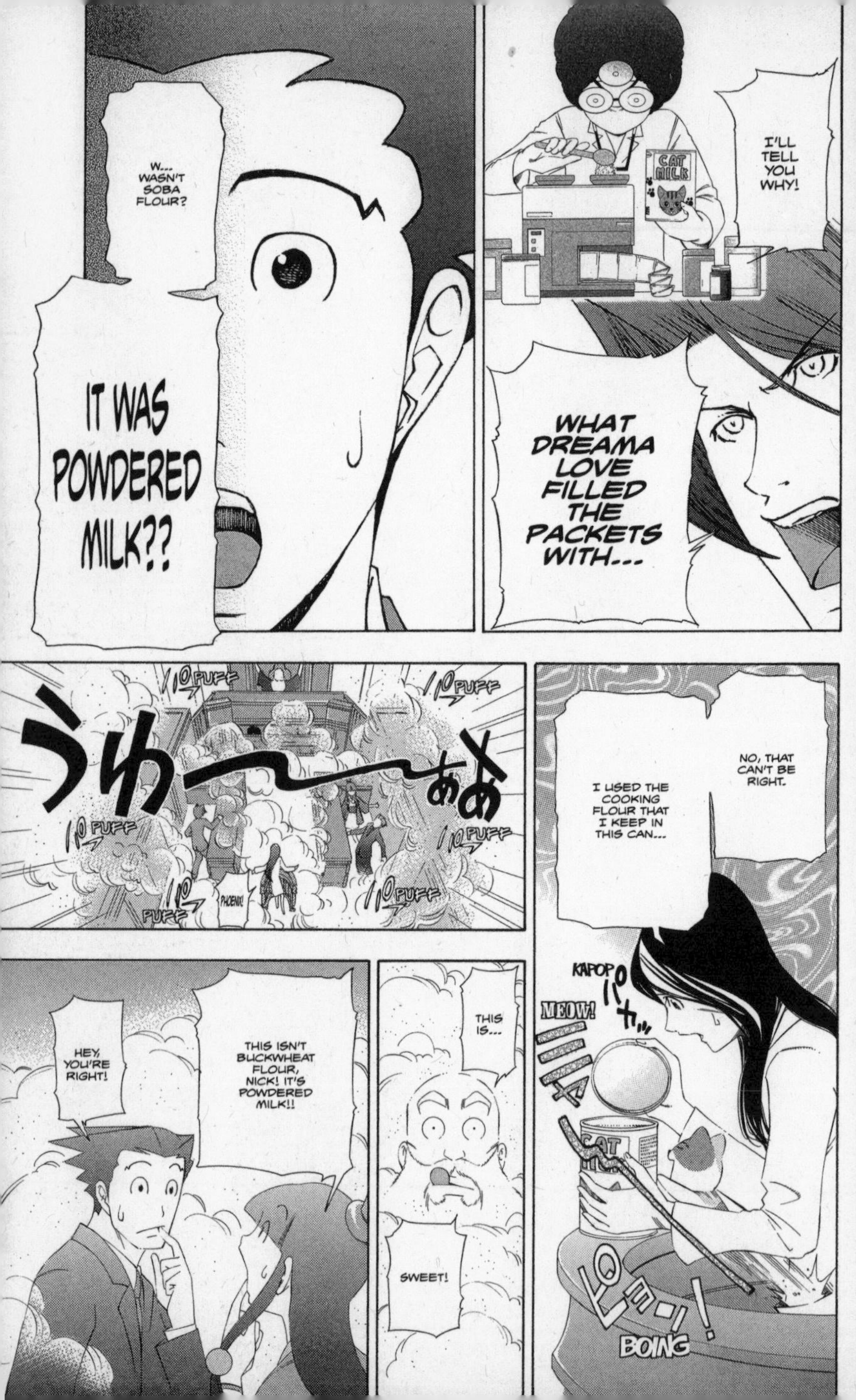
I'LL TELL YOU WHY!
WHAT DREAMA LOVE FILLED THE PACKETS WITH...
W... WASN'T SOBA FLOUR?
IT WAS POWDERED MILK??
NO, THAT CAN'T BE RIGHT.
I USED THE COOKING FLOUR THAT I KEEP IN THIS CAN...
KAPOP
MEOW!
BOING
うゅ〜〜ぁあ
PUFF
PUFF
PUFF
PUFF
PUFF
PUFF
PHOENIX!
THIS IS...
SWEET!
THIS ISN'T BUCKWHEAT FLOUR, NICK! IT'S POWDERED MILK!!
HEY, YOU'RE RIGHT!

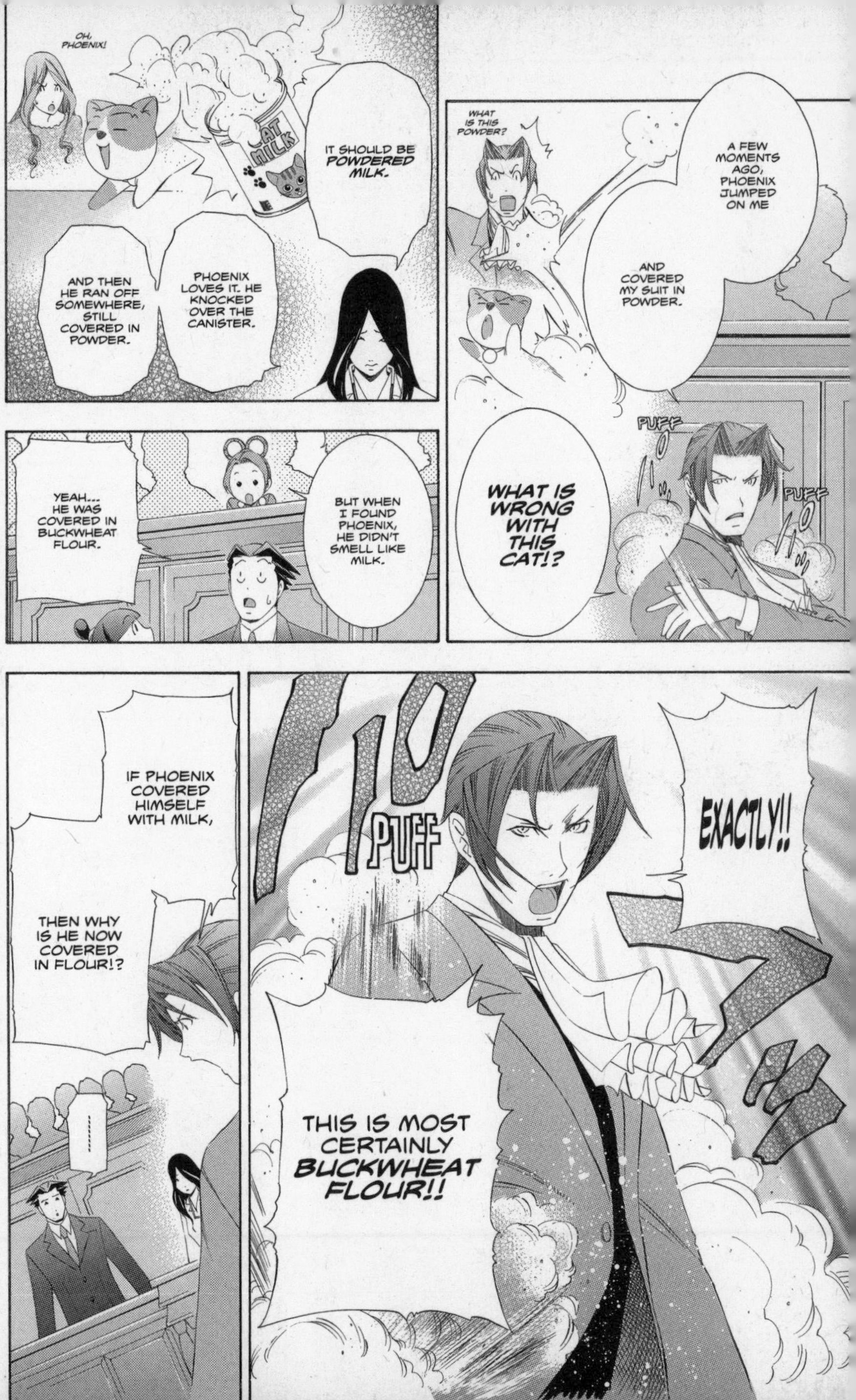
WHAT IS THIS POWDER?
A FEW MOMENTS AGO, PHOENIX JUMPED ON ME
AND COVERED MY SUIT IN POWDER.
PUFF
PUFF
WHAT IS WRONG WITH THIS CAT!?
OH, PHOENIX!
CAT MILK
IT SHOULD BE POWDERED MILK.
PHOENIX LOVES IT. HE KNOCKED OVER THE CANISTER.
AND THEN HE RAN OFF SOMEWHERE, STILL COVERED IN POWDER.
BUT WHEN I FOUND PHOENIX, HE DIDN'T SMELL LIKE MILK.
YEAH... HE WAS COVERED IN BUCKWHEAT FLOUR.
EXACTLY!!
PUFF
THIS IS MOST CERTAINLY BUCKWHEAT FLOUR!!
IF PHOENIX COVERED HIMSELF WITH MILK,
THEN WHY IS HE NOW COVERED IN FLOUR!?
......

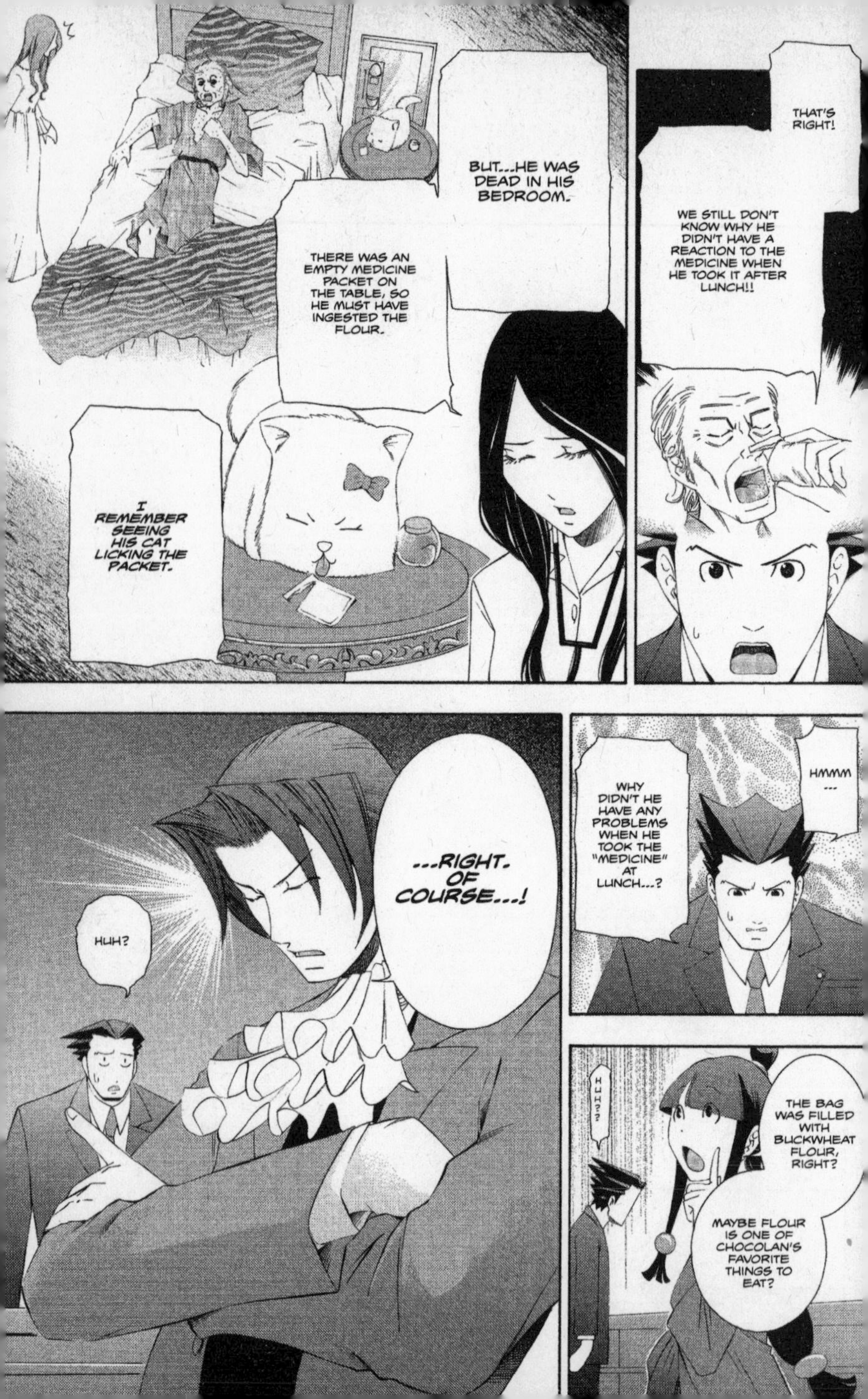
THAT'S RIGHT!
WE STILL DON'T KNOW WHY HE DIDN'T HAVE A REACTION TO THE MEDICINE WHEN HE TOOK IT AFTER LUNCH!!
BUT...HE WAS DEAD IN HIS BEDROOM.
THERE WAS AN EMPTY MEDICINE PACKET ON THE TABLE, SO HE MUST HAVE INGESTED THE FLOUR.
I REMEMBER SEEING HIS CAT LICKING THE PACKET.
HMMM...
WHY DIDN'T HE HAVE ANY PROBLEMS WHEN HE TOOK THE "MEDICINE" AT LUNCH...?
HUH??
THE BAG WAS FILLED WITH BUCKWHEAT FLOUR, RIGHT?
MAYBE FLOUR IS ONE OF CHOCOLAN'S FAVORITE THINGS TO EAT?
...RIGHT. OF COURSE...!
HUH?

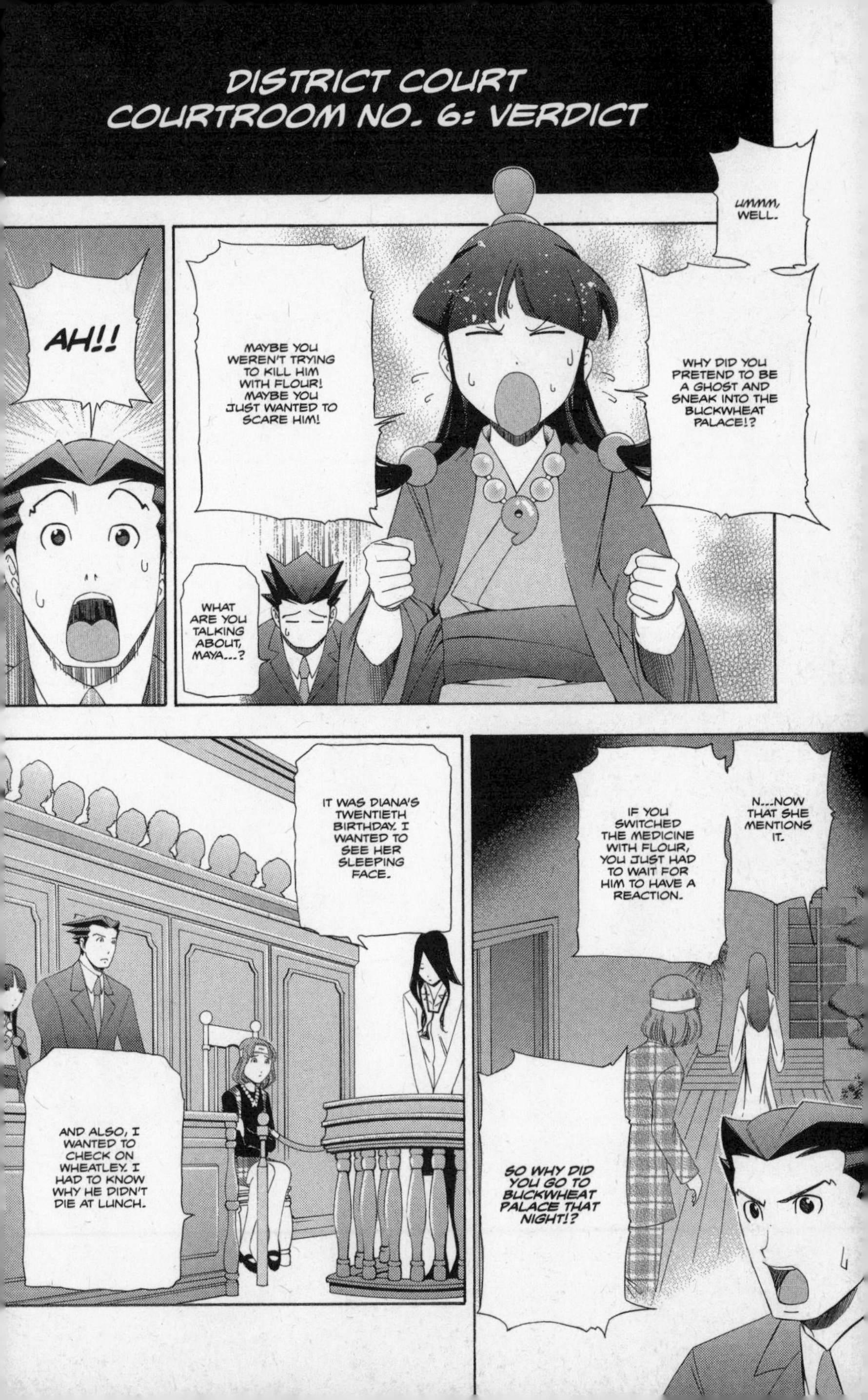
DISTRICT COURT
COURTROOM NO. 6: VERDICT
UMMM, WELL.
WHY DID YOU PRETEND TO BE A GHOST AND SNEAK INTO THE BUCKWHEAT PALACE!?
MAYBE YOU WEREN'T TRYING TO KILL HIM WITH FLOUR! MAYBE YOU JUST WANTED TO SCARE HIM!
WHAT ARE YOU TALKING ABOUT, MAYA...?
AH!!
N...NOW THAT SHE MENTIONS IT.
IF YOU SWITCHED THE MEDICINE WITH FLOUR, YOU JUST HAD TO WAIT FOR HIM TO HAVE A REACTION.
SO WHY DID YOU GO TO BUCKWHEAT PALACE THAT NIGHT!?
IT WAS DIANA'S TWENTIETH BIRTHDAY. I WANTED TO SEE HER SLEEPING FACE.
AND ALSO, I WANTED TO CHECK ON WHEATLEY. I HAD TO KNOW WHY HE DIDN'T DIE AT LUNCH.

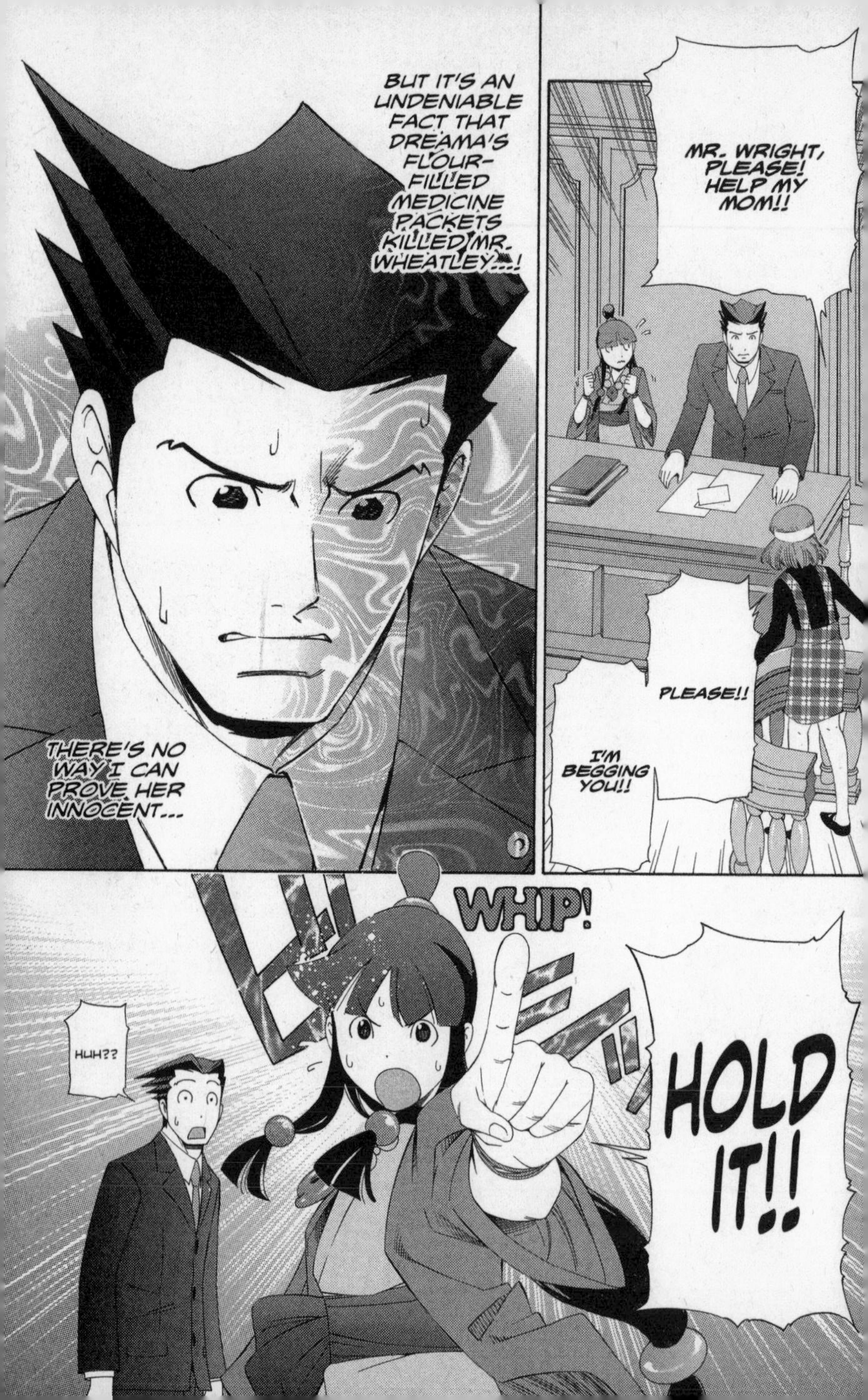
MR. WRIGHT, PLEASE! HELP MY MOM!!
PLEASE!!
I'M BEGGING YOU!!
BUT IT'S AN UNDENIABLE FACT THAT DREAMA'S FLOUR-FILLED MEDICINE PACKETS KILLED MR. WHEATLEY...!
THERE'S NO WAY I CAN PROVE HER INNOCENT...
WHIP!
HOLD IT!!
HUH??

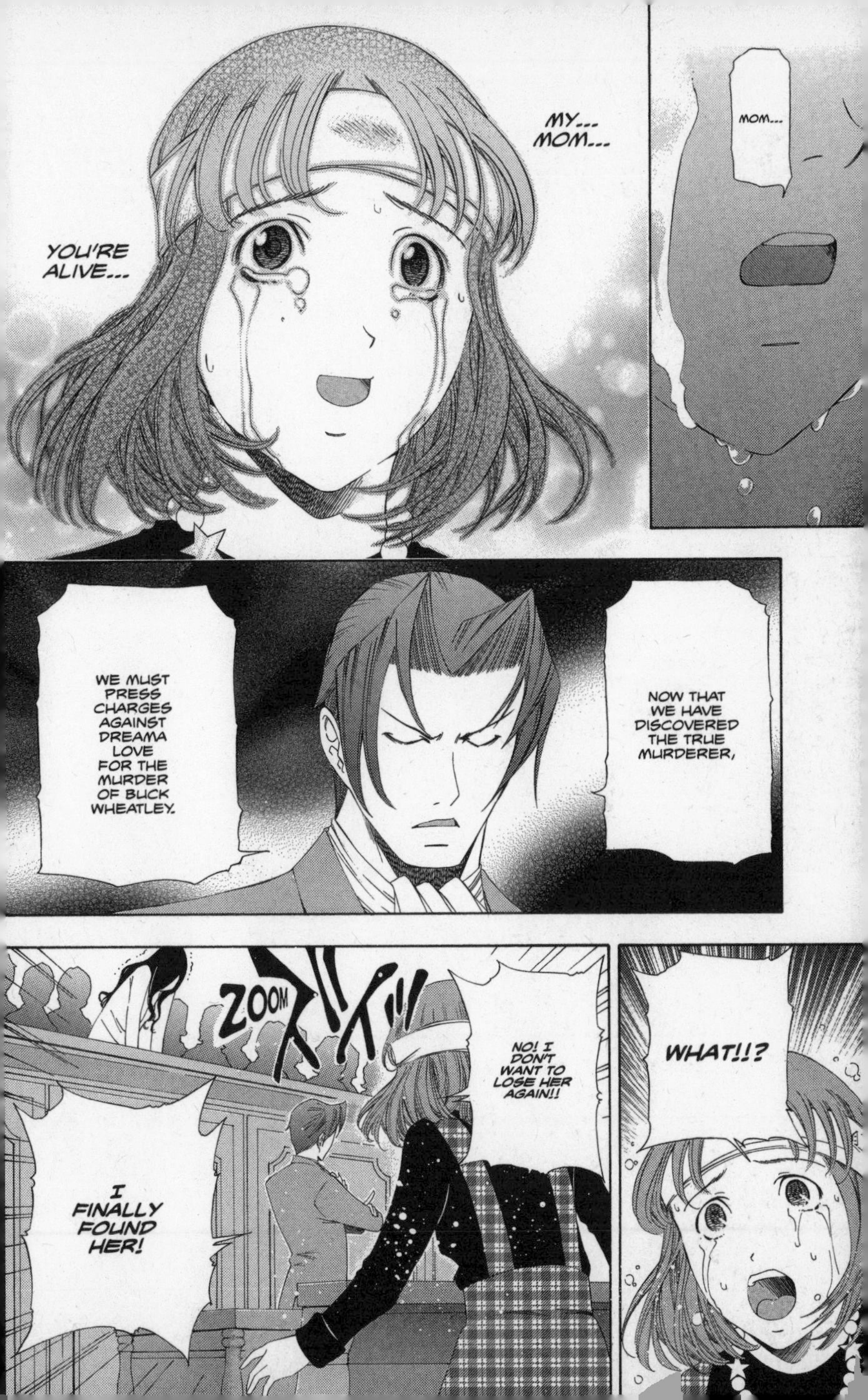
MOM...
MY... MOM...
YOU'RE ALIVE...
NOW THAT WE HAVE DISCOVERED THE TRUE MURDERER,
WE MUST PRESS CHARGES AGAINST DREAMA LOVE FOR THE MURDER OF BUCK WHEATLEY.
WHAT!!?
NO! I DON'T WANT TO LOSE HER AGAIN!!
ZOOM
I FINALLY FOUND HER!

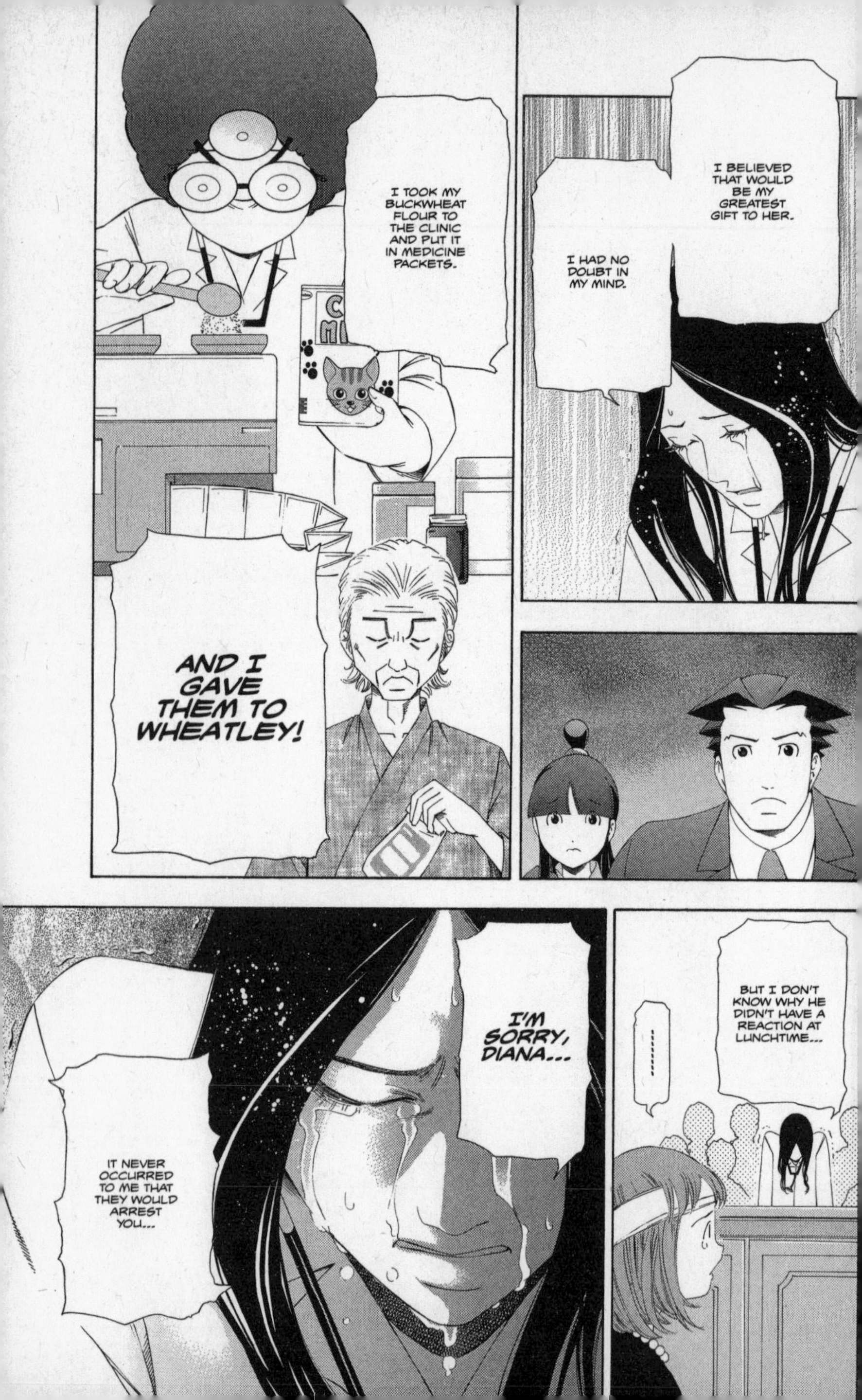
I BELIEVED THAT WOULD BE MY GREATEST GIFT TO HER.
I HAD NO DOUBT IN MY MIND.
I TOOK MY BUCKWHEAT FLOUR TO THE CLINIC AND PUT IT IN MEDICINE PACKETS.
AND I GAVE THEM TO WHEATLEY!
BUT I DON'T KNOW WHY HE DIDN'T HAVE A REACTION AT LUNCHTIME...
......
I'M SORRY, DIANA...
IT NEVER OCCURRED TO ME THAT THEY WOULD ARREST YOU...

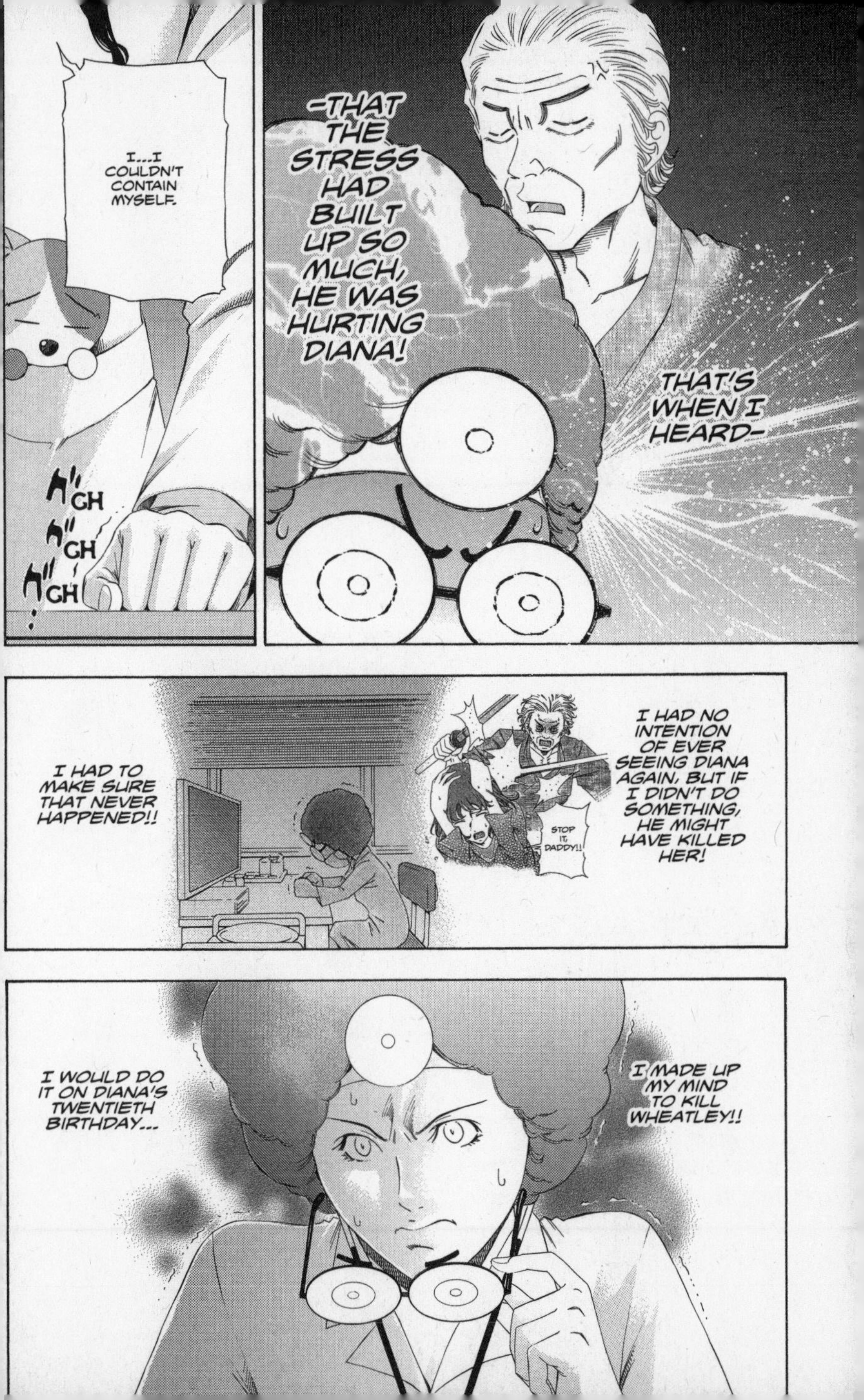
THAT'S WHEN I HEARD-
-THAT THE STRESS HAD BUILT UP SO MUCH, HE WAS HURTING DIANA!
I...I COULDN'T CONTAIN MYSELF.
GH
GH
GH
I HAD NO INTENTION OF EVER SEEING DIANA AGAIN, BUT IF I DIDN'T DO SOMETHING, HE MIGHT HAVE KILLED HER!
STOP IT, DADDY!!
I HAD TO MAKE SURE THAT NEVER HAPPENED!!
I MADE UP MY MIND TO KILL WHEATLEY!!
I WOULD DO IT ON DIANA'S TWENTIETH BIRTHDAY...

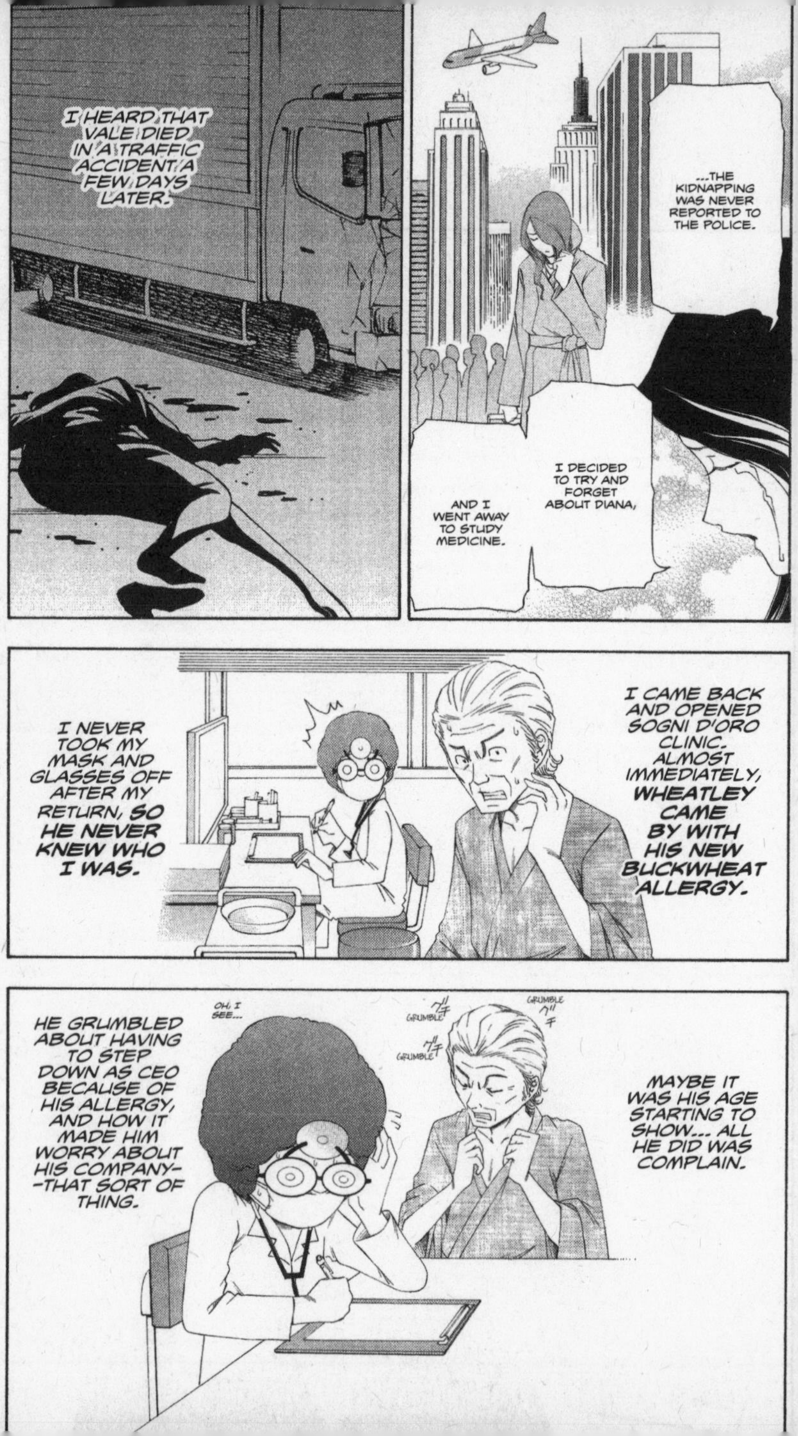
...THE KIDNAPPING WAS NEVER REPORTED TO THE POLICE.
I DECIDED TO TRY AND FORGET ABOUT DIANA,
AND I WENT AWAY TO STUDY MEDICINE.
I HEARD THAT VALE DIED IN A TRAFFIC ACCIDENT A FEW DAYS LATER.
I CAME BACK AND OPENED SOGNI D'ORO CLINIC. ALMOST IMMEDIATELY, **WHEATLEY CAME BY WITH HIS NEW BUCKWHEAT ALLERGY.**
I NEVER TOOK MY MASK AND GLASSES OFF AFTER MY RETURN, **SO HE NEVER KNEW WHO I WAS.**
MAYBE IT WAS HIS AGE STARTING TO SHOW... ALL HE DID WAS COMPLAIN.
GRUMBLE
GRUMBLE
GRUMBLE
OH, I SEE...
HE GRUMBLED ABOUT HAVING TO STEP DOWN AS CEO BECAUSE OF HIS ALLERGY, AND HOW IT MADE HIM WORRY ABOUT HIS COMPANY--THAT SORT OF THING.

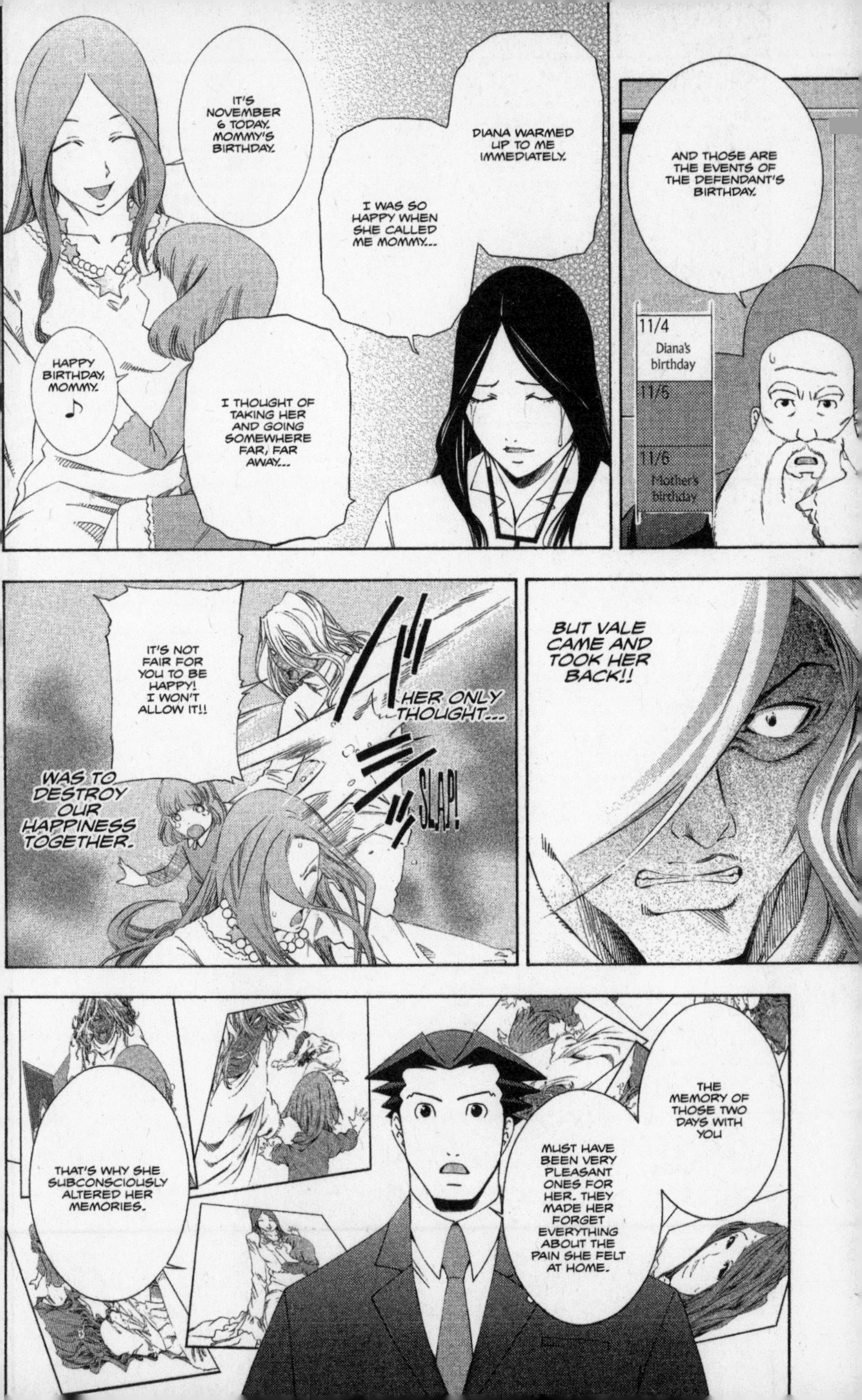
AND THOSE ARE THE EVENTS OF THE DEFENDANT'S BIRTHDAY.
11/4
Diana's birthday
11/5
11/6
Mother's birthday
DIANA WARMED UP TO ME IMMEDIATELY.
I WAS SO HAPPY WHEN SHE CALLED ME MOMMY...
IT'S NOVEMBER 6 TODAY. MOMMY'S BIRTHDAY.
HAPPY BIRTHDAY, MOMMY. ♪
I THOUGHT OF TAKING HER AND GOING SOMEWHERE FAR, FAR AWAY...
BUT VALE CAME AND TOOK HER BACK!!
HER ONLY THOUGHT...
IT'S NOT FAIR FOR YOU TO BE HAPPY! I WON'T ALLOW IT!!
SLAP!
WAS TO DESTROY OUR HAPPINESS TOGETHER.
THE MEMORY OF THOSE TWO DAYS WITH YOU
MUST HAVE BEEN VERY PLEASANT ONES FOR HER. THEY MADE HER FORGET EVERYTHING ABOUT THE PAIN SHE FELT AT HOME.
THAT'S WHY SHE SUBCONSCIOUSLY ALTERED HER MEMORIES.

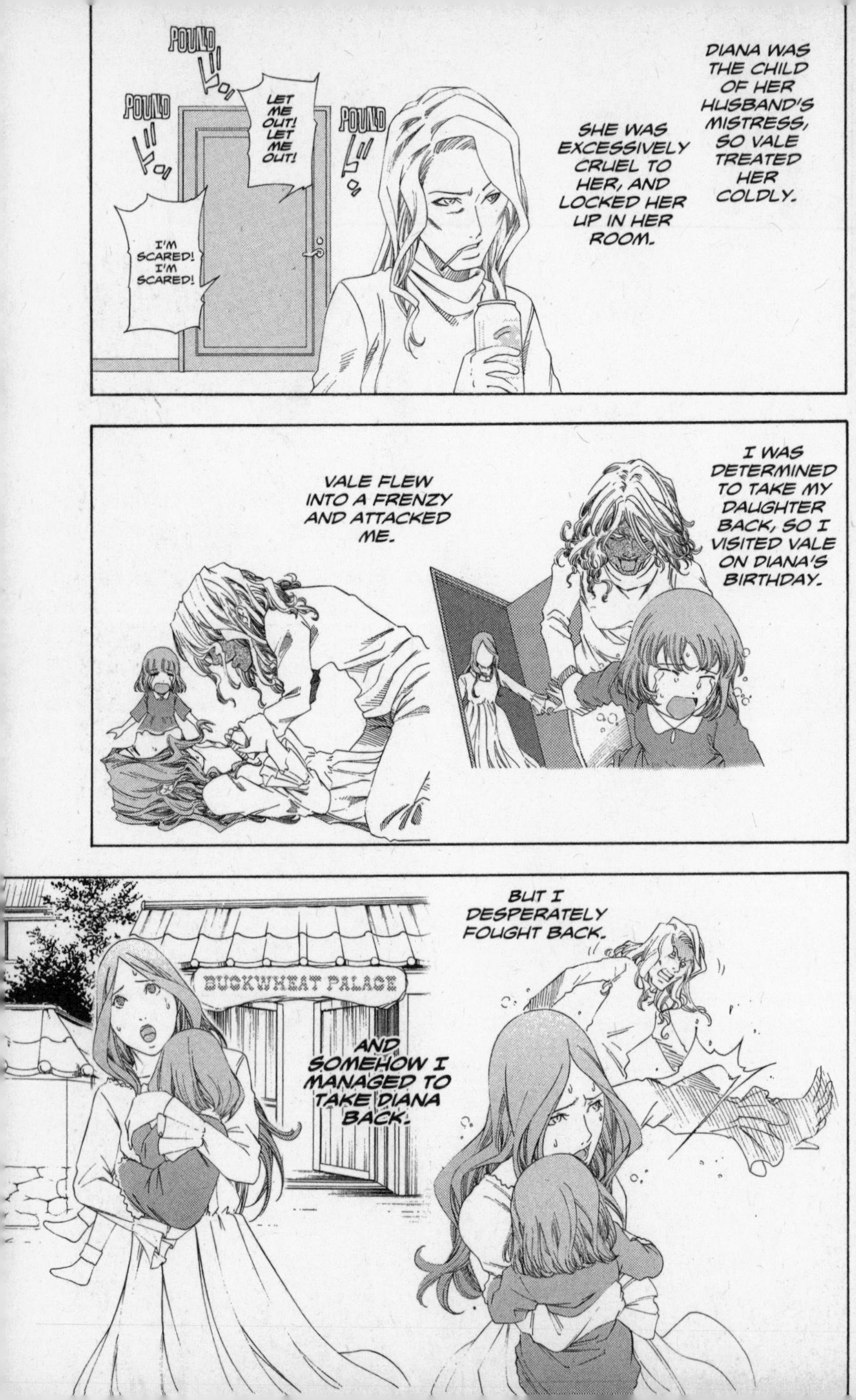
DIANA WAS THE CHILD OF HER HUSBAND'S MISTRESS, SO VALE TREATED HER COLDLY.
SHE WAS EXCESSIVELY CRUEL TO HER, AND LOCKED HER UP IN HER ROOM.
POUND
POUND
LET ME OUT! LET ME OUT!
POUND
I'M SCARED! I'M SCARED!
I WAS DETERMINED TO TAKE MY DAUGHTER BACK, SO I VISITED VALE ON DIANA'S BIRTHDAY.
VALE FLEW INTO A FRENZY AND ATTACKED ME.
BUT I DESPERATELY FOUGHT BACK.
AND SOMEHOW I MANAGED TO TAKE DIANA BACK.
BUCKWHEAT PALACE

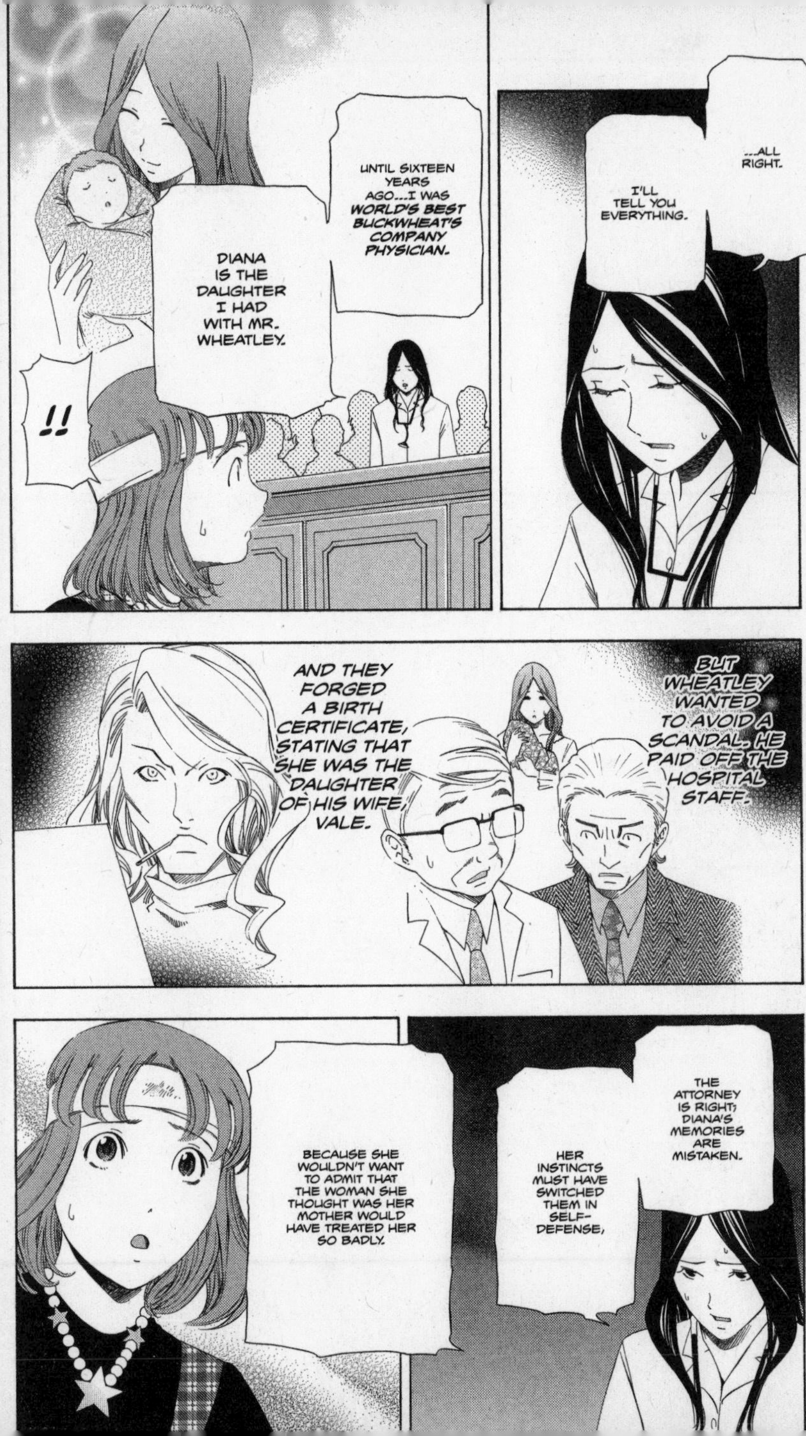
...ALL RIGHT.
I'LL TELL YOU EVERYTHING.
UNTIL SIXTEEN YEARS AGO...I WAS WORLD'S BEST BUCKWHEAT'S COMPANY PHYSICIAN.
DIANA IS THE DAUGHTER I HAD WITH MR. WHEATLEY.
!!
BUT WHEATLEY WANTED TO AVOID A SCANDAL. HE PAID OFF THE HOSPITAL STAFF.
AND THEY FORGED A BIRTH CERTIFICATE, STATING THAT SHE WAS THE DAUGHTER OF HIS WIFE, VALE.
THE ATTORNEY IS RIGHT; DIANA'S MEMORIES ARE MISTAKEN.
HER INSTINCTS MUST HAVE SWITCHED THEM IN SELF-DEFENSE,
BECAUSE SHE WOULDN'T WANT TO ADMIT THAT THE WOMAN SHE THOUGHT WAS HER MOTHER WOULD HAVE TREATED HER SO BADLY.

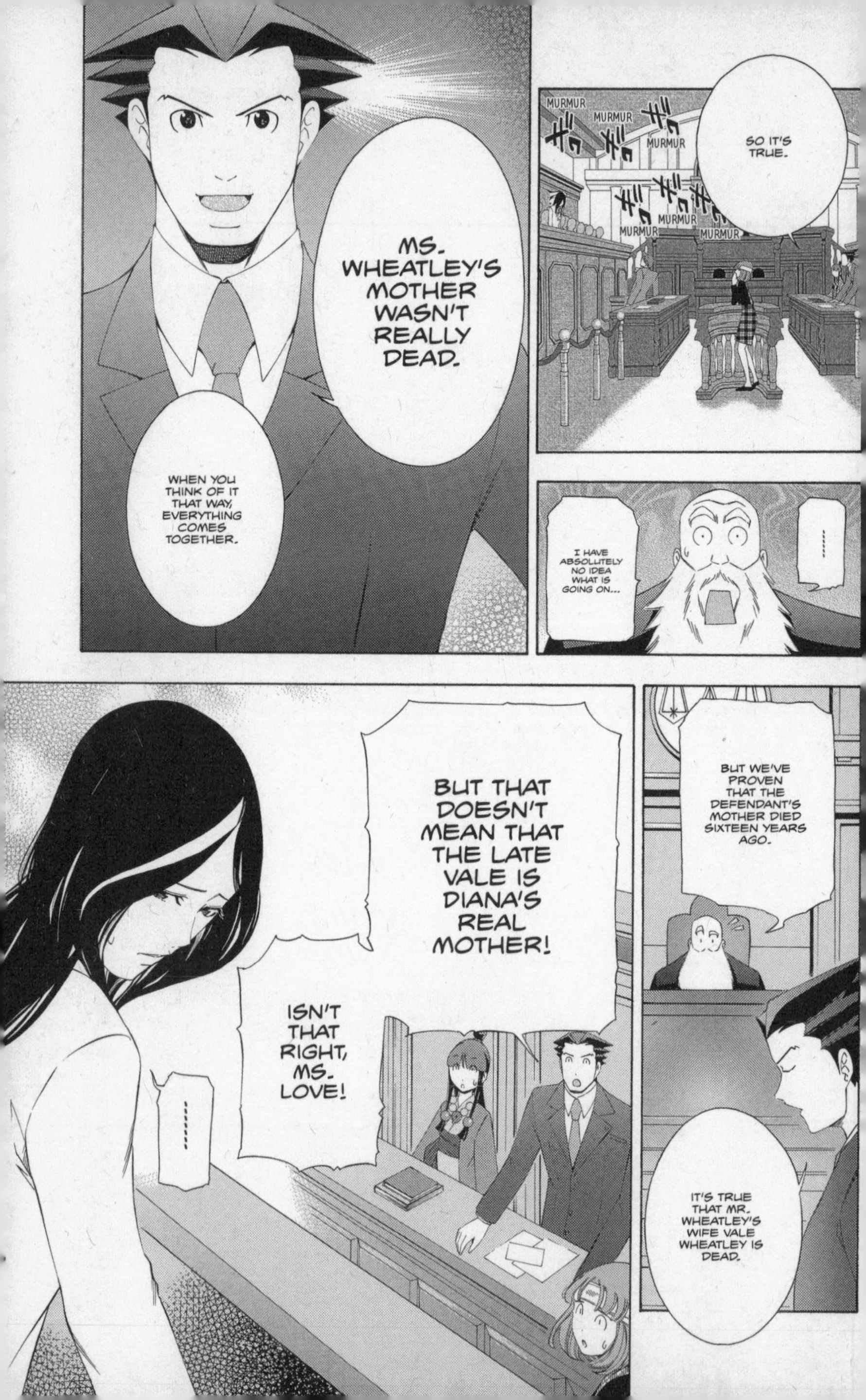
MURMUR
MURMUR
MURMUR
MURMUR
MURMUR
MURMUR
SO IT'S TRUE.
I HAVE ABSOLUTELY NO IDEA WHAT IS GOING ON...
......
MS. WHEATLEY'S MOTHER WASN'T REALLY DEAD.
WHEN YOU THINK OF IT THAT WAY, EVERYTHING COMES TOGETHER.
BUT WE'VE PROVEN THAT THE DEFENDANT'S MOTHER DIED SIXTEEN YEARS AGO.
IT'S TRUE THAT MR. WHEATLEY'S WIFE VALE WHEATLEY IS DEAD.
BUT THAT DOESN'T MEAN THAT THE LATE VALE IS DIANA'S REAL MOTHER!
ISN'T THAT RIGHT, MS. LOVE!
......

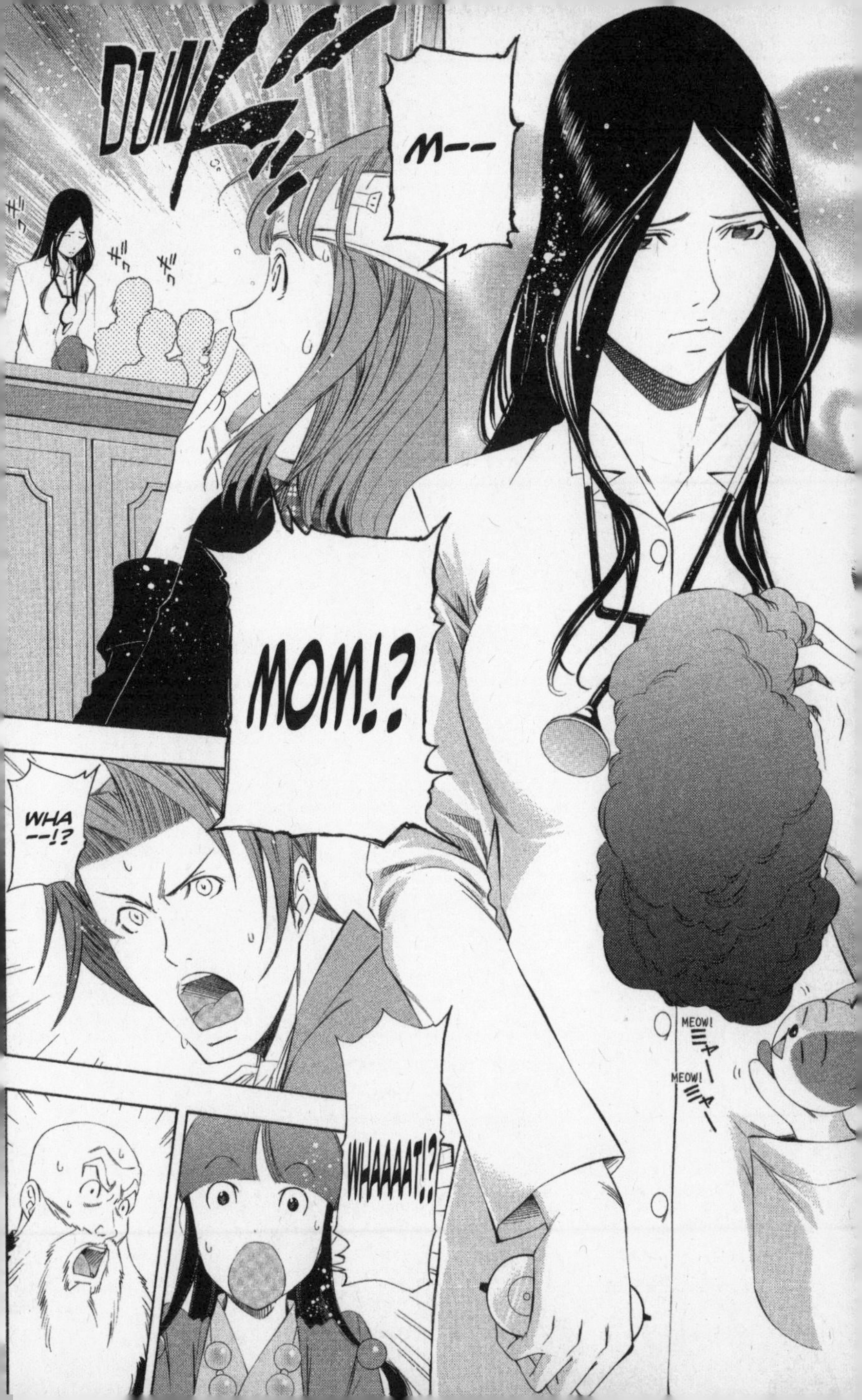
MEOW!
MEOW!
DUN
M--
MOM!?
WHA--!?
WHAAAAT!?

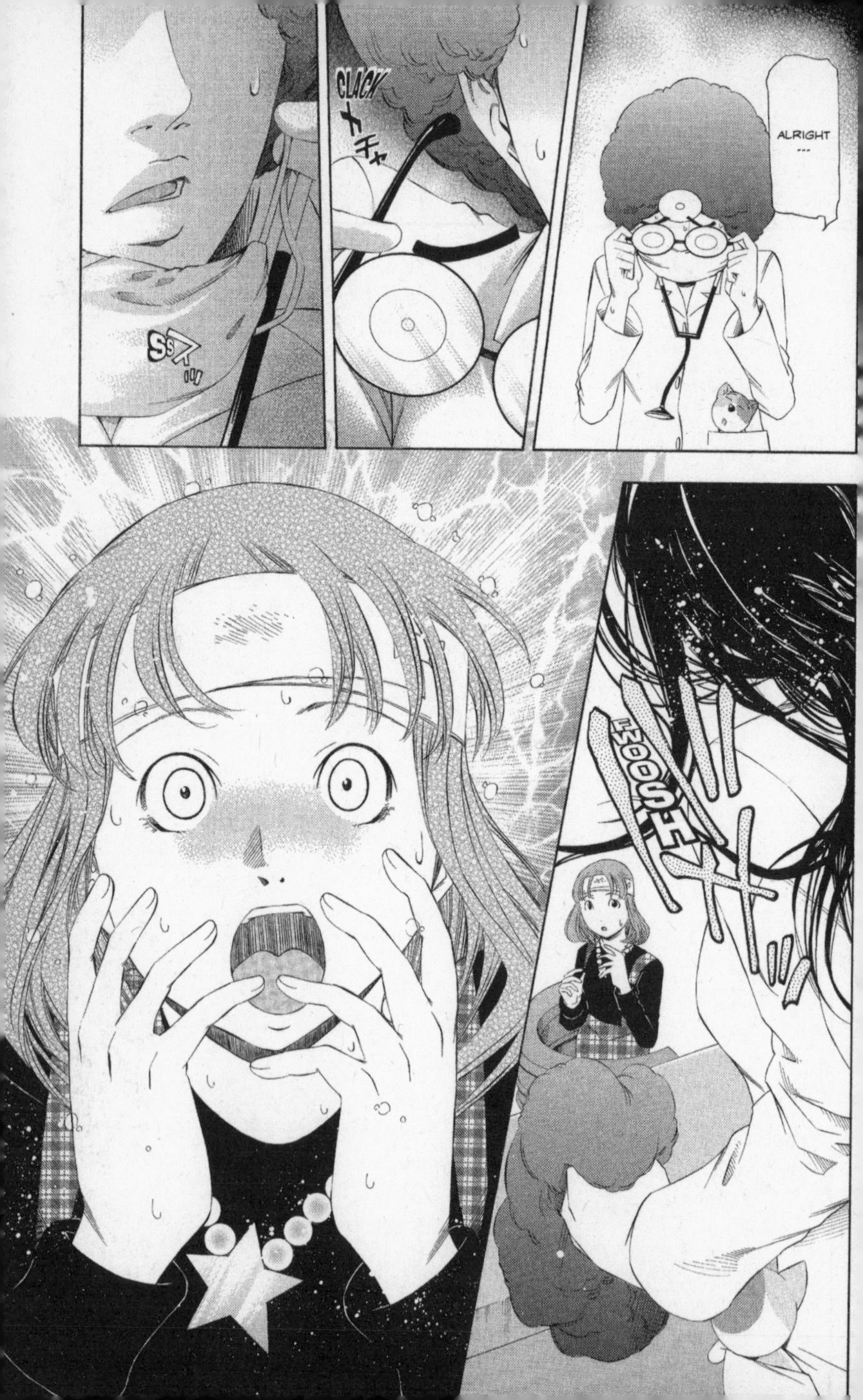
ALRIGHT ---
CLACK
カチャ
Sss
スッ
FWOOSH

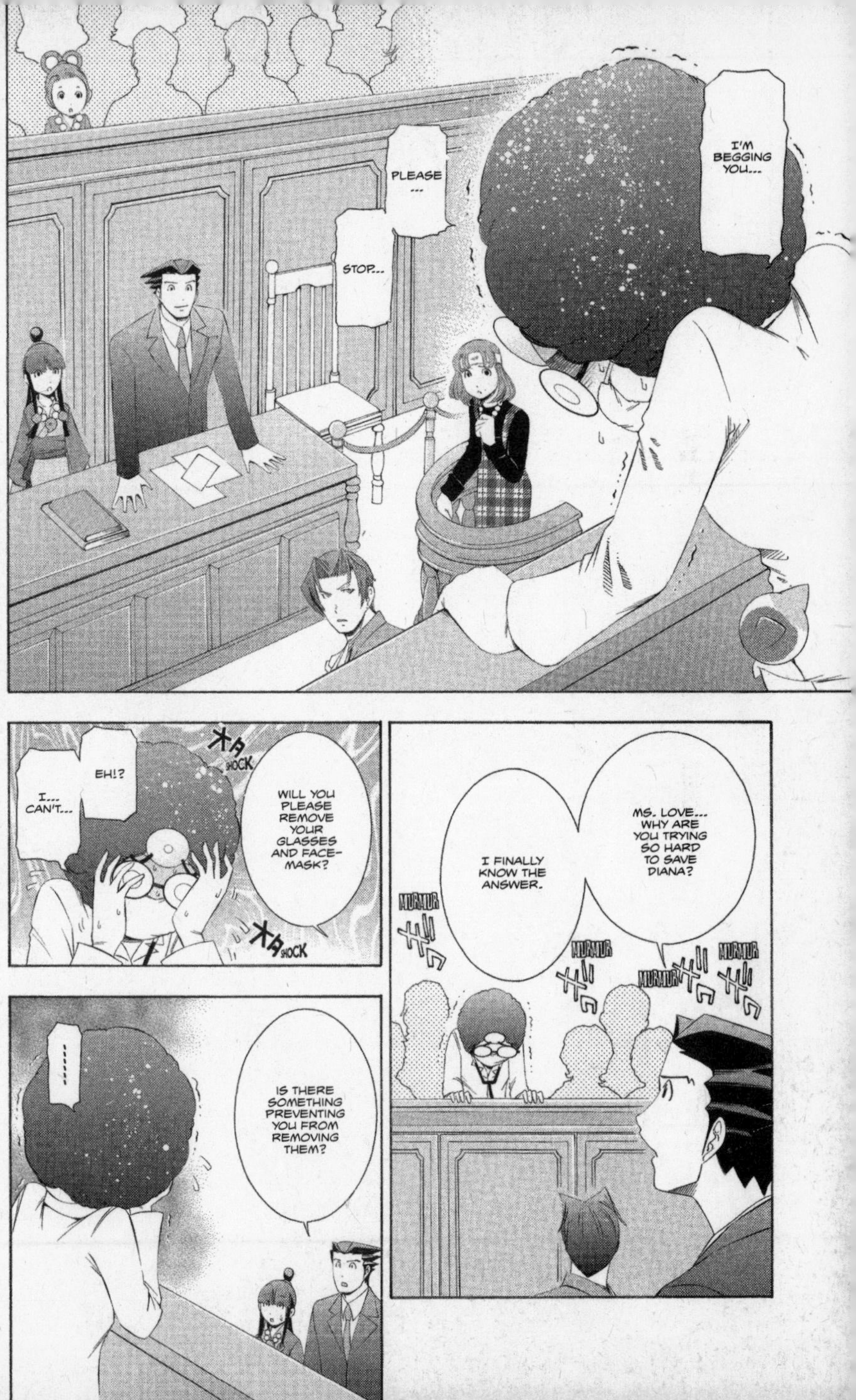
I'M BEGGING YOU...
PLEASE ...
STOP...
MS. LOVE... WHY ARE YOU TRYING SO HARD TO SAVE DIANA?
I FINALLY KNOW THE ANSWER.
MURMUR
MURMUR
MURMUR
MURMUR
WILL YOU PLEASE REMOVE YOUR GLASSES AND FACE-MASK?
SHOCK
EH!?
I... CAN'T...
SHOCK
IS THERE SOMETHING PREVENTING YOU FROM REMOVING THEM?
......

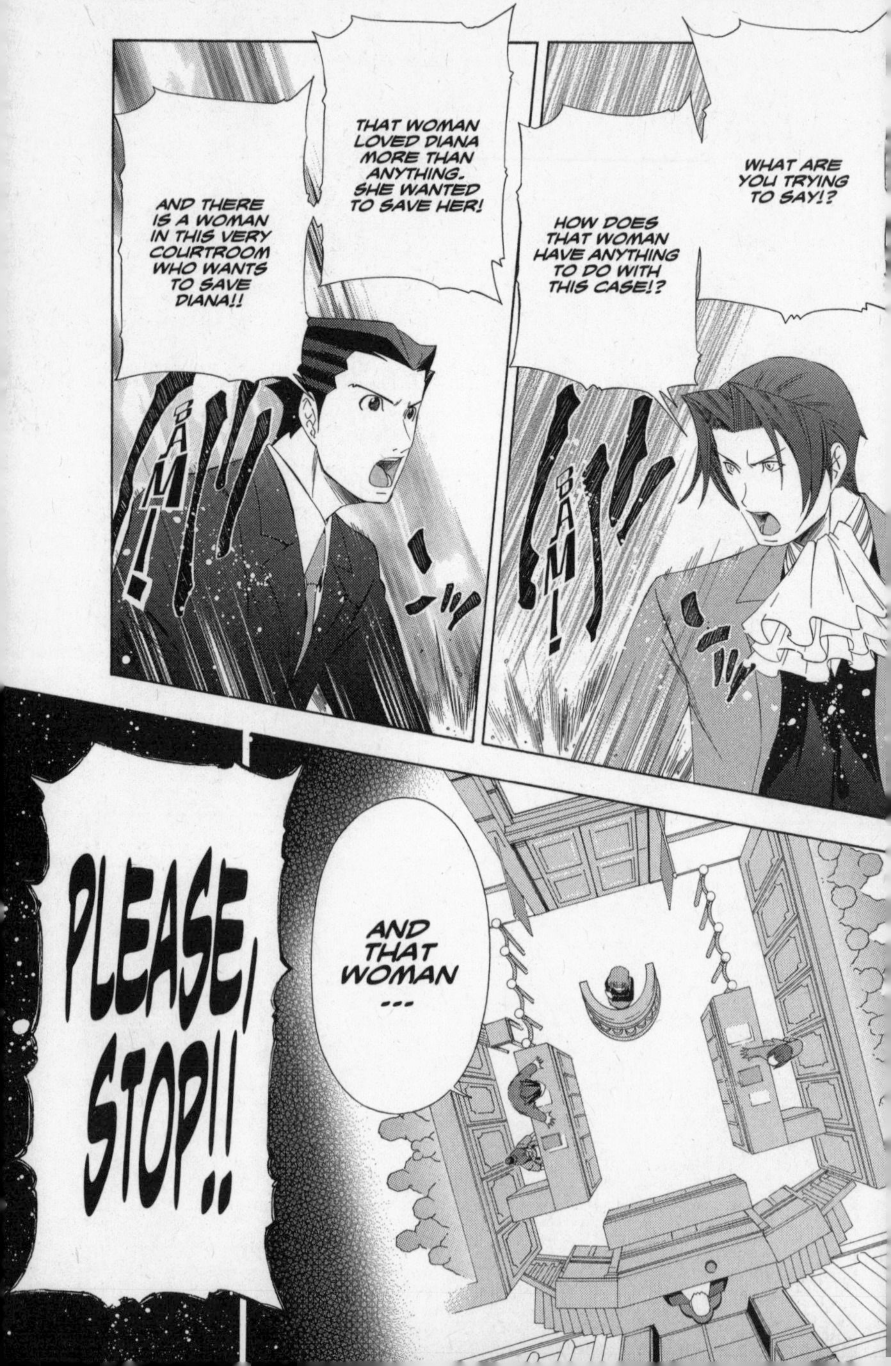

WHAT ARE YOU TRYING TO SAY!?
HOW DOES THAT WOMAN HAVE ANYTHING TO DO WITH THIS CASE!?
BAM!
THAT WOMAN LOVED DIANA MORE THAN ANYTHING. SHE WANTED TO SAVE HER!
AND THERE IS A WOMAN IN THIS VERY COURTROOM WHO WANTS TO SAVE DIANA!!
BAM!
AND THAT WOMAN ---
PLEASE, STOP!!

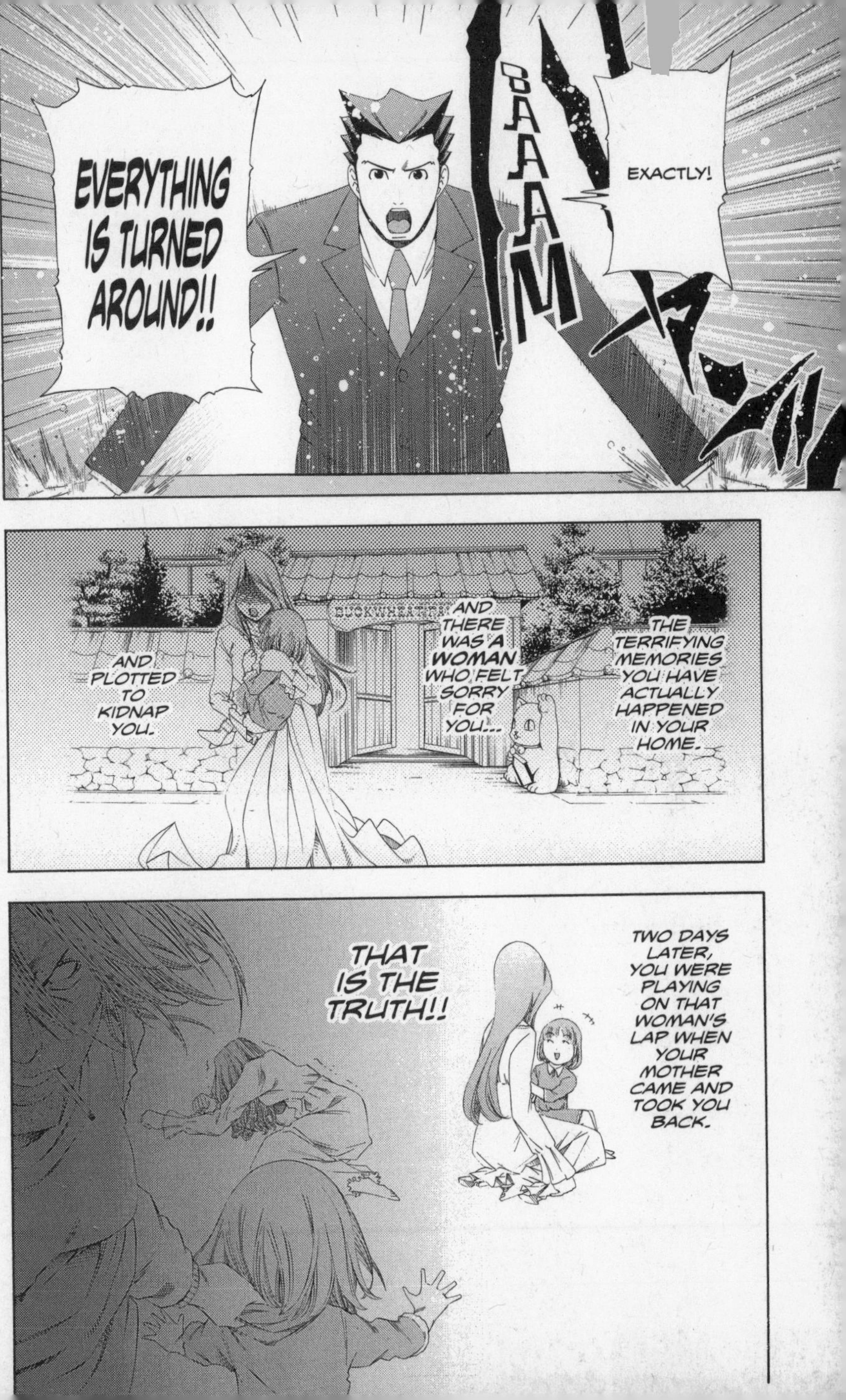

EXACTLY!
BAAAM
EVERYTHING IS TURNED AROUND!!
THE TERRIFYING MEMORIES YOU HAVE ACTUALLY HAPPENED IN YOUR HOME.
AND THERE WAS A WOMAN WHO FELT SORRY FOR YOU...
AND PLOTTED TO KIDNAP YOU.
TWO DAYS LATER, YOU WERE PLAYING ON THAT WOMAN'S LAP WHEN YOUR MOTHER CAME AND TOOK YOU BACK.
THAT IS THE TRUTH!!

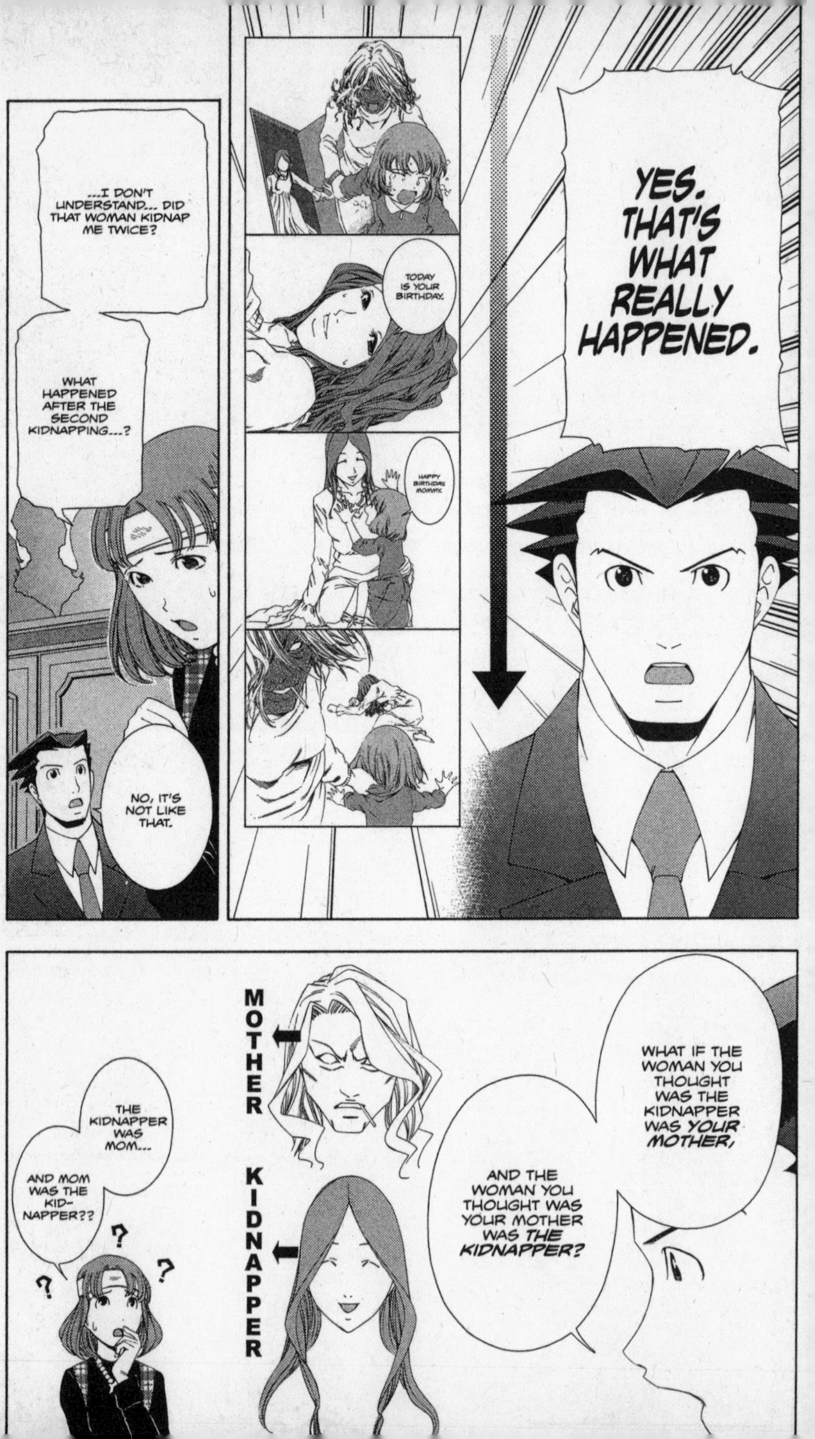
YES. THAT'S WHAT REALLY HAPPENED.
TODAY IS YOUR BIRTHDAY.
HAPPY BIRTHDAY MOMMY.
...I DON'T UNDERSTAND... DID THAT WOMAN KIDNAP ME TWICE?
WHAT HAPPENED AFTER THE SECOND KIDNAPPING...?
NO, IT'S NOT LIKE THAT.
WHAT IF THE WOMAN YOU THOUGHT WAS THE KIDNAPPER WAS *YOUR MOTHER,*
AND THE WOMAN YOU THOUGHT WAS YOUR MOTHER WAS *THE KIDNAPPER?*
MOTHER
KIDNAPPER
THE KIDNAPPER WAS MOM...
AND MOM WAS THE KID-NAPPER??
? ? ?

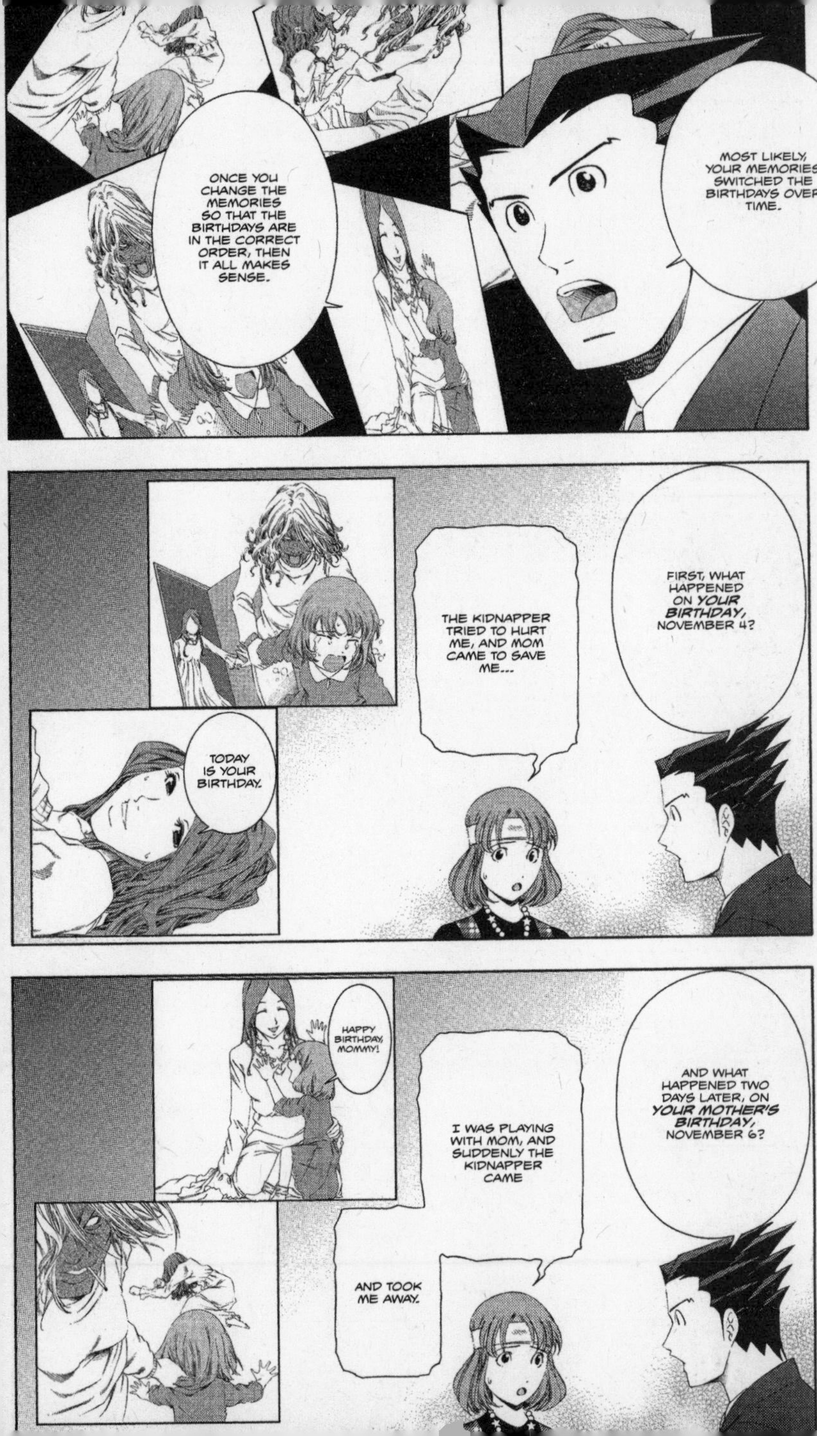
MOST LIKELY, YOUR MEMORIES SWITCHED THE BIRTHDAYS OVER TIME.
ONCE YOU CHANGE THE MEMORIES SO THAT THE BIRTHDAYS ARE IN THE CORRECT ORDER, THEN IT ALL MAKES SENSE.
FIRST, WHAT HAPPENED ON *YOUR BIRTHDAY,* NOVEMBER 4?
THE KIDNAPPER TRIED TO HURT ME, AND MOM CAME TO SAVE ME...
TODAY IS YOUR BIRTHDAY.
AND WHAT HAPPENED TWO DAYS LATER, ON *YOUR MOTHER'S BIRTHDAY,* NOVEMBER 6?
I WAS PLAYING WITH MOM, AND SUDDENLY THE KIDNAPPER CAME
AND TOOK ME AWAY.
HAPPY BIRTHDAY, MOMMY!

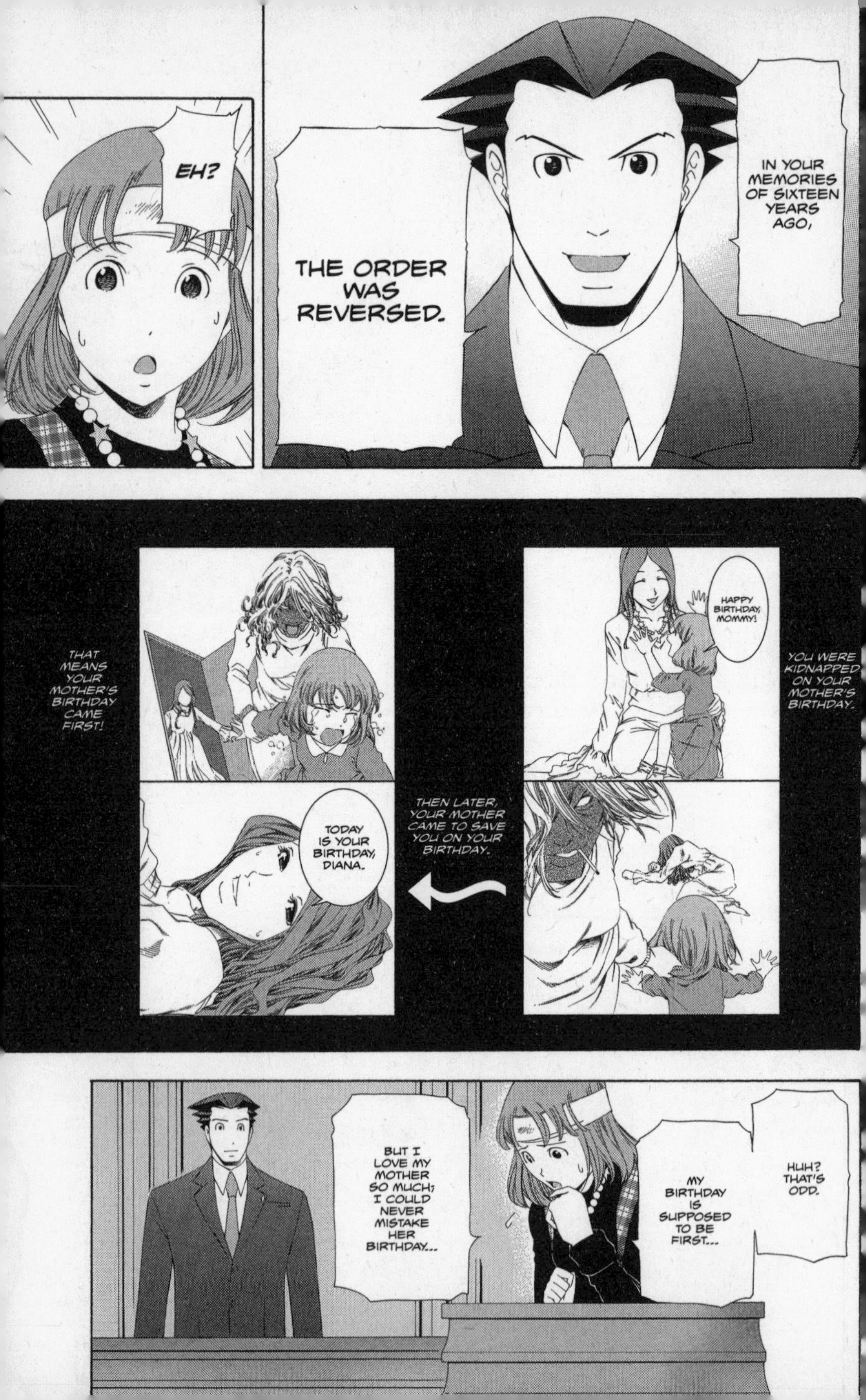
IN YOUR MEMORIES OF SIXTEEN YEARS AGO,
THE ORDER WAS REVERSED.
EH?
YOU WERE KIDNAPPED ON YOUR MOTHER'S BIRTHDAY.
HAPPY BIRTHDAY, MOMMY!
THEN LATER, YOUR MOTHER CAME TO SAVE YOU ON YOUR BIRTHDAY.
TODAY IS YOUR BIRTHDAY, DIANA.
THAT MEANS YOUR MOTHER'S BIRTHDAY CAME FIRST!
HUH? THAT'S ODD.
MY BIRTHDAY IS SUPPOSED TO BE FIRST...
BUT I LOVE MY MOTHER SO MUCH; I COULD NEVER MISTAKE HER BIRTHDAY...

YES.... THAT'S WHY I WANT TO GO VISIT HER GRAVE. TO GIVE HER A BIRTHDAY PRESENT.

AND TO THANK HER FOR THE NECKLACE.

MS. WHEATLEY.

YOUR MOTHER'S BIRTHDAY IS TOMORROW. ...NOVEMBER 6, CORRECT?

YES.

SHE PROMISED TO GIVE IT TO ME ON MY TWENTIETH BIRTHDAY.

THAT NECKLACE.

YOUR MOTHER GAVE IT TO YOU *FOR YOUR BIRTHDAY YESTERDAY.* IS THAT RIGHT?

11/4	Diana's birthday
11/5	
11/6	Mother's birthday

IN OTHER WORDS, *YOUR MOTHER'S BIRTHDAY*

IS *TWO DAYS AFTER YOURS.*

HOWEVER ...

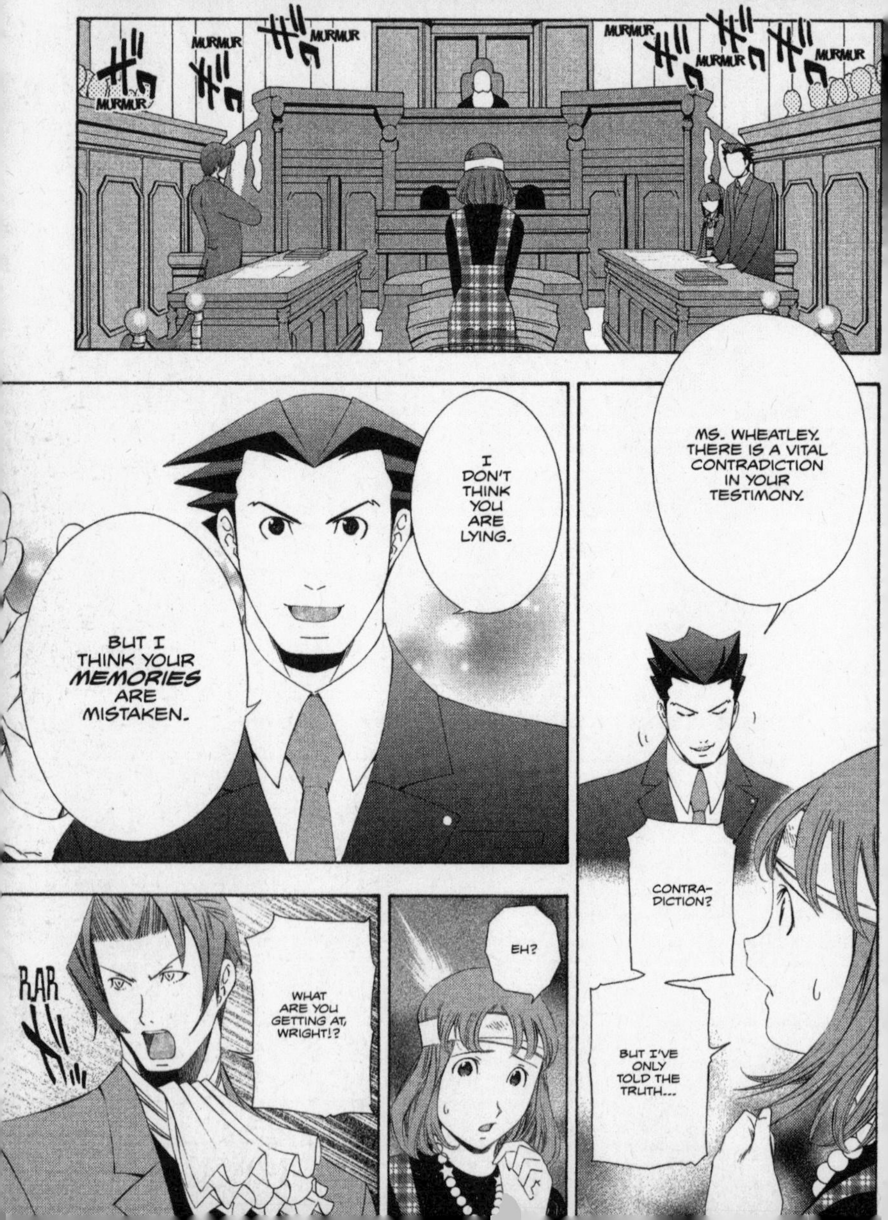
MURMUR
MURMUR
MURMUR
MURMUR
MURMUR
MURMUR
MS. WHEATLEY. THERE IS A VITAL CONTRADICTION IN YOUR TESTIMONY.
CONTRA-DICTION?
BUT I'VE ONLY TOLD THE TRUTH...
I DON'T THINK YOU ARE LYING.
BUT I THINK YOUR *MEMORIES* ARE MISTAKEN.
EH?
WHAT ARE YOU GETTING AT, WRIGHT!?
RAR

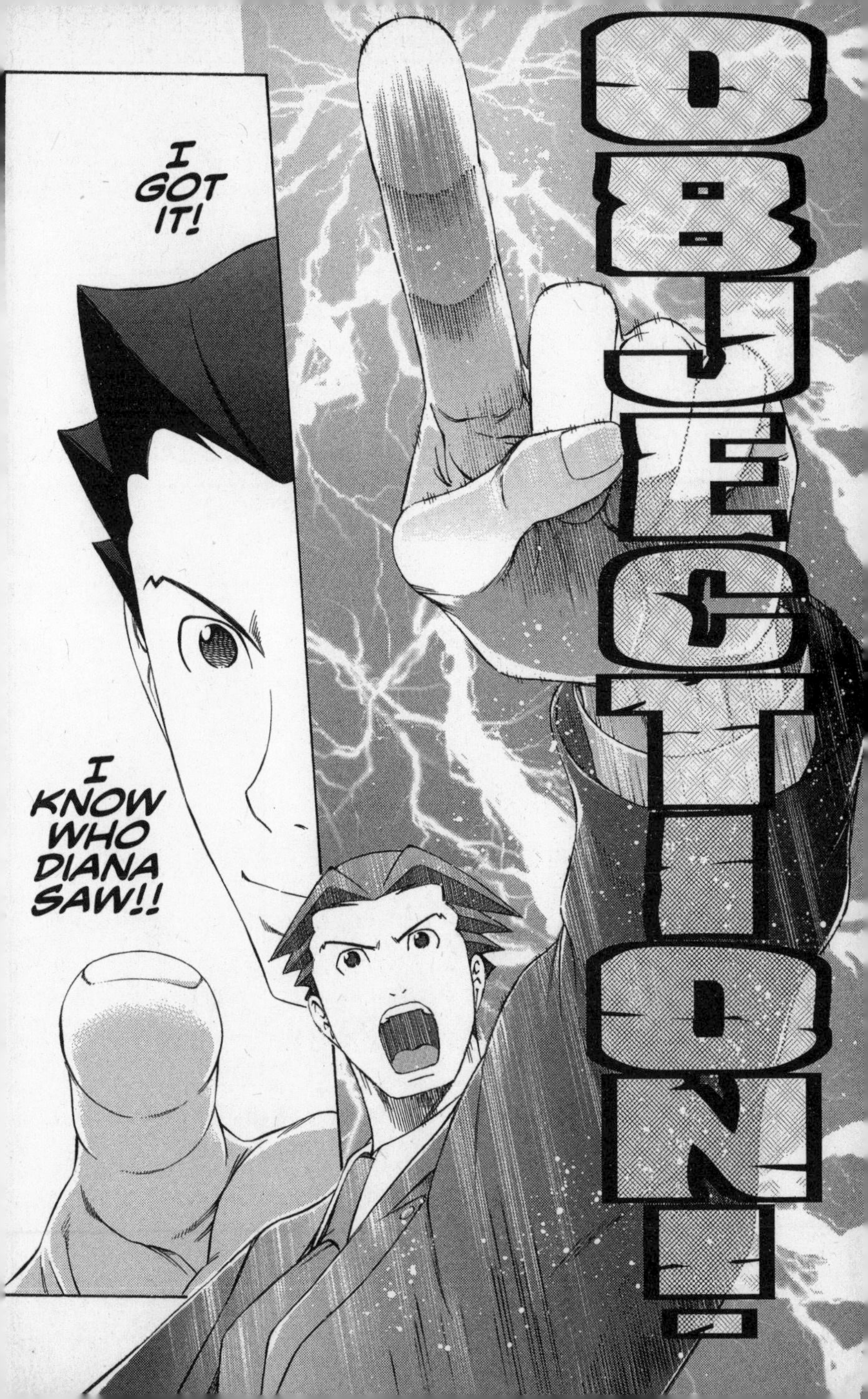
OBJECTION!
I GOT IT!
I KNOW WHO DIANA SAW!!

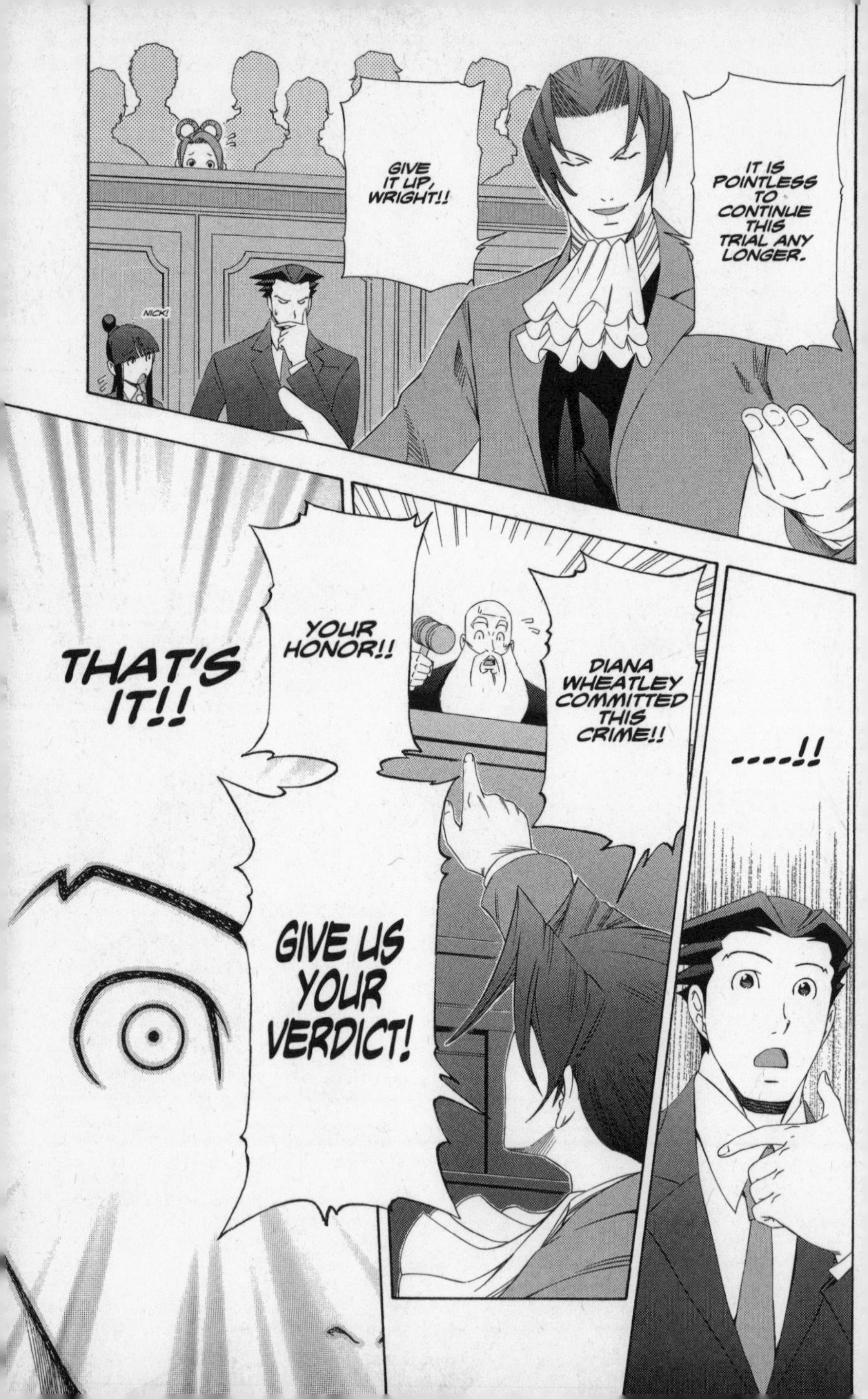
IT IS POINTLESS TO CONTINUE THIS TRIAL ANY LONGER.
GIVE IT UP, WRIGHT!!
NICK!
....!!
YOUR HONOR!!
DIANA WHEATLEY COMMITTED THIS CRIME!!
THAT'S IT!!
GIVE US YOUR VERDICT!

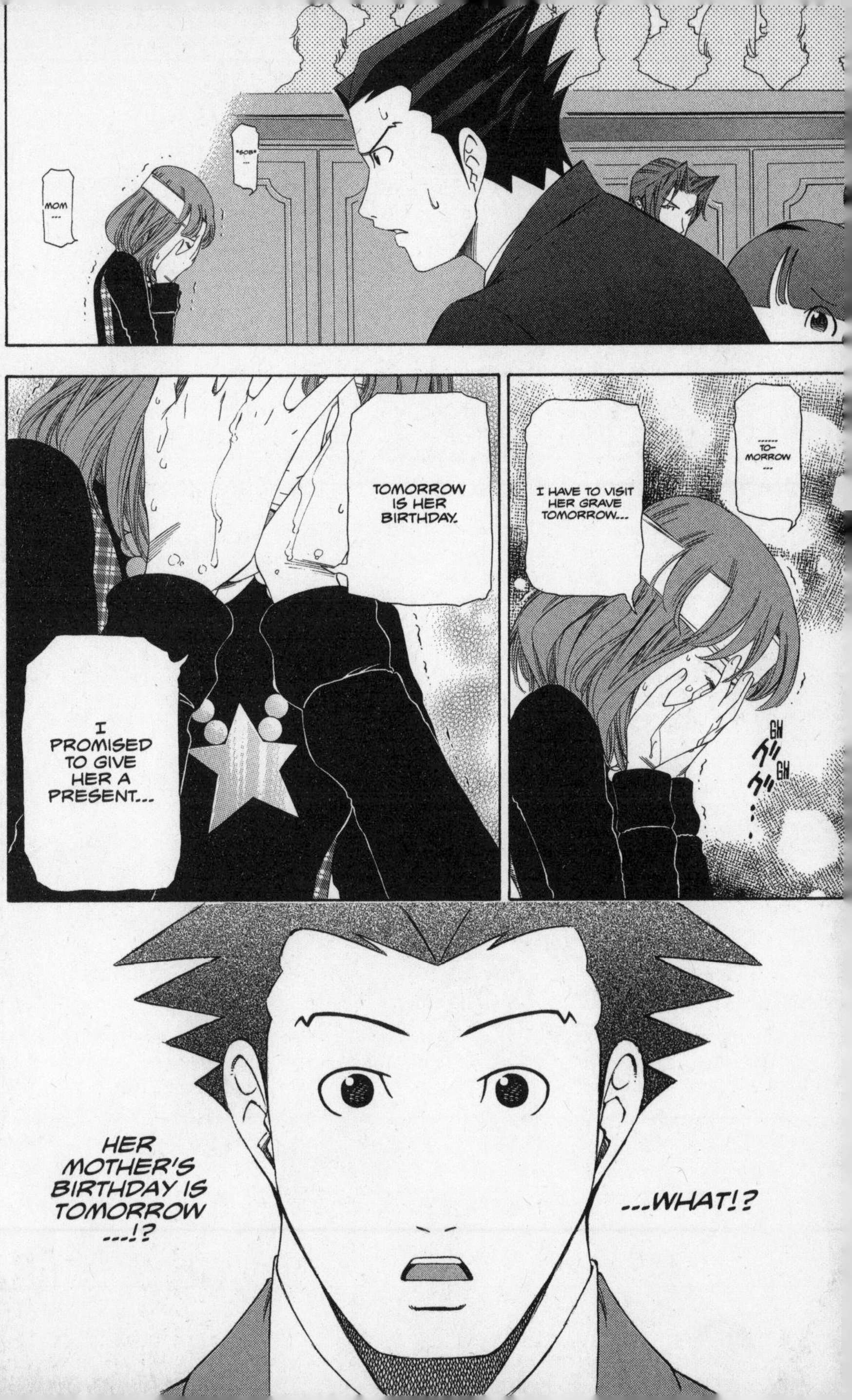
SOB ...
MOM ...
...... TO-MORROW ...
I HAVE TO VISIT HER GRAVE TOMORROW...
GW GW
TOMORROW IS HER BIRTHDAY.
I PROMISED TO GIVE HER A PRESENT...
...WHAT!?
HER MOTHER'S BIRTHDAY IS TOMORROW ...!?

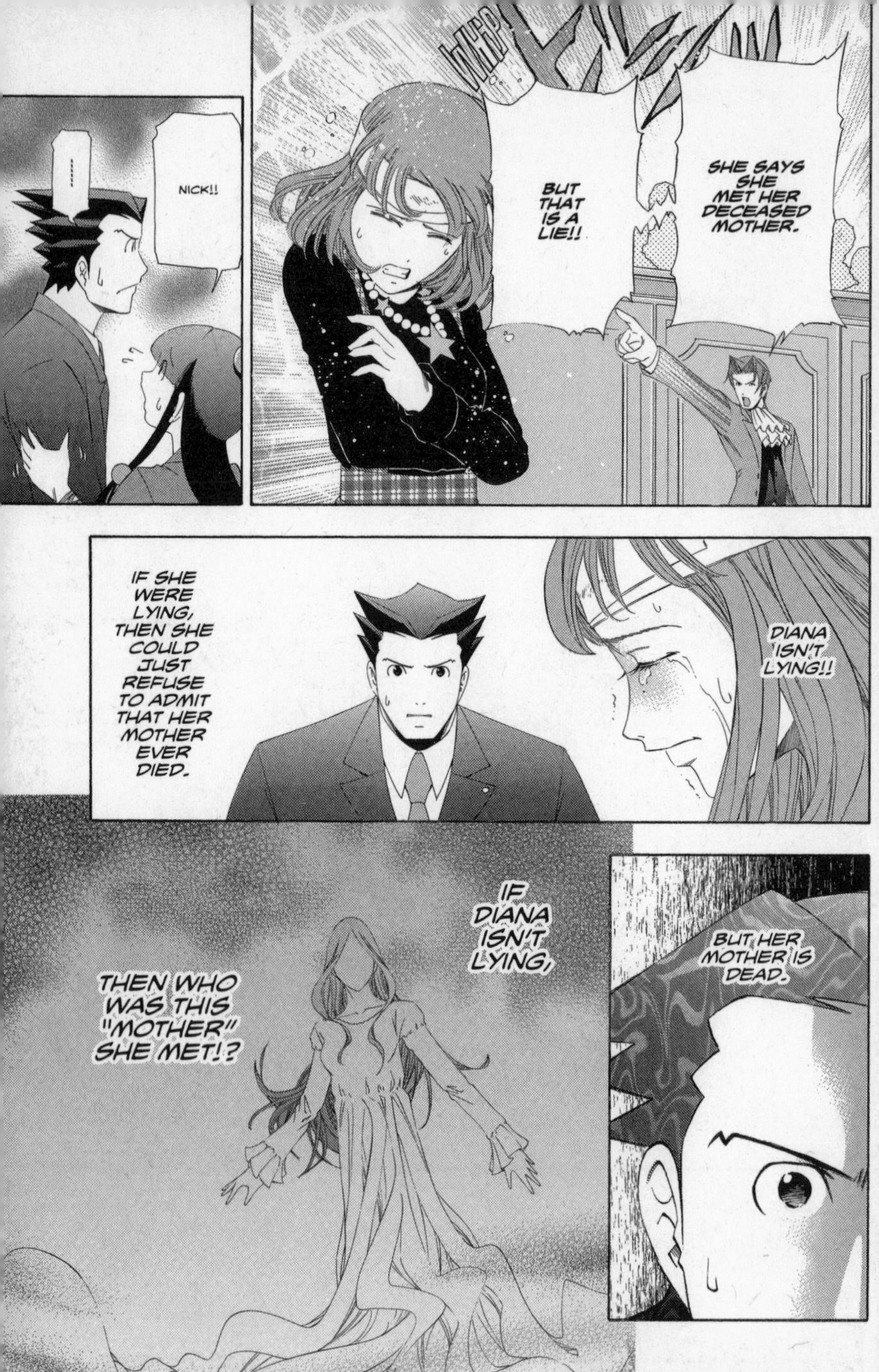
SHE SAYS SHE MET HER DECEASED MOTHER.
BUT THAT IS A LIE!!
NICK!!
......
DIANA ISN'T LYING!!
IF SHE WERE LYING, THEN SHE COULD JUST REFUSE TO ADMIT THAT HER MOTHER EVER DIED.
BUT HER MOTHER IS DEAD.
IF DIANA ISN'T LYING,
THEN WHO WAS THIS "MOTHER" SHE MET!?

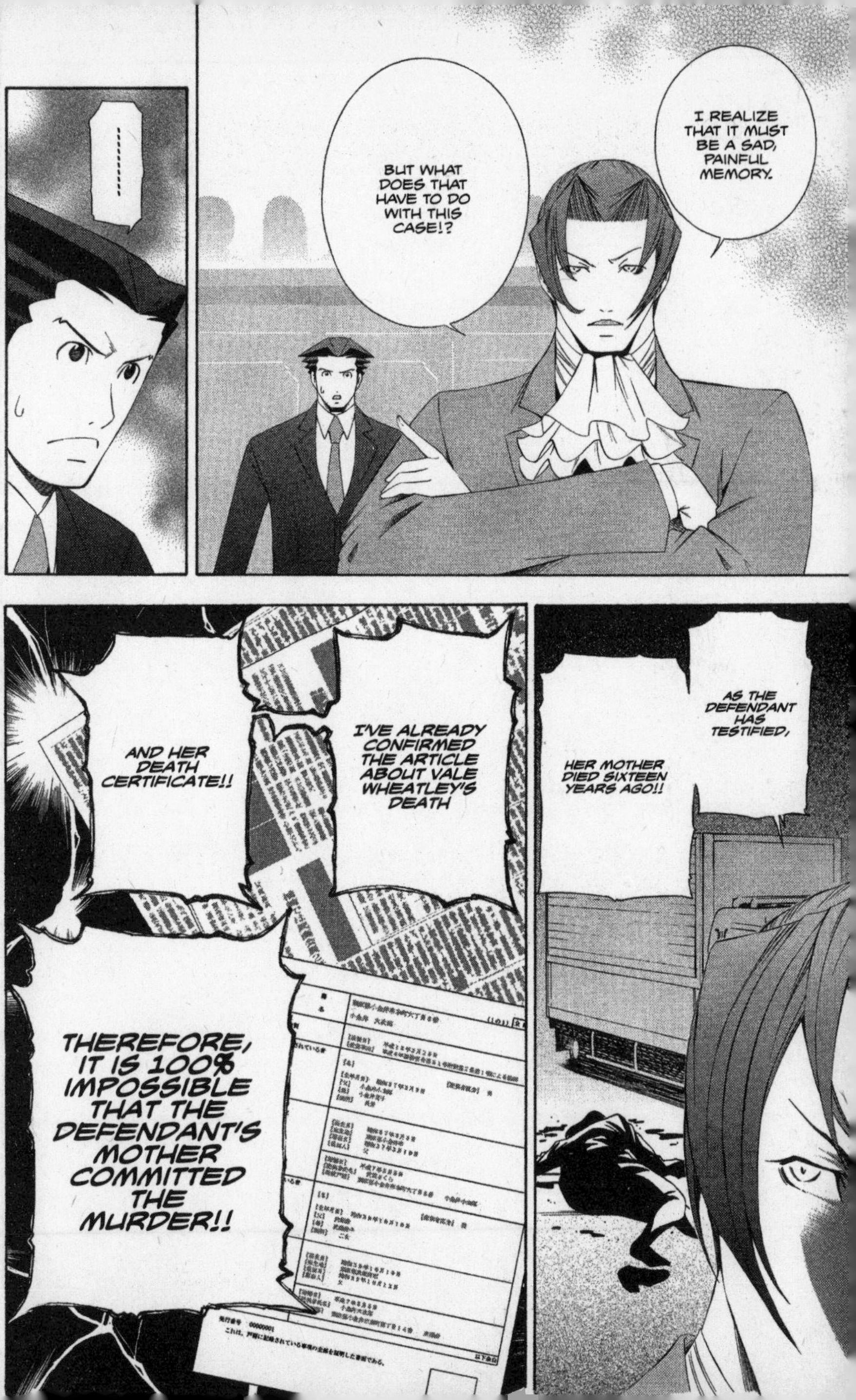
I REALIZE THAT IT MUST BE A SAD, PAINFUL MEMORY.
BUT WHAT DOES THAT HAVE TO DO WITH THIS CASE!?
......
AS THE DEFENDANT HAS TESTIFIED,
HER MOTHER DIED SIXTEEN YEARS AGO!!
I'VE ALREADY CONFIRMED THE ARTICLE ABOUT VALE WHEATLEY'S DEATH
AND HER DEATH CERTIFICATE!!
THEREFORE, IT IS 100% IMPOSSIBLE THAT THE DEFENDANT'S MOTHER COMMITTED THE MURDER!!

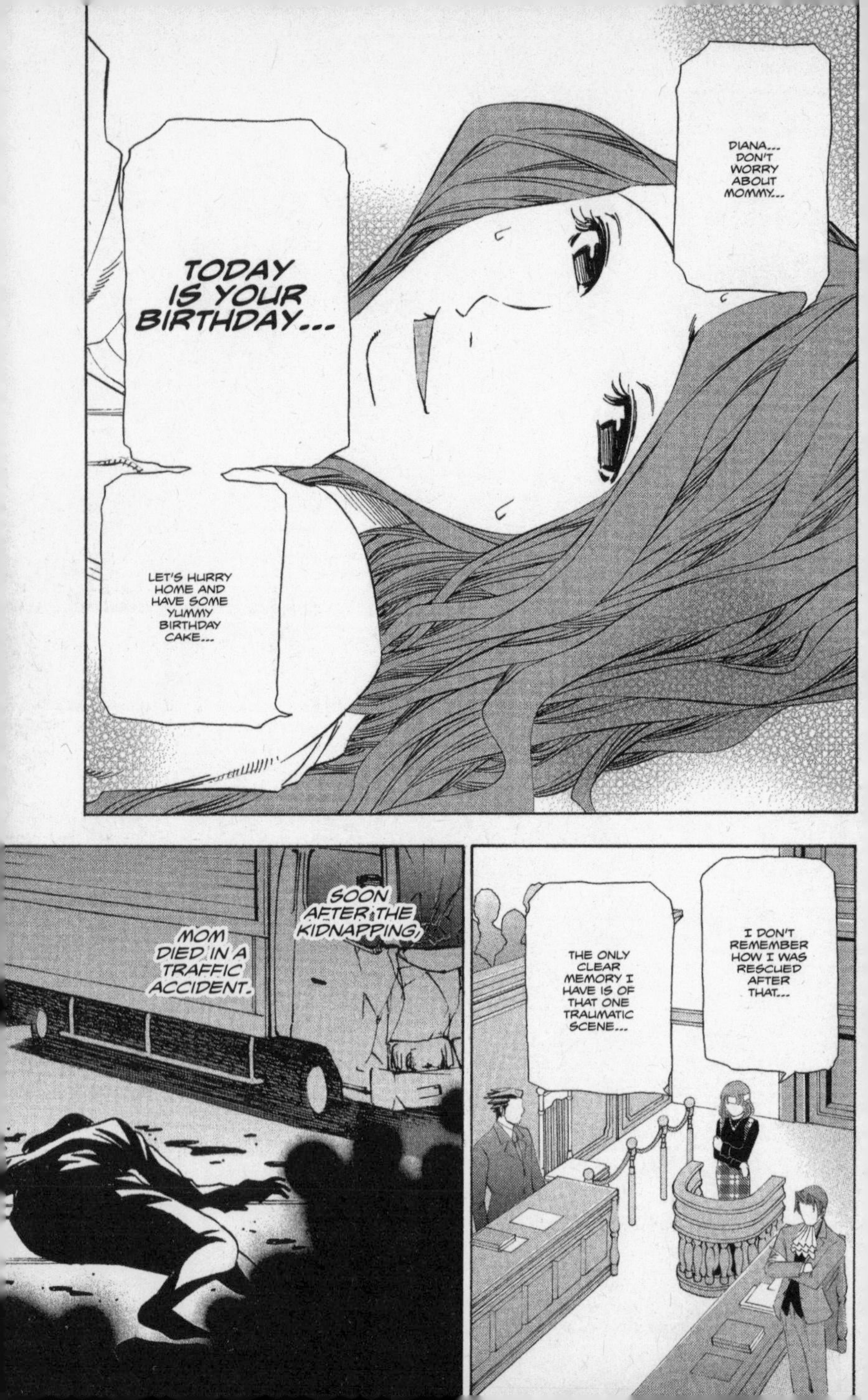
DIANA... DON'T WORRY ABOUT MOMMY...
TODAY IS YOUR BIRTHDAY...
LET'S HURRY HOME AND HAVE SOME YUMMY BIRTHDAY CAKE...
I DON'T REMEMBER HOW I WAS RESCUED AFTER THAT...
THE ONLY CLEAR MEMORY I HAVE IS OF THAT ONE TRAUMATIC SCENE...
SOON AFTER THE KIDNAPPING,
MOM DIED IN A TRAFFIC ACCIDENT.

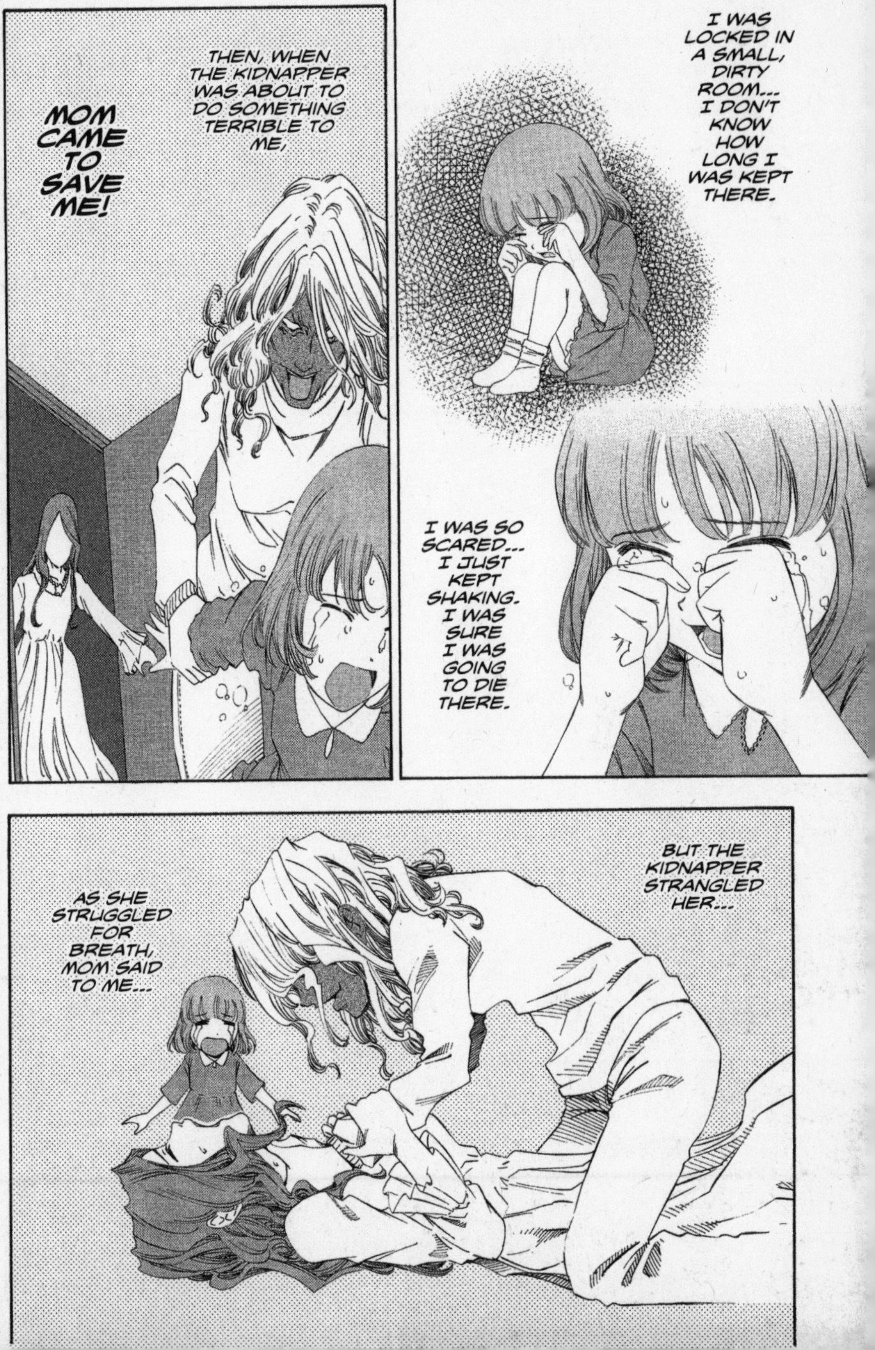
I WAS LOCKED IN A SMALL, DIRTY ROOM... I DON'T KNOW HOW LONG I WAS KEPT THERE.
I WAS SO SCARED... I JUST KEPT SHAKING. I WAS SURE I WAS GOING TO DIE THERE.
THEN, WHEN THE KIDNAPPER WAS ABOUT TO DO SOMETHING TERRIBLE TO ME,
MOM CAME TO SAVE ME!
BUT THE KIDNAPPER STRANGLED HER...
AS SHE STRUGGLED FOR BREATH, MOM SAID TO ME...

DISTRICT COURT
COURTROOM NO. 6: DEFENDANT CROSS-EXAMINATION 2

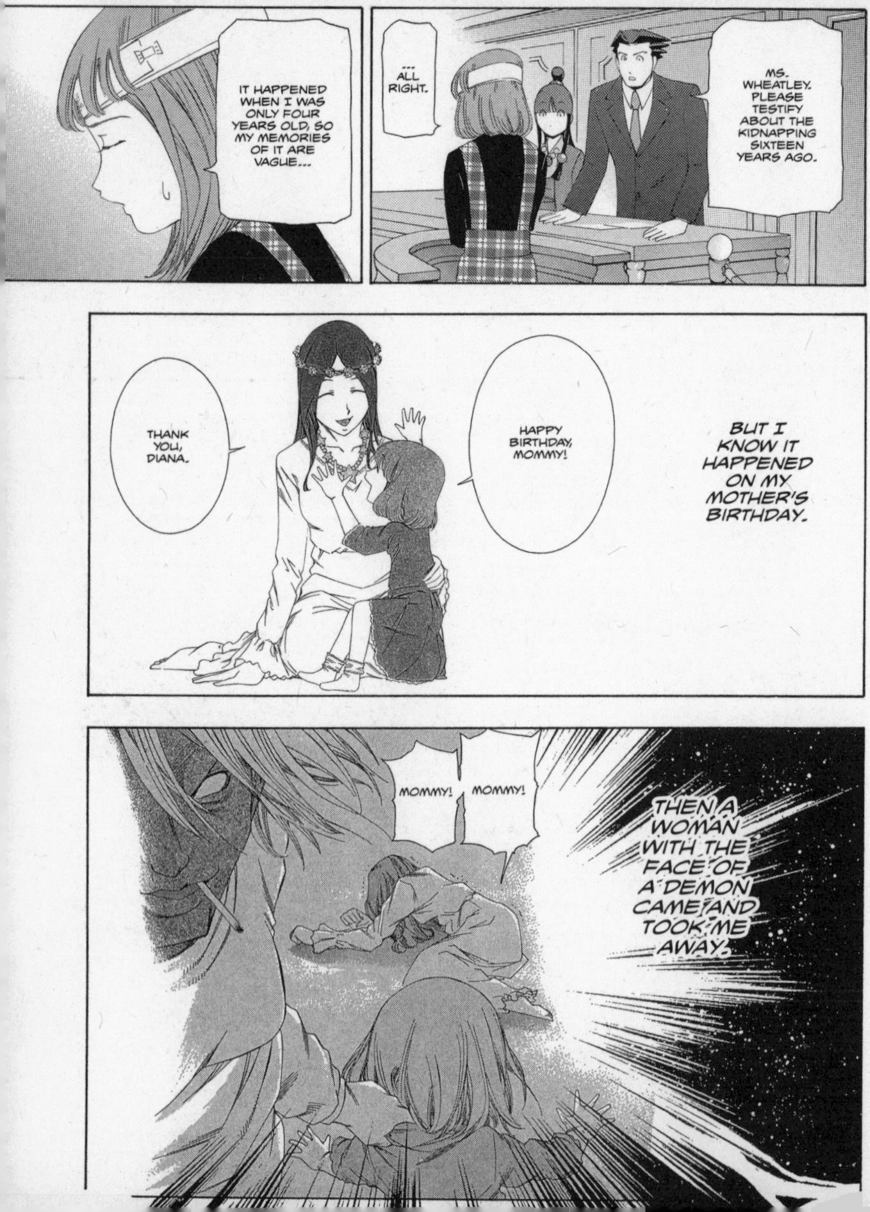
MS. WHEATLEY. PLEASE TESTIFY ABOUT THE KIDNAPPING SIXTEEN YEARS AGO.
... ALL RIGHT.
IT HAPPENED WHEN I WAS ONLY FOUR YEARS OLD, SO MY MEMORIES OF IT ARE VAGUE...
BUT I KNOW IT HAPPENED ON MY MOTHER'S BIRTHDAY.
HAPPY BIRTHDAY, MOMMY!
THANK YOU, DIANA.
MOMMY!
MOMMY!
THEN A WOMAN WITH THE FACE OF A DEMON CAME AND TOOK ME AWAY.

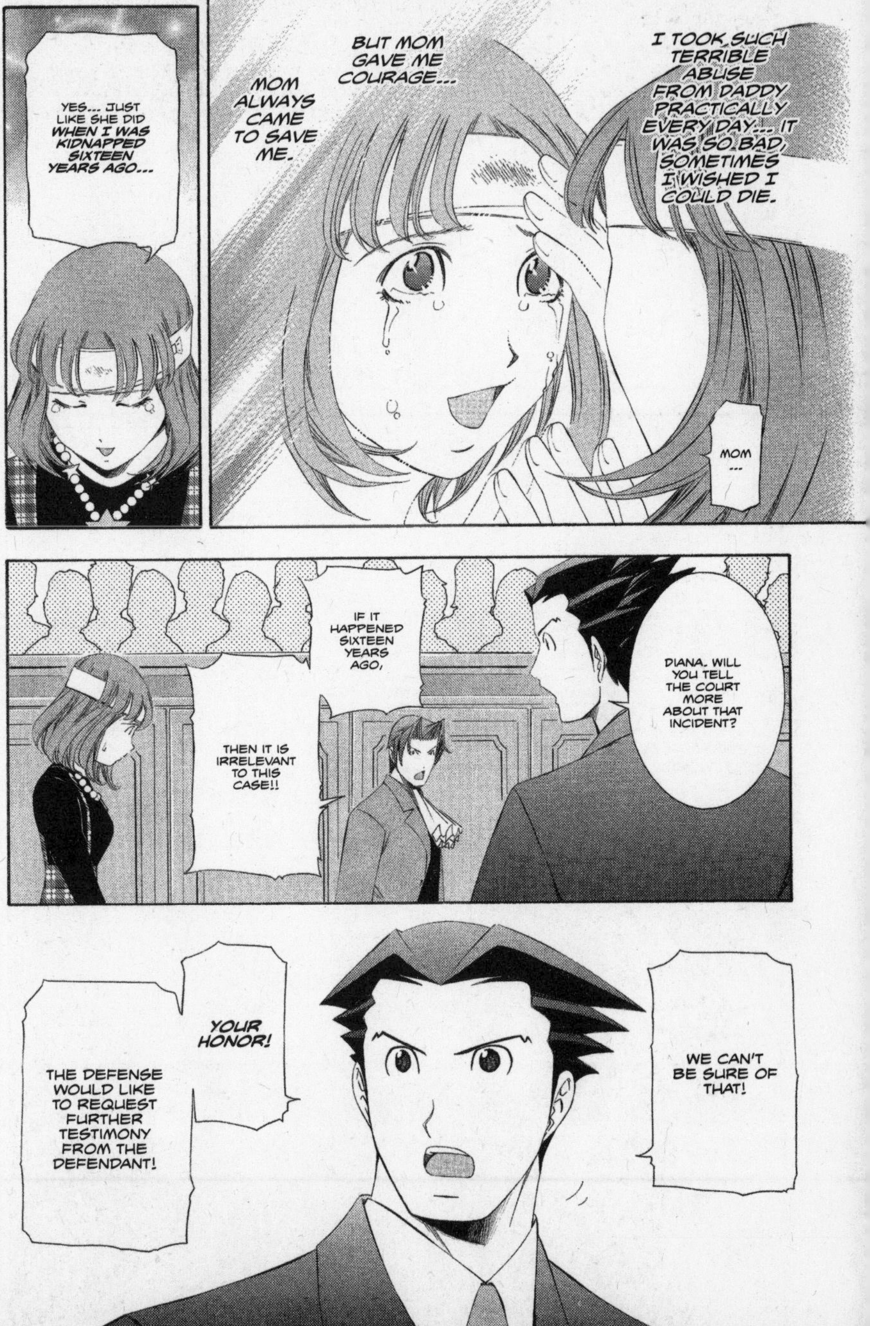
I TOOK SUCH TERRIBLE ABUSE FROM DADDY PRACTICALLY EVERY DAY... IT WAS SO BAD, SOMETIMES I WISHED I COULD DIE.
BUT MOM GAVE ME COURAGE...
MOM ALWAYS CAME TO SAVE ME.
MOM ...
YES... JUST LIKE SHE DID WHEN I WAS KIDNAPPED SIXTEEN YEARS AGO...
DIANA. WILL YOU TELL THE COURT MORE ABOUT THAT INCIDENT?
IF IT HAPPENED SIXTEEN YEARS AGO,
THEN IT IS IRRELEVANT TO THIS CASE!!
WE CAN'T BE SURE OF THAT!
YOUR HONOR!
THE DEFENSE WOULD LIKE TO REQUEST FURTHER TESTIMONY FROM THE DEFENDANT!

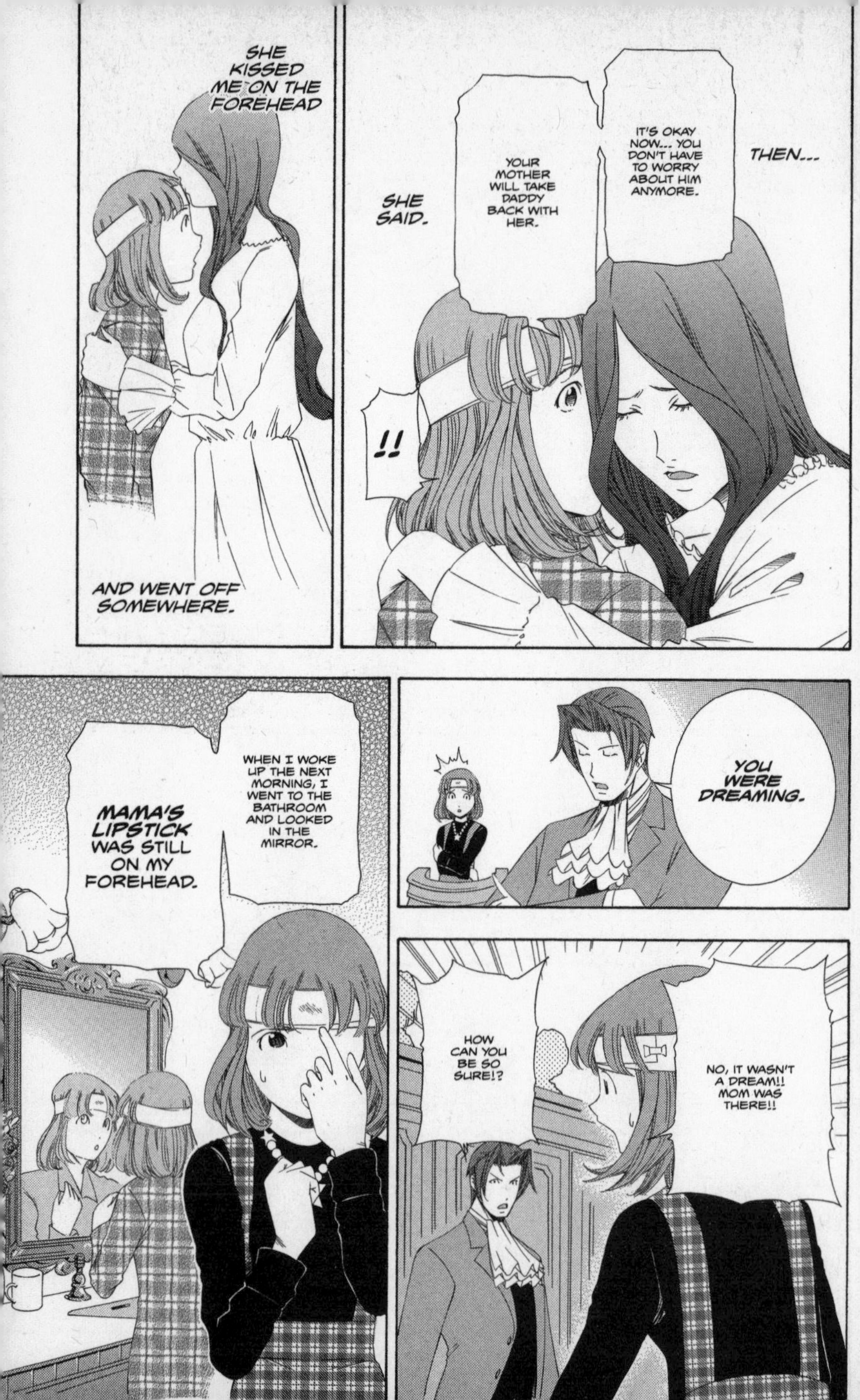
THEN...
IT'S OKAY NOW... YOU DON'T HAVE TO WORRY ABOUT HIM ANYMORE.
YOUR MOTHER WILL TAKE DADDY BACK WITH HER.
SHE SAID.
!!
SHE KISSED ME ON THE FOREHEAD
AND WENT OFF SOMEWHERE.
YOU WERE DREAMING.
NO, IT WASN'T A DREAM!! MOM WAS THERE!!
HOW CAN YOU BE SO SURE!?
WHEN I WOKE UP THE NEXT MORNING, I WENT TO THE BATHROOM AND LOOKED IN THE MIRROR.
MAMA'S LIPSTICK WAS STILL ON MY FOREHEAD.

COURTROOM NO. 6: DEFENDANT CROSS-EXAMINATION 1

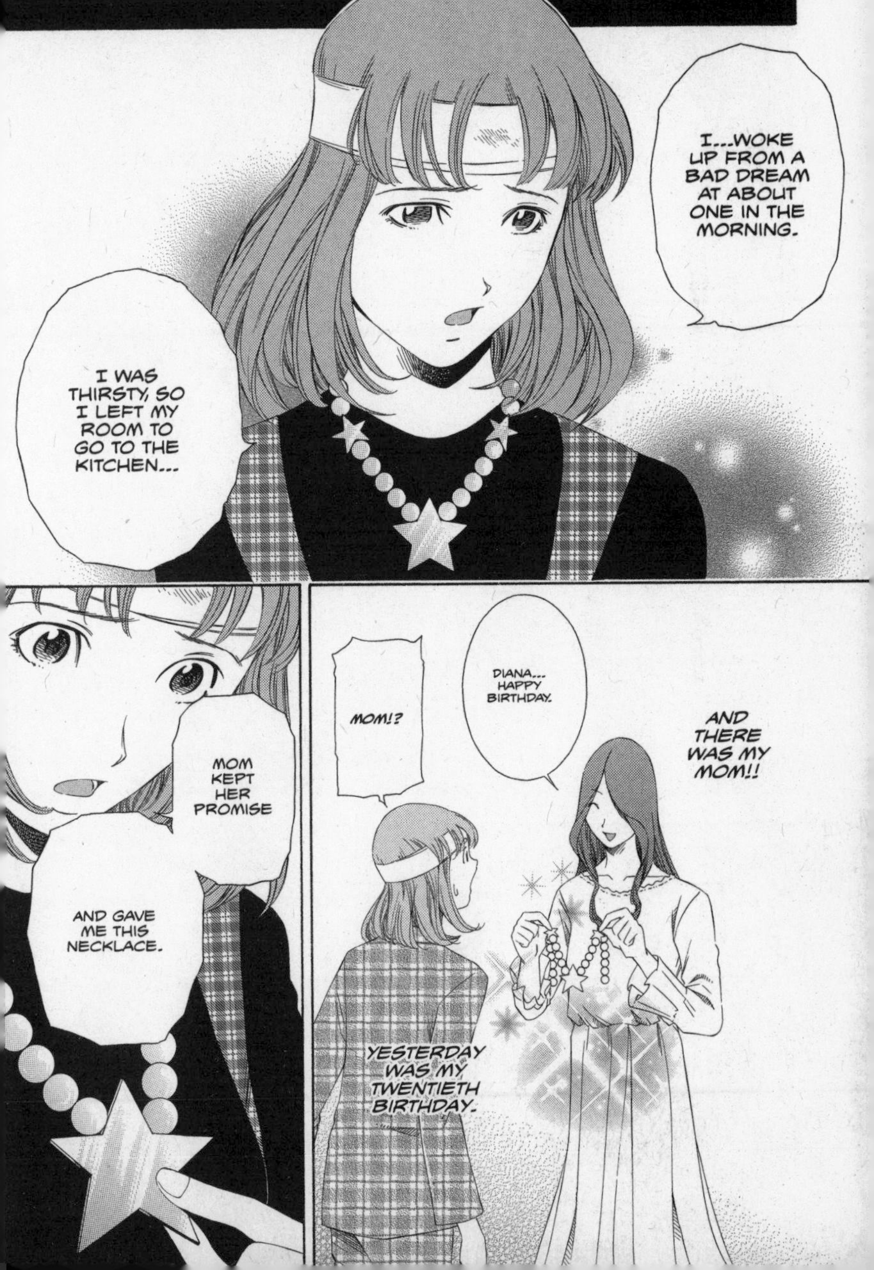

I...WOKE UP FROM A BAD DREAM AT ABOUT ONE IN THE MORNING.
I WAS THIRSTY, SO I LEFT MY ROOM TO GO TO THE KITCHEN...
AND THERE WAS MY MOM!!
DIANA... HAPPY BIRTHDAY.
MOM!?
YESTERDAY WAS MY TWENTIETH BIRTHDAY.
MOM KEPT HER PROMISE
AND GAVE ME THIS NECKLACE.

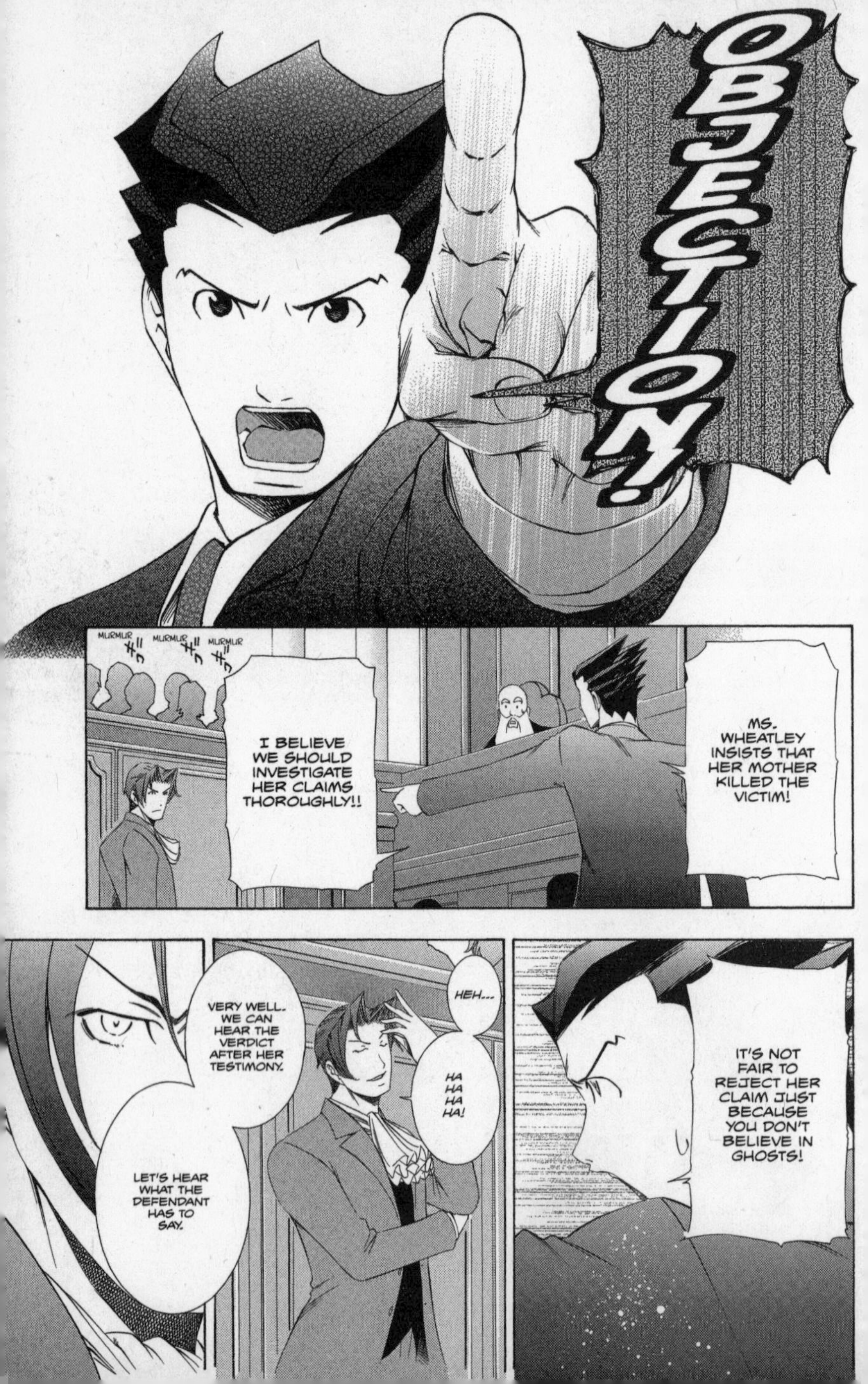
OBJECTION!
MS. WHEATLEY INSISTS THAT HER MOTHER KILLED THE VICTIM!
MURMUR MURMUR MURMUR
I BELIEVE WE SHOULD INVESTIGATE HER CLAIMS THOROUGHLY!!
IT'S NOT FAIR TO REJECT HER CLAIM JUST BECAUSE YOU DON'T BELIEVE IN GHOSTS!
HEH...
HA HA HA HA!
VERY WELL. WE CAN HEAR THE VERDICT AFTER HER TESTIMONY.
LET'S HEAR WHAT THE DEFENDANT HAS TO SAY.

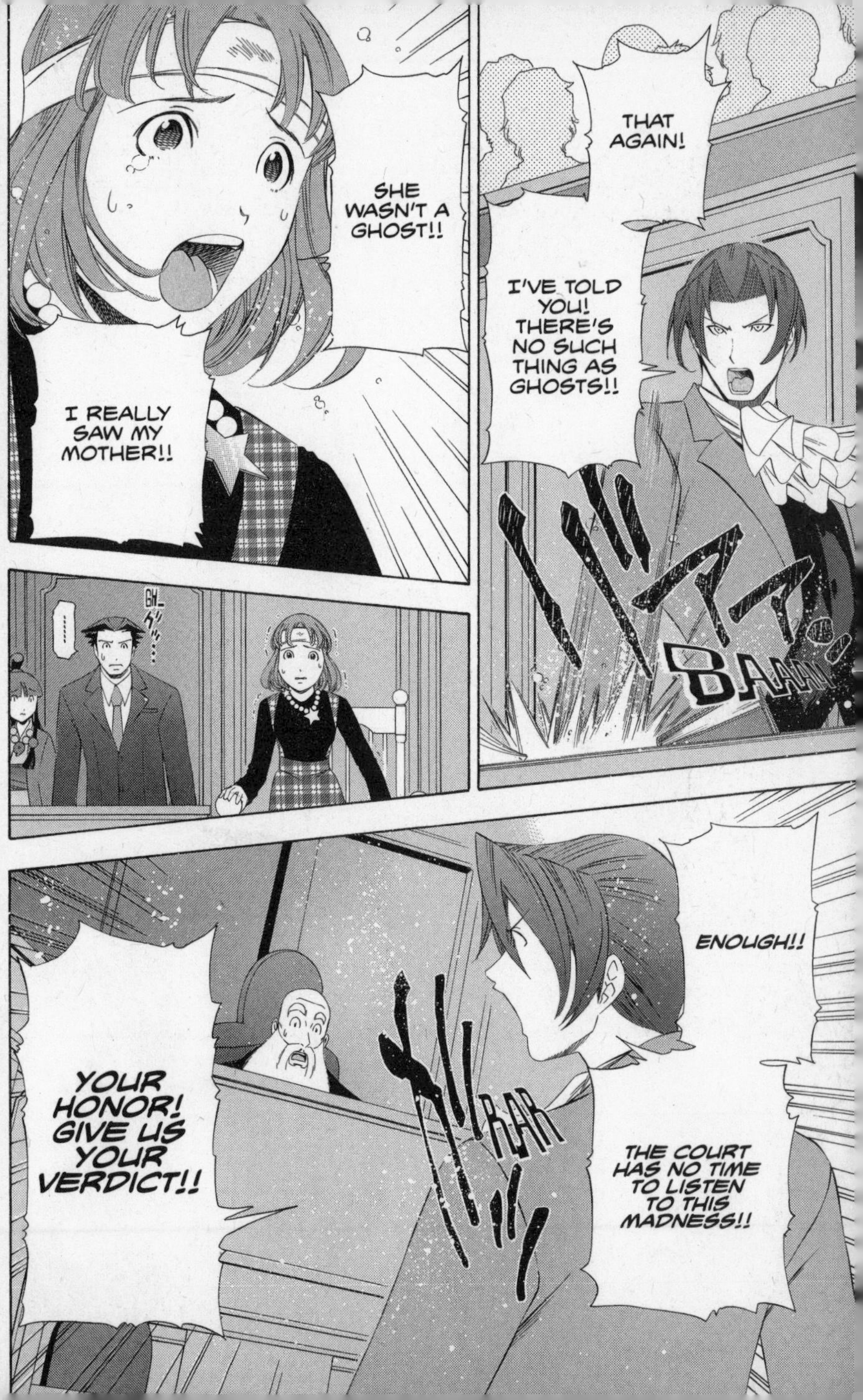
THAT AGAIN!
I'VE TOLD YOU! THERE'S NO SUCH THING AS GHOSTS!!
BAAAN
SHE WASN'T A GHOST!!
I REALLY SAW MY MOTHER!!
ENOUGH!!
THE COURT HAS NO TIME TO LISTEN TO THIS MADNESS!!
RAR
YOUR HONOR! GIVE US YOUR VERDICT!!

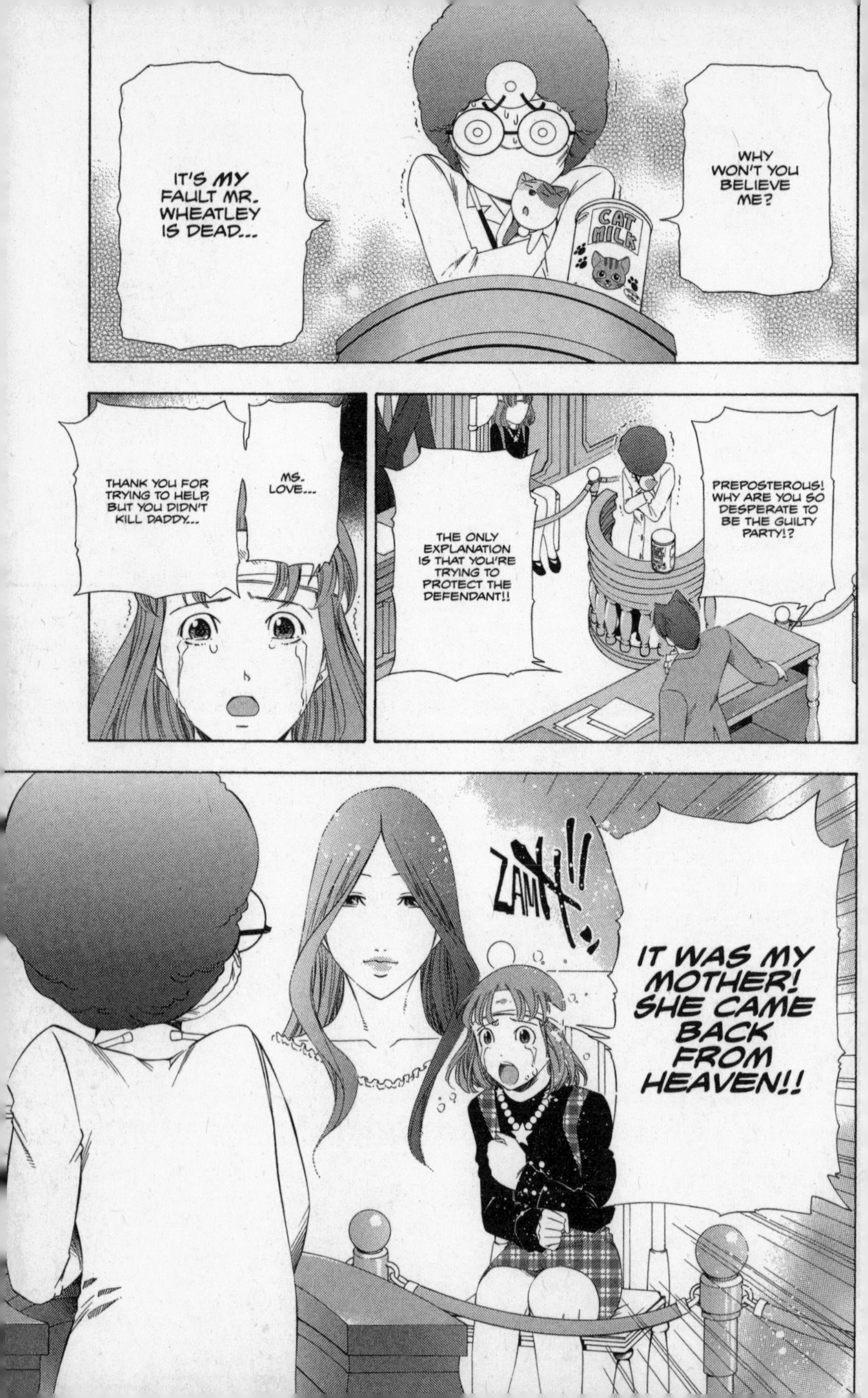
WHY WON'T YOU BELIEVE ME?
IT'S *MY* FAULT MR. WHEATLEY IS DEAD...
PREPOSTEROUS! WHY ARE YOU SO DESPERATE TO BE THE GUILTY PARTY!?
THE ONLY EXPLANATION IS THAT YOU'RE TRYING TO PROTECT THE DEFENDANT!!
MS. LOVE...
THANK YOU FOR TRYING TO HELP, BUT YOU DIDN'T KILL DADDY...
ZAM!!
IT WAS MY MOTHER! SHE CAME BACK FROM HEAVEN!!

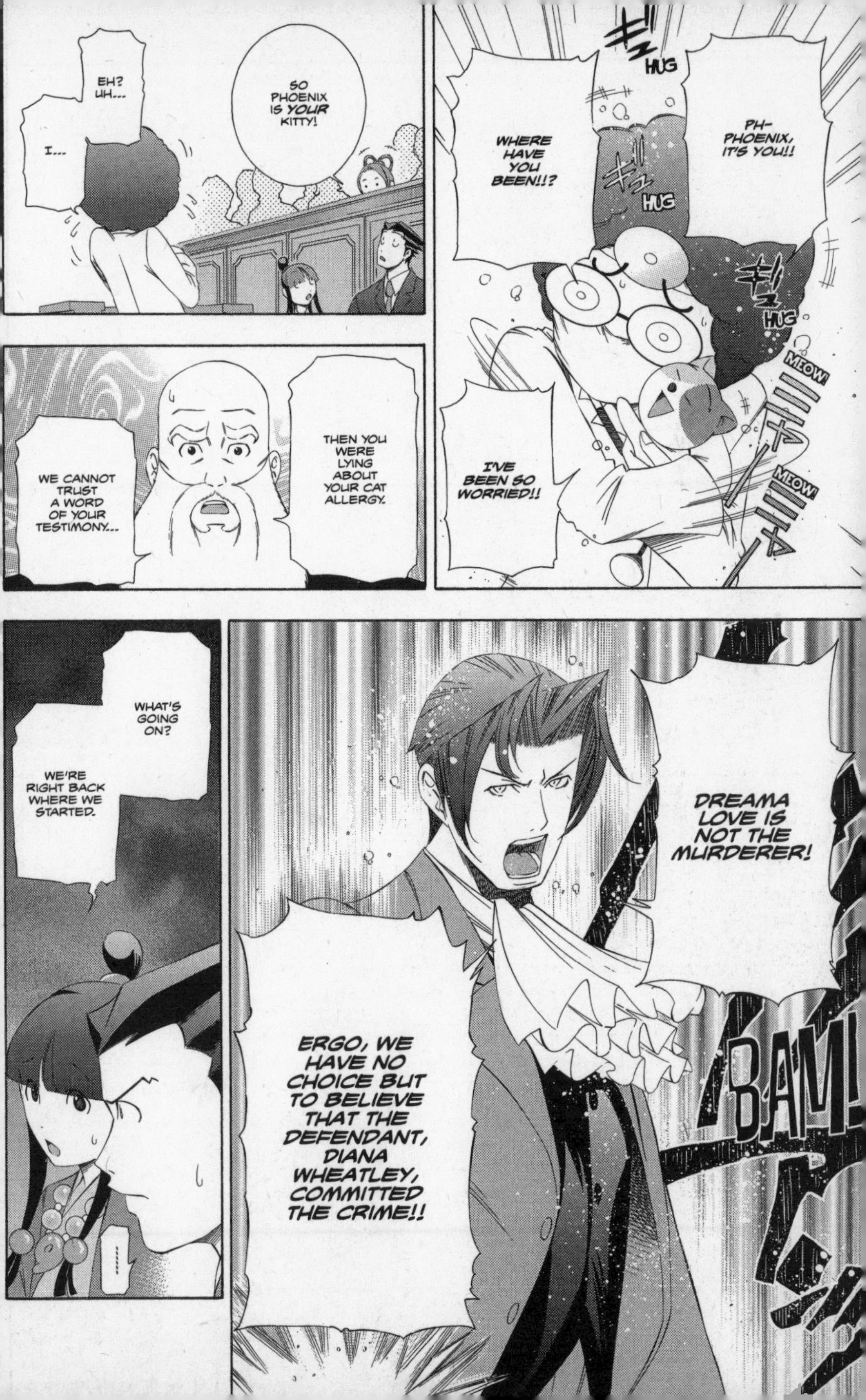
HUG
PH-PHOENIX, IT'S YOU!!
WHERE HAVE YOU BEEN!!?
HUG
HUG
MEOW!
MEOW!
I'VE BEEN SO WORRIED!!
SO PHOENIX IS YOUR KITTY!
EH? UH...
I...
THEN YOU WERE LYING ABOUT YOUR CAT ALLERGY.
WE CANNOT TRUST A WORD OF YOUR TESTIMONY...
DREAMA LOVE IS NOT THE MURDERER!
BAM!
ERGO, WE HAVE NO CHOICE BUT TO BELIEVE THAT THE DEFENDANT, DIANA WHEATLEY, COMMITTED THE CRIME!!
WHAT'S GOING ON?
WE'RE RIGHT BACK WHERE WE STARTED.
......

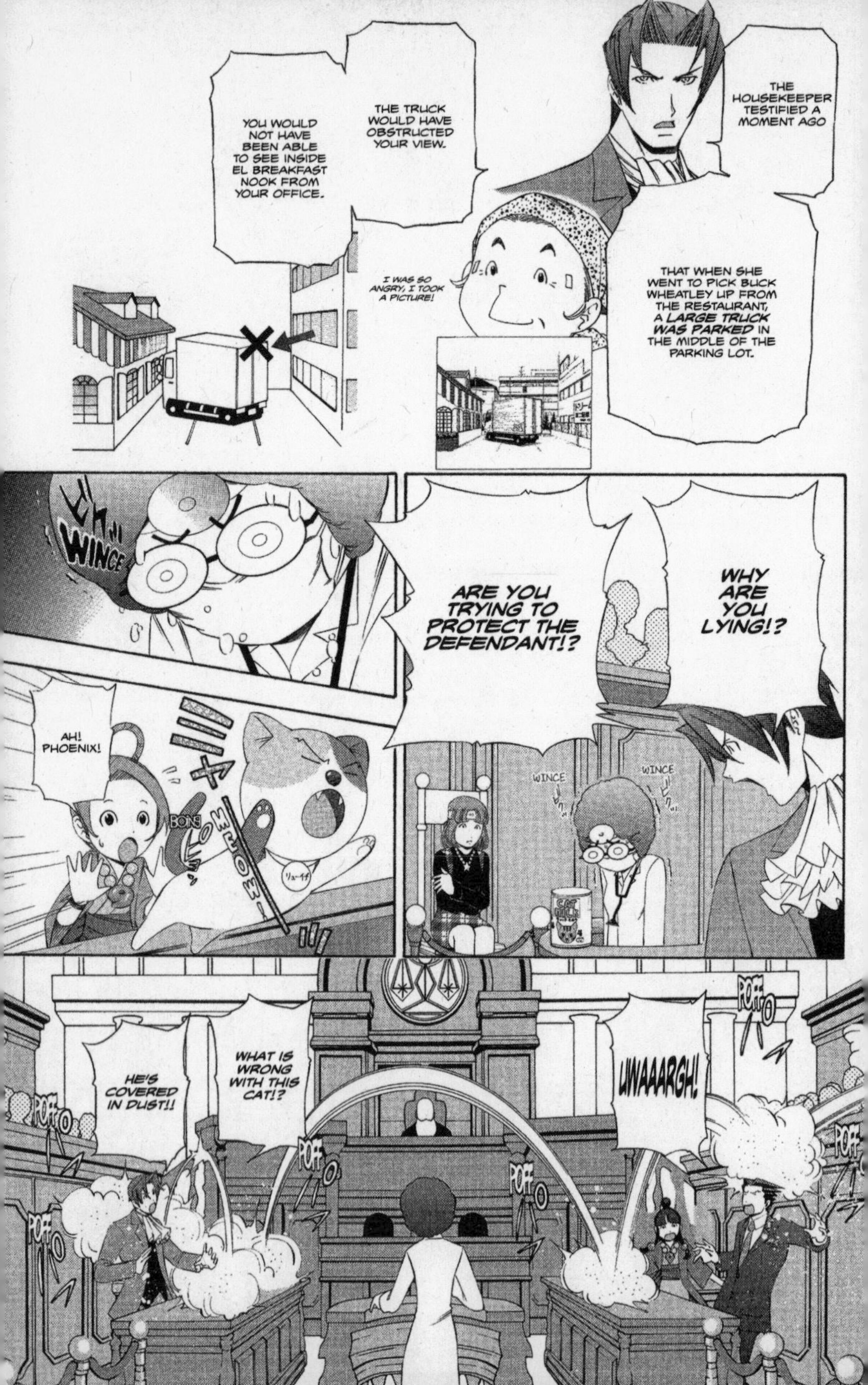
THE HOUSEKEEPER TESTIFIED A MOMENT AGO
THAT WHEN SHE WENT TO PICK BUCK WHEATLEY UP FROM THE RESTAURANT, A **LARGE TRUCK WAS PARKED** IN THE MIDDLE OF THE PARKING LOT.
I WAS SO ANGRY, I TOOK A PICTURE!
THE TRUCK WOULD HAVE OBSTRUCTED YOUR VIEW.
YOU WOULD NOT HAVE BEEN ABLE TO SEE INSIDE EL BREAKFAST NOOK FROM YOUR OFFICE.
WHY ARE YOU LYING!?
ARE YOU TRYING TO PROTECT THE DEFENDANT!?
WINCE
WINCE
WINCE
AH! PHOENIX!
BONG
MEOW!
POFF
UWAAARGH!
WHAT IS WRONG WITH THIS CAT!?
HE'S COVERED IN DUST!!
POFF
POFF
POFF
POFF

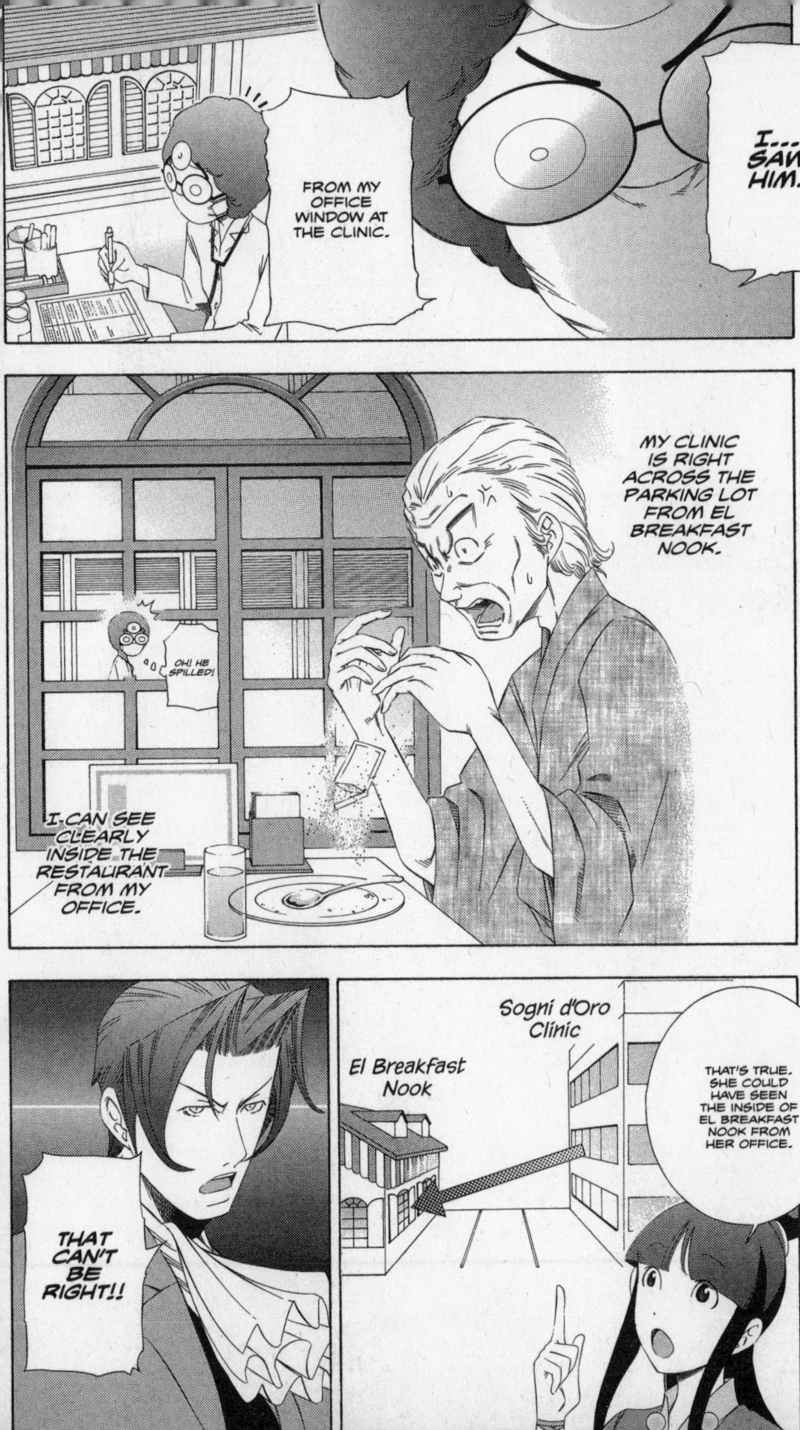
I... SAW HIM.
FROM MY OFFICE WINDOW AT THE CLINIC.
MY CLINIC IS RIGHT ACROSS THE PARKING LOT FROM EL BREAKFAST NOOK.
OH! HE SPILLED!
I CAN SEE CLEARLY INSIDE THE RESTAURANT FROM MY OFFICE.
Sogni d'Oro Clinic
El Breakfast Nook
THAT'S TRUE. SHE COULD HAVE SEEN THE INSIDE OF EL BREAKFAST NOOK FROM HER OFFICE.
THAT CAN'T BE RIGHT!!

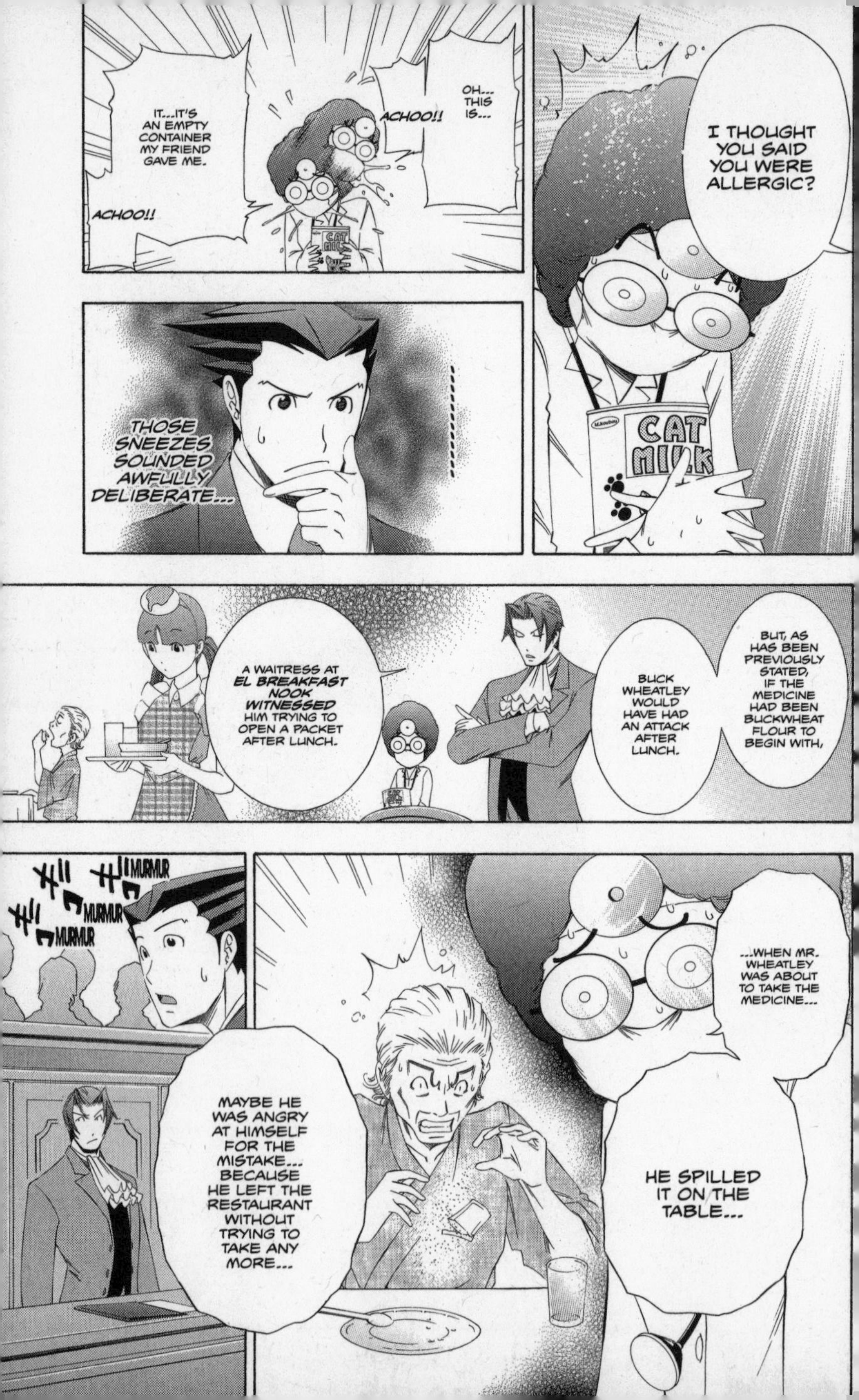
I THOUGHT YOU SAID YOU WERE ALLERGIC?
CAT MILK
OH... THIS IS...
ACHOO!!
IT...IT'S AN EMPTY CONTAINER MY FRIEND GAVE ME.
ACHOO!!
CAT MILK
......
THOSE SNEEZES SOUNDED AWFULLY DELIBERATE...
BUT, AS HAS BEEN PREVIOUSLY STATED, IF THE MEDICINE HAD BEEN BUCKWHEAT FLOUR TO BEGIN WITH,
BUCK WHEATLEY WOULD HAVE HAD AN ATTACK AFTER LUNCH.
A WAITRESS AT EL BREAKFAST NOOK WITNESSED HIM TRYING TO OPEN A PACKET AFTER LUNCH.
...WHEN MR. WHEATLEY WAS ABOUT TO TAKE THE MEDICINE...
HE SPILLED IT ON THE TABLE...
MAYBE HE WAS ANGRY AT HIMSELF FOR THE MISTAKE... BECAUSE HE LEFT THE RESTAURANT WITHOUT TRYING TO TAKE ANY MORE...
MURMUR
MURMUR
MURMUR

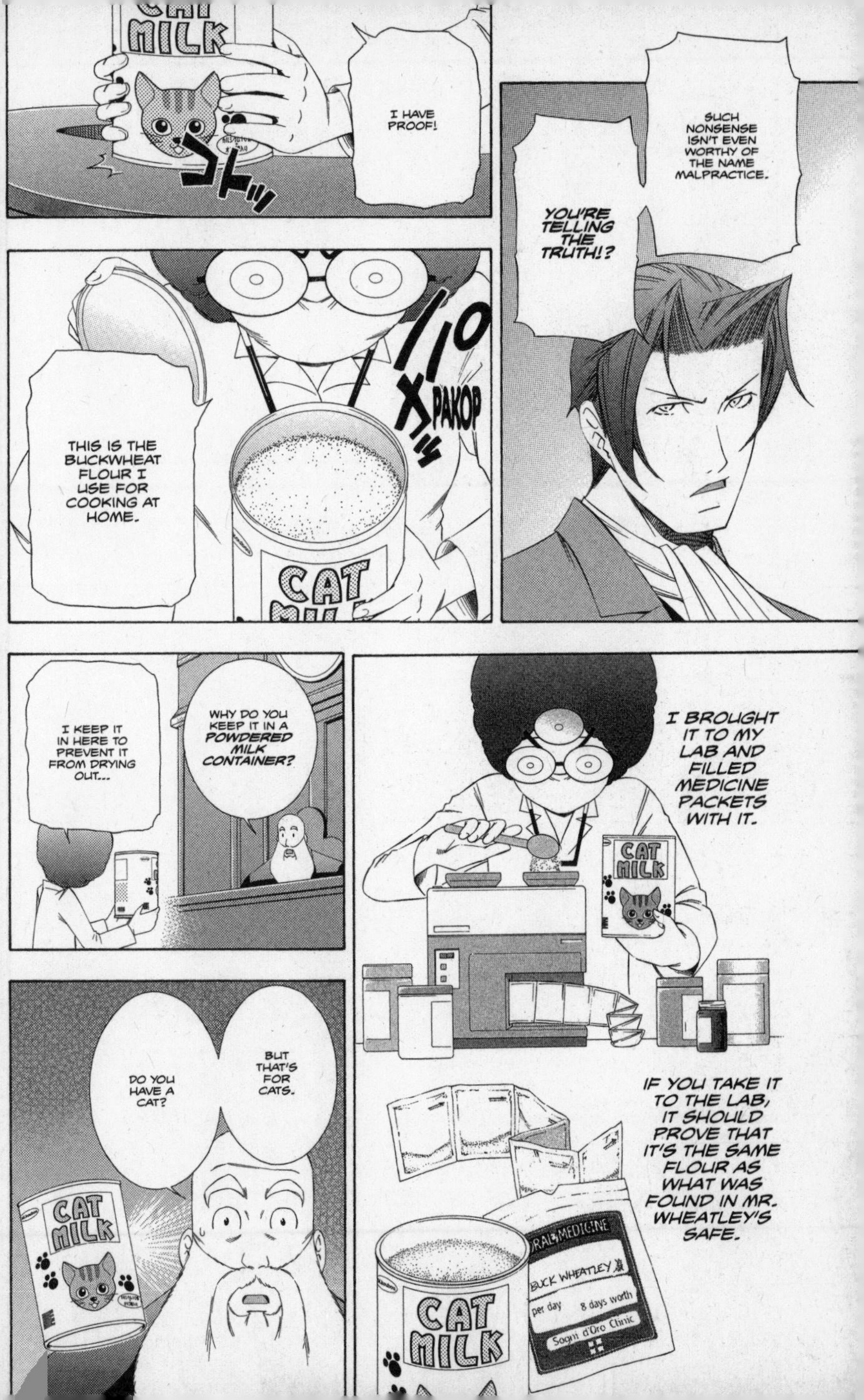

SUCH NONSENSE ISN'T EVEN WORTHY OF THE NAME MALPRACTICE.
YOU'RE TELLING THE TRUTH!?
I HAVE PROOF!
THIS IS THE BUCKWHEAT FLOUR I USE FOR COOKING AT HOME.
PAKOP
CAT MILK
I BROUGHT IT TO MY LAB AND FILLED MEDICINE PACKETS WITH IT.
CAT MILK
IF YOU TAKE IT TO THE LAB, IT SHOULD PROVE THAT IT'S THE SAME FLOUR AS WHAT WAS FOUND IN MR. WHEATLEY'S SAFE.
ORAL MEDICINE
BUCK WHEATLEY
per day 8 days worth
Sogni d'Oro Clinic
CAT MILK
WHY DO YOU KEEP IT IN A POWDERED MILK CONTAINER?
I KEEP IT IN HERE TO PREVENT IT FROM DRYING OUT...
BUT THAT'S FOR CATS.
DO YOU HAVE A CAT?
CAT MILK

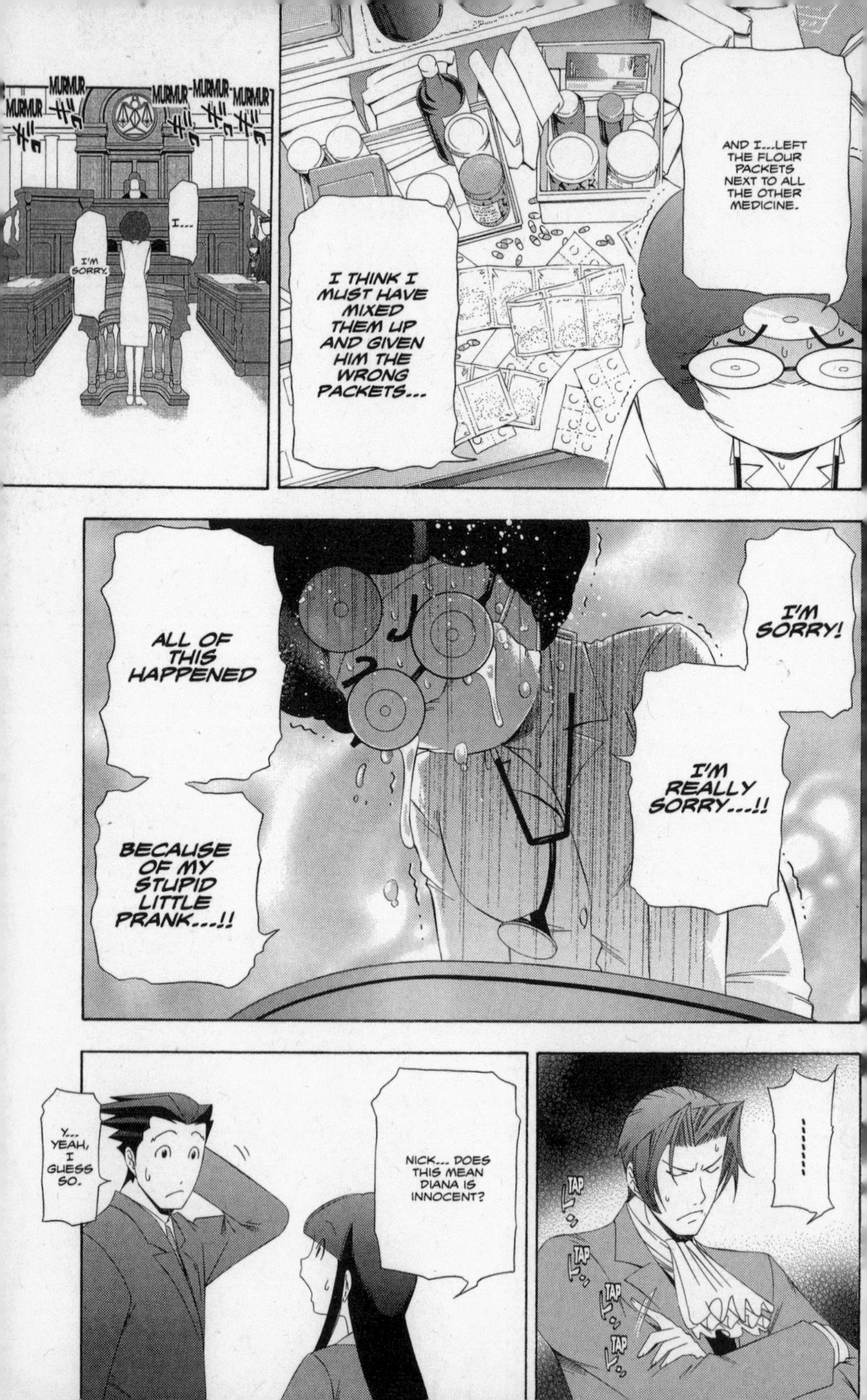
AND I...LEFT THE FLOUR PACKETS NEXT TO ALL THE OTHER MEDICINE.
I THINK I MUST HAVE MIXED THEM UP AND GIVEN HIM THE WRONG PACKETS...
MURMUR
MURMUR
MURMUR
MURMUR
MURMUR
I...
I'M SORRY.
I'M SORRY!
I'M REALLY SORRY...!!
ALL OF THIS HAPPENED
BECAUSE OF MY STUPID LITTLE PRANK...!!
......
TAP
TAP
TAP
TAP
NICK... DOES THIS MEAN DIANA IS INNOCENT?
Y... YEAH, I GUESS SO.

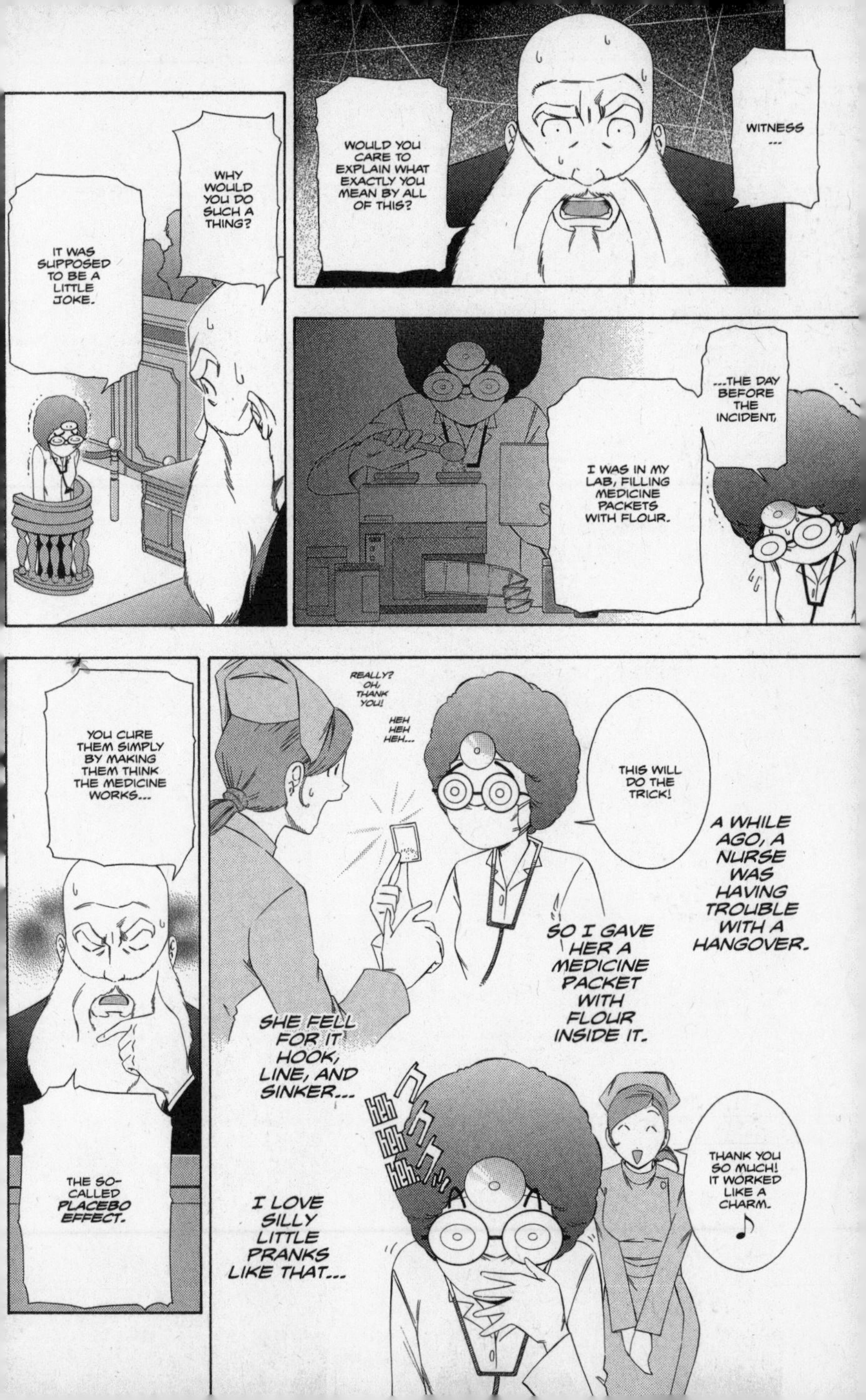
WITNESS ---
WOULD YOU CARE TO EXPLAIN WHAT EXACTLY YOU MEAN BY ALL OF THIS?
...THE DAY BEFORE THE INCIDENT,
I WAS IN MY LAB, FILLING MEDICINE PACKETS WITH FLOUR.
WHY WOULD YOU DO SUCH A THING?
IT WAS SUPPOSED TO BE A LITTLE JOKE.
A WHILE AGO, A NURSE WAS HAVING TROUBLE WITH A HANGOVER.
THIS WILL DO THE TRICK!
HEH HEH HEH...
REALLY? OH, THANK YOU!
SO I GAVE HER A MEDICINE PACKET WITH FLOUR INSIDE IT.
SHE FELL FOR IT HOOK, LINE, AND SINKER...
THANK YOU SO MUCH! IT WORKED LIKE A CHARM. ♪
heh heh heh
I LOVE SILLY LITTLE PRANKS LIKE THAT...
YOU CURE THEM SIMPLY BY MAKING THEM THINK THE MEDICINE WORKS...
THE SO-CALLED PLACEBO EFFECT.

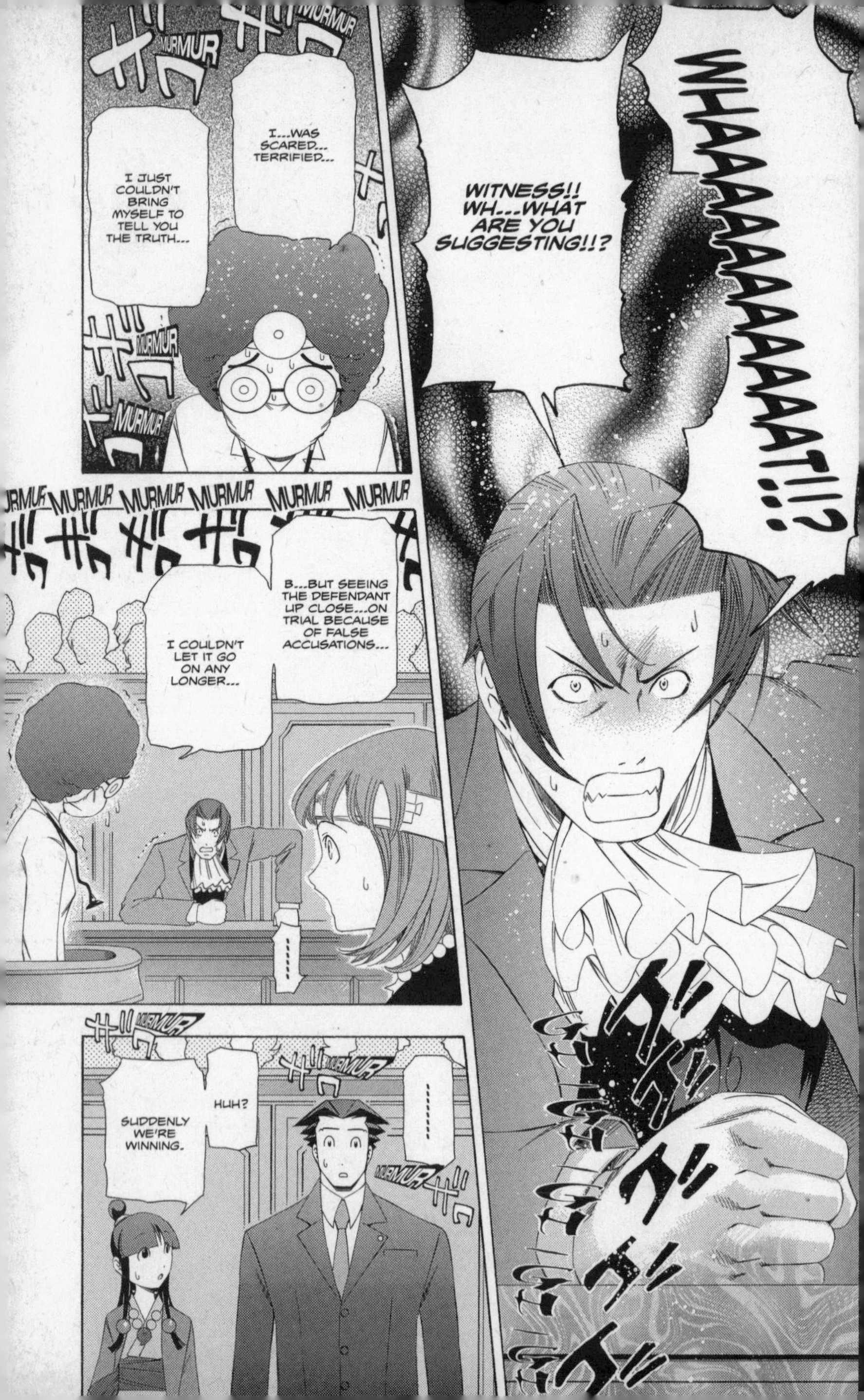
WHAAAAAAAAAAAT!!!?
WITNESS!! WH...WHAT ARE YOU SUGGESTING!!?
MURMUR
MURMUR
I...WAS SCARED... TERRIFIED...
I JUST COULDN'T BRING MYSELF TO TELL YOU THE TRUTH...
MURMUR
MURMUR
MURMUR MURMUR MURMUR MURMUR MURMUR MURMUR
B...BUT SEEING THE DEFENDANT UP CLOSE...ON TRIAL BECAUSE OF FALSE ACCUSATIONS...
I COULDN'T LET IT GO ON ANY LONGER...
......
MURMUR
MURMUR
......
HUH?
SUDDENLY WE'RE WINNING.
MURMUR

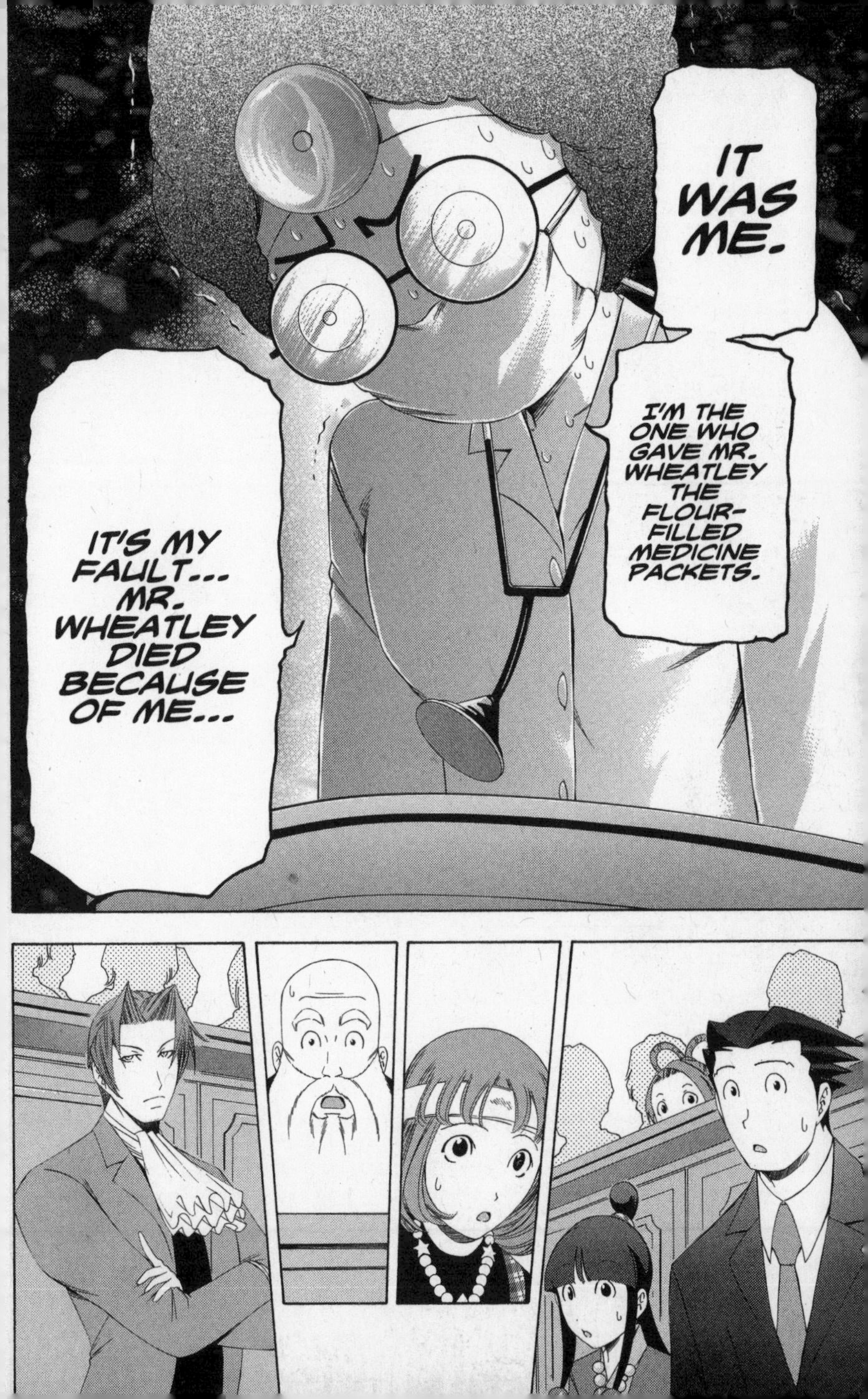
IT WAS ME.
I'M THE ONE WHO GAVE MR. WHEATLEY THE FLOUR-FILLED MEDICINE PACKETS.
IT'S MY FAULT... MR. WHEATLEY DIED BECAUSE OF ME...

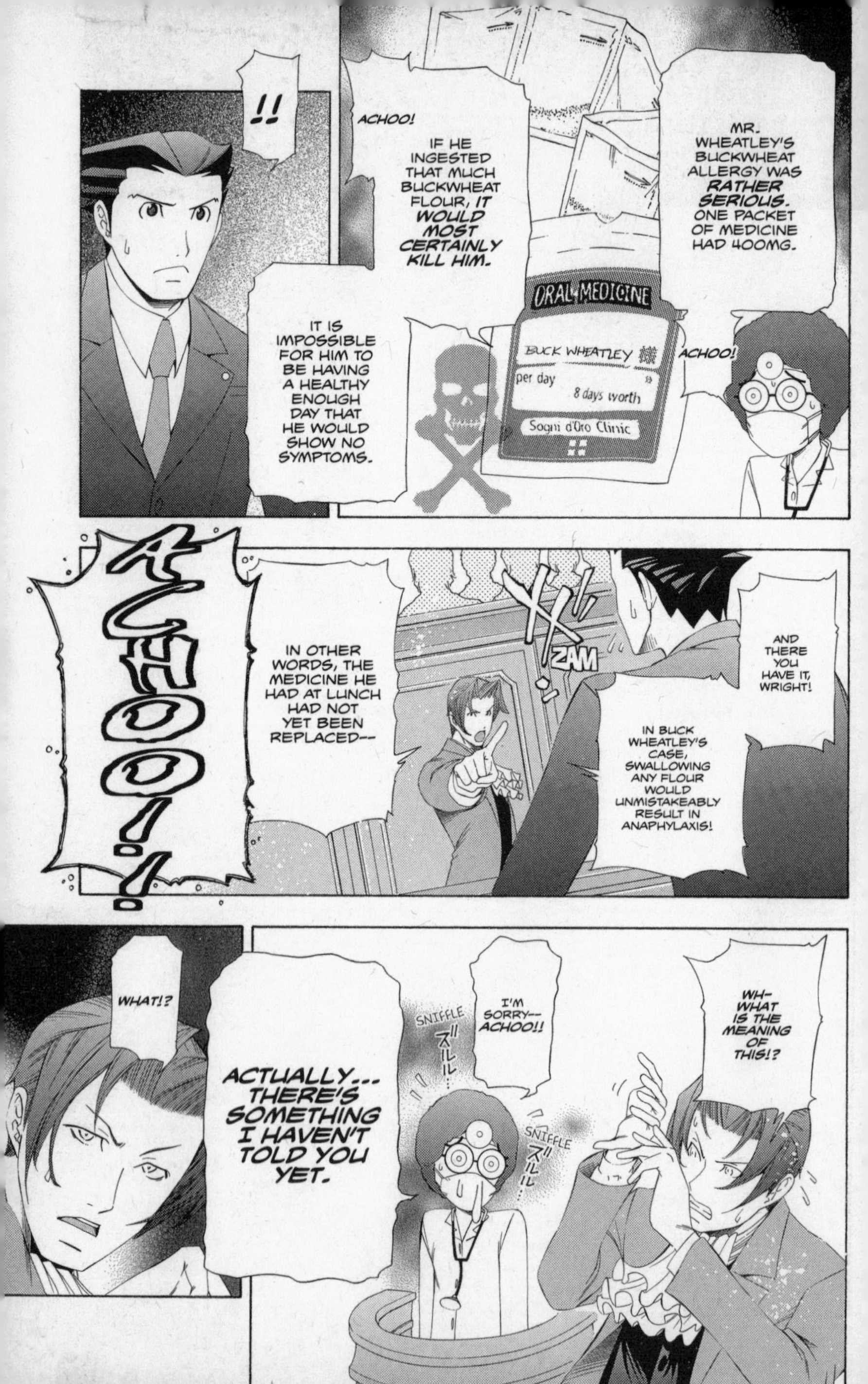
MR. WHEATLEY'S BUCKWHEAT ALLERGY WAS RATHER SERIOUS. ONE PACKET OF MEDICINE HAD 400MG.
ACHOO!
ORAL MEDICINE
BUCK WHEATLEY
per day
8 days worth
Sogni d'Oro Clinic
ACHOO!
IF HE INGESTED THAT MUCH BUCKWHEAT FLOUR, IT WOULD MOST CERTAINLY KILL HIM.
IT IS IMPOSSIBLE FOR HIM TO BE HAVING A HEALTHY ENOUGH DAY THAT HE WOULD SHOW NO SYMPTOMS.
!!
AND THERE YOU HAVE IT, WRIGHT!
IN BUCK WHEATLEY'S CASE, SWALLOWING ANY FLOUR WOULD UNMISTAKEABLY RESULT IN ANAPHYLAXIS!
ZAM
IN OTHER WORDS, THE MEDICINE HE HAD AT LUNCH HAD NOT YET BEEN REPLACED--
ACHOOO!!
WH-WHAT IS THE MEANING OF THIS!?
SNIFFLE ズルル…
I'M SORRY-- ACHOO!!
SNIFFLE ズルル…
ACTUALLY... THERE'S SOMETHING I HAVEN'T TOLD YOU YET.
WHAT!?

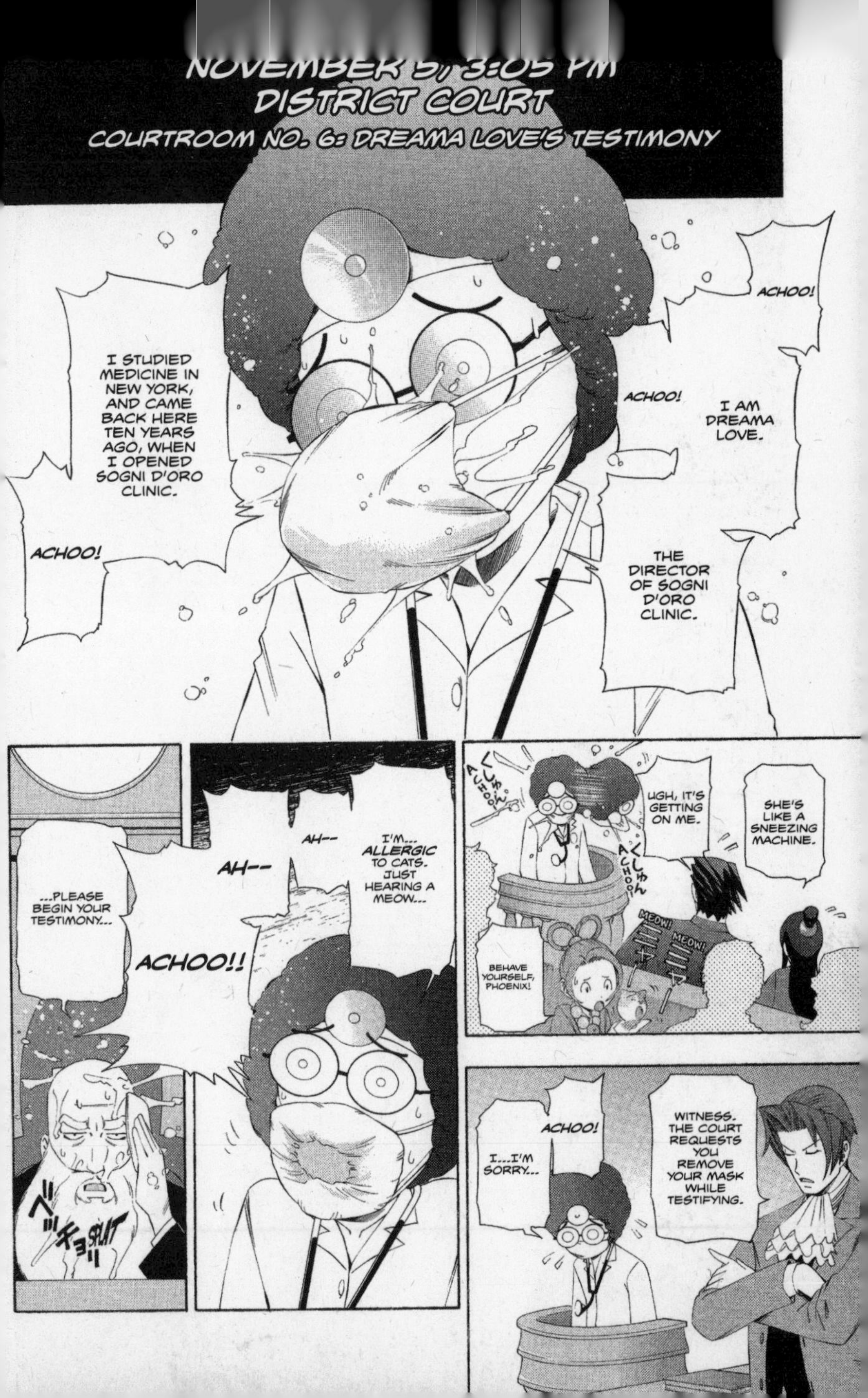
NOVEMBER 5, 3:05 PM
DISTRICT COURT
COURTROOM NO. 6: DREAMA LOVE'S TESTIMONY
ACHOO!
I AM DREAMA LOVE.
ACHOO!
THE DIRECTOR OF SOGNI D'ORO CLINIC.
I STUDIED MEDICINE IN NEW YORK, AND CAME BACK HERE TEN YEARS AGO, WHEN I OPENED SOGNI D'ORO CLINIC.
ACHOO!
SHE'S LIKE A SNEEZING MACHINE.
UGH, IT'S GETTING ON ME.
ACHOO!
ACHOO!
MEOW!
MEOW!
BEHAVE YOURSELF, PHOENIX!
WITNESS. THE COURT REQUESTS YOU REMOVE YOUR MASK WHILE TESTIFYING.
ACHOO!
I...I'M SORRY...
I'M... ALLERGIC TO CATS. JUST HEARING A MEOW...
AH--
AH--
ACHOO!!
...PLEASE BEGIN YOUR TESTIMONY...
SPLAT

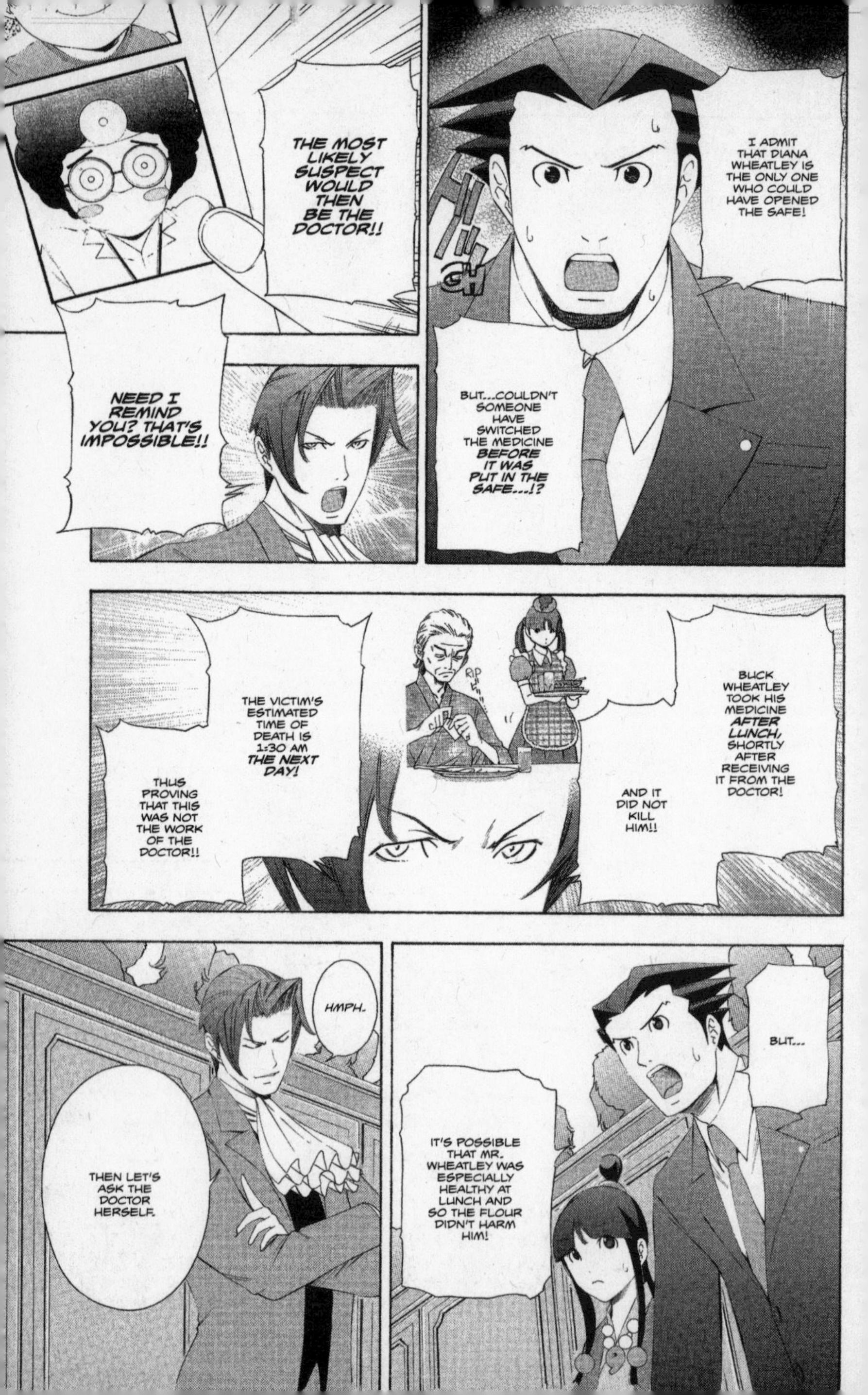
I ADMIT THAT DIANA WHEATLEY IS THE ONLY ONE WHO COULD HAVE OPENED THE SAFE!
BUT...COULDN'T SOMEONE HAVE SWITCHED THE MEDICINE BEFORE IT WAS PUT IN THE SAFE...!?
THE MOST LIKELY SUSPECT WOULD THEN BE THE DOCTOR!!
NEED I REMIND YOU? THAT'S IMPOSSIBLE!!
BUCK WHEATLEY TOOK HIS MEDICINE AFTER LUNCH, SHORTLY AFTER RECEIVING IT FROM THE DOCTOR!
AND IT DID NOT KILL HIM!!
RIP
THE VICTIM'S ESTIMATED TIME OF DEATH IS 1:30 AM THE NEXT DAY!
THUS PROVING THAT THIS WAS NOT THE WORK OF THE DOCTOR!!
BUT...
IT'S POSSIBLE THAT MR. WHEATLEY WAS ESPECIALLY HEALTHY AT LUNCH AND SO THE FLOUR DIDN'T HARM HIM!
HMPH.
THEN LET'S ASK THE DOCTOR HERSELF.

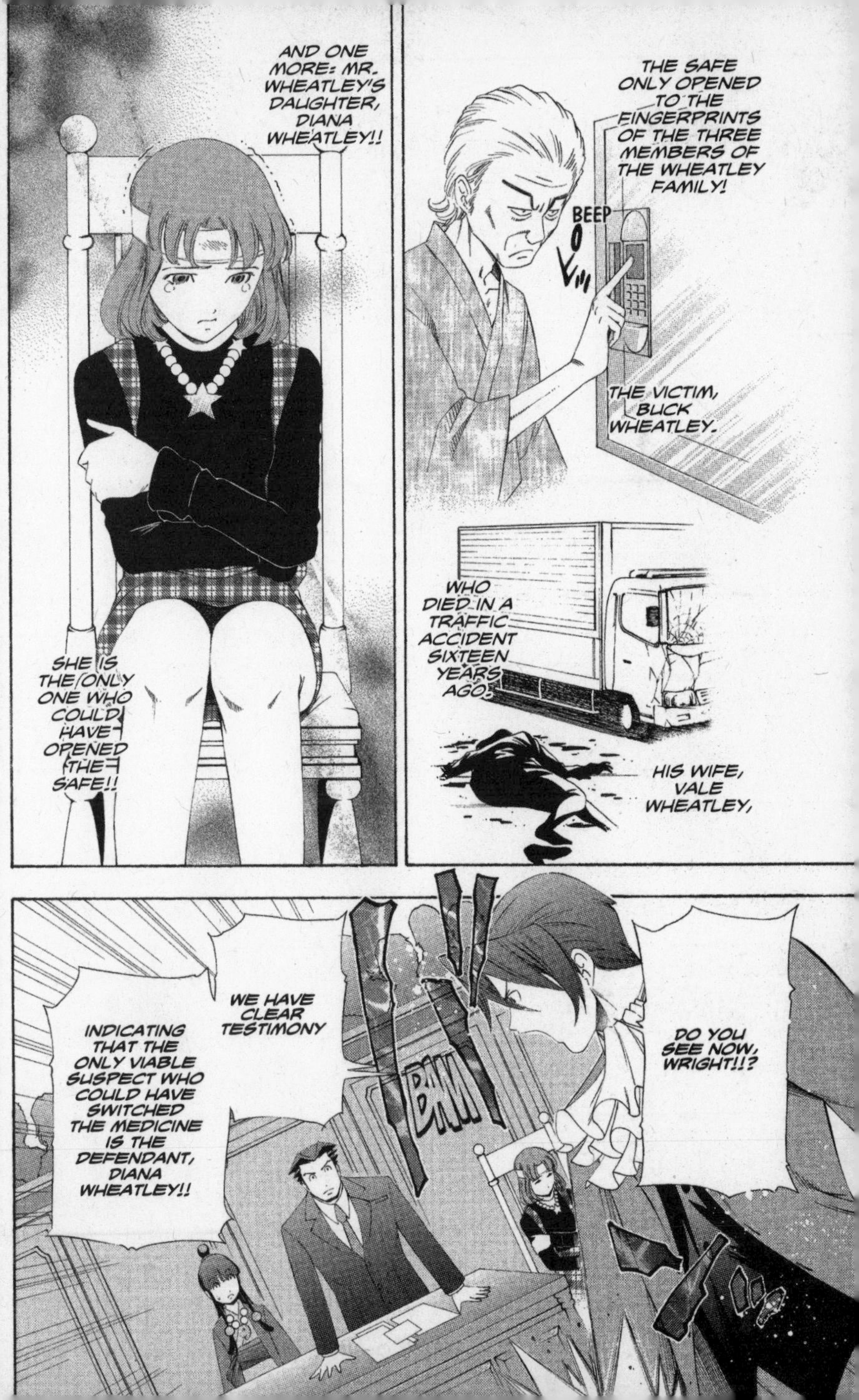
THE SAFE ONLY OPENED TO THE FINGERPRINTS OF THE THREE MEMBERS OF THE WHEATLEY FAMILY!
BEEP
THE VICTIM, BUCK WHEATLEY.
HIS WIFE, VALE WHEATLEY,
WHO DIED IN A TRAFFIC ACCIDENT SIXTEEN YEARS AGO.
AND ONE MORE: MR. WHEATLEY'S DAUGHTER, DIANA WHEATLEY!!
SHE IS THE ONLY ONE WHO COULD HAVE OPENED THE SAFE!!
DO YOU SEE NOW, WRIGHT!!?
BAM
WE HAVE CLEAR TESTIMONY
INDICATING THAT THE ONLY VIABLE SUSPECT WHO COULD HAVE SWITCHED THE MEDICINE IS THE DEFENDANT, DIANA WHEATLEY!!

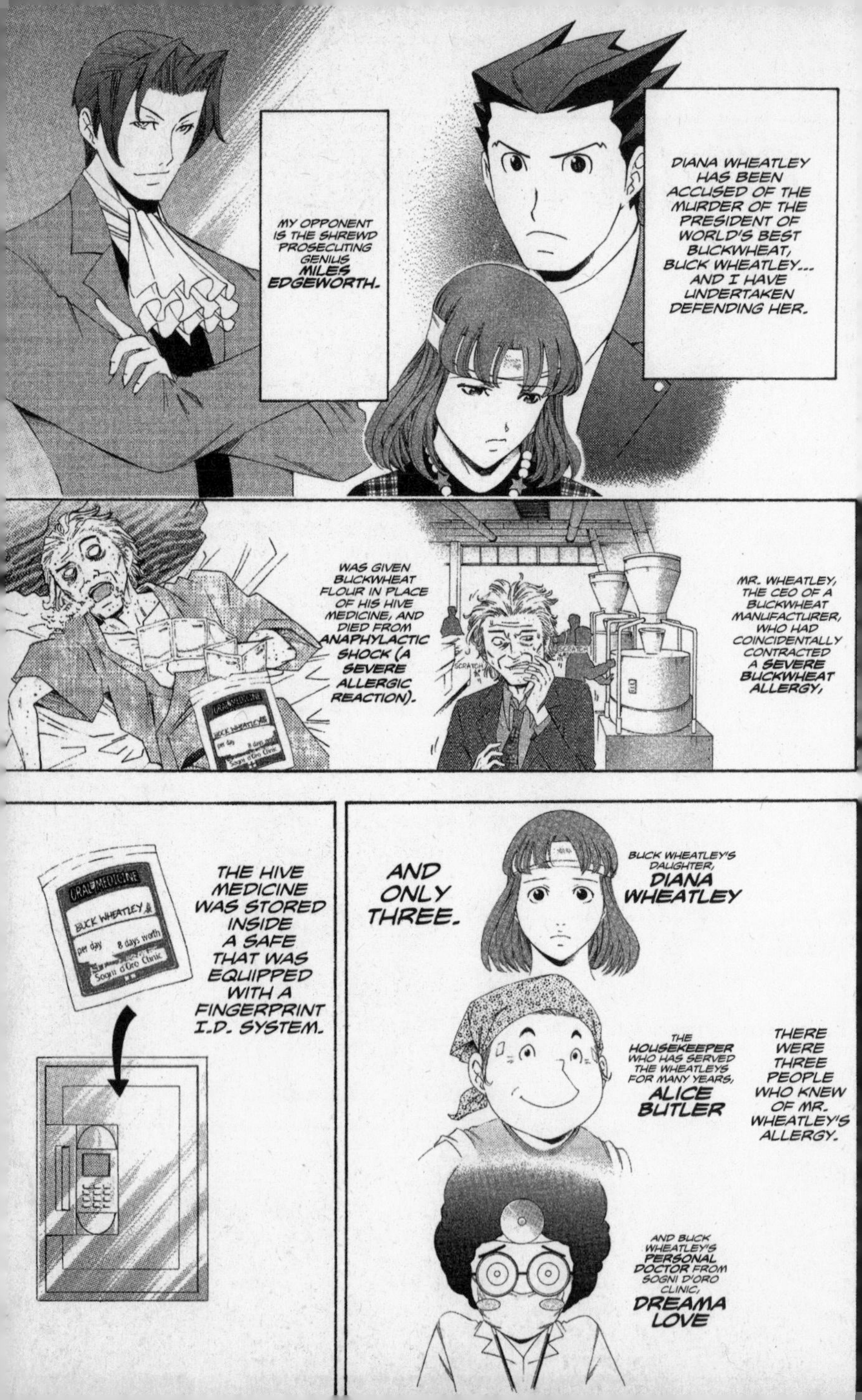

DIANA WHEATLEY HAS BEEN ACCUSED OF THE MURDER OF THE PRESIDENT OF WORLD'S BEST BUCKWHEAT, BUCK WHEATLEY... AND I HAVE UNDERTAKEN DEFENDING HER.
MY OPPONENT IS THE SHREWD PROSECUTING GENIUS MILES EDGEWORTH.
MR. WHEATLEY, THE CEO OF A BUCKWHEAT MANUFACTURER, WHO HAD COINCIDENTALLY CONTRACTED A SEVERE BUCKWHEAT ALLERGY,
SCRATCH
SCRATCH
WAS GIVEN BUCKWHEAT FLOUR IN PLACE OF HIS HIVE MEDICINE, AND DIED FROM ANAPHYLACTIC SHOCK (A SEVERE ALLERGIC REACTION).
THERE WERE THREE PEOPLE WHO KNEW OF MR. WHEATLEY'S ALLERGY.
AND ONLY THREE.
BUCK WHEATLEY'S DAUGHTER, DIANA WHEATLEY
THE HOUSEKEEPER WHO HAS SERVED THE WHEATLEYS FOR MANY YEARS, ALICE BUTLER
AND BUCK WHEATLEY'S PERSONAL DOCTOR FROM SOGNI D'ORO CLINIC, DREAMA LOVE
THE HIVE MEDICINE WAS STORED INSIDE A SAFE THAT WAS EQUIPPED WITH A FINGERPRINT I.D. SYSTEM.
ORAL MEDICINE
BUCK WHEATLEY
per day
8 days worth
Sogni d'Oro Clinic

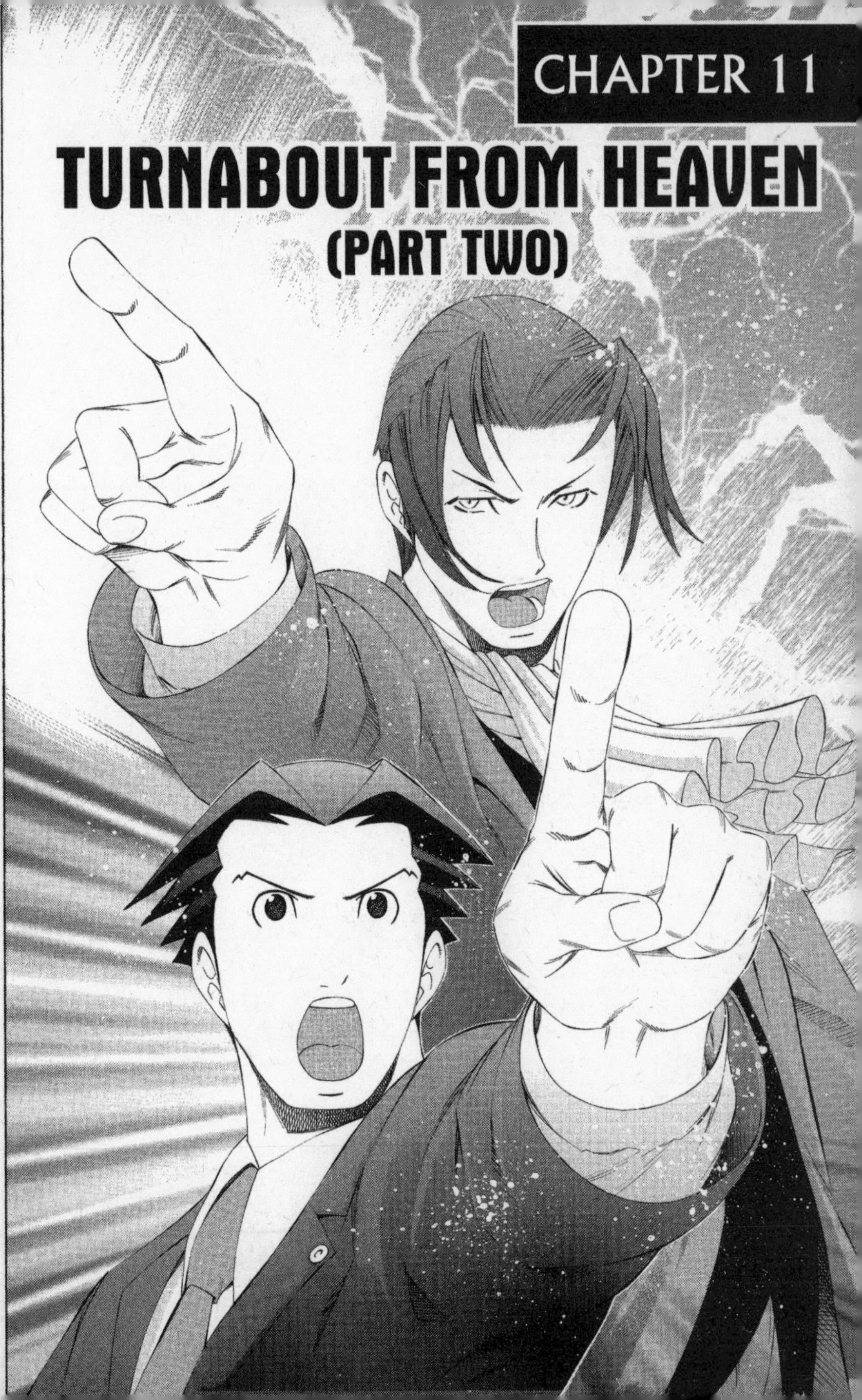
CHAPTER 11
TURNABOUT FROM HEAVEN
(PART TWO)

Ace Attorney

Phoenix Wright

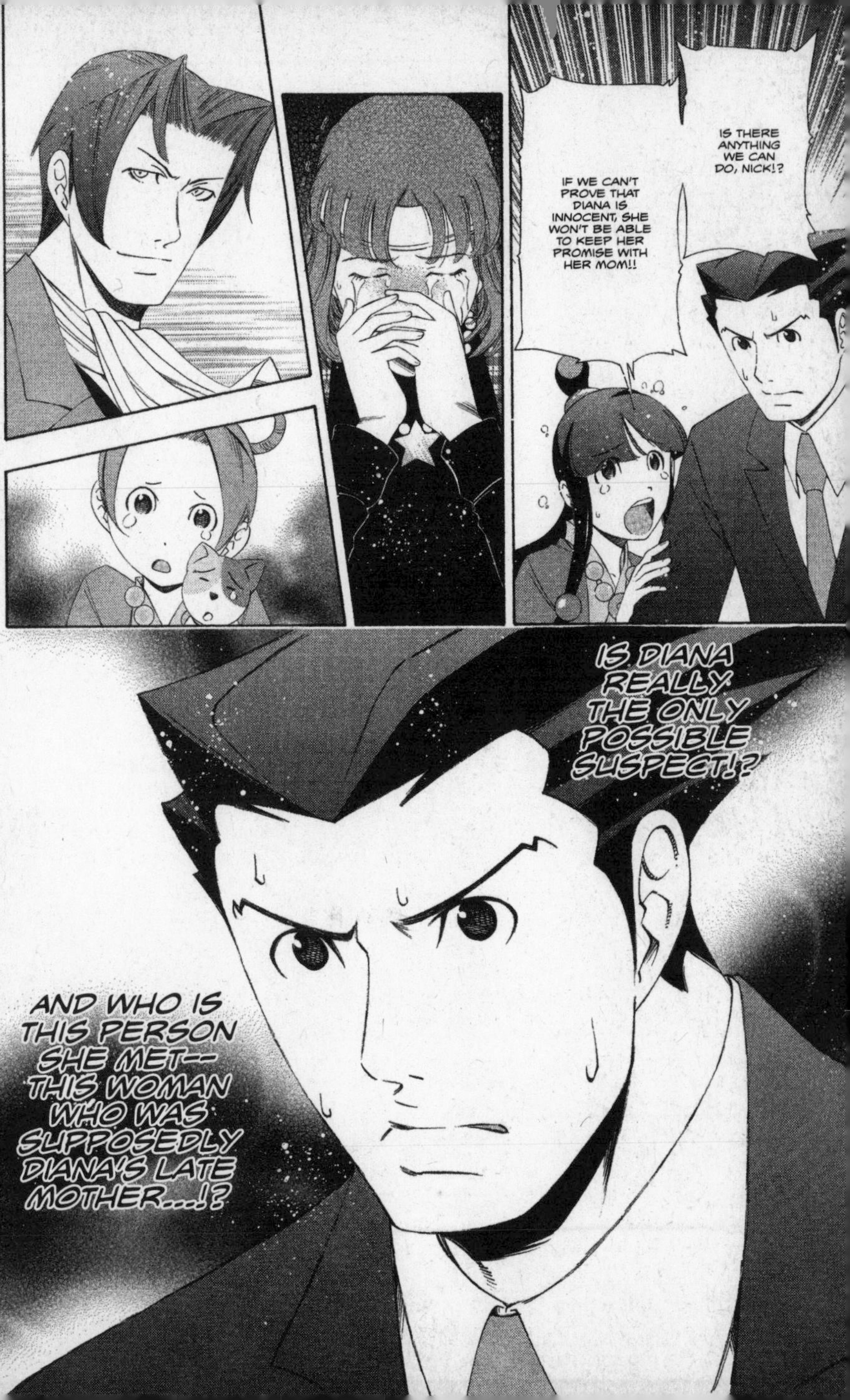
IS THERE ANYTHING WE CAN DO, NICK!?
IF WE CAN'T PROVE THAT DIANA IS INNOCENT, SHE WON'T BE ABLE TO KEEP HER PROMISE WITH HER MOM!!
IS DIANA REALLY THE ONLY POSSIBLE SUSPECT!?
AND WHO IS THIS PERSON SHE MET-- THIS WOMAN WHO WAS SUPPOSEDLY DIANA'S LATE MOTHER...!?

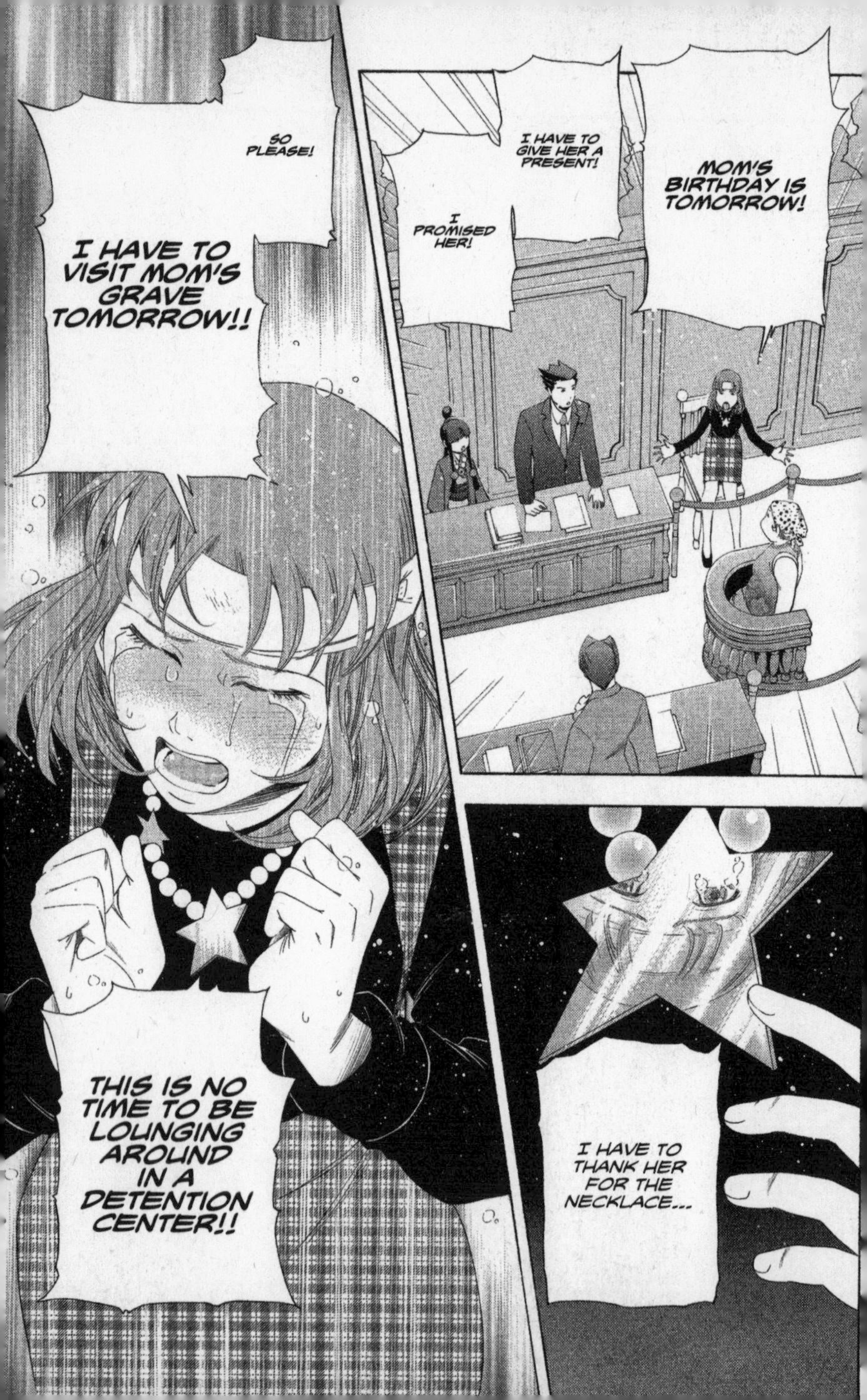
MOM'S BIRTHDAY IS TOMORROW!
I HAVE TO GIVE HER A PRESENT!
I PROMISED HER!
I HAVE TO THANK HER FOR THE NECKLACE...
SO PLEASE!
I HAVE TO VISIT MOM'S GRAVE TOMORROW!!
THIS IS NO TIME TO BE LOUNGING AROUND IN A DETENTION CENTER!!

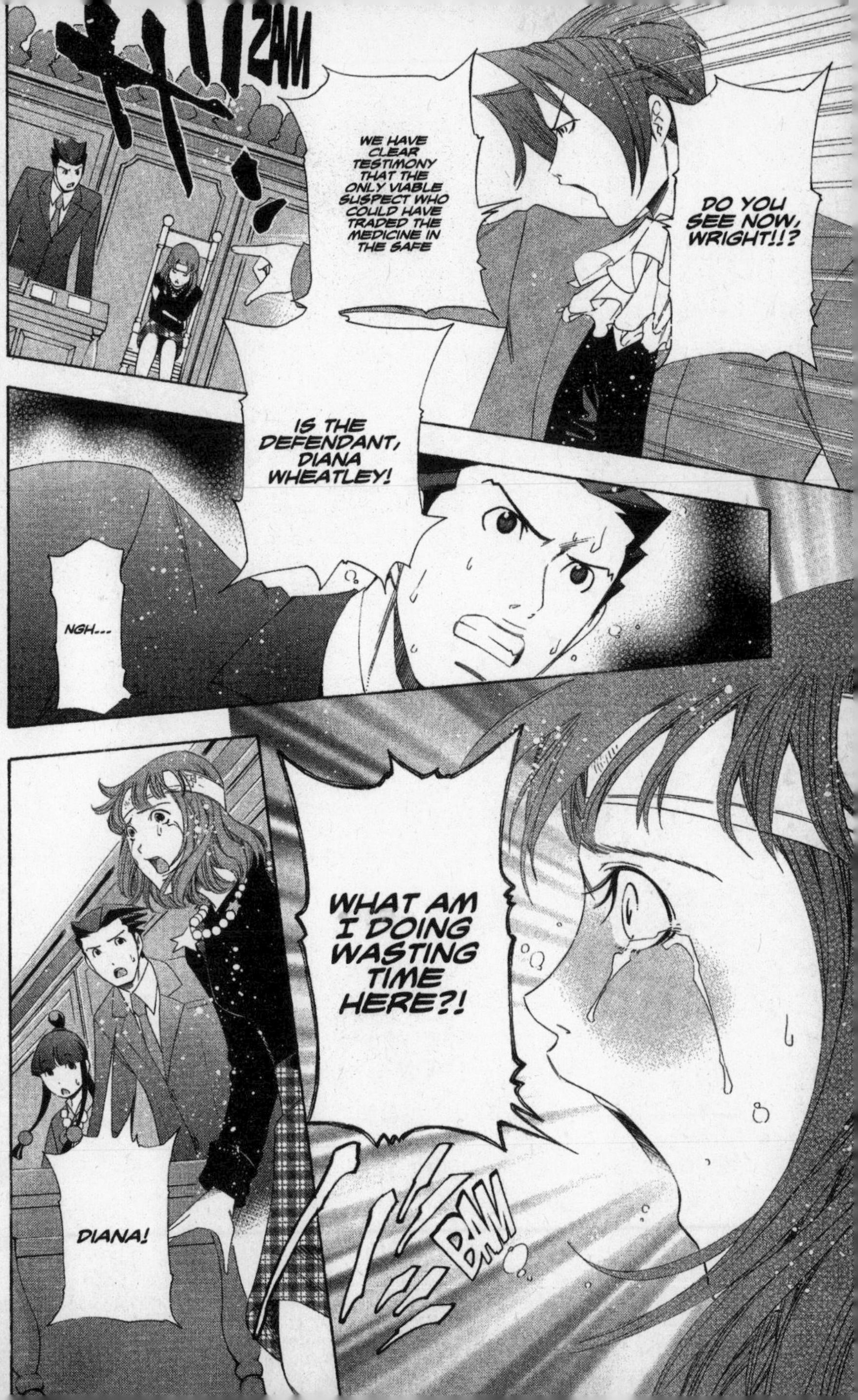
DO YOU SEE NOW, WRIGHT!!?
WE HAVE CLEAR TESTIMONY THAT THE ONLY VIABLE SUSPECT WHO COULD HAVE TRADED THE MEDICINE IN THE SAFE
ZAM
IS THE DEFENDANT, DIANA WHEATLEY!
NGH...
WHAT AM I DOING WASTING TIME HERE?!
BAM
DIANA!

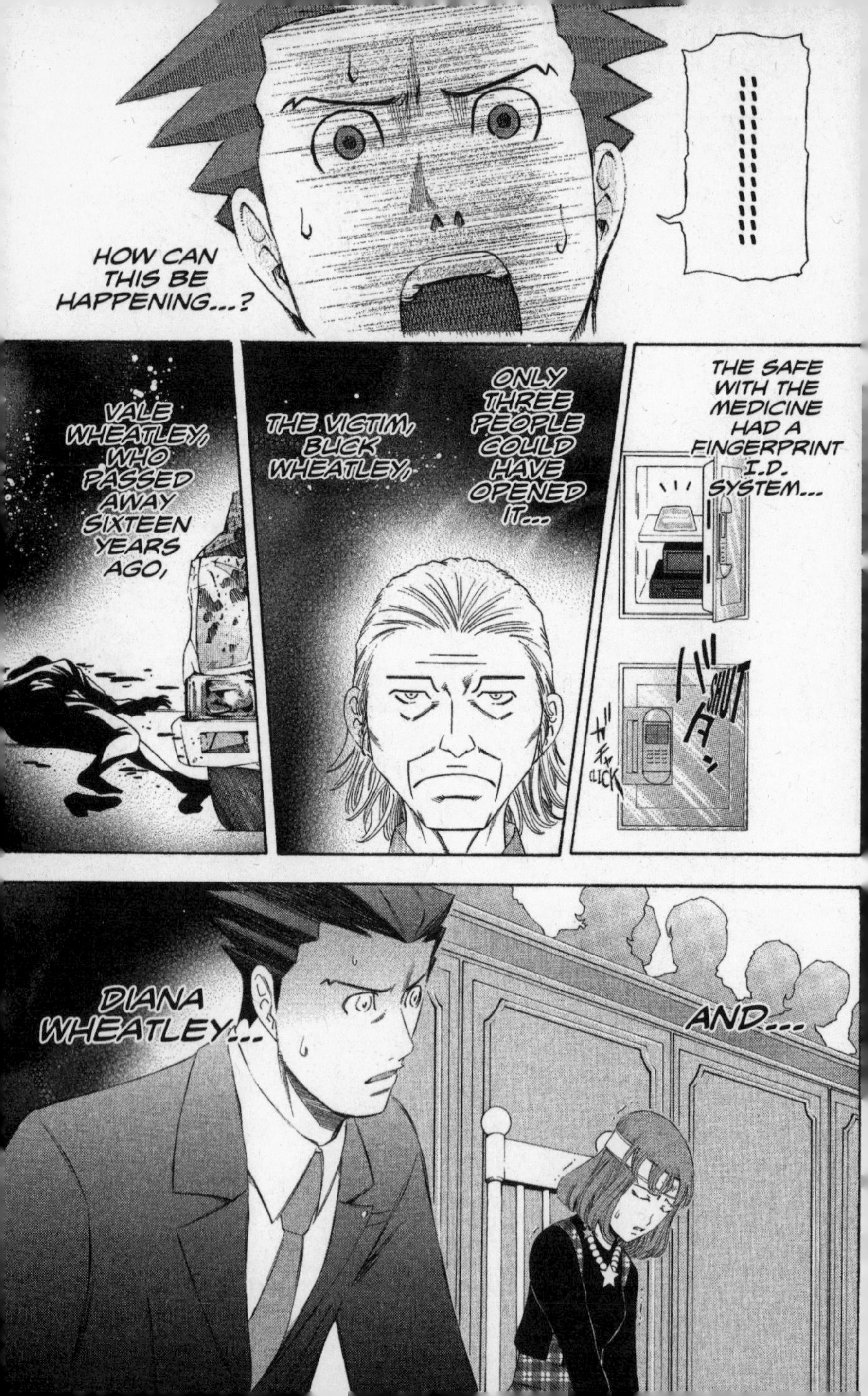

HOW CAN THIS BE HAPPENING...?
THE SAFE WITH THE MEDICINE HAD A FINGERPRINT I.D. SYSTEM...
SHUT
CLICK
ONLY THREE PEOPLE COULD HAVE OPENED IT...
THE VICTIM, BUCK WHEATLEY,
VALE WHEATLEY, WHO PASSED AWAY SIXTEEN YEARS AGO,
AND...
DIANA WHEATLEY...

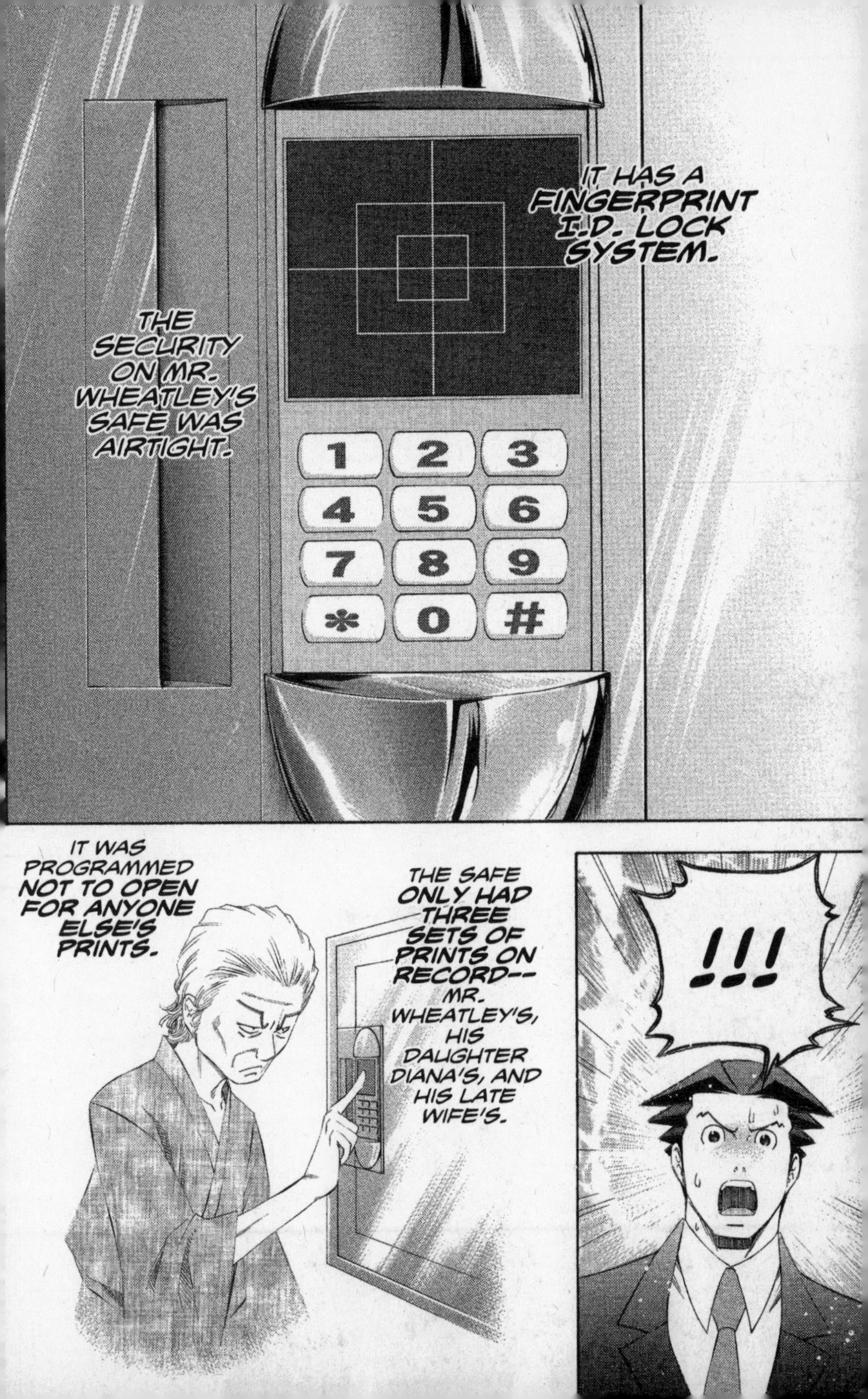
IT HAS A FINGERPRINT I.D. LOCK SYSTEM.
THE SECURITY ON MR. WHEATLEY'S SAFE WAS AIRTIGHT.
!!!
THE SAFE ONLY HAD THREE SETS OF PRINTS ON RECORD-- MR. WHEATLEY'S, HIS DAUGHTER DIANA'S, AND HIS LATE WIFE'S.
IT WAS PROGRAMMED NOT TO OPEN FOR ANYONE ELSE'S PRINTS.

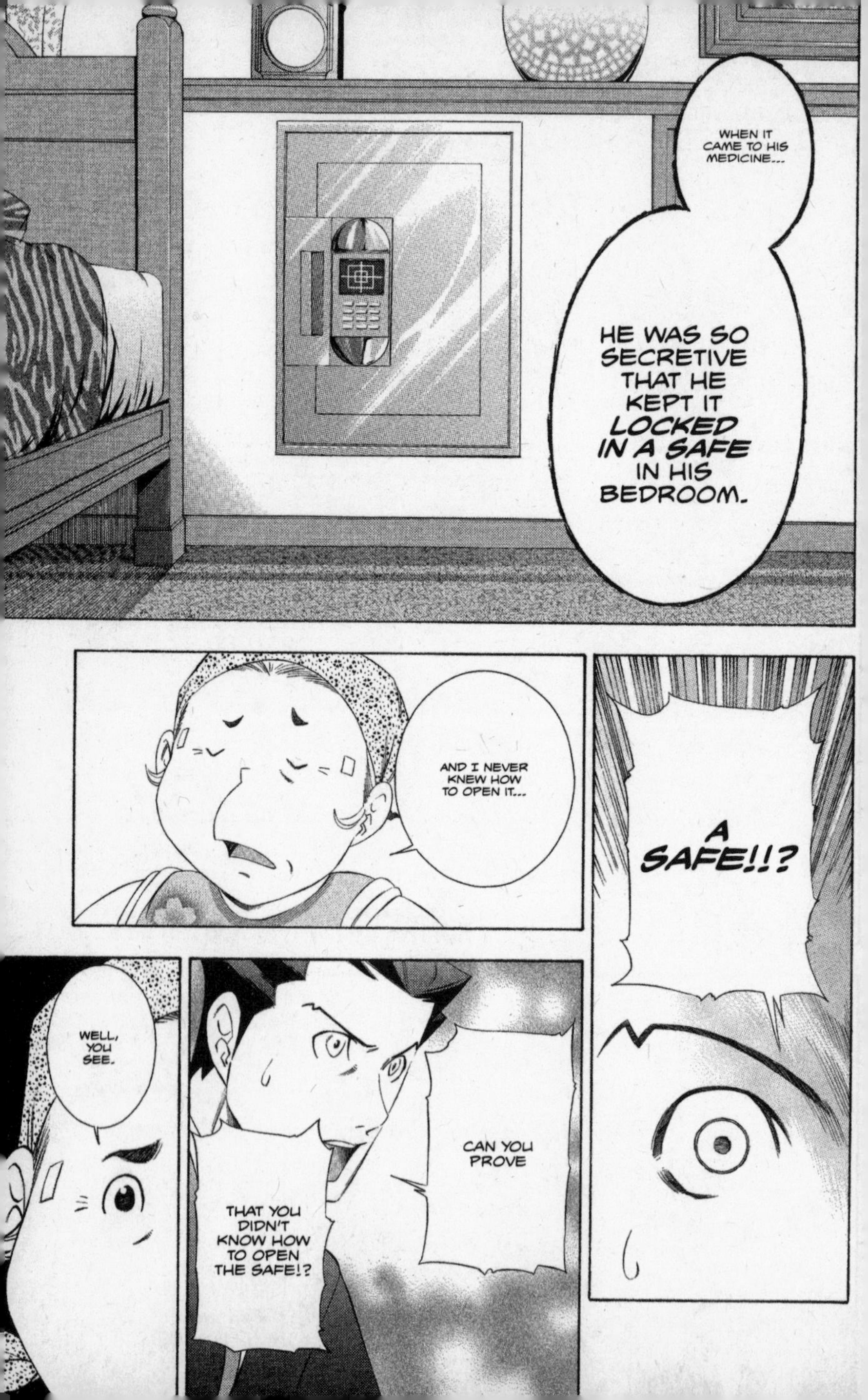
WHEN IT CAME TO HIS MEDICINE...
HE WAS SO SECRETIVE THAT HE KEPT IT *LOCKED IN A SAFE* IN HIS BEDROOM.
A SAFE!!?
AND I NEVER KNEW HOW TO OPEN IT...
CAN YOU PROVE
THAT YOU DIDN'T KNOW HOW TO OPEN THE SAFE!?
WELL, YOU SEE.

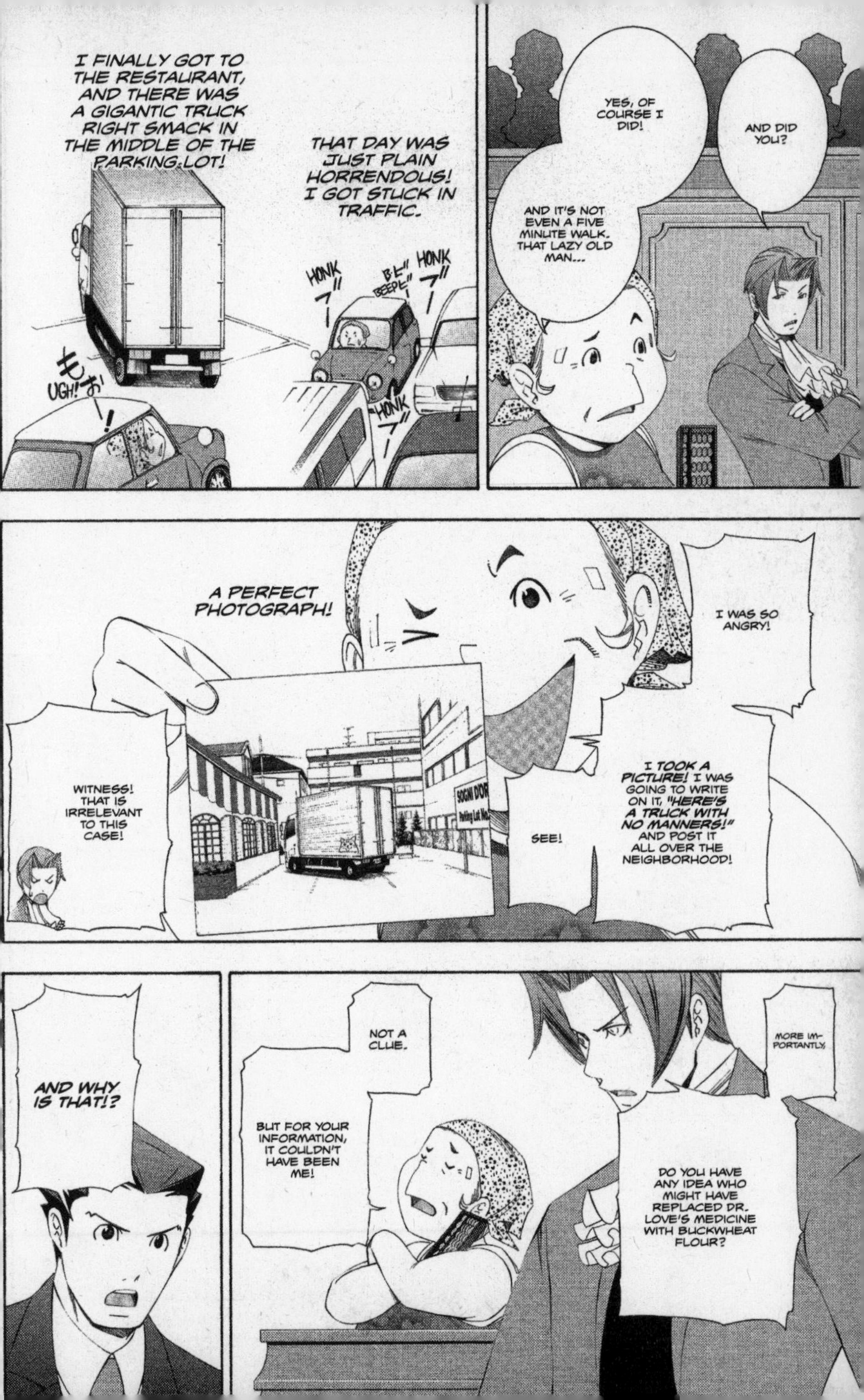
AND DID YOU?
YES, OF COURSE I DID!
AND IT'S NOT EVEN A FIVE MINUTE WALK. THAT LAZY OLD MAN...
THAT DAY WAS JUST PLAIN HORRENDOUS! I GOT STUCK IN TRAFFIC.
HONK
BEEP
HONK
HONK
I FINALLY GOT TO THE RESTAURANT, AND THERE WAS A GIGANTIC TRUCK RIGHT SMACK IN THE MIDDLE OF THE PARKING LOT!
UGH!
I WAS SO ANGRY!
I TOOK A PICTURE! I WAS GOING TO WRITE ON IT, "HERE'S A TRUCK WITH NO MANNERS!" AND POST IT ALL OVER THE NEIGHBORHOOD!
SEE!
A PERFECT PHOTOGRAPH!
SOGNI D'OR
WITNESS! THAT IS IRRELEVANT TO THIS CASE!
MORE IMPORTANTLY,
DO YOU HAVE ANY IDEA WHO MIGHT HAVE REPLACED DR. LOVE'S MEDICINE WITH BUCKWHEAT FLOUR?
NOT A CLUE.
BUT FOR YOUR INFORMATION, IT COULDN'T HAVE BEEN ME!
AND WHY IS THAT!?

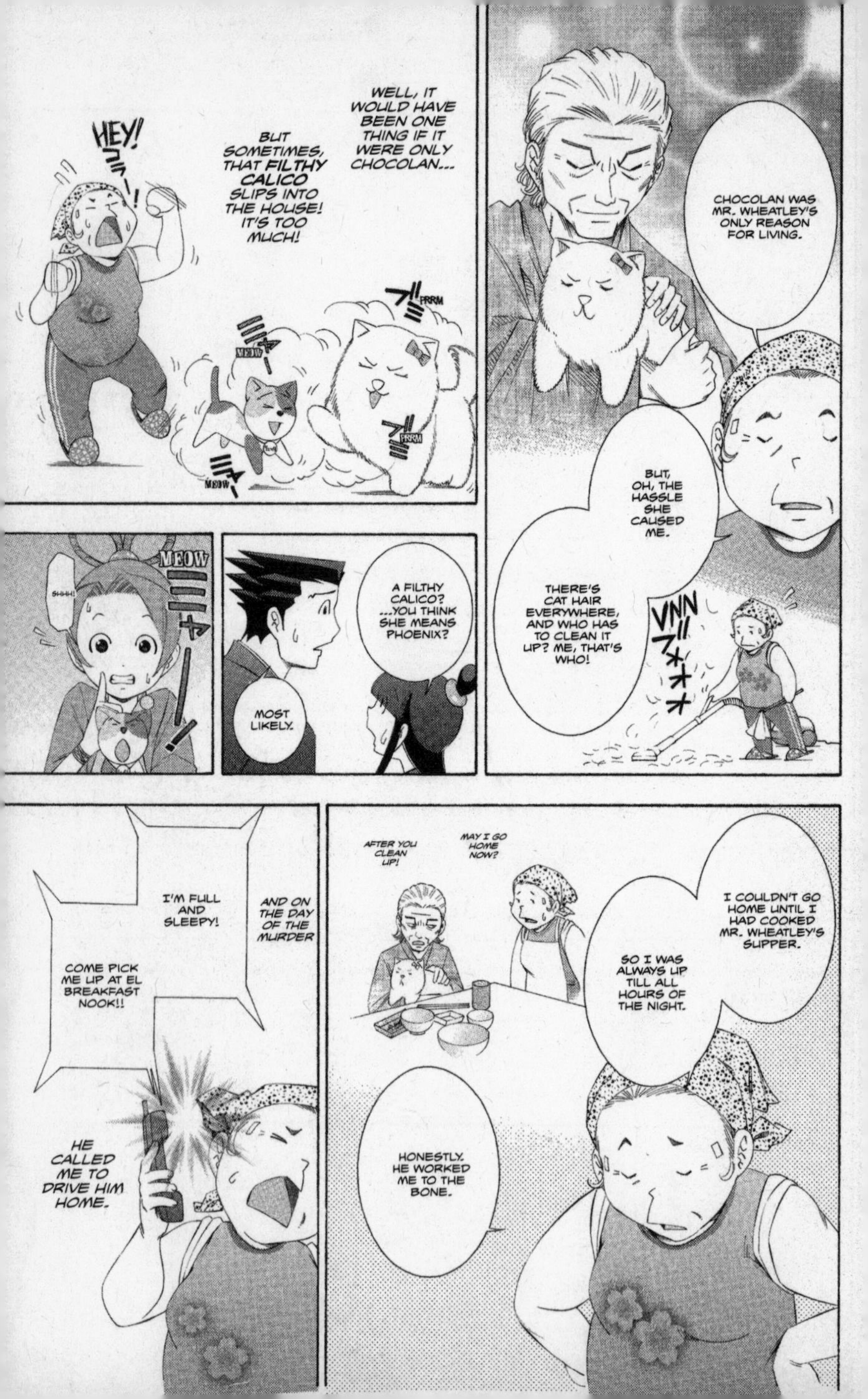
CHOCOLAN WAS MR. WHEATLEY'S ONLY REASON FOR LIVING.
BUT, OH, THE HASSLE SHE CAUSED ME.
THERE'S CAT HAIR EVERYWHERE, AND WHO HAS TO CLEAN IT UP? ME, THAT'S WHO!
VNN
WELL, IT WOULD HAVE BEEN ONE THING IF IT WERE ONLY CHOCOLAN...
BUT SOMETIMES, THAT FILTHY CALICO SLIPS INTO THE HOUSE! IT'S TOO MUCH!
HEY!
PRRM
MEOW
PRRM
MEOW
A FILTHY CALICO? ...YOU THINK SHE MEANS PHOENIX?
MOST LIKELY.
MEOW
SHHH!
I COULDN'T GO HOME UNTIL I HAD COOKED MR. WHEATLEY'S SUPPER.
SO I WAS ALWAYS UP TILL ALL HOURS OF THE NIGHT.
MAY I GO HOME NOW?
AFTER YOU CLEAN UP!
HONESTLY. HE WORKED ME TO THE BONE.
AND ON THE DAY OF THE MURDER
I'M FULL AND SLEEPY!
COME PICK ME UP AT EL BREAKFAST NOOK!!
HE CALLED ME TO DRIVE HIM HOME.

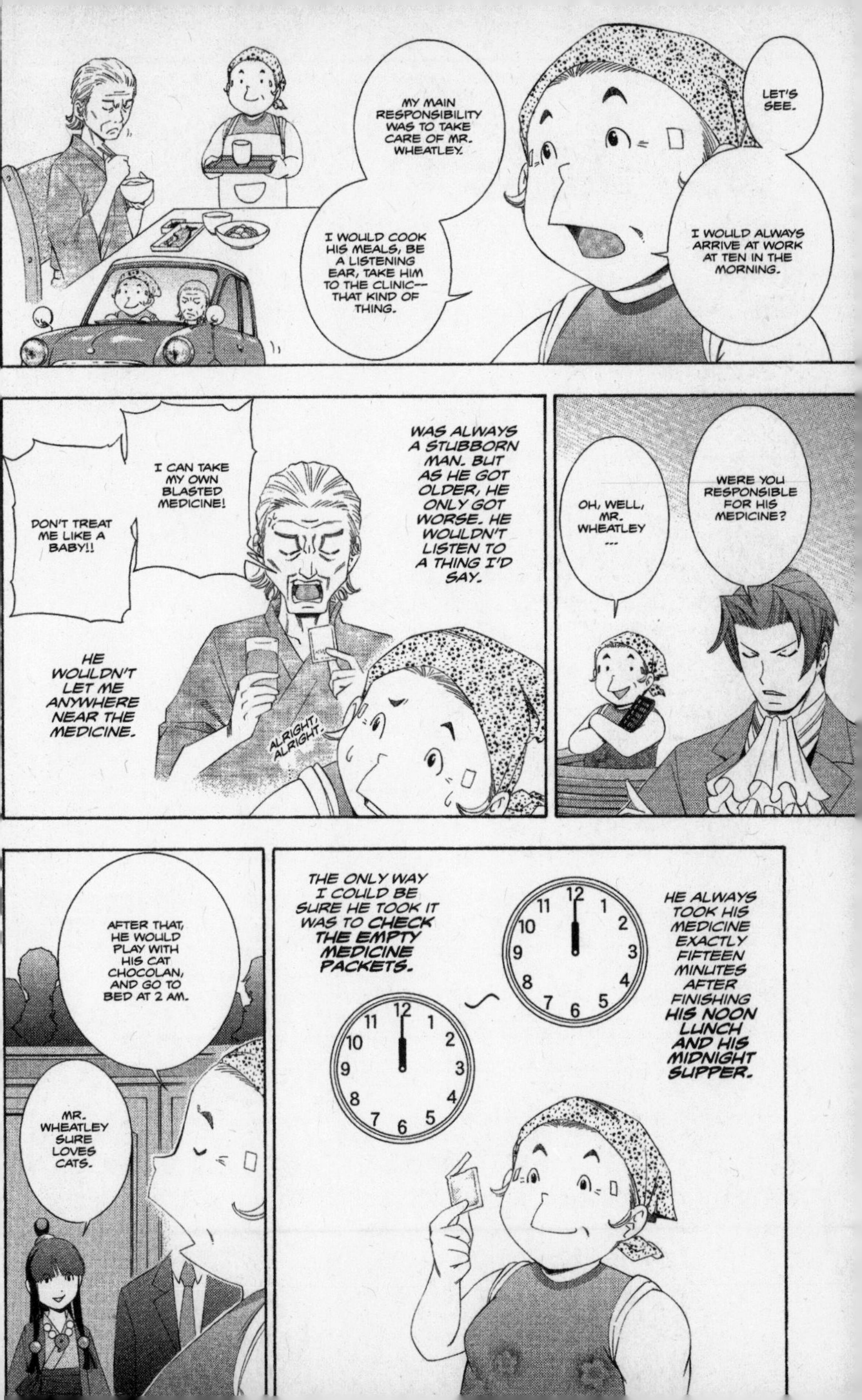
LET'S SEE.
I WOULD ALWAYS ARRIVE AT WORK AT TEN IN THE MORNING.
MY MAIN RESPONSIBILITY WAS TO TAKE CARE OF MR. WHEATLEY.
I WOULD COOK HIS MEALS, BE A LISTENING EAR, TAKE HIM TO THE CLINIC-- THAT KIND OF THING.
WERE YOU RESPONSIBLE FOR HIS MEDICINE?
OH, WELL, MR. WHEATLEY ---
WAS ALWAYS A STUBBORN MAN. BUT AS HE GOT OLDER, HE ONLY GOT WORSE. HE WOULDN'T LISTEN TO A THING I'D SAY.
I CAN TAKE MY OWN BLASTED MEDICINE!
DON'T TREAT ME LIKE A BABY!!
HE WOULDN'T LET ME ANYWHERE NEAR THE MEDICINE.
ALRIGHT, ALRIGHT.
HE ALWAYS TOOK HIS MEDICINE EXACTLY FIFTEEN MINUTES AFTER FINISHING HIS NOON LUNCH AND HIS MIDNIGHT SUPPER.
THE ONLY WAY I COULD BE SURE HE TOOK IT WAS TO CHECK THE EMPTY MEDICINE PACKETS.
AFTER THAT, HE WOULD PLAY WITH HIS CAT CHOCOLAN, AND GO TO BED AT 2 AM.
MR. WHEATLEY SURE LOVES CATS.

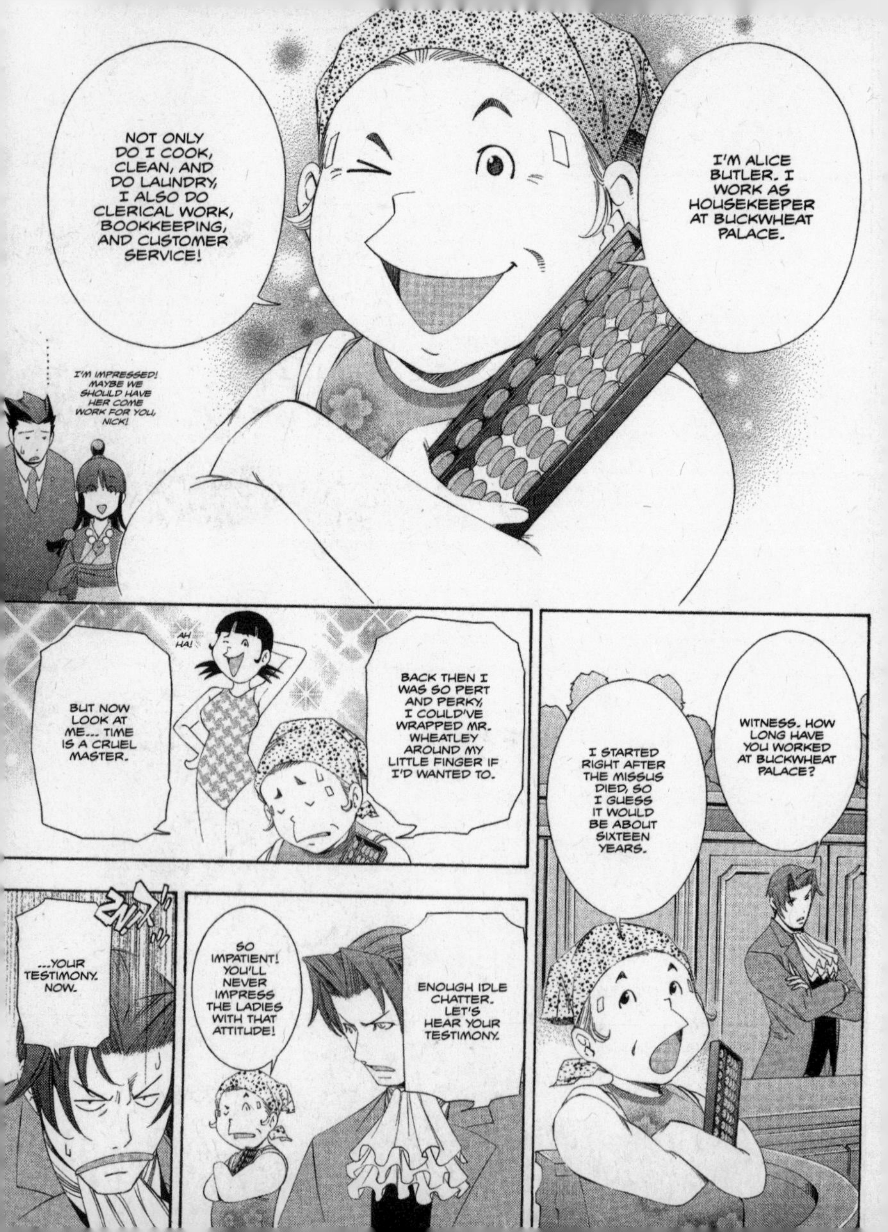
I'M ALICE BUTLER. I WORK AS HOUSEKEEPER AT BUCKWHEAT PALACE.
NOT ONLY DO I COOK, CLEAN, AND DO LAUNDRY, I ALSO DO CLERICAL WORK, BOOKKEEPING, AND CUSTOMER SERVICE!
I'M IMPRESSED! MAYBE WE SHOULD HAVE HER COME WORK FOR YOU, NICK!
WITNESS. HOW LONG HAVE YOU WORKED AT BUCKWHEAT PALACE?
I STARTED RIGHT AFTER THE MISSUS DIED, SO I GUESS IT WOULD BE ABOUT SIXTEEN YEARS.
BACK THEN I WAS SO PERT AND PERKY, I COULD'VE WRAPPED MR. WHEATLEY AROUND MY LITTLE FINGER IF I'D WANTED TO.
AH HA!
BUT NOW LOOK AT ME... TIME IS A CRUEL MASTER.
ENOUGH IDLE CHATTER. LET'S HEAR YOUR TESTIMONY.
SO IMPATIENT! YOU'LL NEVER IMPRESS THE LADIES WITH THAT ATTITUDE!
...YOUR TESTIMONY. NOW.

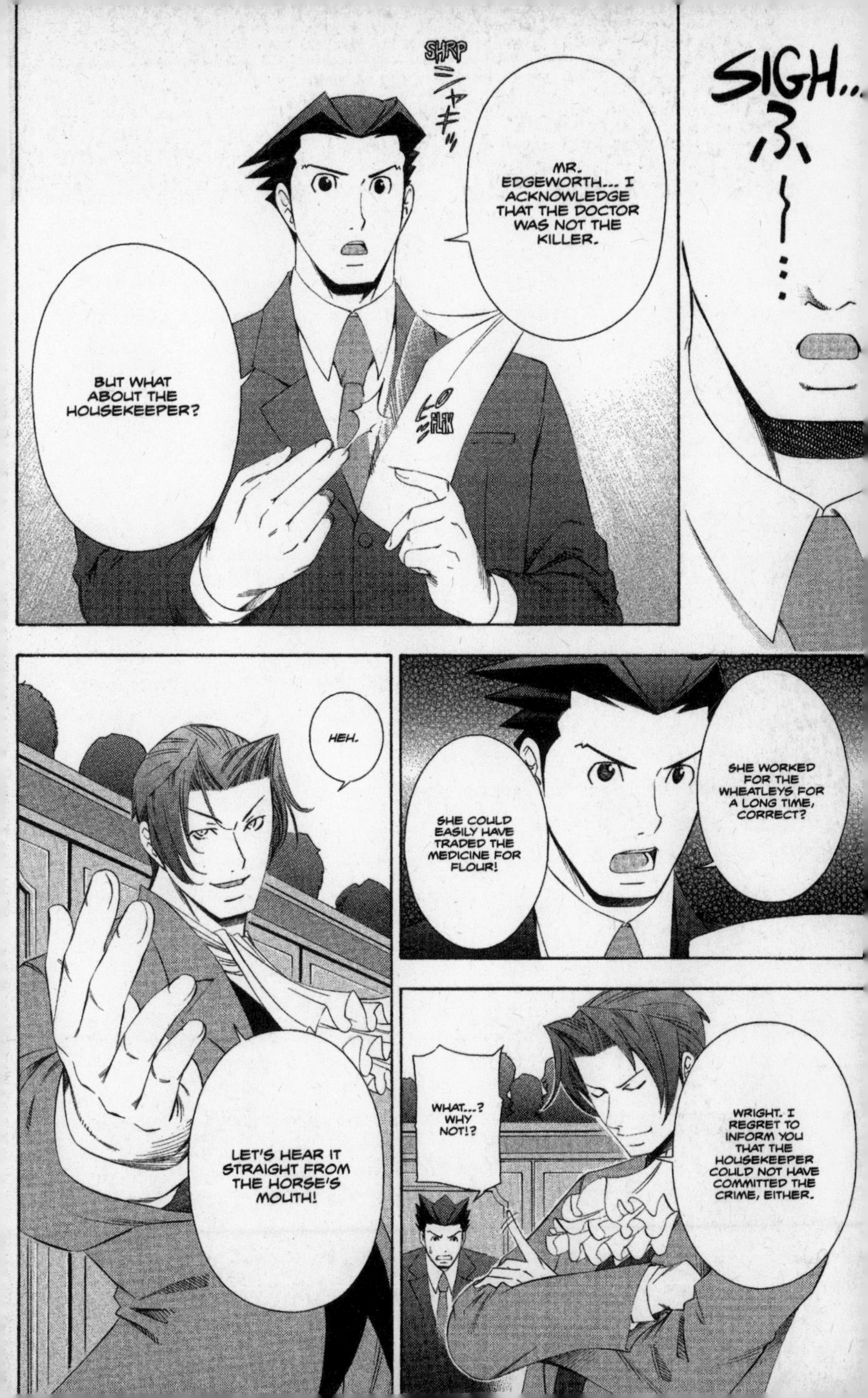
SIGH...
ふ〜〜…
SHRP
シャキッ
MR. EDGEWORTH... I ACKNOWLEDGE THAT THE DOCTOR WAS NOT THE KILLER.
BUT WHAT ABOUT THE HOUSEKEEPER?
FLIK
SHE WORKED FOR THE WHEATLEYS FOR A LONG TIME, CORRECT?
SHE COULD EASILY HAVE TRADED THE MEDICINE FOR FLOUR!
WRIGHT. I REGRET TO INFORM YOU THAT THE HOUSEKEEPER COULD NOT HAVE COMMITTED THE CRIME, EITHER.
WHAT...? WHY NOT!?
HEH.
LET'S HEAR IT STRAIGHT FROM THE HORSE'S MOUTH!

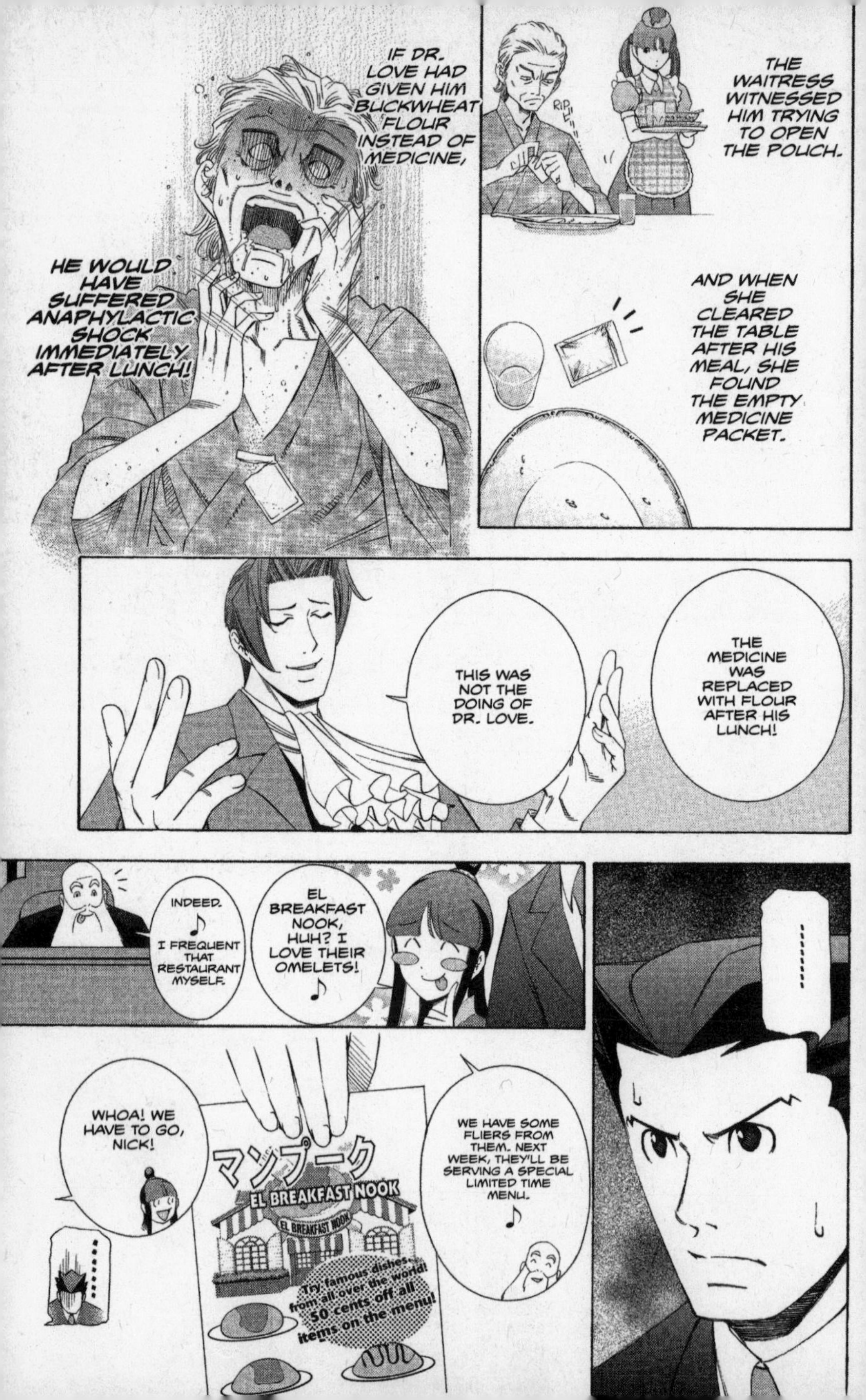
THE WAITRESS WITNESSED HIM TRYING TO OPEN THE POUCH.
RIP
AND WHEN SHE CLEARED THE TABLE AFTER HIS MEAL, SHE FOUND THE EMPTY MEDICINE PACKET.
IF DR. LOVE HAD GIVEN HIM BUCKWHEAT FLOUR INSTEAD OF MEDICINE,
HE WOULD HAVE SUFFERED ANAPHYLACTIC SHOCK IMMEDIATELY AFTER LUNCH!
THE MEDICINE WAS REPLACED WITH FLOUR AFTER HIS LUNCH!
THIS WAS NOT THE DOING OF DR. LOVE.
......
EL BREAKFAST NOOK, HUH? I LOVE THEIR OMELETS! ♪
INDEED. ♪ I FREQUENT THAT RESTAURANT MYSELF.
WE HAVE SOME FLIERS FROM THEM. NEXT WEEK, THEY'LL BE SERVING A SPECIAL LIMITED TIME MENU. ♪
WHOA! WE HAVE TO GO, NICK!
......
マンプーク
EL BREAKFAST NOOK
EL BREAKFAST NOOK
Try famous dishes from all over the world! 50 cents off all items on the menu!

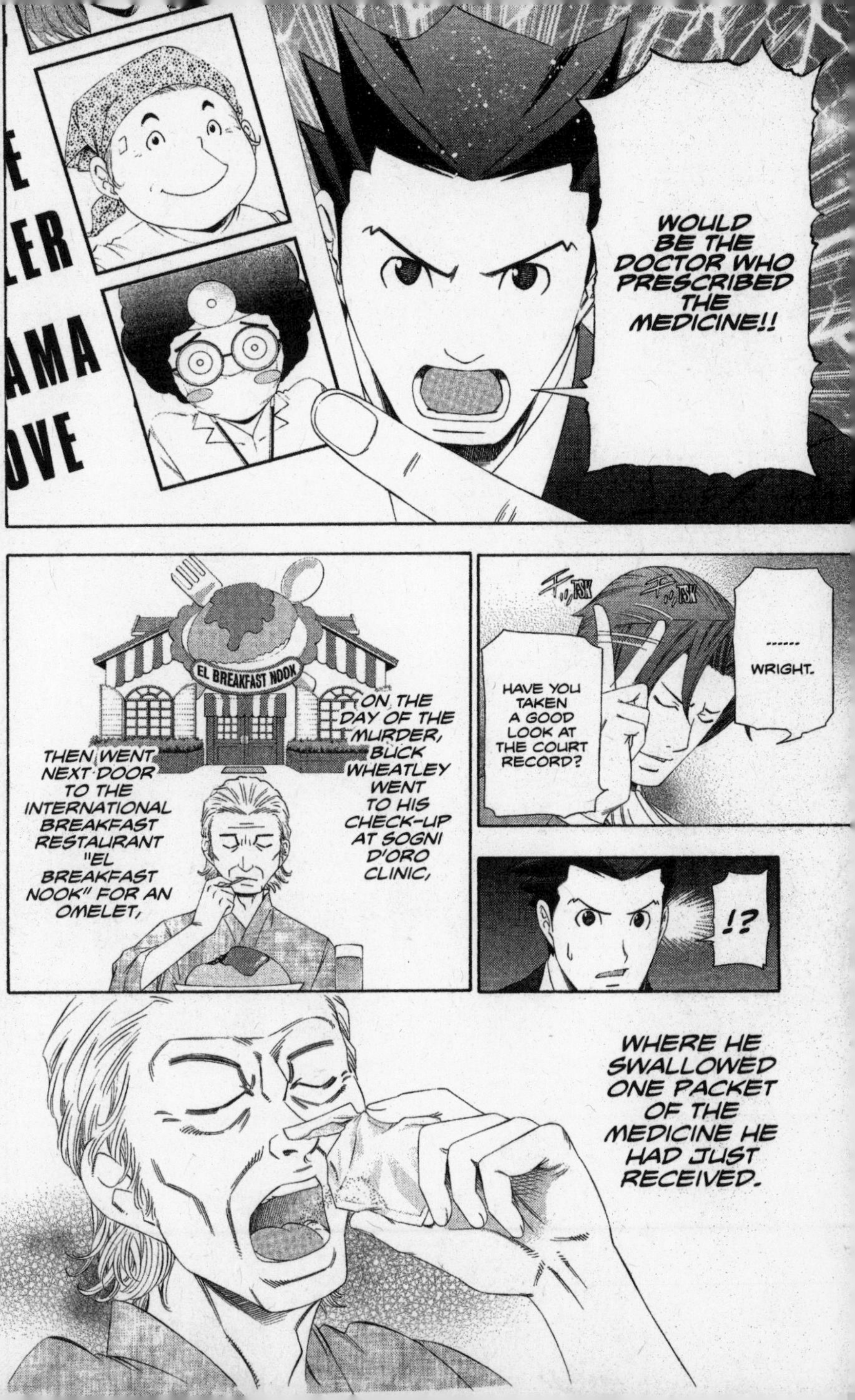
WOULD BE THE DOCTOR WHO PRESCRIBED THE MEDICINE!!
TSK
TSK
...... WRIGHT.
HAVE YOU TAKEN A GOOD LOOK AT THE COURT RECORD?
!?
EL BREAKFAST NOOK
ON THE DAY OF THE MURDER, BUCK WHEATLEY WENT TO HIS CHECK-UP AT SOGNI D'ORO CLINIC,
THEN WENT NEXT DOOR TO THE INTERNATIONAL BREAKFAST RESTAURANT "EL BREAKFAST NOOK" FOR AN OMELET,
WHERE HE SWALLOWED ONE PACKET OF THE MEDICINE HE HAD JUST RECEIVED.

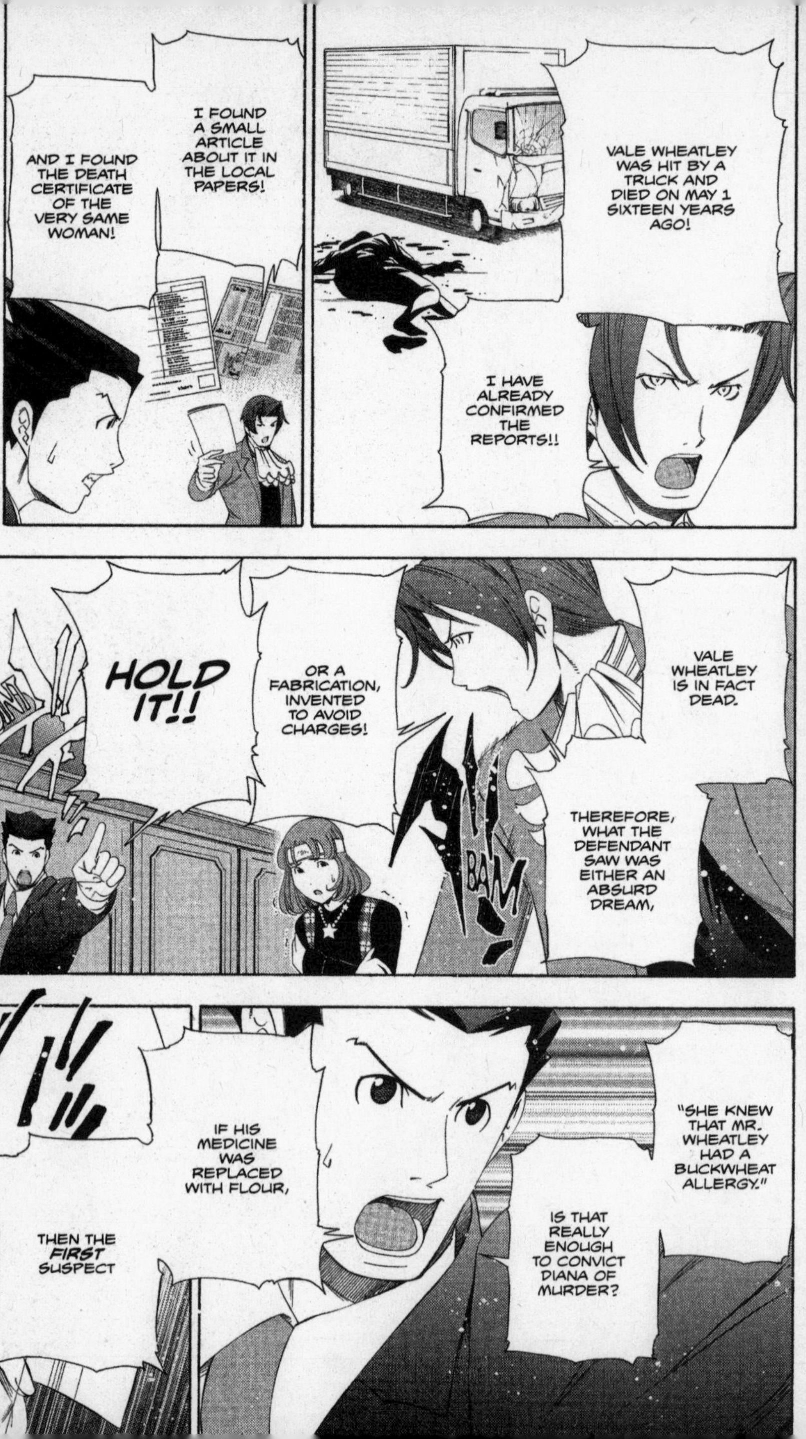
VALE WHEATLEY WAS HIT BY A TRUCK AND DIED ON MAY 1 SIXTEEN YEARS AGO!
I HAVE ALREADY CONFIRMED THE REPORTS!!
I FOUND A SMALL ARTICLE ABOUT IT IN THE LOCAL PAPERS!
AND I FOUND THE DEATH CERTIFICATE OF THE VERY SAME WOMAN!
VALE WHEATLEY IS IN FACT DEAD.
THEREFORE, WHAT THE DEFENDANT SAW WAS EITHER AN ABSURD DREAM,
BAM
OR A FABRICATION, INVENTED TO AVOID CHARGES!
HOLD IT!!
POINT
"SHE KNEW THAT MR. WHEATLEY HAD A BUCKWHEAT ALLERGY."
IS THAT REALLY ENOUGH TO CONVICT DIANA OF MURDER?
IF HIS MEDICINE WAS REPLACED WITH FLOUR,
THEN THE *FIRST* SUSPECT

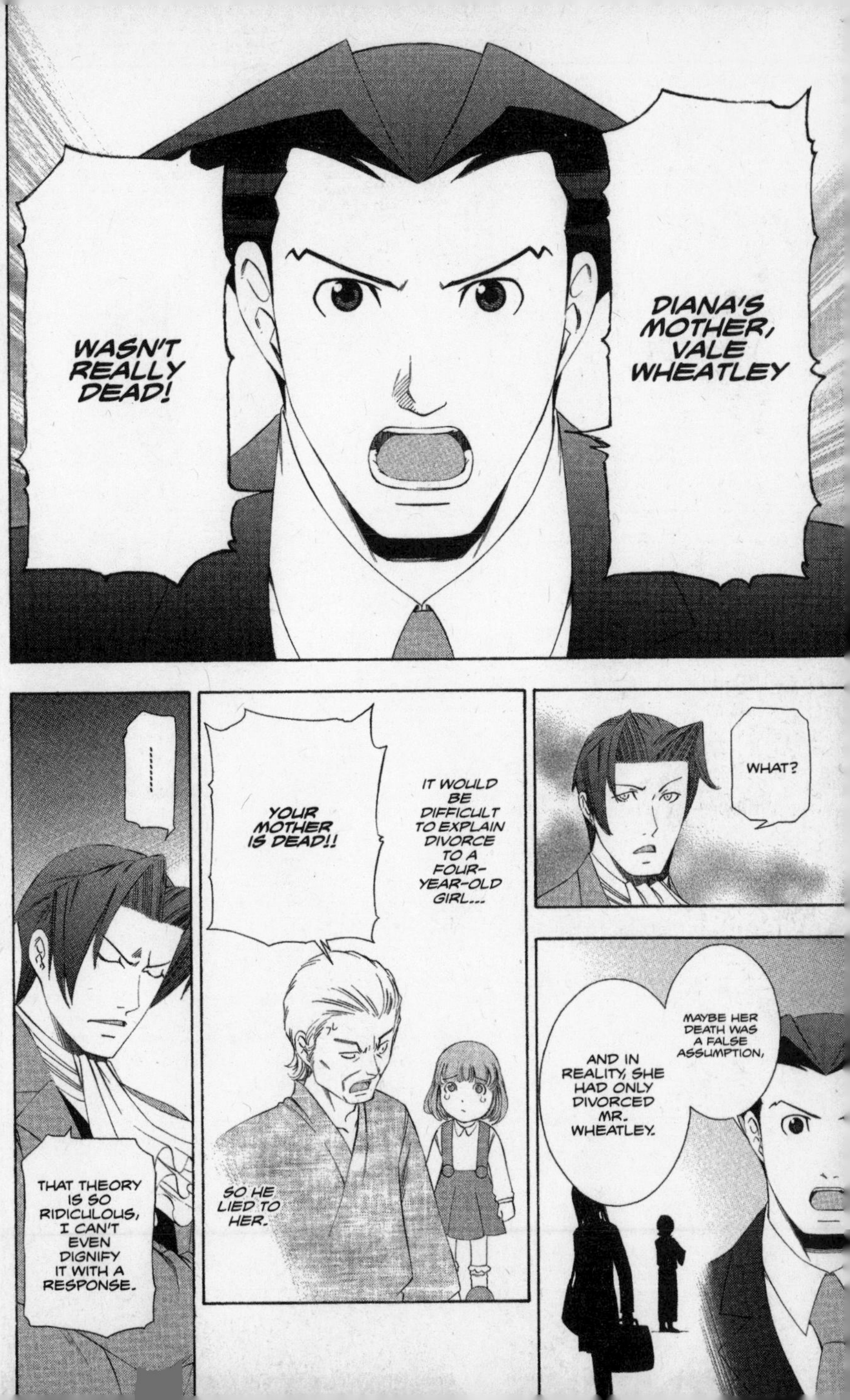
DIANA'S MOTHER, VALE WHEATLEY
WASN'T REALLY DEAD!
WHAT?
MAYBE HER DEATH WAS A FALSE ASSUMPTION,
AND IN REALITY, SHE HAD ONLY DIVORCED MR. WHEATLEY.
IT WOULD BE DIFFICULT TO EXPLAIN DIVORCE TO A FOUR-YEAR-OLD GIRL...
YOUR MOTHER IS DEAD!!
SO HE LIED TO HER.
......
THAT THEORY IS SO RIDICULOUS, I CAN'T EVEN DIGNIFY IT WITH A RESPONSE.

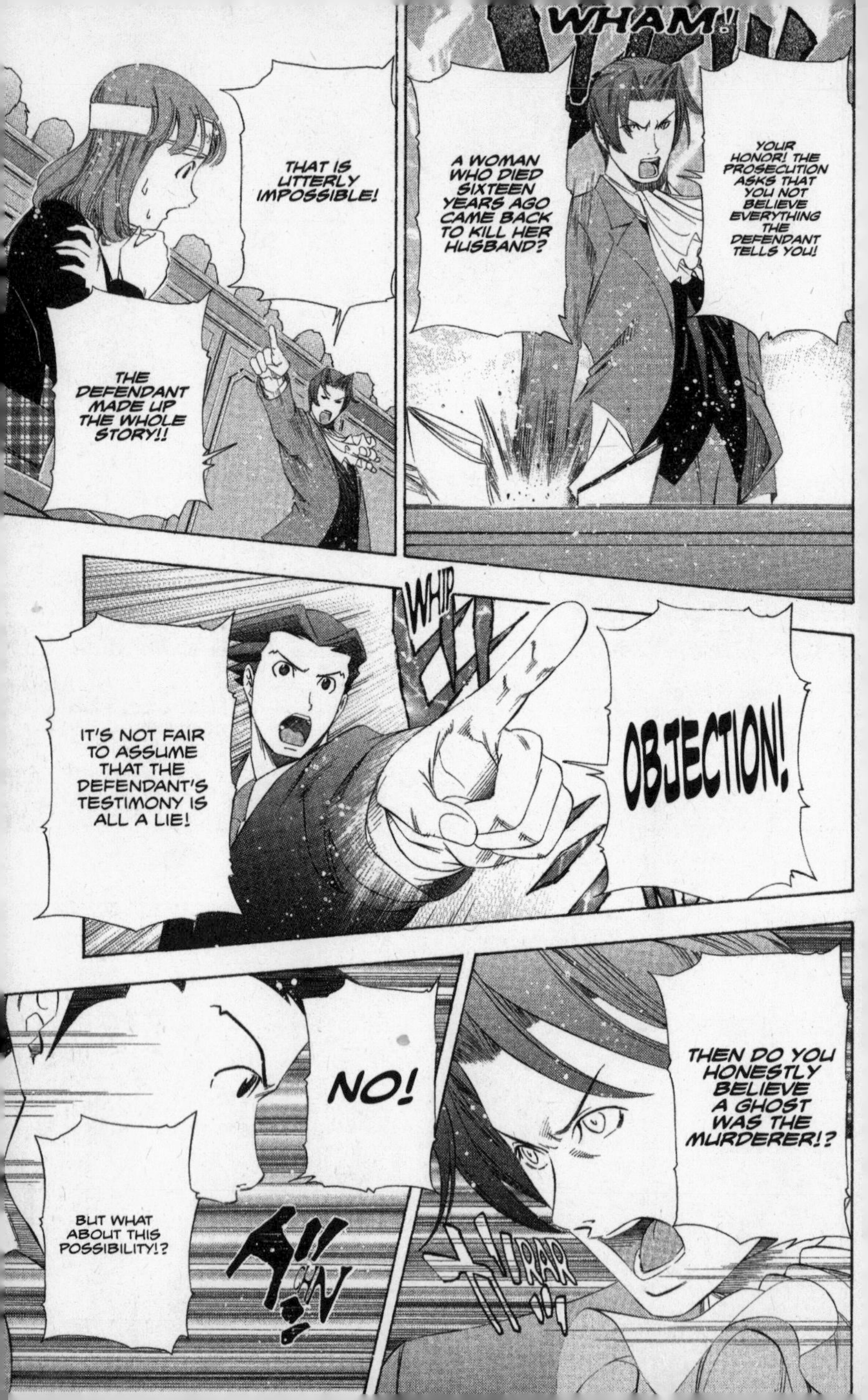
WHAM!
YOUR HONOR! THE PROSECUTION ASKS THAT YOU NOT BELIEVE EVERYTHING THE DEFENDANT TELLS YOU!
A WOMAN WHO DIED SIXTEEN YEARS AGO CAME BACK TO KILL HER HUSBAND?
THAT IS UTTERLY IMPOSSIBLE!
THE DEFENDANT MADE UP THE WHOLE STORY!!
WHIP
OBJECTION!
IT'S NOT FAIR TO ASSUME THAT THE DEFENDANT'S TESTIMONY IS ALL A LIE!
THEN DO YOU HONESTLY BELIEVE A GHOST WAS THE MURDERER!?
NO!
BUT WHAT ABOUT THIS POSSIBILITY!?

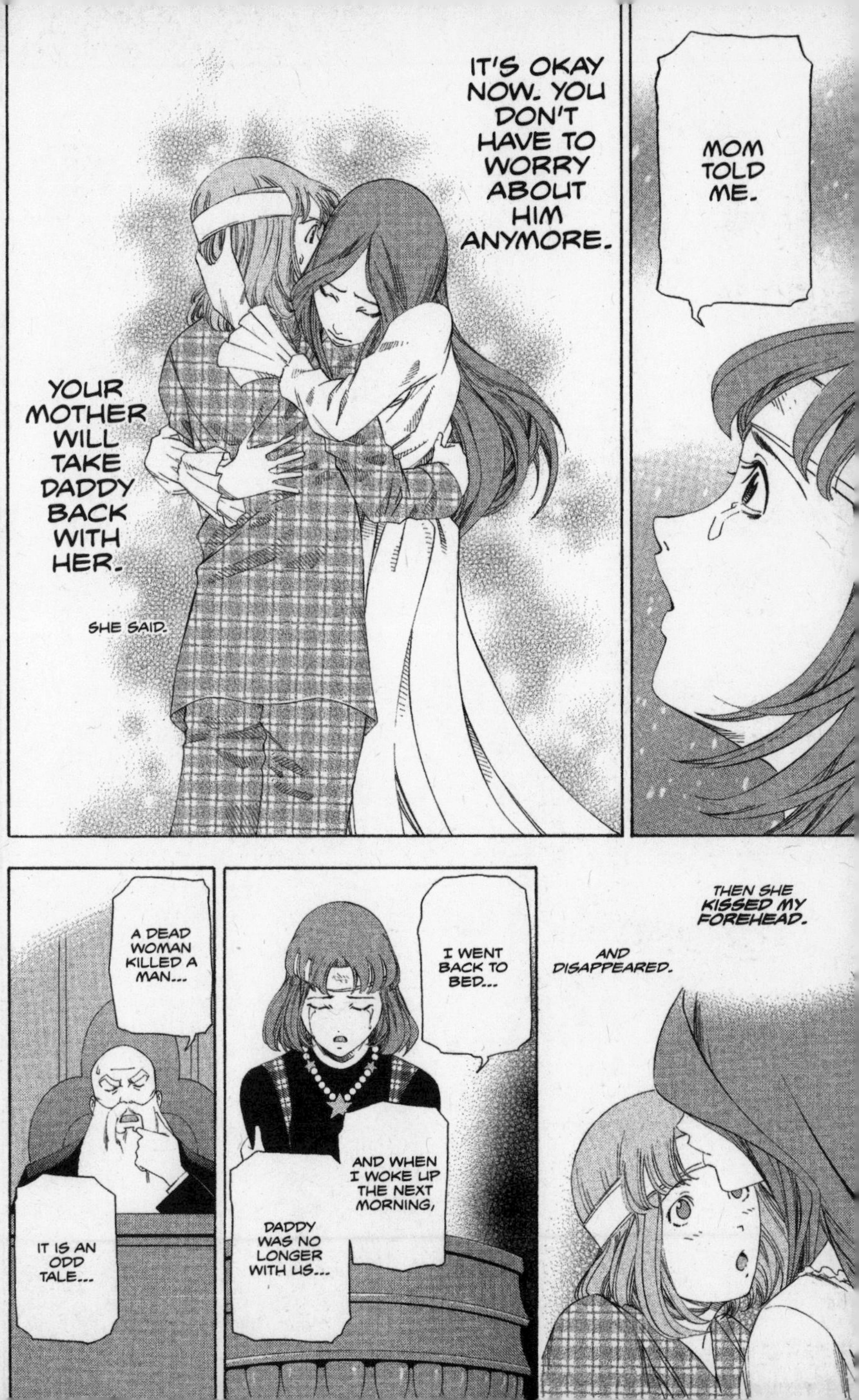
MOM TOLD ME.
IT'S OKAY NOW. YOU DON'T HAVE TO WORRY ABOUT HIM ANYMORE.
YOUR MOTHER WILL TAKE DADDY BACK WITH HER.
SHE SAID.
THEN SHE KISSED MY FOREHEAD.
AND DISAPPEARED.
I WENT BACK TO BED...
AND WHEN I WOKE UP THE NEXT MORNING,
DADDY WAS NO LONGER WITH US...
A DEAD WOMAN KILLED A MAN...
IT IS AN ODD TALE...

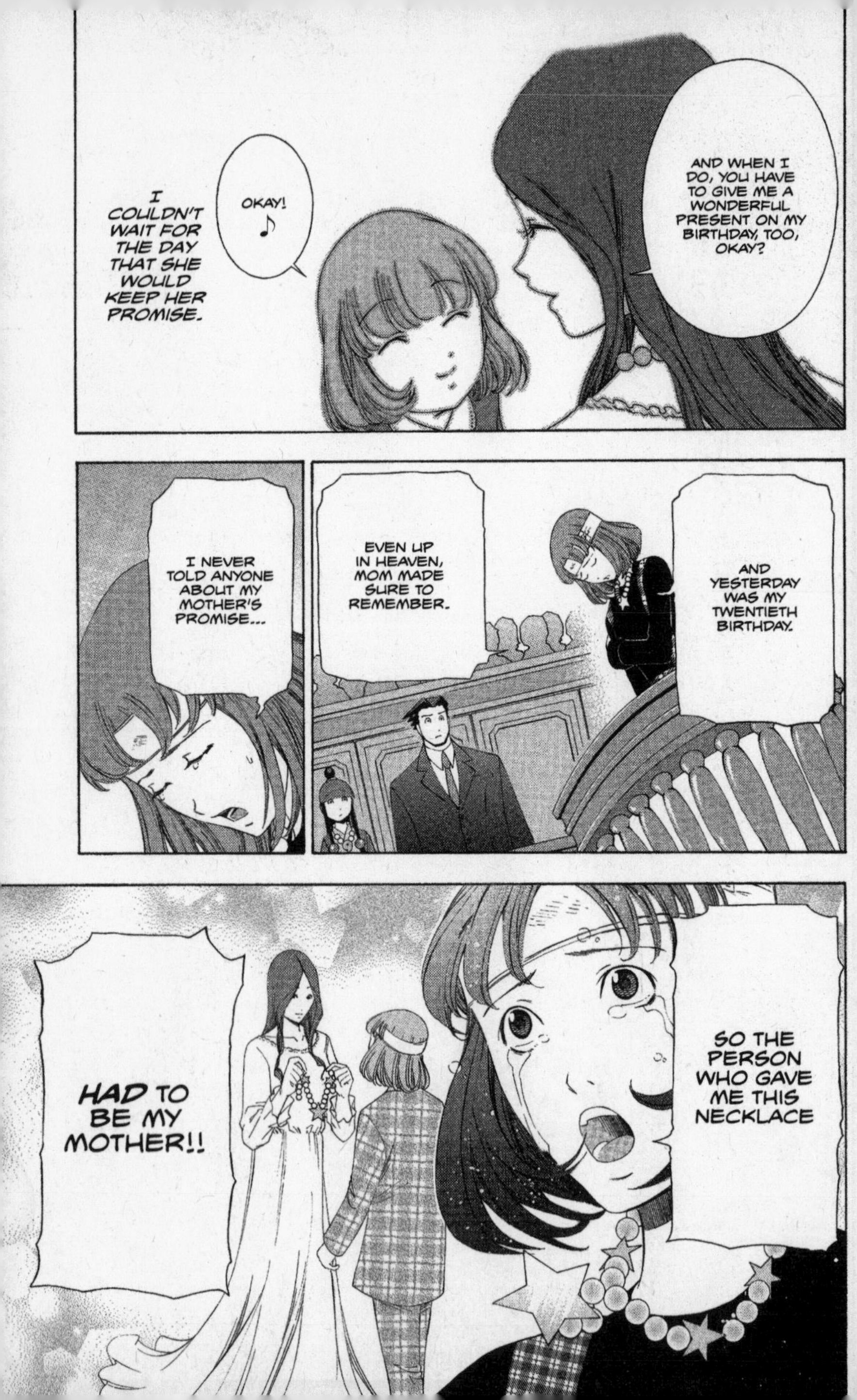
AND WHEN I DO, YOU HAVE TO GIVE ME A WONDERFUL PRESENT ON MY BIRTHDAY, TOO, OKAY?
OKAY! ♪
I COULDN'T WAIT FOR THE DAY THAT SHE WOULD KEEP HER PROMISE.
AND YESTERDAY WAS MY TWENTIETH BIRTHDAY.
EVEN UP IN HEAVEN, MOM MADE SURE TO REMEMBER.
I NEVER TOLD ANYONE ABOUT MY MOTHER'S PROMISE...
SO THE PERSON WHO GAVE ME THIS NECKLACE
HAD TO BE MY MOTHER!!

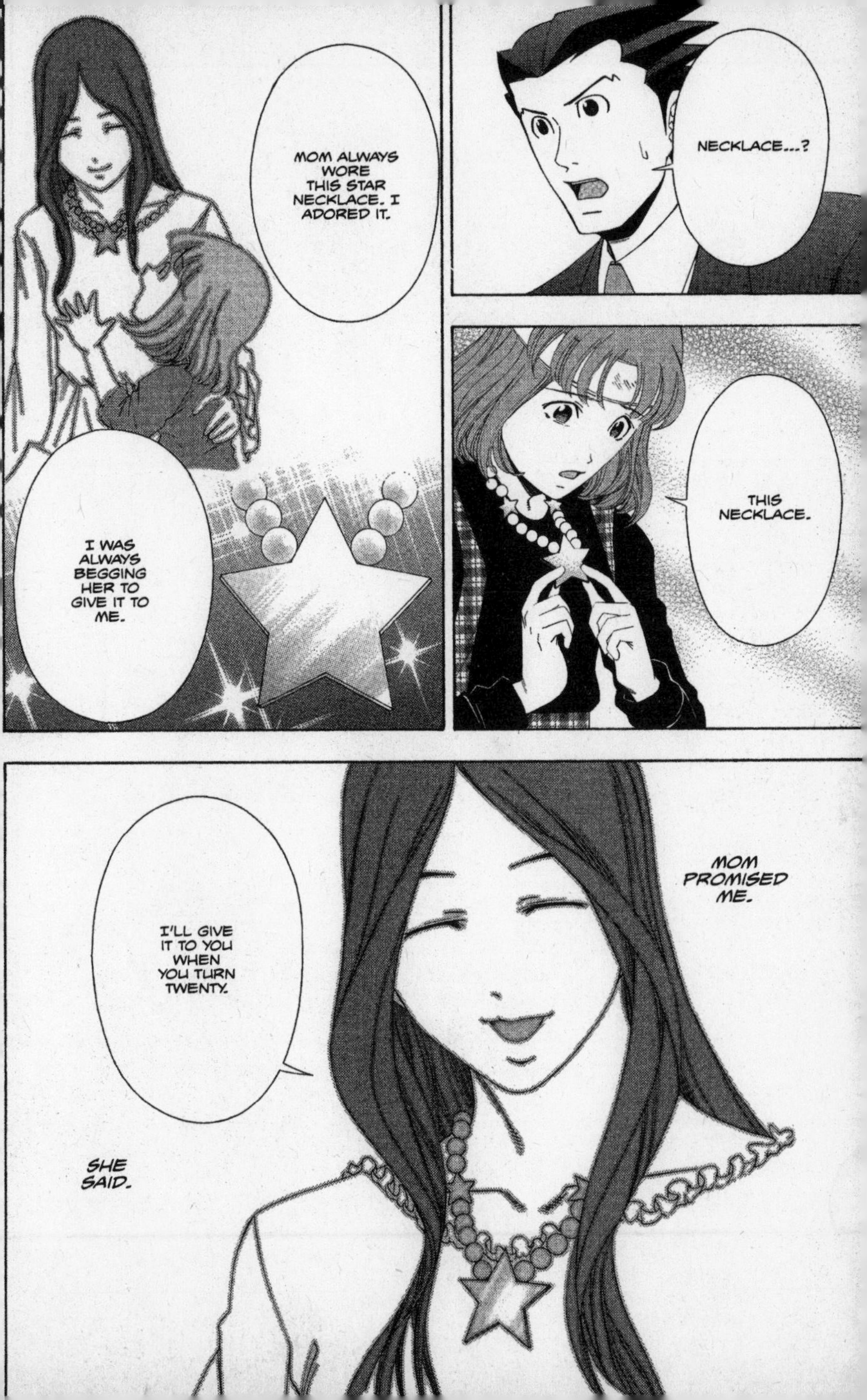
NECKLACE...?
THIS NECKLACE.
MOM ALWAYS WORE THIS STAR NECKLACE. I ADORED IT.
I WAS ALWAYS BEGGING HER TO GIVE IT TO ME.
MOM PROMISED ME.
I'LL GIVE IT TO YOU WHEN YOU TURN TWENTY.
SHE SAID.

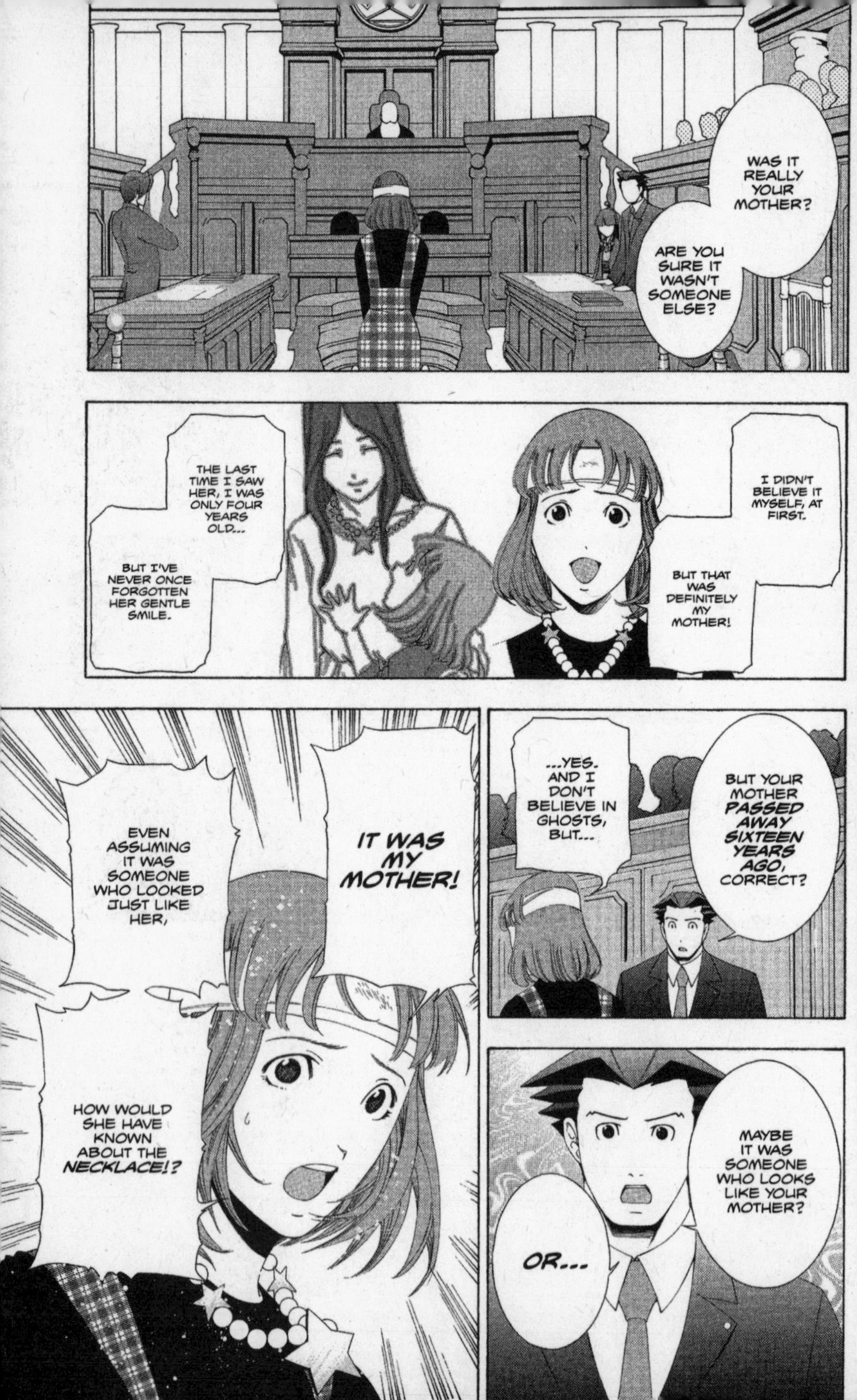

WAS IT REALLY YOUR MOTHER?
ARE YOU SURE IT WASN'T SOMEONE ELSE?
I DIDN'T BELIEVE IT MYSELF, AT FIRST.
BUT THAT WAS DEFINITELY MY MOTHER!
THE LAST TIME I SAW HER, I WAS ONLY FOUR YEARS OLD...
BUT I'VE NEVER ONCE FORGOTTEN HER GENTLE SMILE.
BUT YOUR MOTHER *PASSED AWAY SIXTEEN YEARS AGO*, CORRECT?
...YES. AND I DON'T BELIEVE IN GHOSTS, BUT...
MAYBE IT WAS SOMEONE WHO LOOKS LIKE YOUR MOTHER?
OR...
IT WAS MY MOTHER!
EVEN ASSUMING IT WAS SOMEONE WHO LOOKED JUST LIKE HER,
HOW WOULD SHE HAVE KNOWN ABOUT THE *NECKLACE!?*

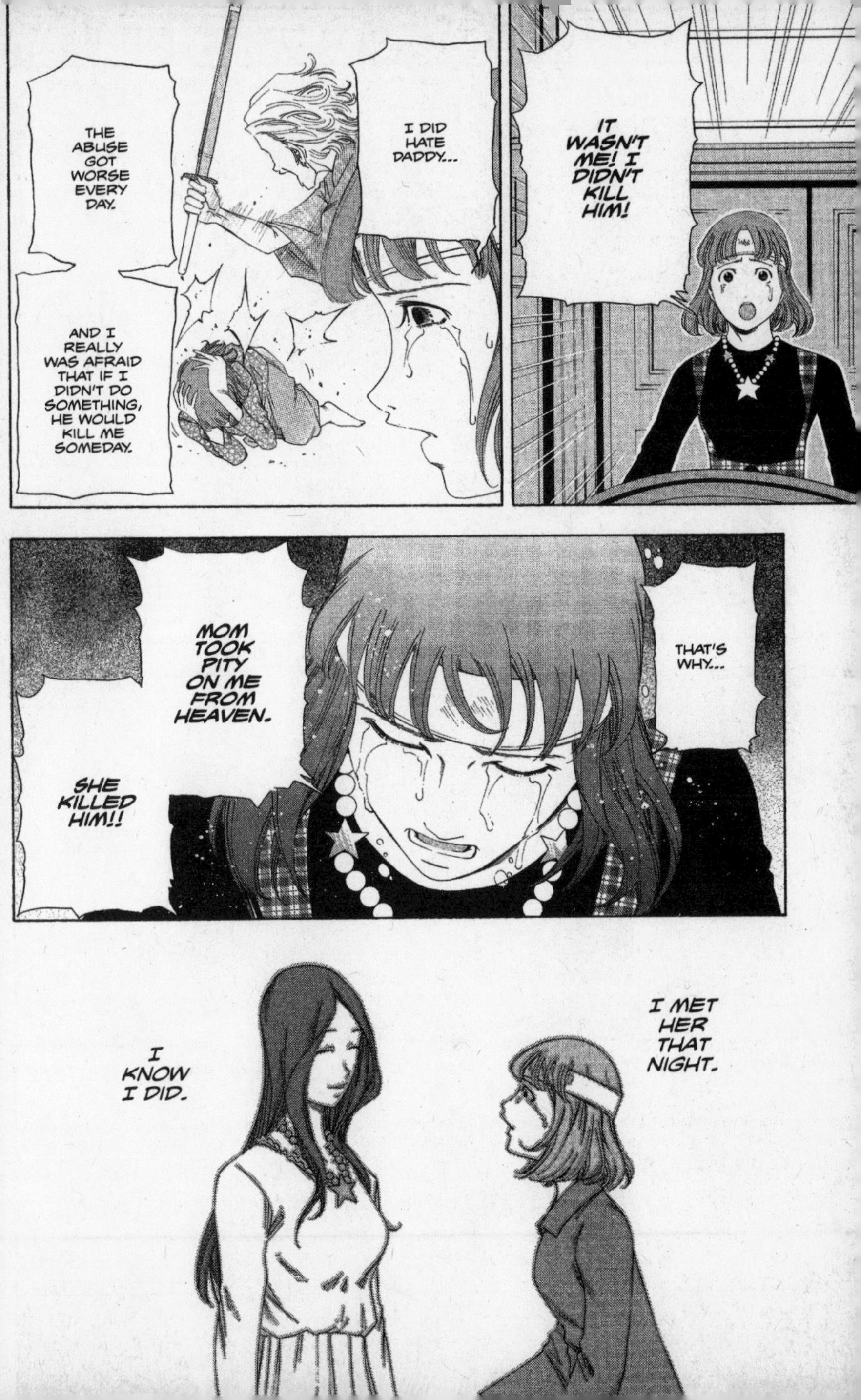
IT WASN'T ME! I DIDN'T KILL HIM!
I DID HATE DADDY...
THE ABUSE GOT WORSE EVERY DAY.
AND I REALLY WAS AFRAID THAT IF I DIDN'T DO SOMETHING, HE WOULD KILL ME SOMEDAY.
THAT'S WHY...
MOM TOOK PITY ON ME FROM HEAVEN.
SHE KILLED HIM!!
I MET HER THAT NIGHT.
I KNOW I DID.

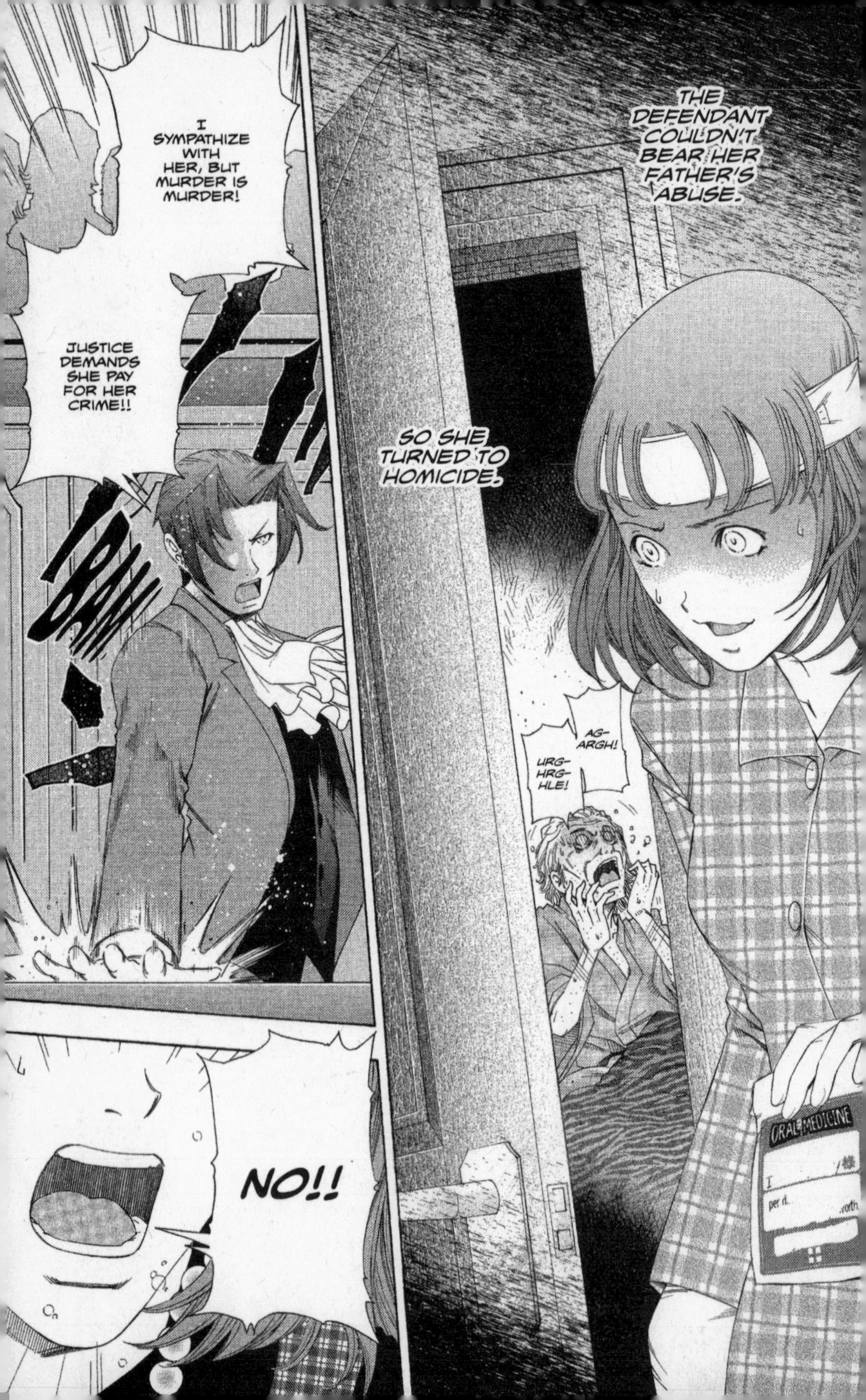
THE DEFENDANT COULDN'T BEAR HER FATHER'S ABUSE.
SO SHE TURNED TO HOMICIDE.
AG-ARGH!
URG-HRG-HLE!
ORAL MEDICINE
I SYMPATHIZE WITH HER, BUT MURDER IS MURDER!
JUSTICE DEMANDS SHE PAY FOR HER CRIME!!
BAM
NO!!

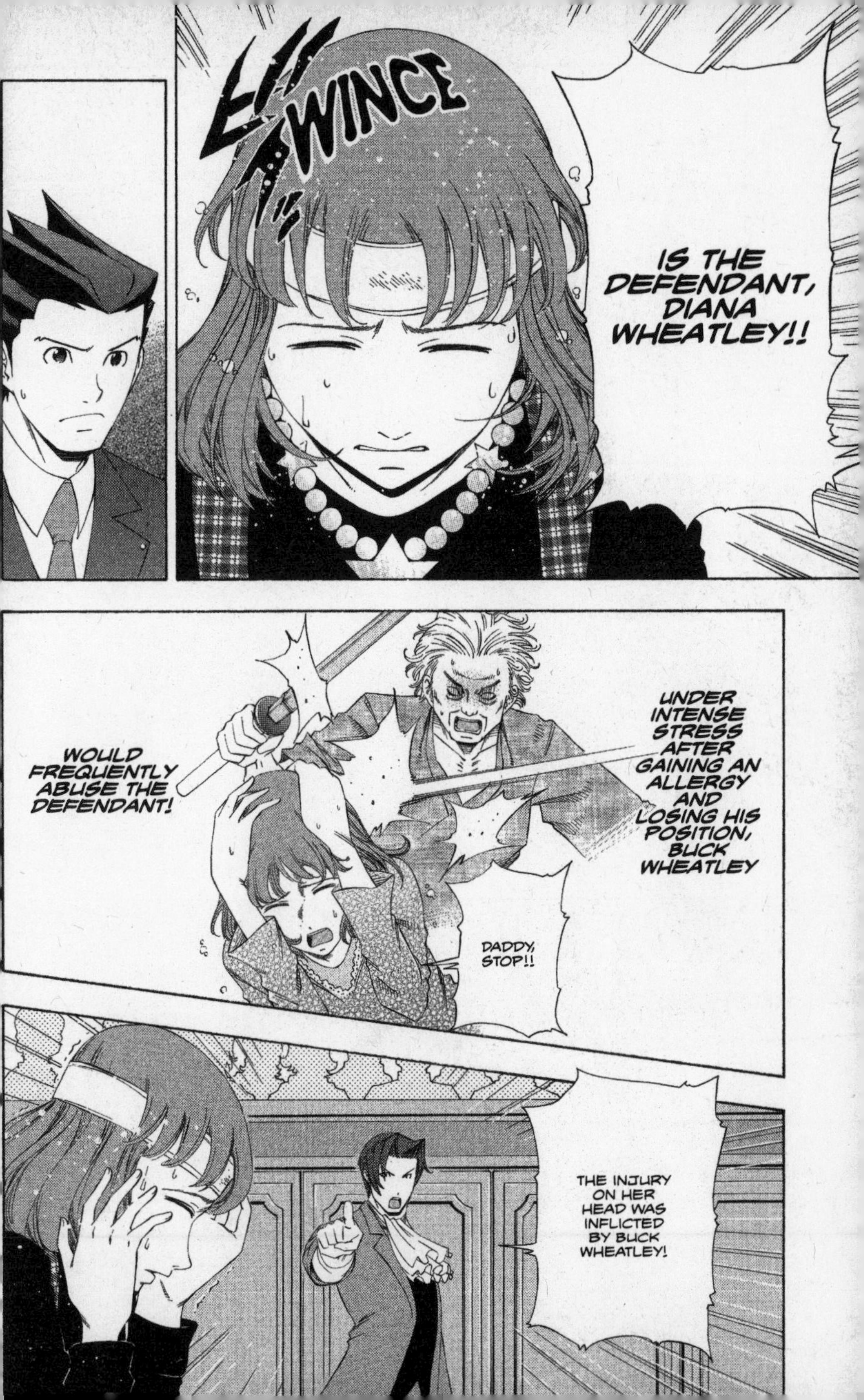
IS THE DEFENDANT, DIANA WHEATLEY!!
WINCE
UNDER INTENSE STRESS AFTER GAINING AN ALLERGY AND LOSING HIS POSITION, BUCK WHEATLEY
WOULD FREQUENTLY ABUSE THE DEFENDANT!
DADDY, STOP!!
THE INJURY ON HER HEAD WAS INFLICTED BY BUCK WHEATLEY!

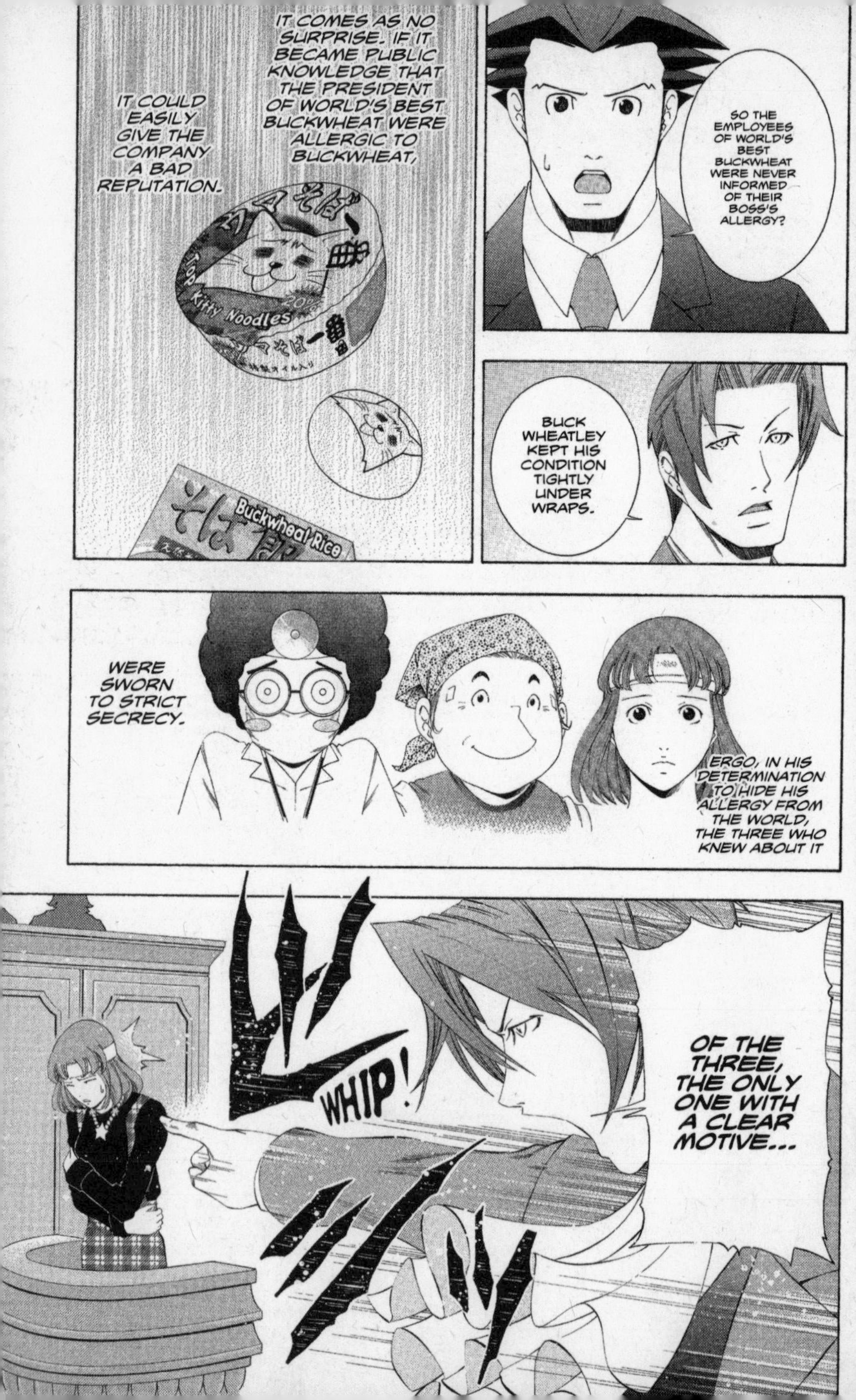
SO THE EMPLOYEES OF WORLD'S BEST BUCKWHEAT WERE NEVER INFORMED OF THEIR BOSS'S ALLERGY?
BUCK WHEATLEY KEPT HIS CONDITION TIGHTLY UNDER WRAPS.
IT COMES AS NO SURPRISE. IF IT BECAME PUBLIC KNOWLEDGE THAT THE PRESIDENT OF WORLD'S BEST BUCKWHEAT WERE ALLERGIC TO BUCKWHEAT,
IT COULD EASILY GIVE THE COMPANY A BAD REPUTATION.
Top Kitty Noodles
Buckwheat Rice
ERGO, IN HIS DETERMINATION TO HIDE HIS ALLERGY FROM THE WORLD, THE THREE WHO KNEW ABOUT IT
WERE SWORN TO STRICT SECRECY.
OF THE THREE, THE ONLY ONE WITH A CLEAR MOTIVE...
WHIP!

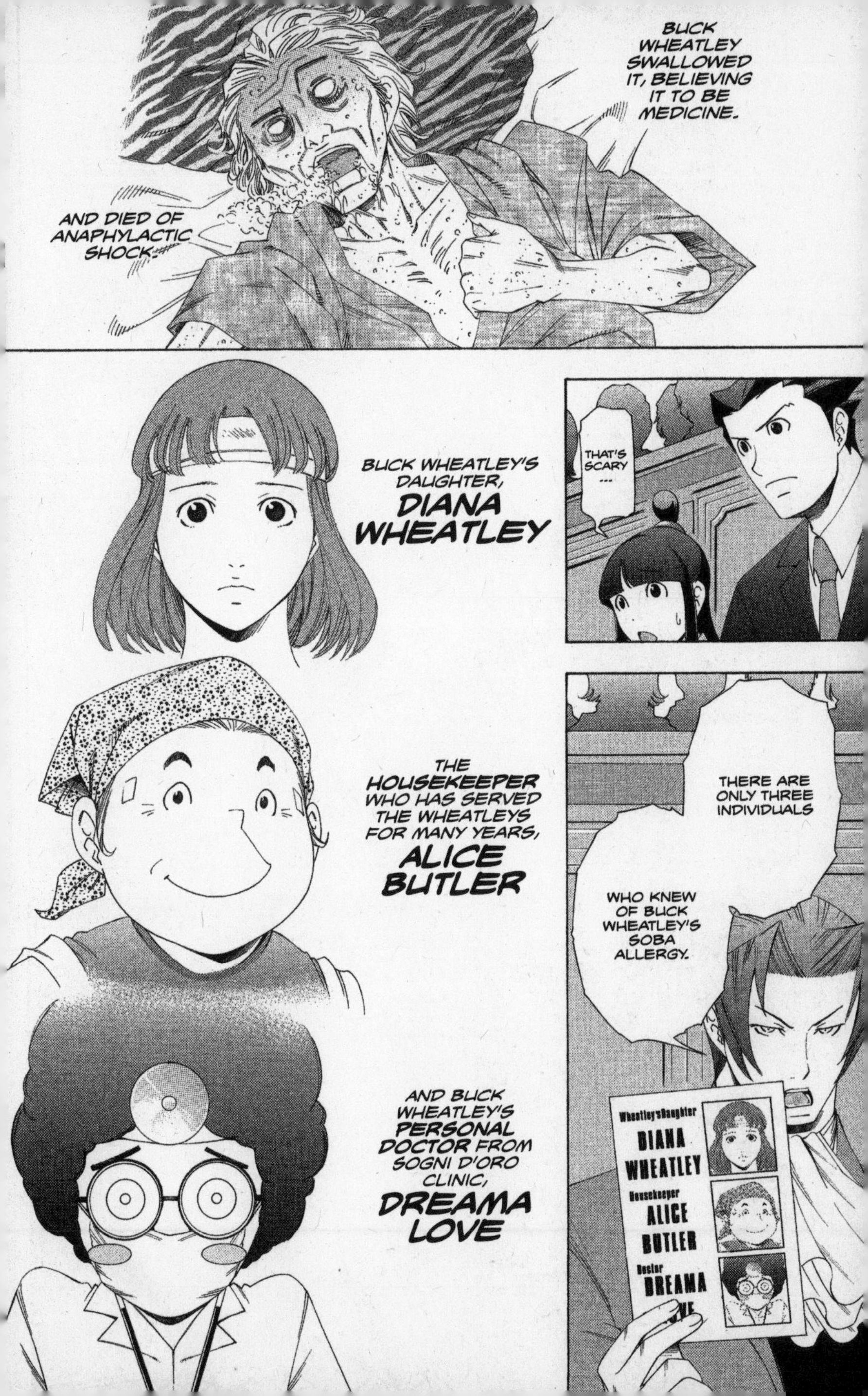
BUCK WHEATLEY SWALLOWED IT, BELIEVING IT TO BE MEDICINE.
AND DIED OF ANAPHYLACTIC SHOCK.
THAT'S SCARY ---
THERE ARE ONLY THREE INDIVIDUALS
WHO KNEW OF BUCK WHEATLEY'S SOBA ALLERGY.
Wheatley's Daughter
DIANA WHEATLEY
Housekeeper
ALICE BUTLER
Doctor
DREAMA
BUCK WHEATLEY'S DAUGHTER, DIANA WHEATLEY
THE HOUSEKEEPER WHO HAS SERVED THE WHEATLEYS FOR MANY YEARS, ALICE BUTLER
AND BUCK WHEATLEY'S PERSONAL DOCTOR FROM SOGNI D'ORO CLINIC, DREAMA LOVE

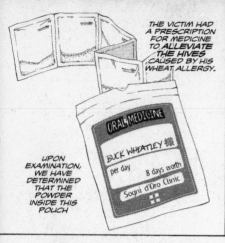

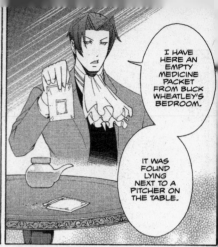

I HAVE HERE AN EMPTY MEDICINE PACKET FROM BUCK WHEATLEY'S BEDROOM.
IT WAS FOUND LYING NEXT TO A PITCHER ON THE TABLE.
THE VICTIM HAD A PRESCRIPTION FOR MEDICINE TO ALLEVIATE THE HIVES CAUSED BY HIS WHEAT ALLERGY.
ORAL MEDICINE
BUCK WHEATLEY 様
per day
8 days worth
Sogni d'Oro Clinic
UPON EXAMINATION, WE HAVE DETERMINED THAT THE POWDER INSIDE THIS POUCH
WAS NOT MEDICINE.
IT WAS BUCKWHEAT FLOUR.
WE'RE STILL WAITING FOR LAB RESULTS ON THE CONTENTS OF THE UNOPENED POUCHES.
BUT THE POWDER'S COLOR AND SHAPE DIFFER FROM THAT OF THE MEDICINE, SO IT IS SAFE TO ASSUME THAT THE REMAINING POUCHES ALL CONTAIN BUCKWHEAT FLOUR.
CUT ALONG LINE
NO DOUBT SOMEONE...
TRADED THE MEDICINE FOR FLOUR!!

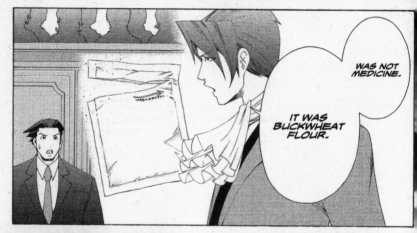

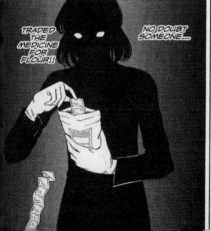

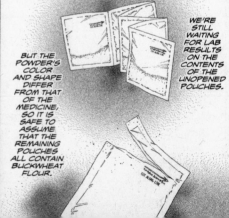

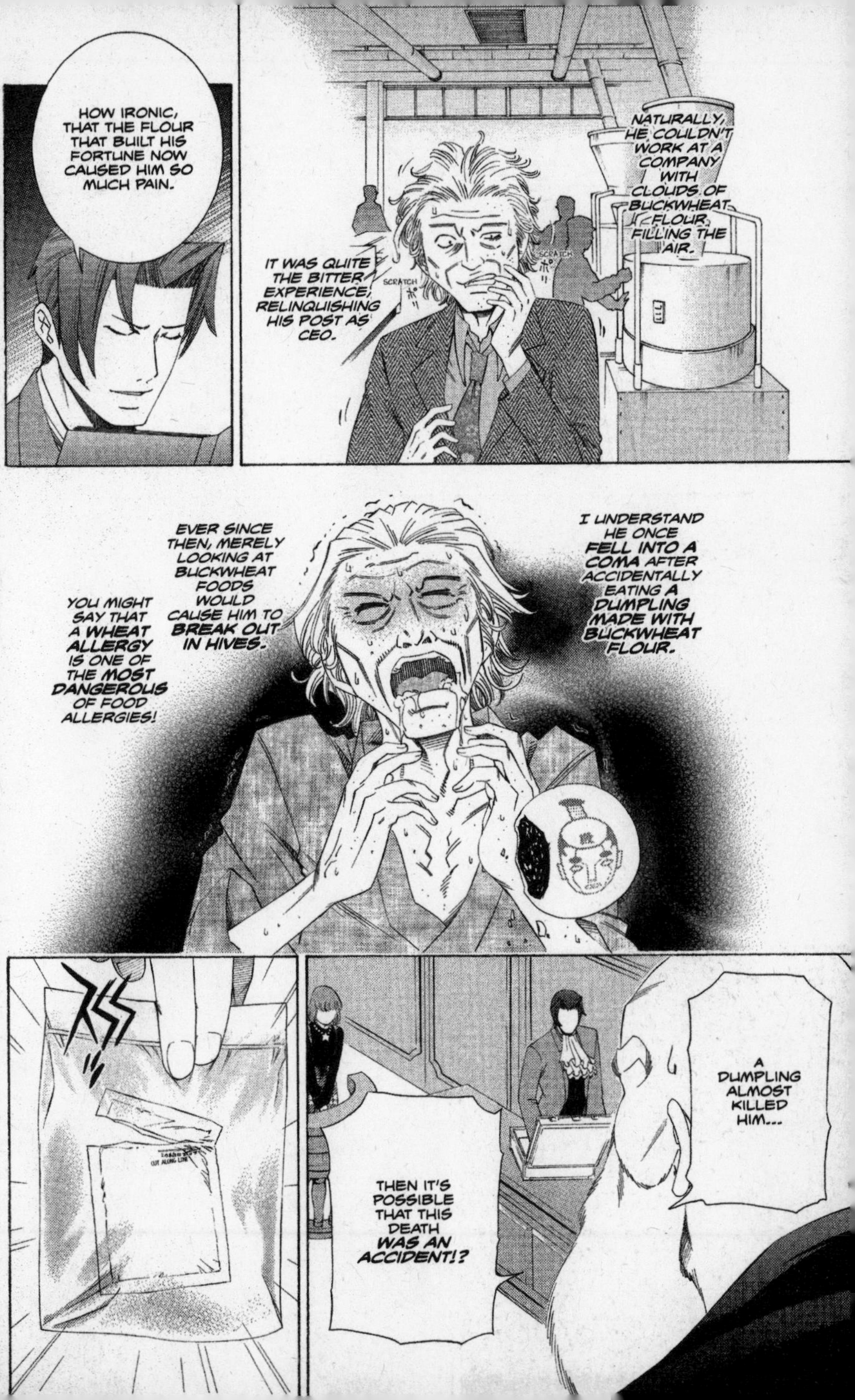
NATURALLY, HE COULDN'T WORK AT A COMPANY WITH CLOUDS OF BUCKWHEAT FLOUR FILLING THE AIR.
SCRATCH
IT WAS QUITE THE BITTER EXPERIENCE, RELINQUISHING HIS POST AS CEO.
SCRATCH
HOW IRONIC, THAT THE FLOUR THAT BUILT HIS FORTUNE NOW CAUSED HIM SO MUCH PAIN.
I UNDERSTAND HE ONCE FELL INTO A COMA AFTER ACCIDENTALLY EATING A DUMPLING MADE WITH BUCKWHEAT FLOUR.
EVER SINCE THEN, MERELY LOOKING AT BUCKWHEAT FOODS WOULD CAUSE HIM TO BREAK OUT IN HIVES.
YOU MIGHT SAY THAT A WHEAT ALLERGY IS ONE OF THE MOST DANGEROUS OF FOOD ALLERGIES!
A DUMPLING ALMOST KILLED HIM...
THEN IT'S POSSIBLE THAT THIS DEATH WAS AN ACCIDENT!?
RSS
CUT ALONG LINE

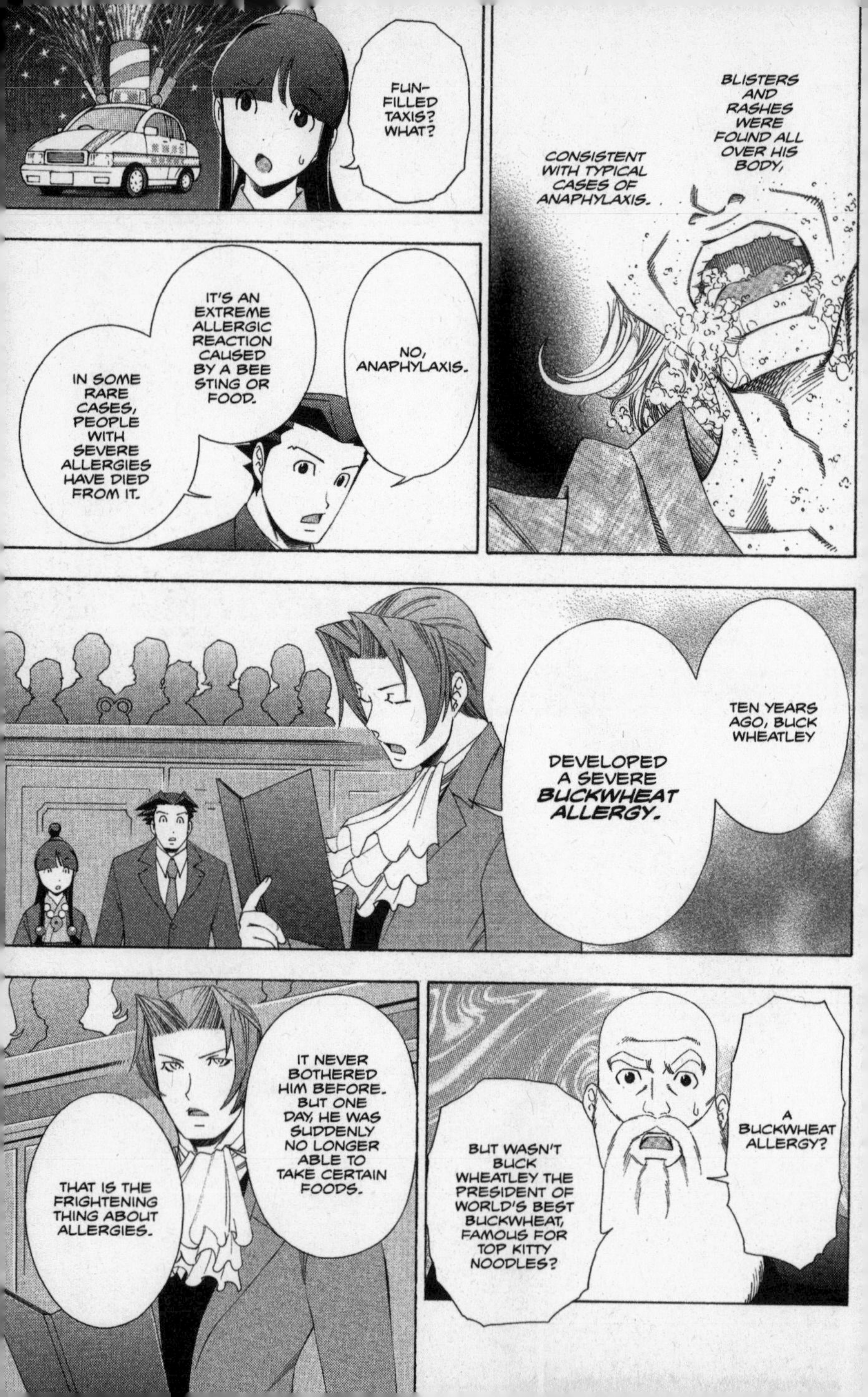
BLISTERS AND RASHES WERE FOUND ALL OVER HIS BODY,
CONSISTENT WITH TYPICAL CASES OF ANAPHYLAXIS.
FUN-FILLED TAXIS? WHAT?
NO, ANAPHYLAXIS.
IT'S AN EXTREME ALLERGIC REACTION CAUSED BY A BEE STING OR FOOD.
IN SOME RARE CASES, PEOPLE WITH SEVERE ALLERGIES HAVE DIED FROM IT.
TEN YEARS AGO, BUCK WHEATLEY
DEVELOPED A SEVERE BUCKWHEAT ALLERGY.
A BUCKWHEAT ALLERGY?
BUT WASN'T BUCK WHEATLEY THE PRESIDENT OF WORLD'S BEST BUCKWHEAT, FAMOUS FOR TOP KITTY NOODLES?
IT NEVER BOTHERED HIM BEFORE. BUT ONE DAY, HE WAS SUDDENLY NO LONGER ABLE TO TAKE CERTAIN FOODS.
THAT IS THE FRIGHTENING THING ABOUT ALLERGIES.

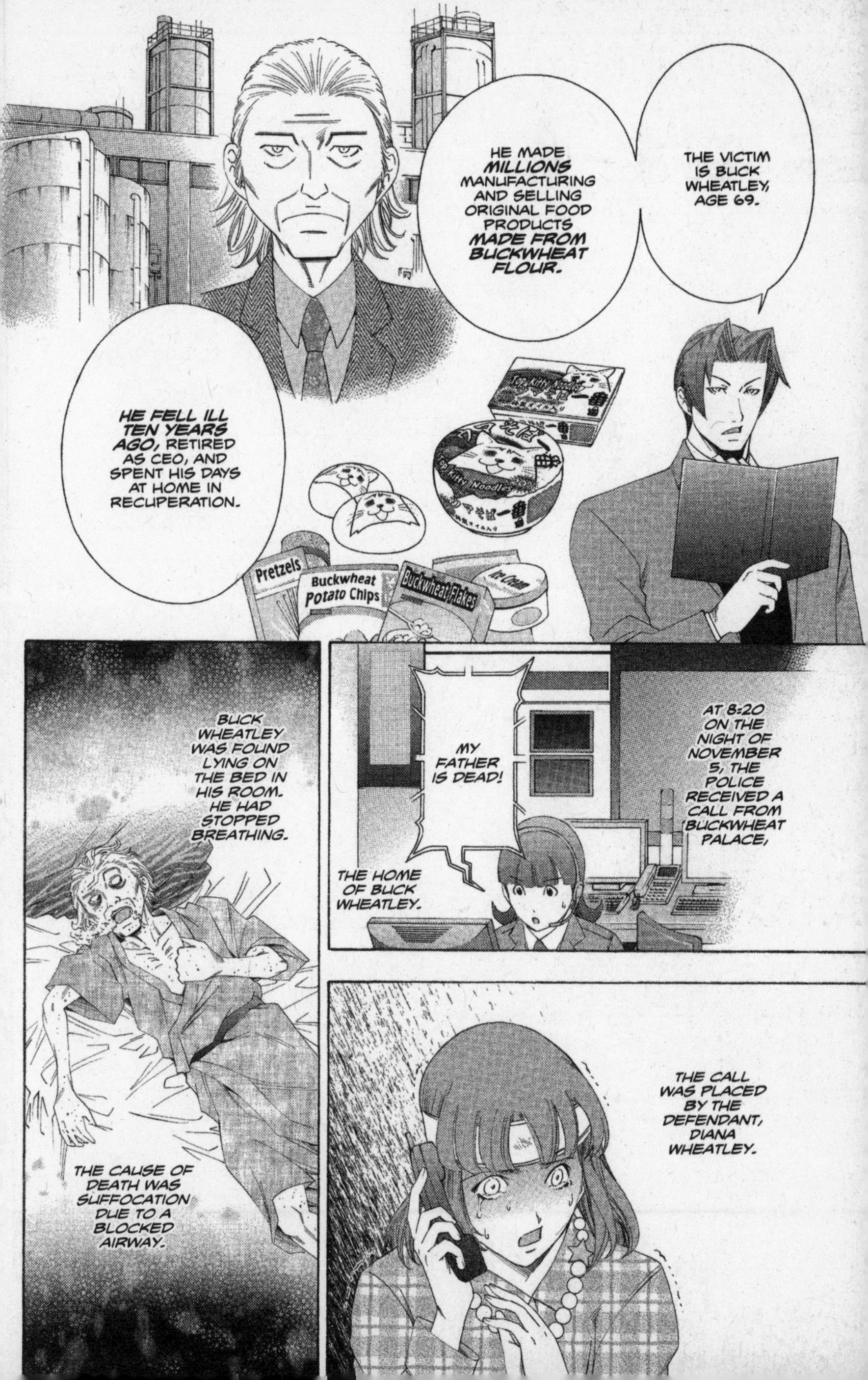
THE VICTIM IS BUCK WHEATLEY, AGE 69.
HE MADE **MILLIONS** MANUFACTURING AND SELLING ORIGINAL FOOD PRODUCTS **MADE FROM BUCKWHEAT FLOUR.**
Top Kitty Noodles
Top Kitty Noodles
HE FELL ILL TEN YEARS AGO, RETIRED AS CEO, AND SPENT HIS DAYS AT HOME IN RECUPERATION.
Ice Cream
Buckwheat Flakes
Buckwheat Potato Chips
Pretzels
AT 8:20 ON THE NIGHT OF NOVEMBER 5, THE POLICE RECEIVED A CALL FROM BUCKWHEAT PALACE,
MY FATHER IS DEAD!
THE HOME OF BUCK WHEATLEY.
THE CALL WAS PLACED BY THE DEFENDANT, DIANA WHEATLEY.
BUCK WHEATLEY WAS FOUND LYING ON THE BED IN HIS ROOM. HE HAD STOPPED BREATHING.
THE CAUSE OF DEATH WAS SUFFOCATION DUE TO A BLOCKED AIRWAY.

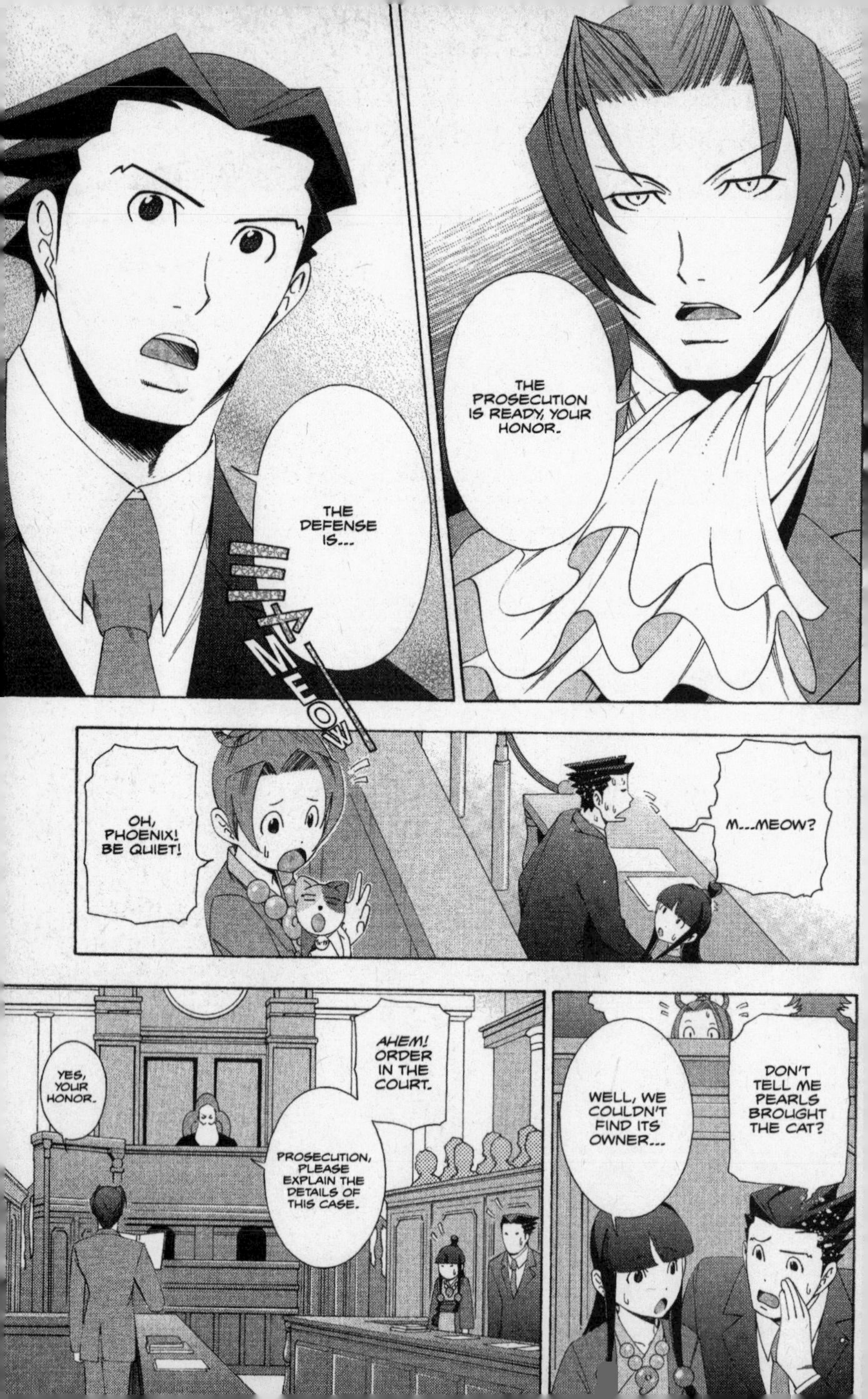
THE PROSECUTION IS READY, YOUR HONOR.
THE DEFENSE IS...
MEOW
M...MEOW?
OH, PHOENIX! BE QUIET!
DON'T TELL ME PEARLS BROUGHT THE CAT?
WELL, WE COULDN'T FIND ITS OWNER...
AHEM! ORDER IN THE COURT.
PROSECUTION, PLEASE EXPLAIN THE DETAILS OF THIS CASE.
YES, YOUR HONOR.

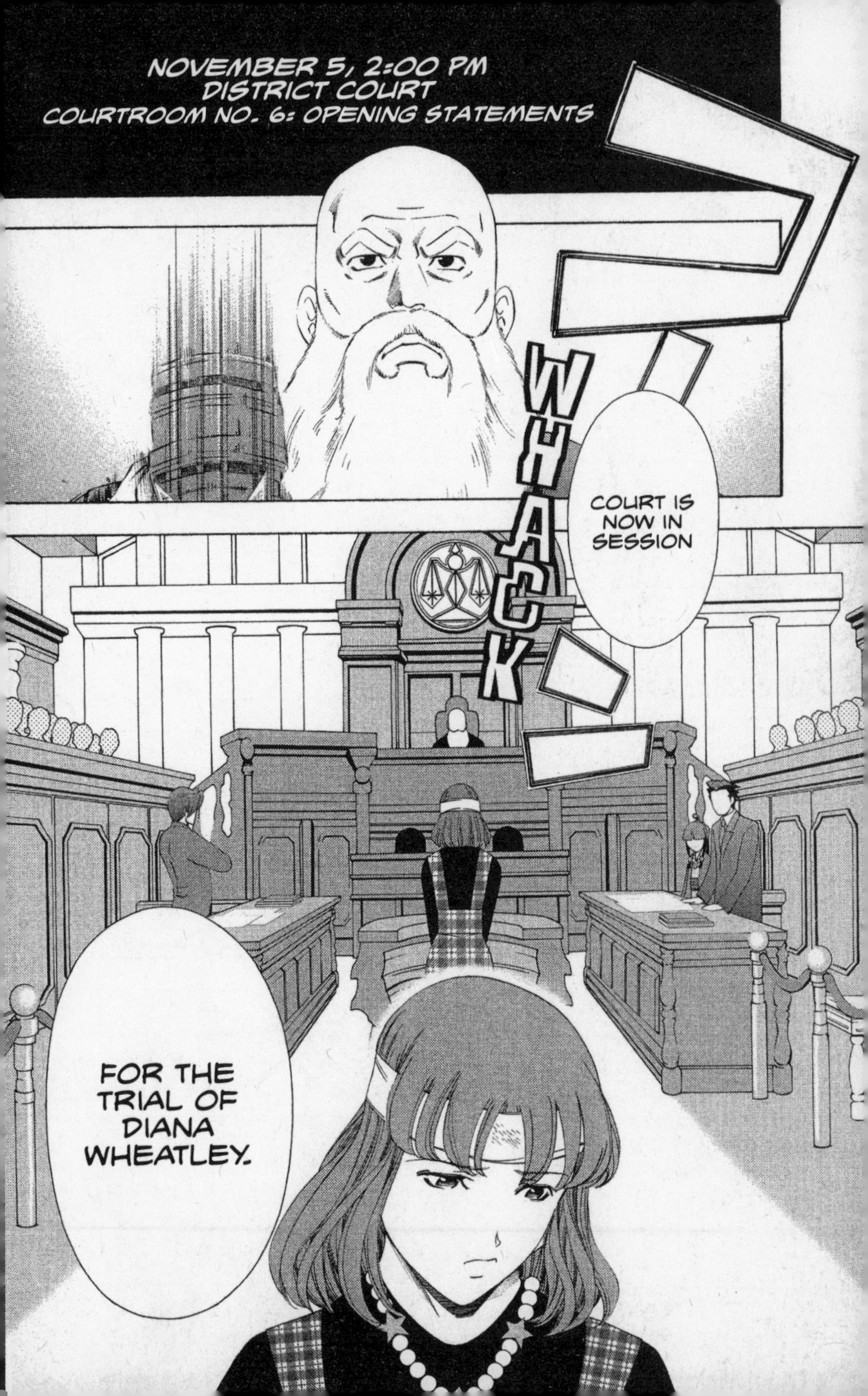
NOVEMBER 5, 2:00 PM
DISTRICT COURT
COURTROOM NO. 6: OPENING STATEMENTS
WHACK
COURT IS NOW IN SESSION
FOR THE TRIAL OF DIANA WHEATLEY.

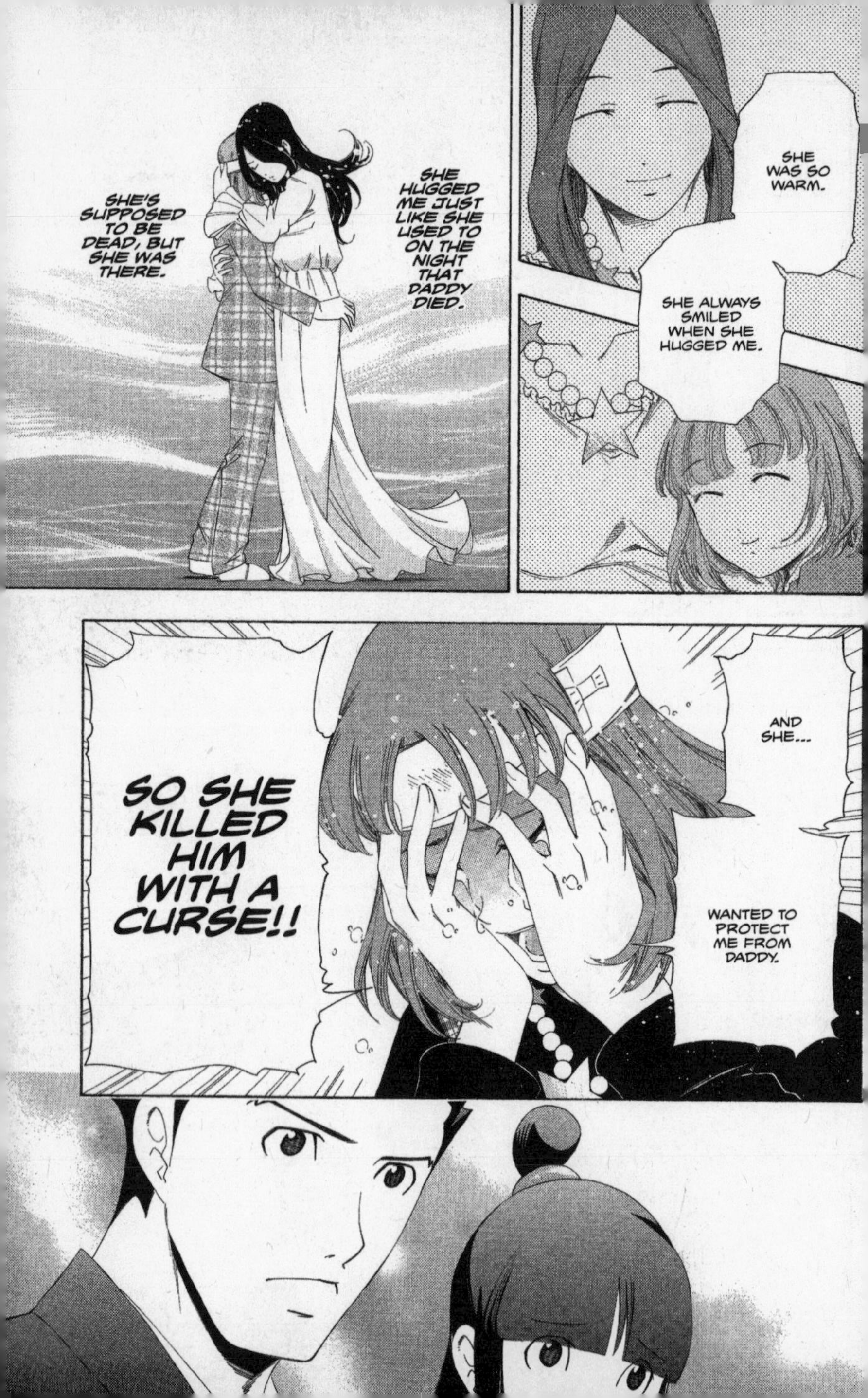
SHE WAS SO WARM.
SHE ALWAYS SMILED WHEN SHE HUGGED ME.
SHE HUGGED ME JUST LIKE SHE USED TO ON THE NIGHT THAT DADDY DIED.
SHE'S SUPPOSED TO BE DEAD, BUT SHE WAS THERE.
AND SHE...
WANTED TO PROTECT ME FROM DADDY.
SO SHE KILLED HIM WITH A CURSE!!

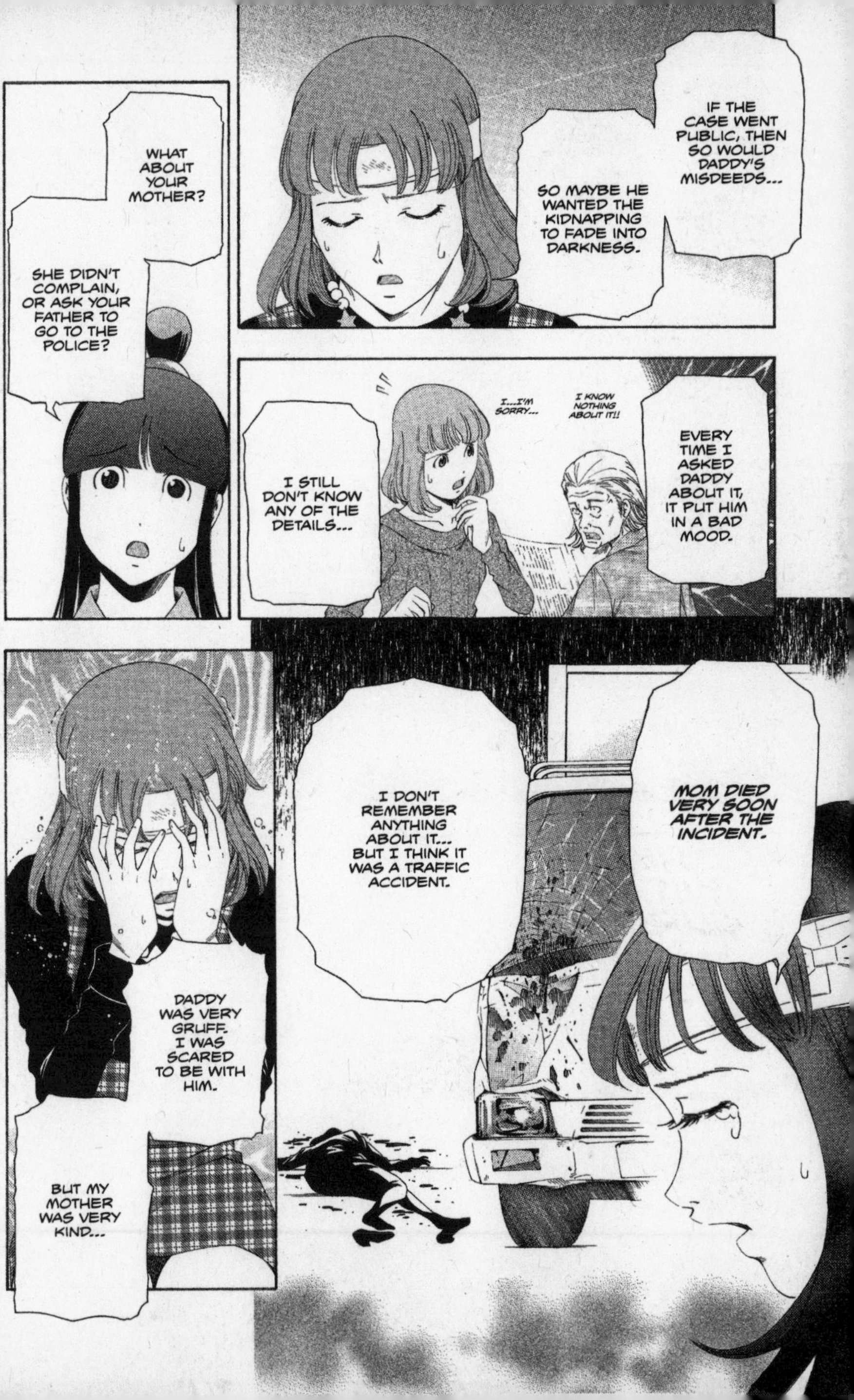
IF THE CASE WENT PUBLIC, THEN SO WOULD DADDY'S MISDEEDS...
SO MAYBE HE WANTED THE KIDNAPPING TO FADE INTO DARKNESS.
EVERY TIME I ASKED DADDY ABOUT IT, IT PUT HIM IN A BAD MOOD.
I KNOW NOTHING ABOUT IT!!
I...I'M SORRY...
I STILL DON'T KNOW ANY OF THE DETAILS...
WHAT ABOUT YOUR MOTHER?
SHE DIDN'T COMPLAIN, OR ASK YOUR FATHER TO GO TO THE POLICE?
MOM DIED VERY SOON AFTER THE INCIDENT.
I DON'T REMEMBER ANYTHING ABOUT IT... BUT I THINK IT WAS A TRAFFIC ACCIDENT.
DADDY WAS VERY GRUFF. I WAS SCARED TO BE WITH HIM.
BUT MY MOTHER WAS VERY KIND...

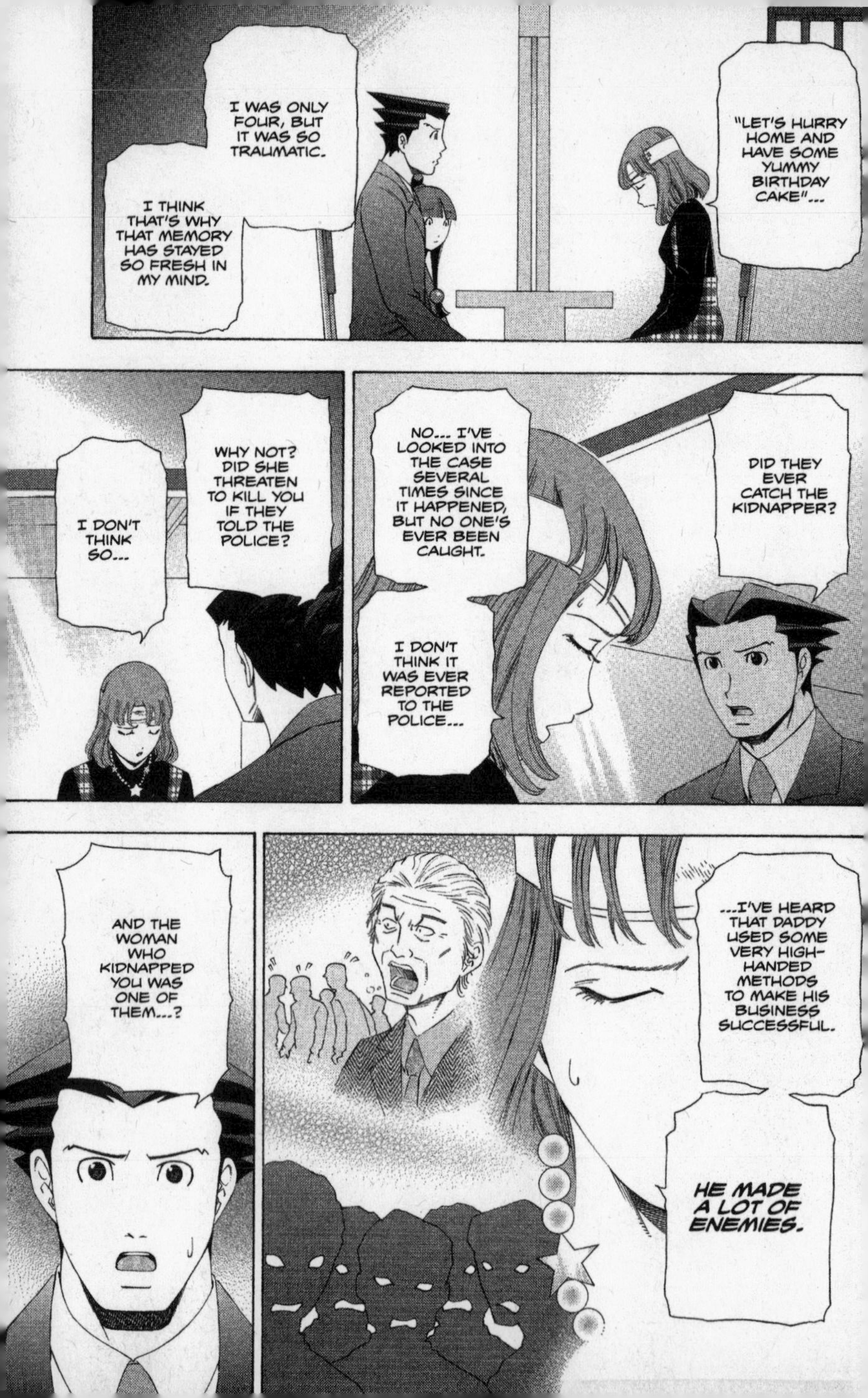
"LET'S HURRY HOME AND HAVE SOME YUMMY BIRTHDAY CAKE"...
I WAS ONLY FOUR, BUT IT WAS SO TRAUMATIC.
I THINK THAT'S WHY THAT MEMORY HAS STAYED SO FRESH IN MY MIND.
DID THEY EVER CATCH THE KIDNAPPER?
NO... I'VE LOOKED INTO THE CASE SEVERAL TIMES SINCE IT HAPPENED, BUT NO ONE'S EVER BEEN CAUGHT.
I DON'T THINK IT WAS EVER REPORTED TO THE POLICE...
WHY NOT? DID SHE THREATEN TO KILL YOU IF THEY TOLD THE POLICE?
I DON'T THINK SO...
...I'VE HEARD THAT DADDY USED SOME VERY HIGH-HANDED METHODS TO MAKE HIS BUSINESS SUCCESSFUL.
HE MADE A LOT OF ENEMIES.
AND THE WOMAN WHO KIDNAPPED YOU WAS ONE OF THEM...?

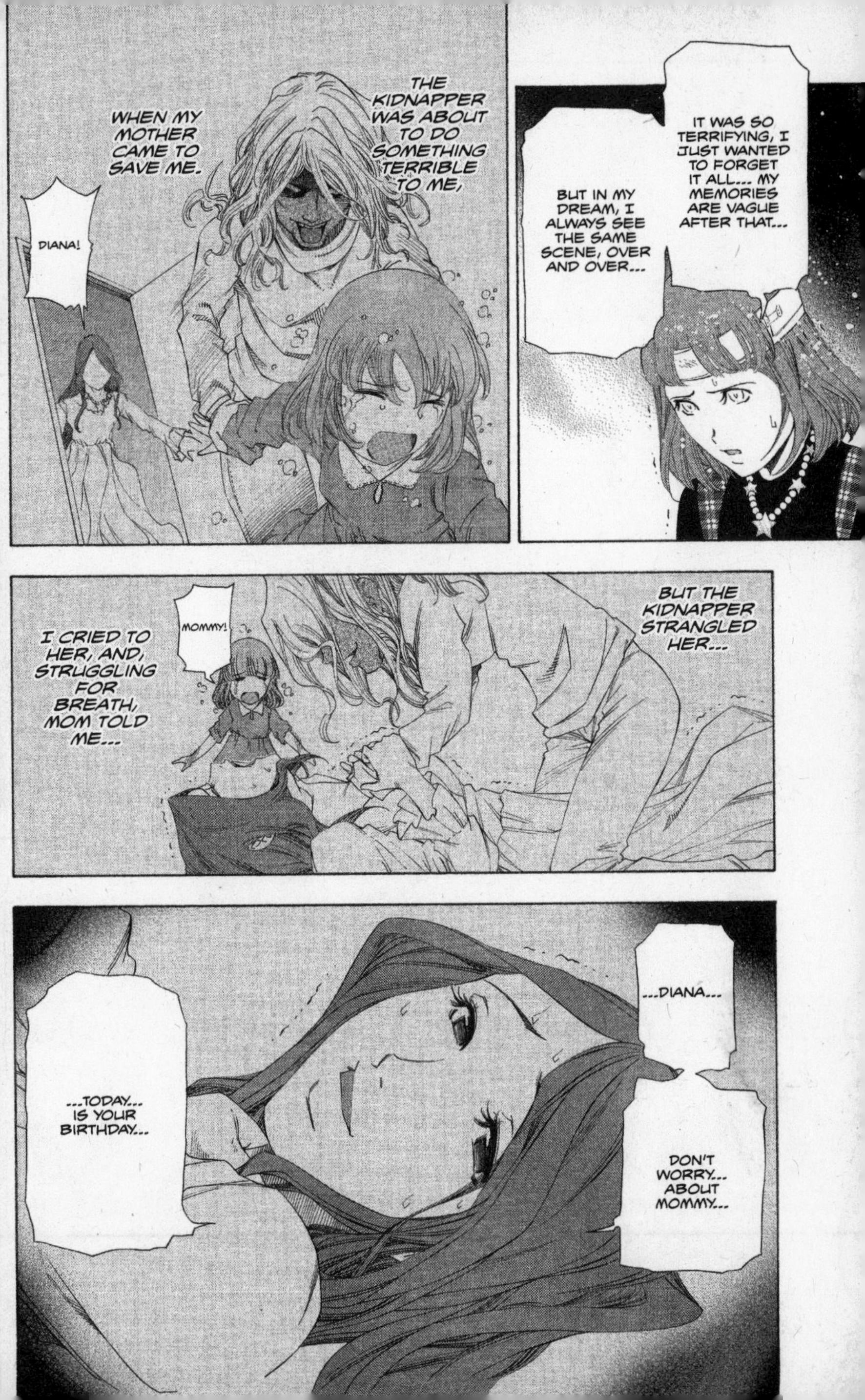
IT WAS SO TERRIFYING, I JUST WANTED TO FORGET IT ALL... MY MEMORIES ARE VAGUE AFTER THAT...
BUT IN MY DREAM, I ALWAYS SEE THE SAME SCENE, OVER AND OVER...
THE KIDNAPPER WAS ABOUT TO DO SOMETHING TERRIBLE TO ME,
WHEN MY MOTHER CAME TO SAVE ME.
DIANA!
BUT THE KIDNAPPER STRANGLED HER...
MOMMY!
I CRIED TO HER, AND, STRUGGLING FOR BREATH, MOM TOLD ME...
...DIANA...
DON'T WORRY... ABOUT MOMMY...
...TODAY... IS YOUR BIRTHDAY...

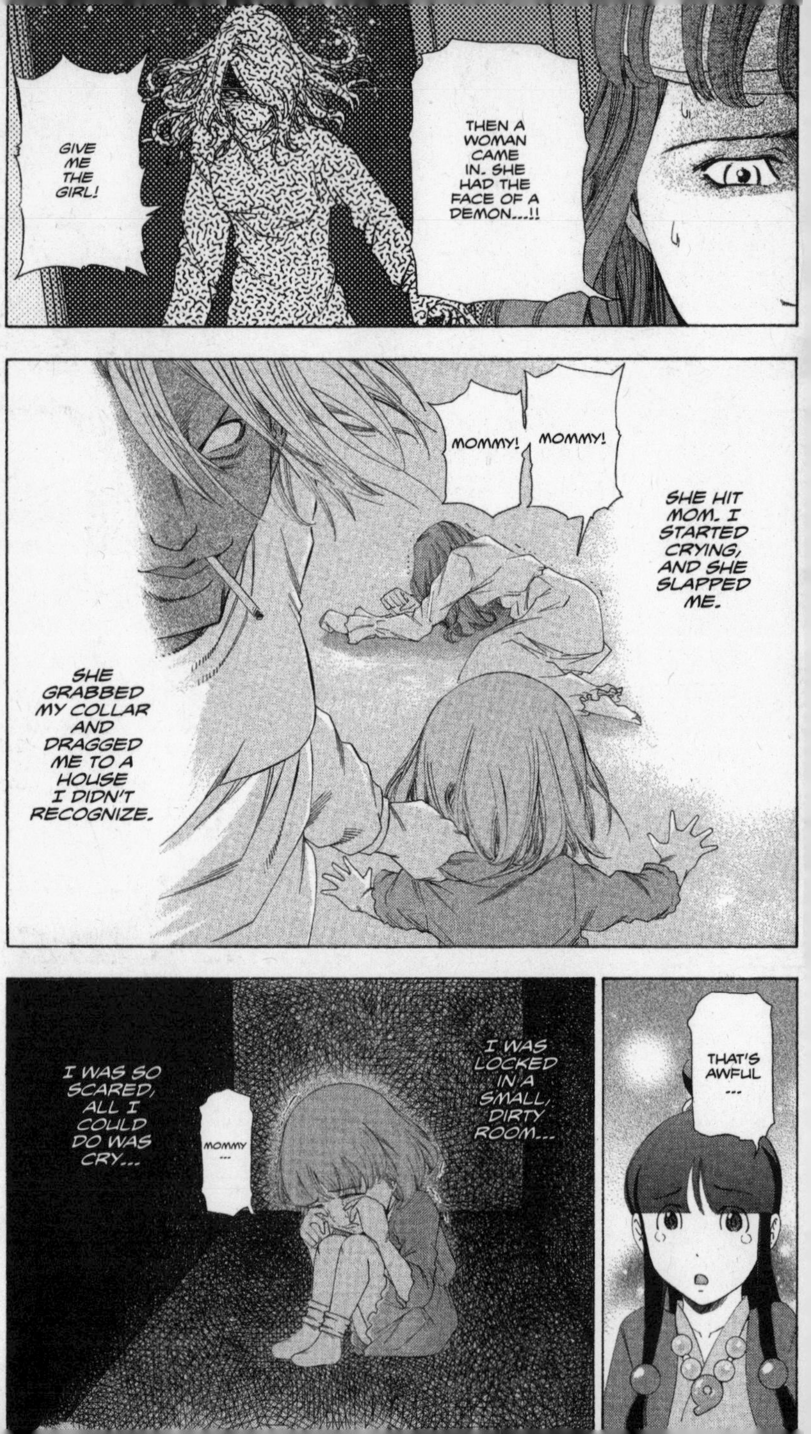
THEN A WOMAN CAME IN. SHE HAD THE FACE OF A DEMON...!!
GIVE ME THE GIRL!
MOMMY!
MOMMY!
SHE HIT MOM. I STARTED CRYING, AND SHE SLAPPED ME.
SHE GRABBED MY COLLAR AND DRAGGED ME TO A HOUSE I DIDN'T RECOGNIZE.
THAT'S AWFUL ...
I WAS LOCKED IN A SMALL, DIRTY ROOM...
MOMMY ...
I WAS SO SCARED, ALL I COULD DO WAS CRY...

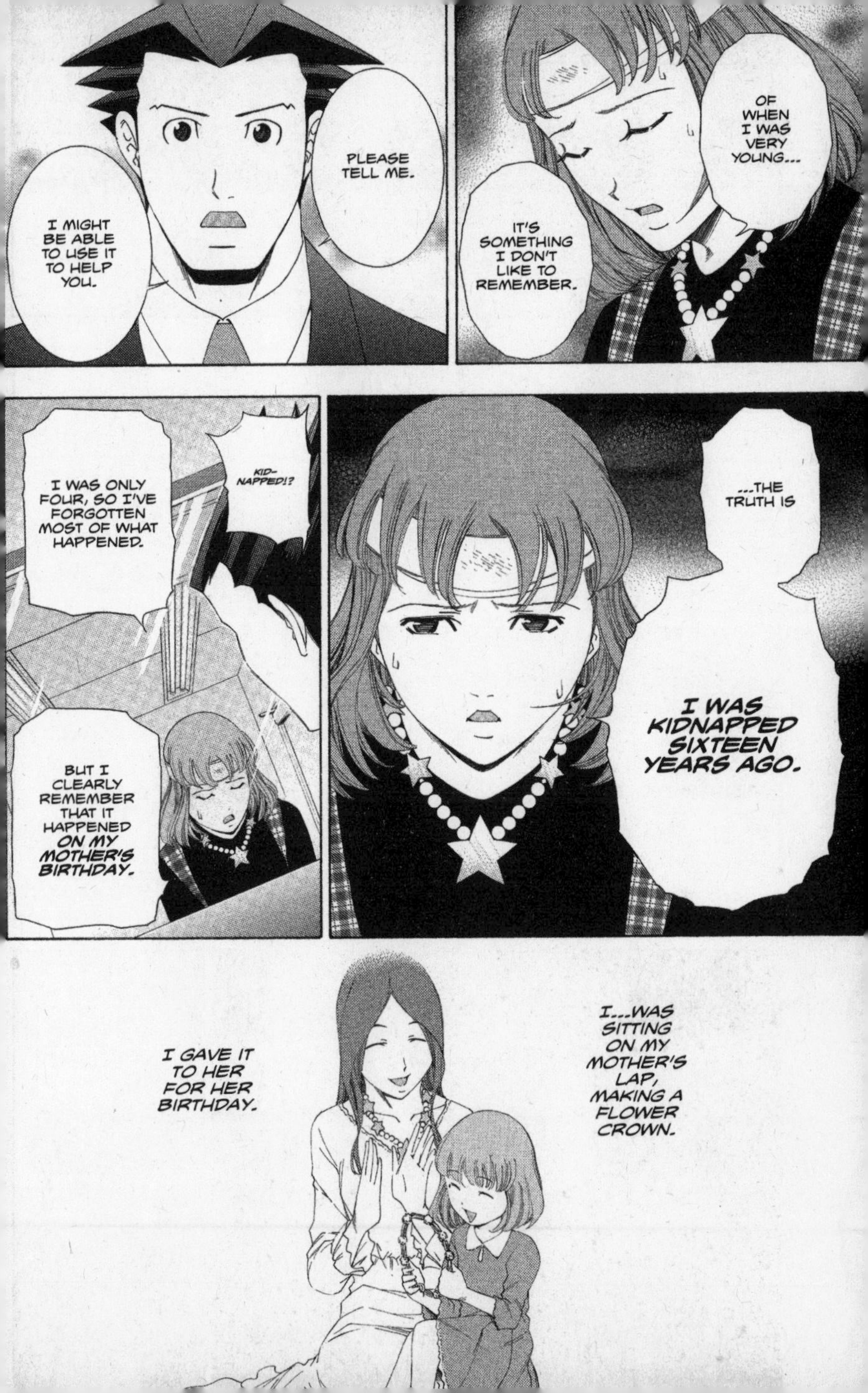
OF WHEN I WAS VERY YOUNG...
IT'S SOMETHING I DON'T LIKE TO REMEMBER.
PLEASE TELL ME.
I MIGHT BE ABLE TO USE IT TO HELP YOU.
...THE TRUTH IS
I WAS KIDNAPPED SIXTEEN YEARS AGO.
KID-NAPPED!?
I WAS ONLY FOUR, SO I'VE FORGOTTEN MOST OF WHAT HAPPENED.
BUT I CLEARLY REMEMBER THAT IT HAPPENED ON MY MOTHER'S BIRTHDAY.
I...WAS SITTING ON MY MOTHER'S LAP, MAKING A FLOWER CROWN.
I GAVE IT TO HER FOR HER BIRTHDAY.

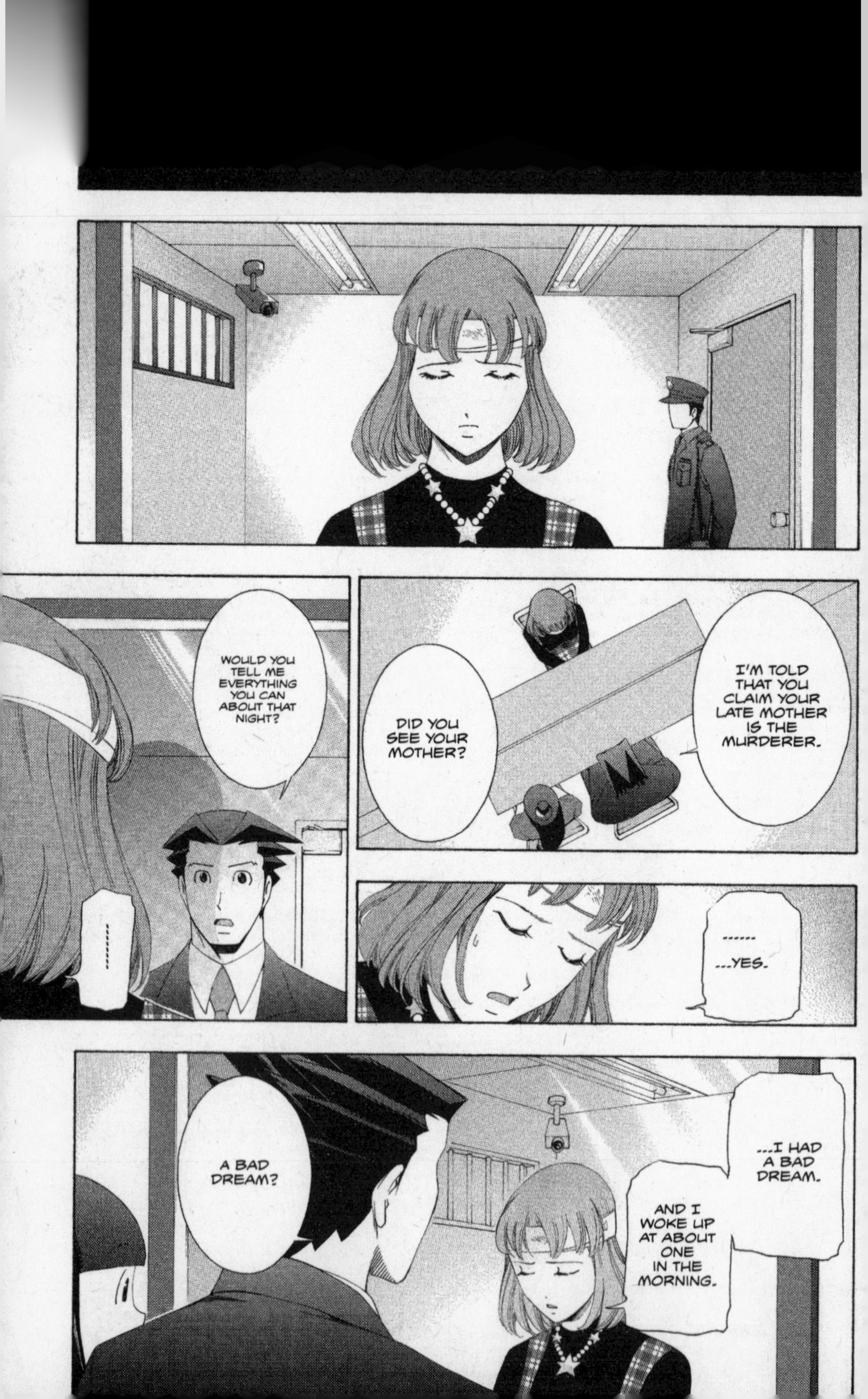
I'M TOLD THAT YOU CLAIM YOUR LATE MOTHER IS THE MURDERER.
DID YOU SEE YOUR MOTHER?
......
...YES.
WOULD YOU TELL ME EVERYTHING YOU CAN ABOUT THAT NIGHT?
......
...I HAD A BAD DREAM.
AND I WOKE UP AT ABOUT ONE IN THE MORNING.
A BAD DREAM?

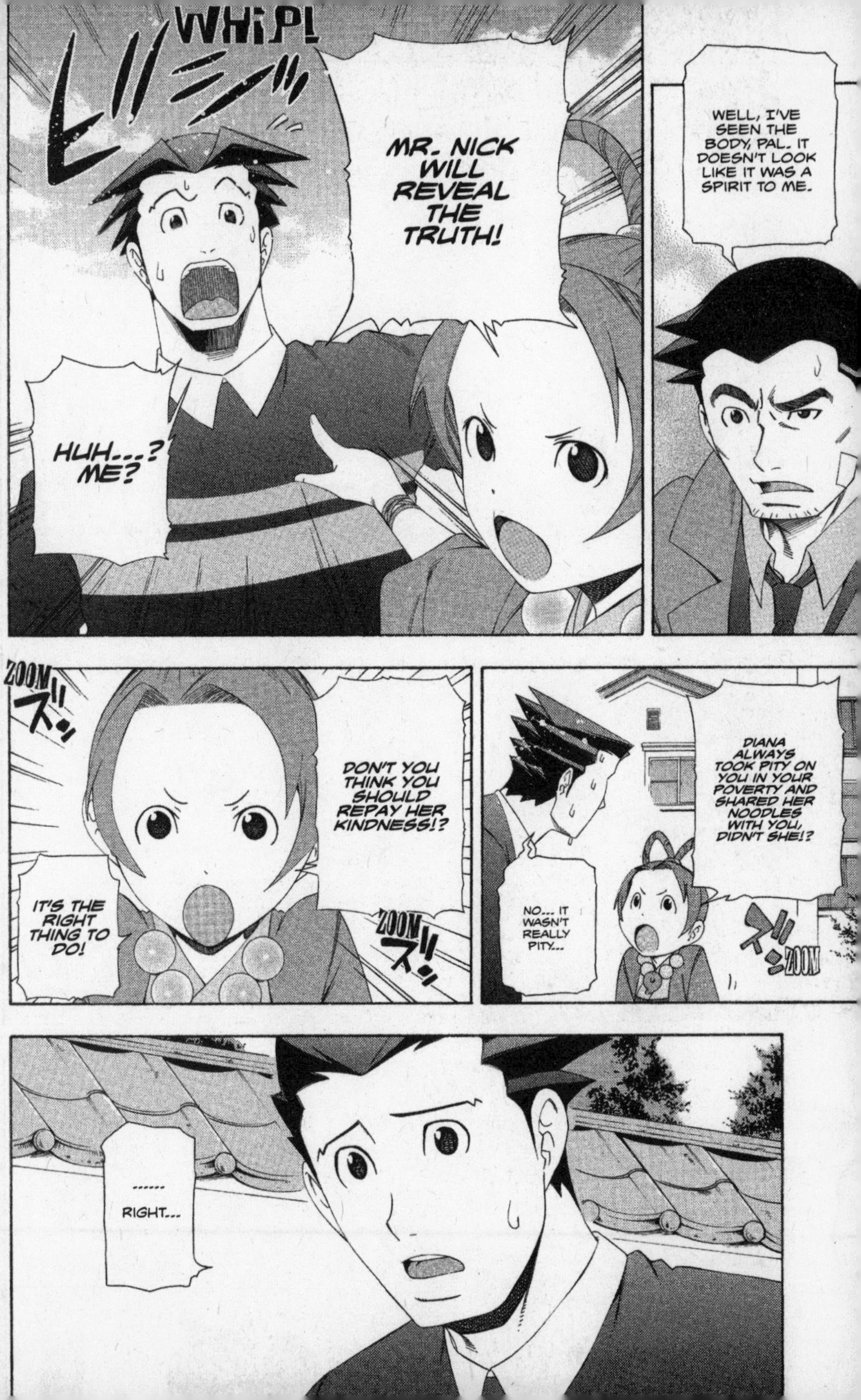

WELL, I'VE SEEN THE BODY, PAL. IT DOESN'T LOOK LIKE IT WAS A SPIRIT TO ME.
WHIP!
MR. NICK WILL REVEAL THE TRUTH!
HUH...? ME?
DIANA ALWAYS TOOK PITY ON YOU IN YOUR POVERTY AND SHARED HER NOODLES WITH YOU, DIDN'T SHE!?
ZOOM
NO... IT WASN'T REALLY PITY...
ZOOM
DON'T YOU THINK YOU SHOULD REPAY HER KINDNESS!?
ZOOM
IT'S THE RIGHT THING TO DO!
......
RIGHT...

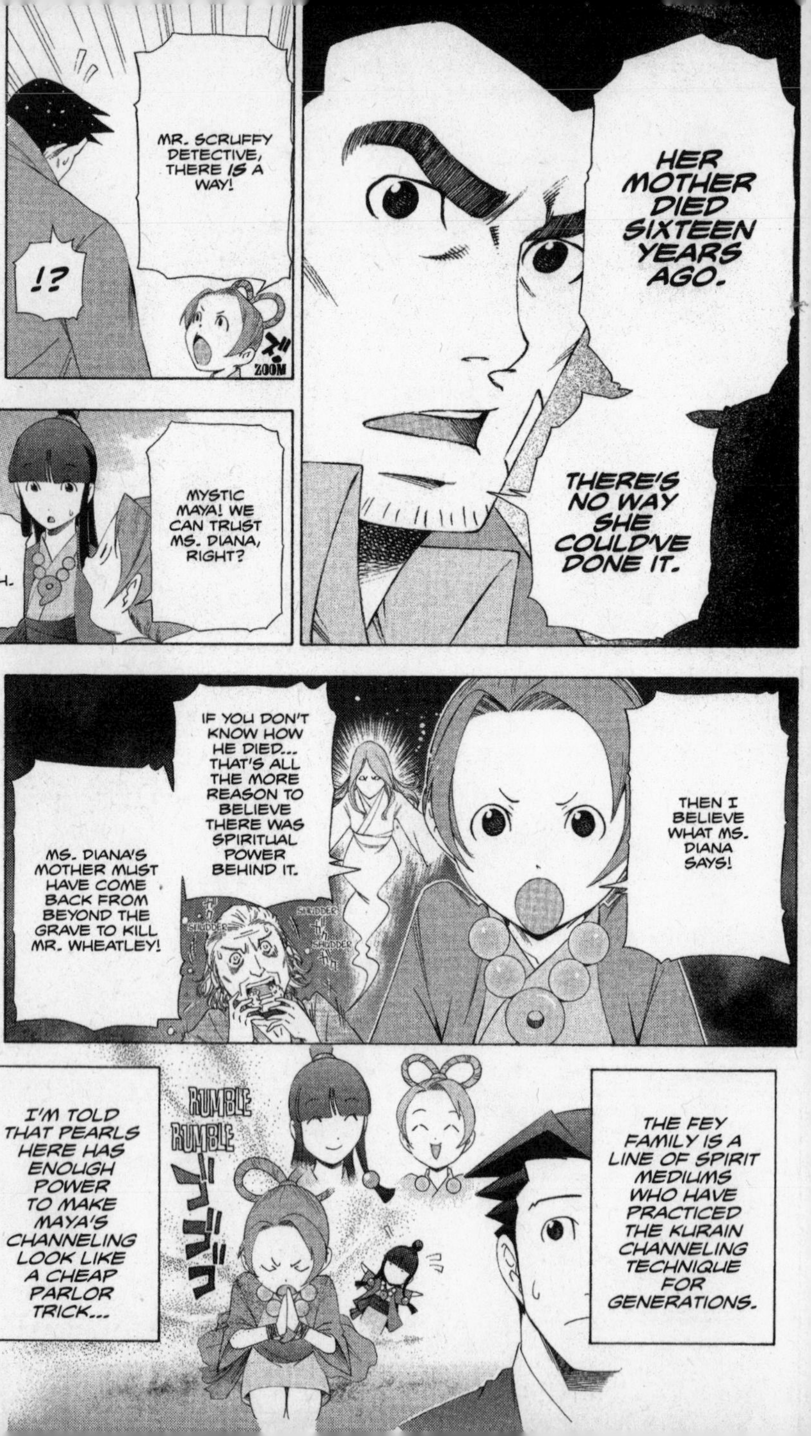
HER MOTHER DIED SIXTEEN YEARS AGO.
THERE'S NO WAY SHE COULD'VE DONE IT.
MR. SCRUFFY DETECTIVE, THERE IS A WAY!
!?
ZOOM
MYSTIC MAYA! WE CAN TRUST MS. DIANA, RIGHT?
Y... YEAH.
THEN I BELIEVE WHAT MS. DIANA SAYS!
IF YOU DON'T KNOW HOW HE DIED... THAT'S ALL THE MORE REASON TO BELIEVE THERE WAS SPIRITUAL POWER BEHIND IT.
SHUDDER
SHUDDER
SHUDDER
MS. DIANA'S MOTHER MUST HAVE COME BACK FROM BEYOND THE GRAVE TO KILL MR. WHEATLEY!
THE FEY FAMILY IS A LINE OF SPIRIT MEDIUMS WHO HAVE PRACTICED THE KURAIN CHANNELING TECHNIQUE FOR GENERATIONS.
RUMBLE
RUMBLE
I'M TOLD THAT PEARLS HERE HAS ENOUGH POWER TO MAKE MAYA'S CHANNELING LOOK LIKE A CHEAP PARLOR TRICK...

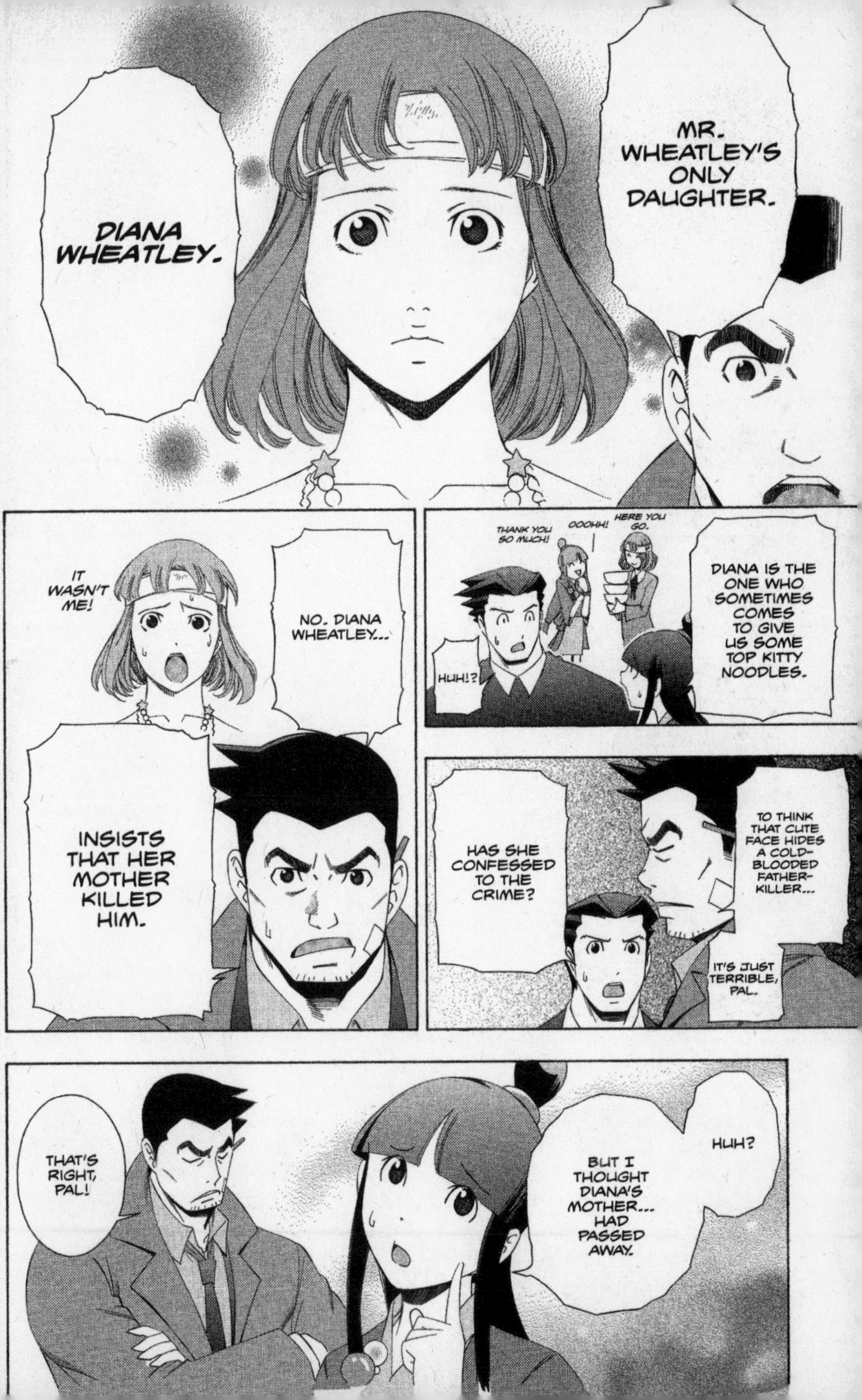
MR. WHEATLEY'S ONLY DAUGHTER.
DIANA WHEATLEY.
DIANA IS THE ONE WHO SOMETIMES COMES TO GIVE US SOME TOP KITTY NOODLES.
HERE YOU GO.
OOOHH!
THANK YOU SO MUCH!
HUH!?
TO THINK THAT CUTE FACE HIDES A COLD-BLOODED FATHER-KILLER...
IT'S JUST TERRIBLE, PAL.
HAS SHE CONFESSED TO THE CRIME?
NO. DIANA WHEATLEY...
IT WASN'T ME!
INSISTS THAT HER MOTHER KILLED HIM.
HUH?
BUT I THOUGHT DIANA'S MOTHER... HAD PASSED AWAY.
THAT'S RIGHT, PAL!

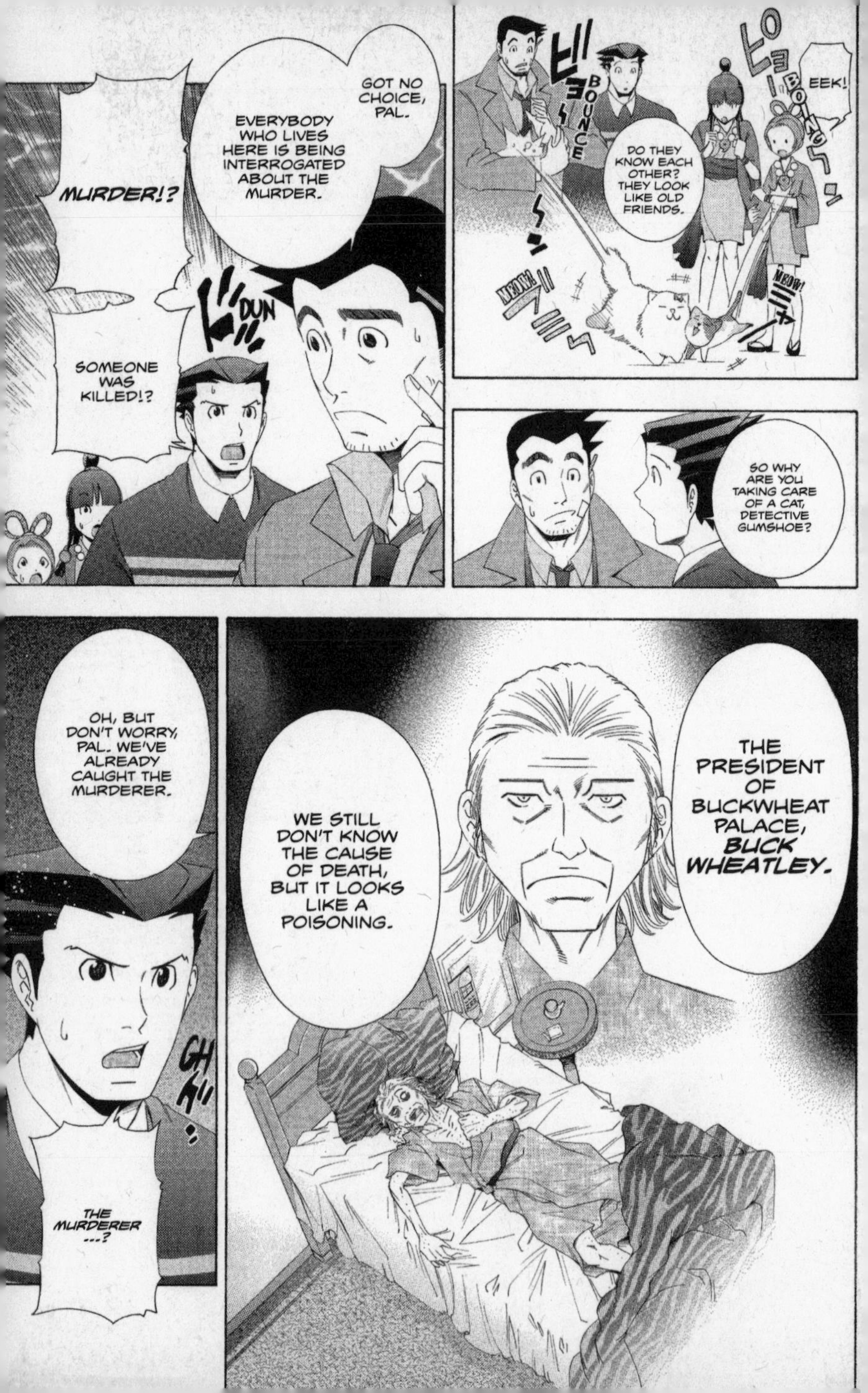
EEK!
BOING
DO THEY KNOW EACH OTHER? THEY LOOK LIKE OLD FRIENDS.
BOUNCE
MEOW!
MEOW
SO WHY ARE YOU TAKING CARE OF A CAT, DETECTIVE GUMSHOE?
GOT NO CHOICE, PAL.
EVERYBODY WHO LIVES HERE IS BEING INTERROGATED ABOUT THE MURDER.
MURDER!?
DUN
SOMEONE WAS KILLED!?
THE PRESIDENT OF BUCKWHEAT PALACE, ***BUCK WHEATLEY.***
WE STILL DON'T KNOW THE CAUSE OF DEATH, BUT IT LOOKS LIKE A POISONING.
OH, BUT DON'T WORRY, PAL. WE'VE ALREADY CAUGHT THE MURDERER.
GH
THE MURDERER...?

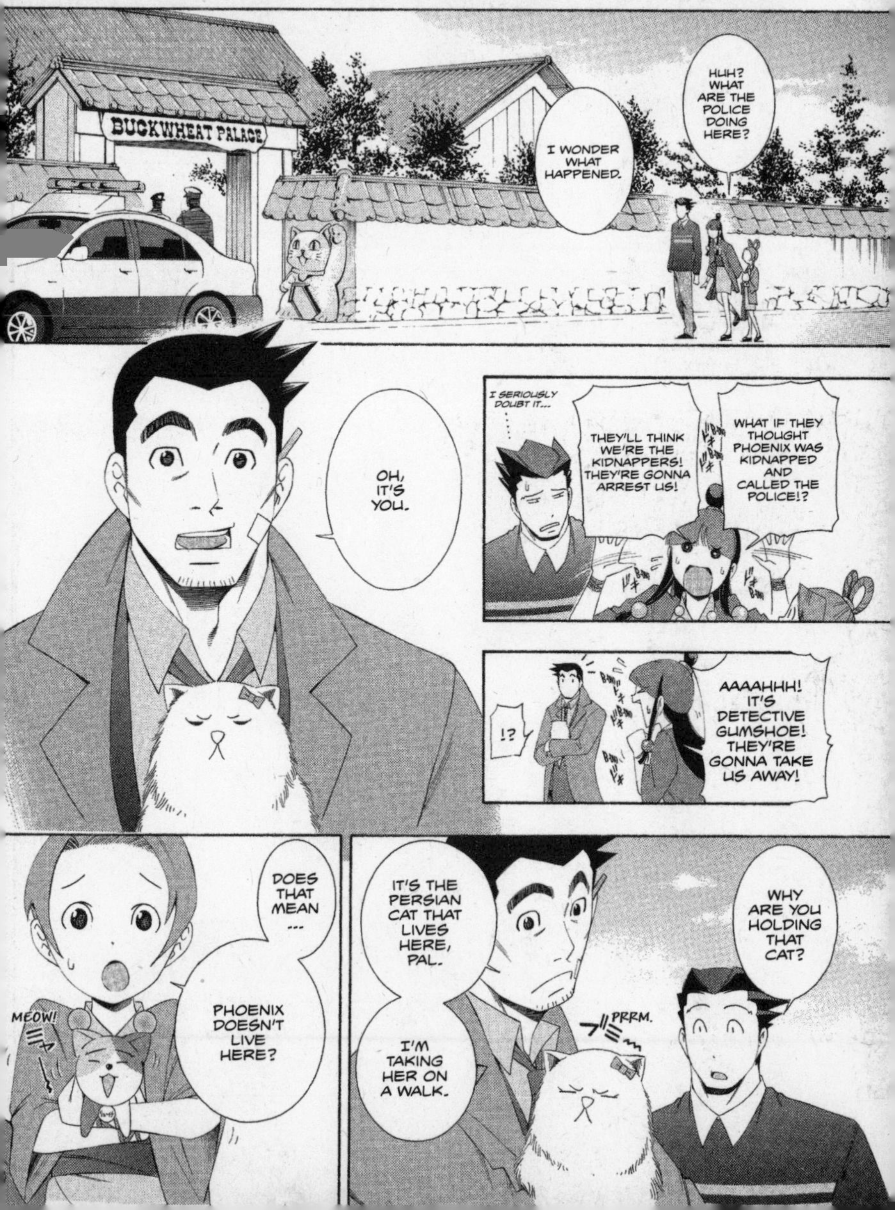
BUCKWHEAT PALACE
HUH? WHAT ARE THE POLICE DOING HERE?
I WONDER WHAT HAPPENED.
WHAT IF THEY THOUGHT PHOENIX WAS KIDNAPPED AND CALLED THE POLICE!?
THEY'LL THINK WE'RE THE KIDNAPPERS! THEY'RE GONNA ARREST US!
I SERIOUSLY DOUBT IT...
AAAAHHH! IT'S DETECTIVE GUMSHOE! THEY'RE GONNA TAKE US AWAY!
!?
OH, IT'S YOU.
WHY ARE YOU HOLDING THAT CAT?
PRRM.
IT'S THE PERSIAN CAT THAT LIVES HERE, PAL.
I'M TAKING HER ON A WALK.
DOES THAT MEAN ...
PHOENIX DOESN'T LIVE HERE?
MEOW!

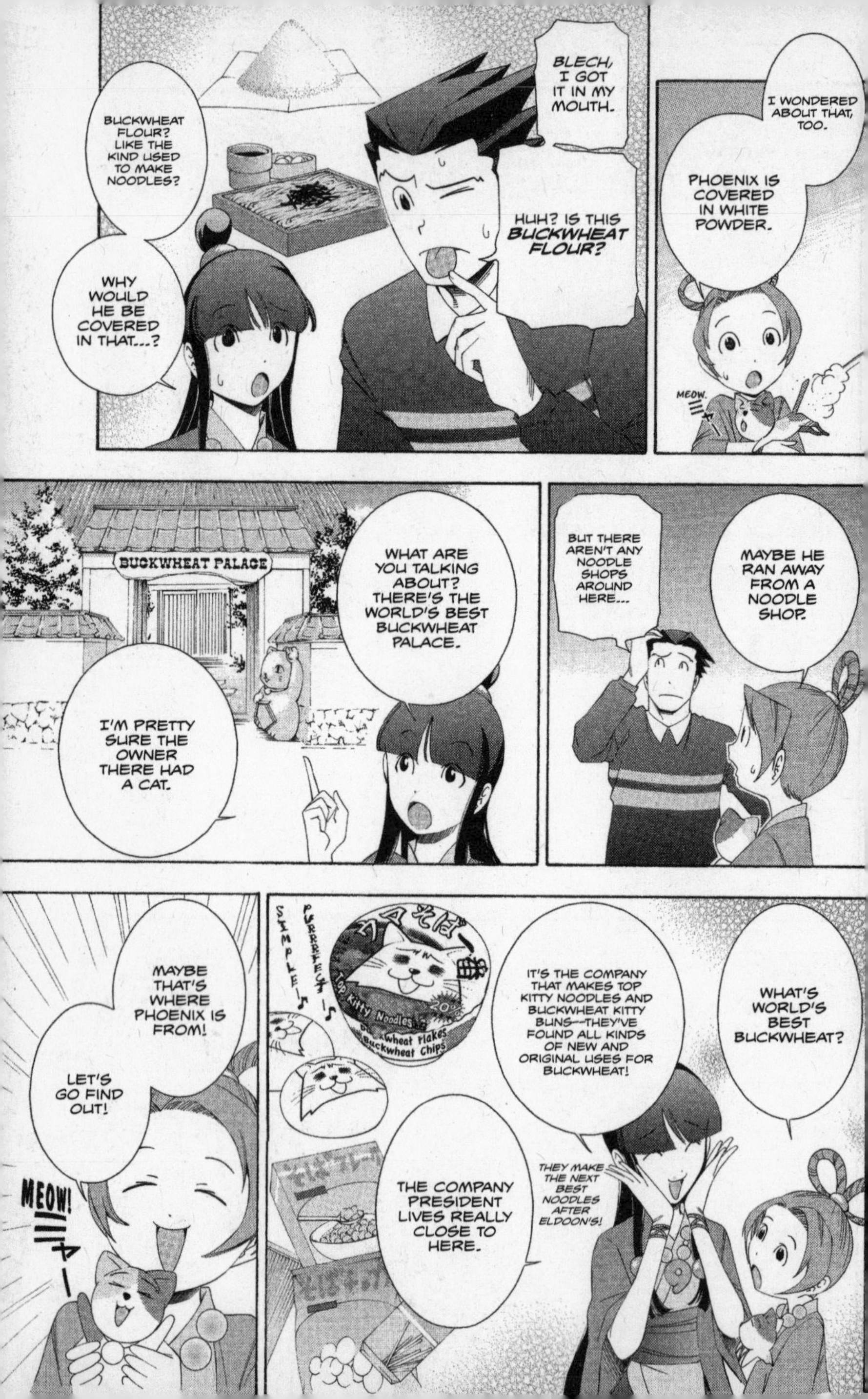
I WONDERED ABOUT THAT, TOO.
PHOENIX IS COVERED IN WHITE POWDER.
MEOW.
BLECH, I GOT IT IN MY MOUTH.
HUH? IS THIS *BUCKWHEAT FLOUR?*
BUCKWHEAT FLOUR? LIKE THE KIND USED TO MAKE NOODLES?
WHY WOULD HE BE COVERED IN THAT...?
MAYBE HE RAN AWAY FROM A NOODLE SHOP.
BUT THERE AREN'T ANY NOODLE SHOPS AROUND HERE...
BUCKWHEAT PALACE
WHAT ARE YOU TALKING ABOUT? THERE'S THE WORLD'S BEST BUCKWHEAT PALACE.
I'M PRETTY SURE THE OWNER THERE HAD A CAT.
WHAT'S WORLD'S BEST BUCKWHEAT?
IT'S THE COMPANY THAT MAKES TOP KITTY NOODLES AND BUCKWHEAT KITTY BUNS--THEY'VE FOUND ALL KINDS OF NEW AND ORIGINAL USES FOR BUCKWHEAT!
THEY MAKE THE NEXT BEST NOODLES AFTER ELDOON'S!
THE COMPANY PRESIDENT LIVES REALLY CLOSE TO HERE.
PURRFECT!
SIMPLE!
Top Kitty Noodles
20%
Buckwheat Flakes
Buckwheat Chips
MAYBE THAT'S WHERE PHOENIX IS FROM!
LET'S GO FIND OUT!
MEOW!

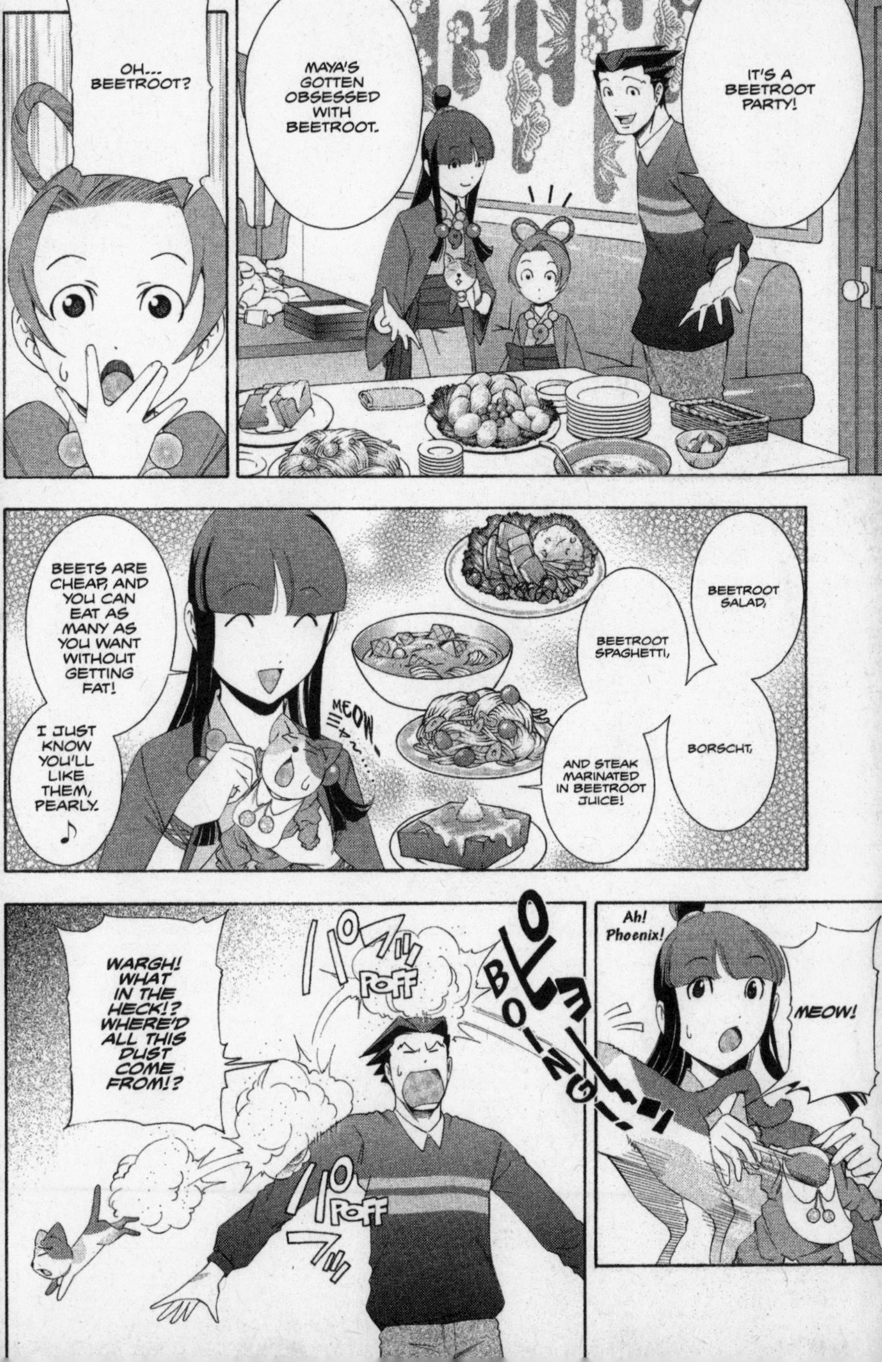
IT'S A BEETROOT PARTY!
MAYA'S GOTTEN OBSESSED WITH BEETROOT.
OH... BEETROOT?
BEETROOT SALAD,
BEETROOT SPAGHETTI,
BORSCHT,
AND STEAK MARINATED IN BEETROOT JUICE!
MEOW
BEETS ARE CHEAP, AND YOU CAN EAT AS MANY AS YOU WANT WITHOUT GETTING FAT!
I JUST KNOW YOU'LL LIKE THEM, PEARLY. ♪
Ah! Phoenix!
MEOW!
BOING
POFF
WARGH! WHAT IN THE HECK!? WHERE'D ALL THIS DUST COME FROM!?
POFF

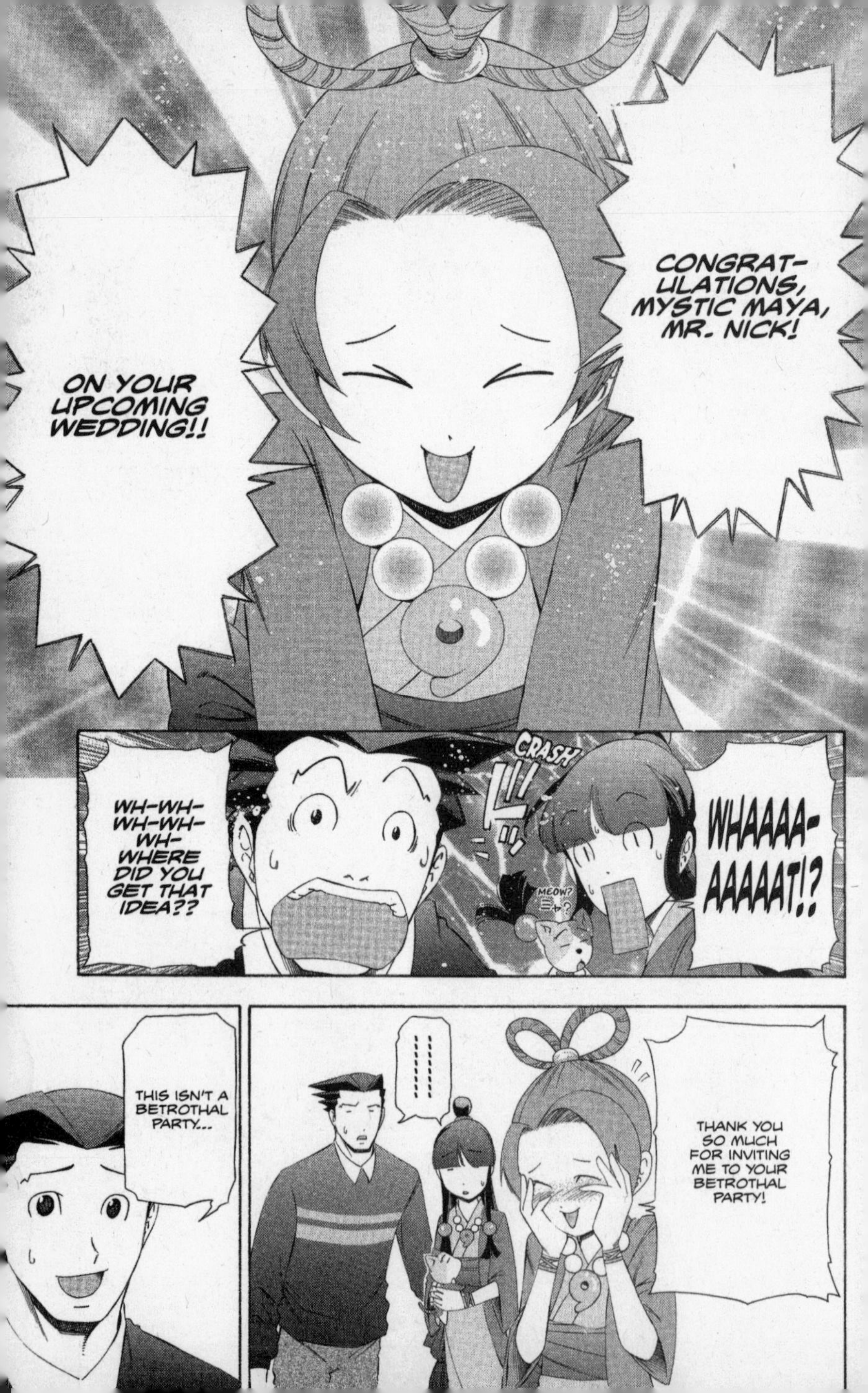
CONGRAT-ULATIONS, MYSTIC MAYA, MR. NICK!
ON YOUR UPCOMING WEDDING!!
WHAAAAA-AAAAAT!?
CRASH
MEOW?
ミャ?
WH-WH-WH-WH-WH-WHERE DID YOU GET THAT IDEA??
THANK YOU SO MUCH FOR INVITING ME TO YOUR BETROTHAL PARTY!
......
THIS ISN'T A BETROTHAL PARTY...

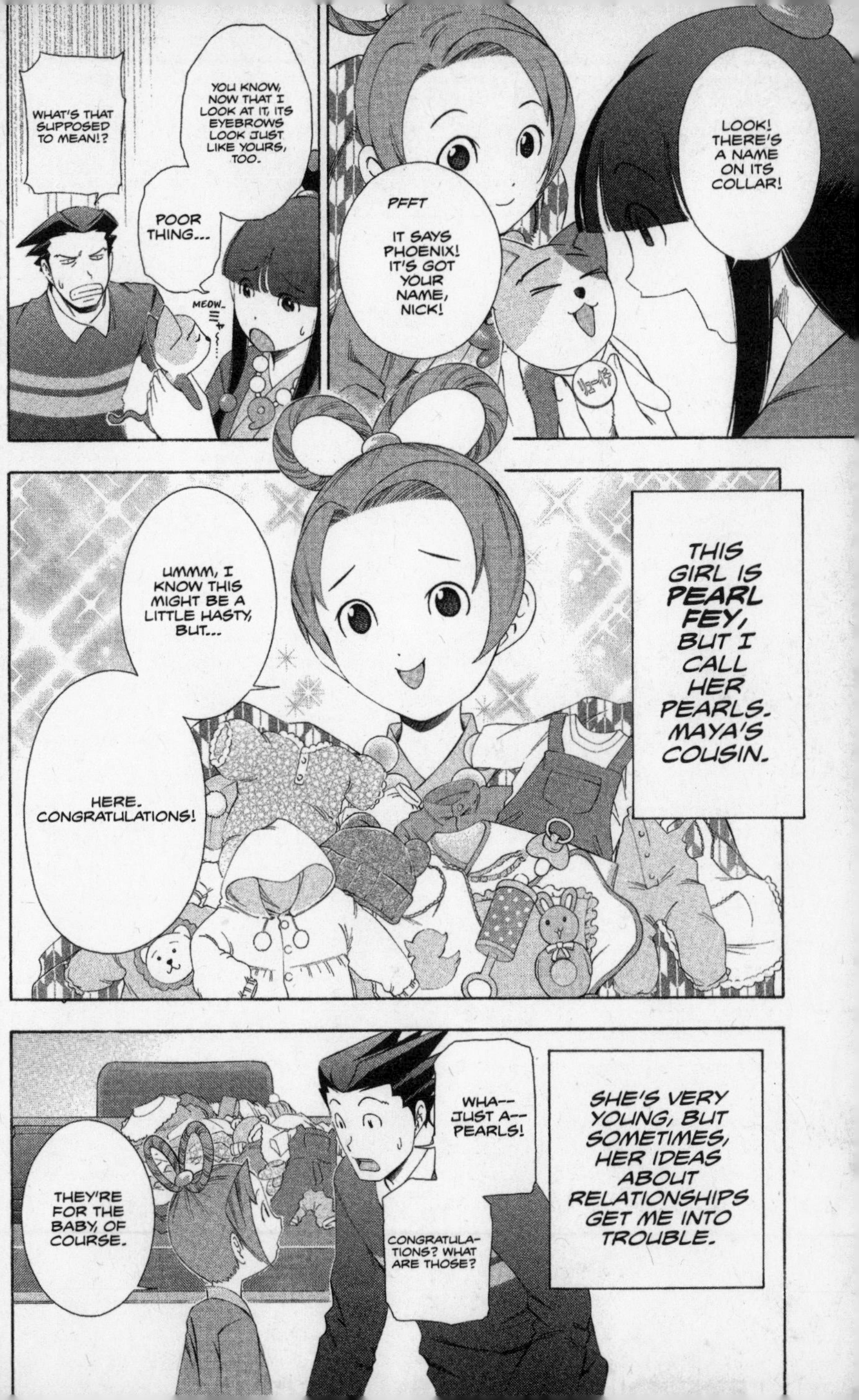
LOOK! THERE'S A NAME ON ITS COLLAR!
PFFT
IT SAYS PHOENIX! IT'S GOT YOUR NAME, NICK!
YOU KNOW, NOW THAT I LOOK AT IT, ITS EYEBROWS LOOK JUST LIKE YOURS, TOO.
WHAT'S THAT SUPPOSED TO MEAN!?
POOR THING...
MEOW...
THIS GIRL IS PEARL FEY, BUT I CALL HER PEARLS. MAYA'S COUSIN.
UMMM, I KNOW THIS MIGHT BE A LITTLE HASTY, BUT...
HERE. CONGRATULATIONS!
SHE'S VERY YOUNG, BUT SOMETIMES, HER IDEAS ABOUT RELATIONSHIPS GET ME INTO TROUBLE.
WHA-- JUST A-- PEARLS!
CONGRATULA-TIONS? WHAT ARE THOSE?
THEY'RE FOR THE BABY, OF COURSE.

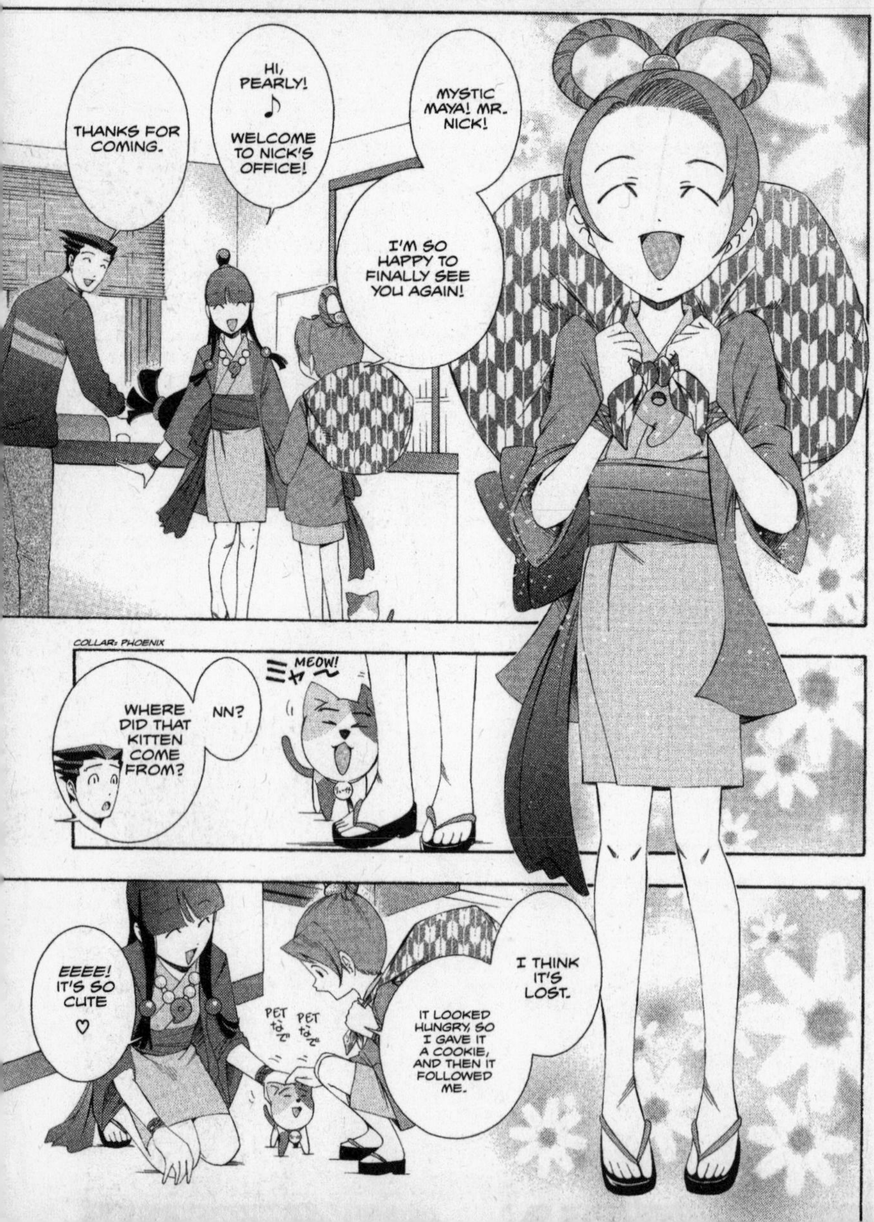
MYSTIC MAYA! MR. NICK!
I'M SO HAPPY TO FINALLY SEE YOU AGAIN!
HI, PEARLY! ♪ WELCOME TO NICK'S OFFICE!
THANKS FOR COMING.
COLLAR: PHOENIX
ミャ〜 MEOW!
NN?
WHERE DID THAT KITTEN COME FROM?
I THINK IT'S LOST.
IT LOOKED HUNGRY, SO I GAVE IT A COOKIE, AND THEN IT FOLLOWED ME.
PET なで PET なで
EEEE! IT'S SO CUTE ♡

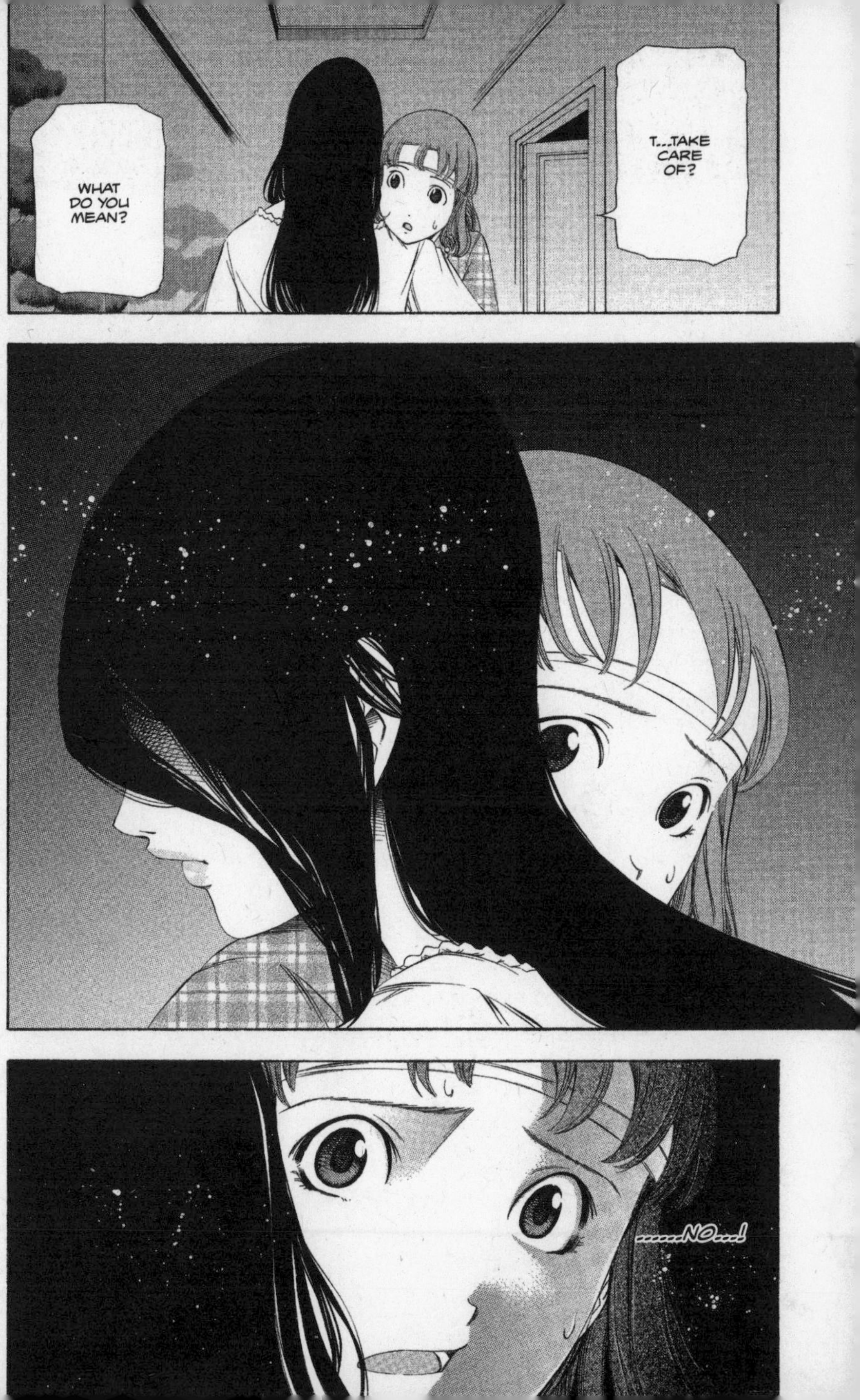
T...TAKE CARE OF?
WHAT DO YOU MEAN?
......NO...!

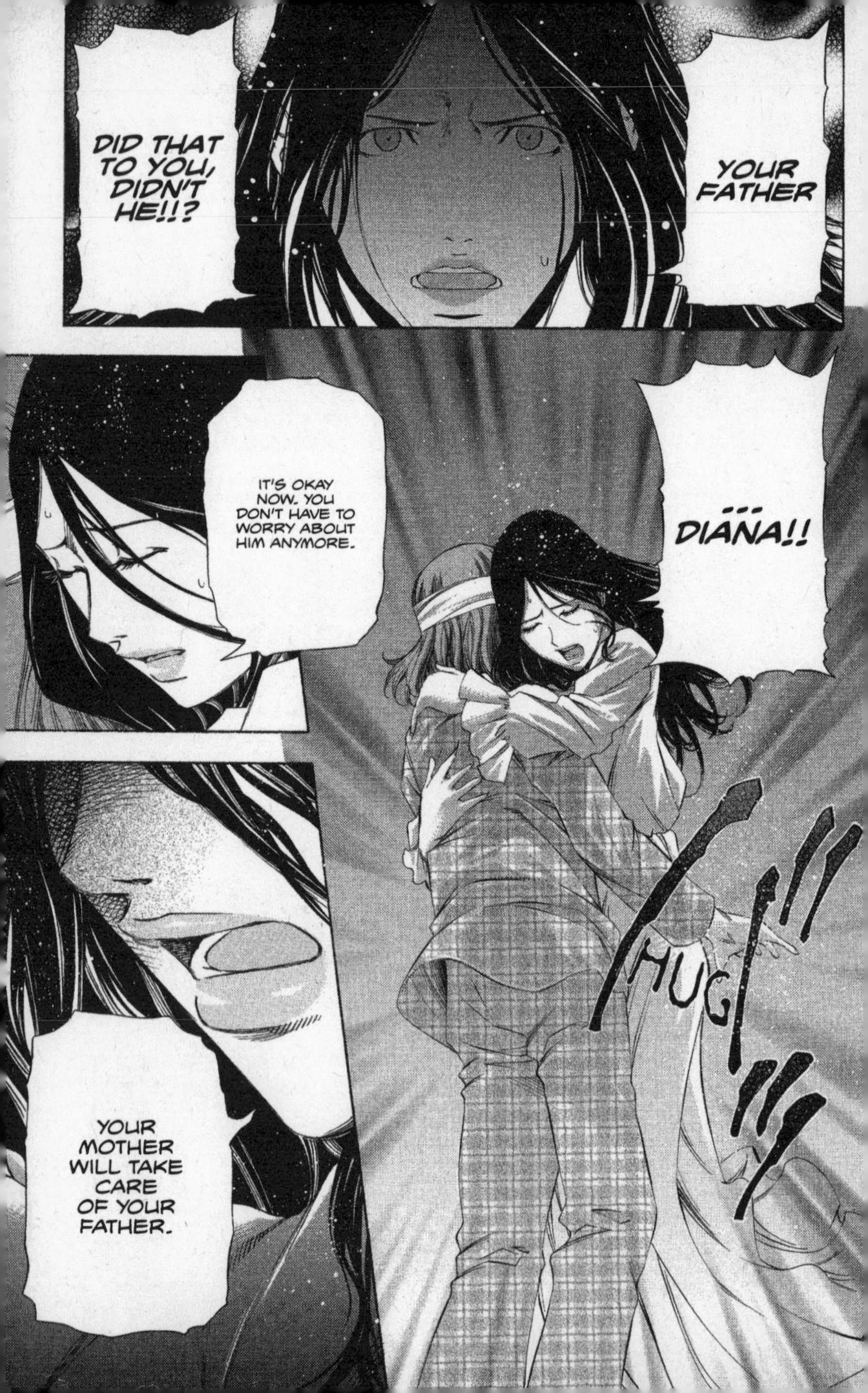

YOUR FATHER
DID THAT TO YOU, DIDN'T HE!!?
...DIANA!!
HUG!!!
IT'S OKAY NOW. YOU DON'T HAVE TO WORRY ABOUT HIM ANYMORE.
YOUR MOTHER WILL TAKE CARE OF YOUR FATHER.

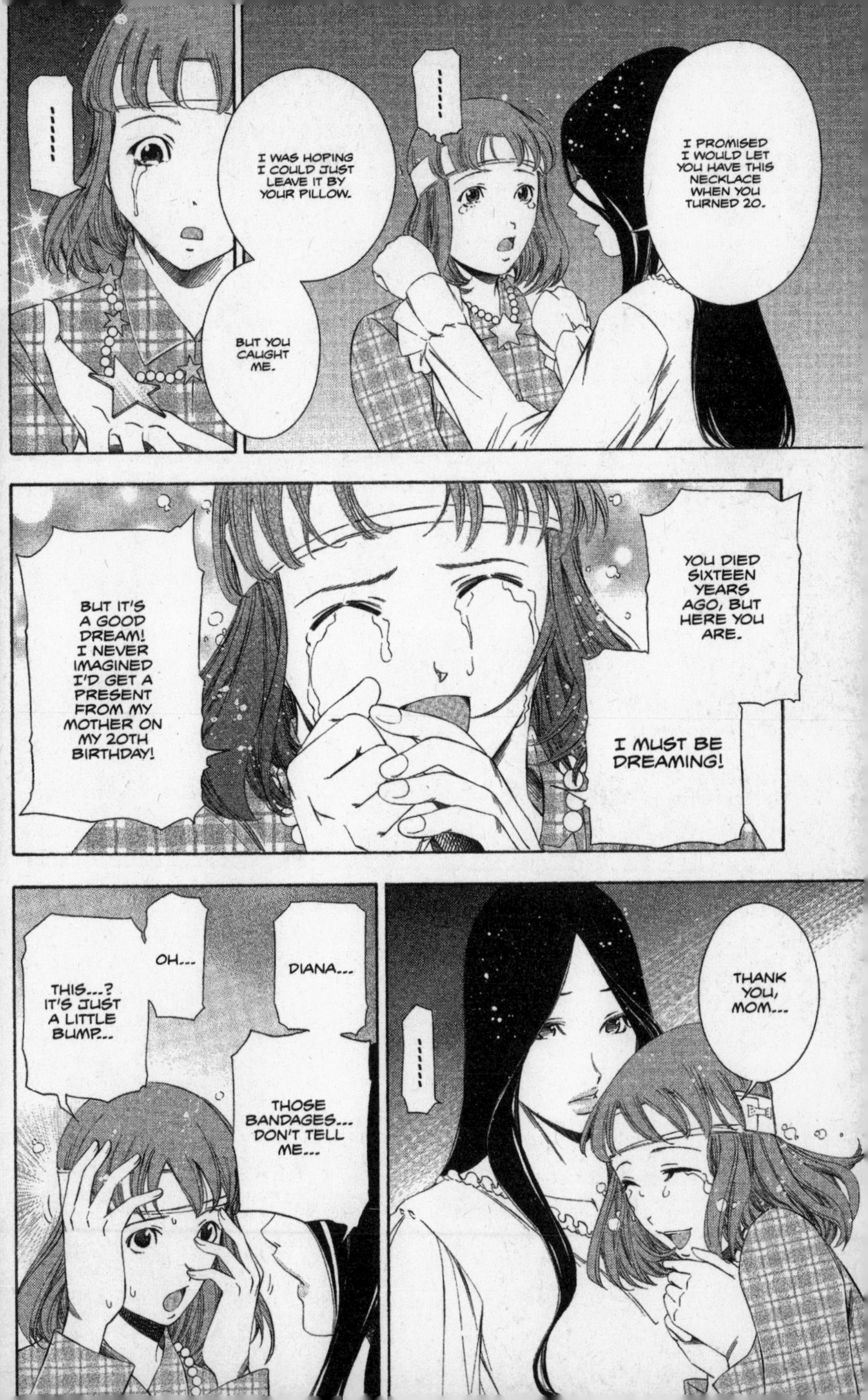
I PROMISED I WOULD LET YOU HAVE THIS NECKLACE WHEN YOU TURNED 20.
......
I WAS HOPING I COULD JUST LEAVE IT BY YOUR PILLOW.
BUT YOU CAUGHT ME.
......
YOU DIED SIXTEEN YEARS AGO, BUT HERE YOU ARE.
I MUST BE DREAMING!
BUT IT'S A GOOD DREAM! I NEVER IMAGINED I'D GET A PRESENT FROM MY MOTHER ON MY 20TH BIRTHDAY!
THANK YOU, MOM...
......
DIANA...
THOSE BANDAGES... DON'T TELL ME...
OH...
THIS...? IT'S JUST A LITTLE BUMP...

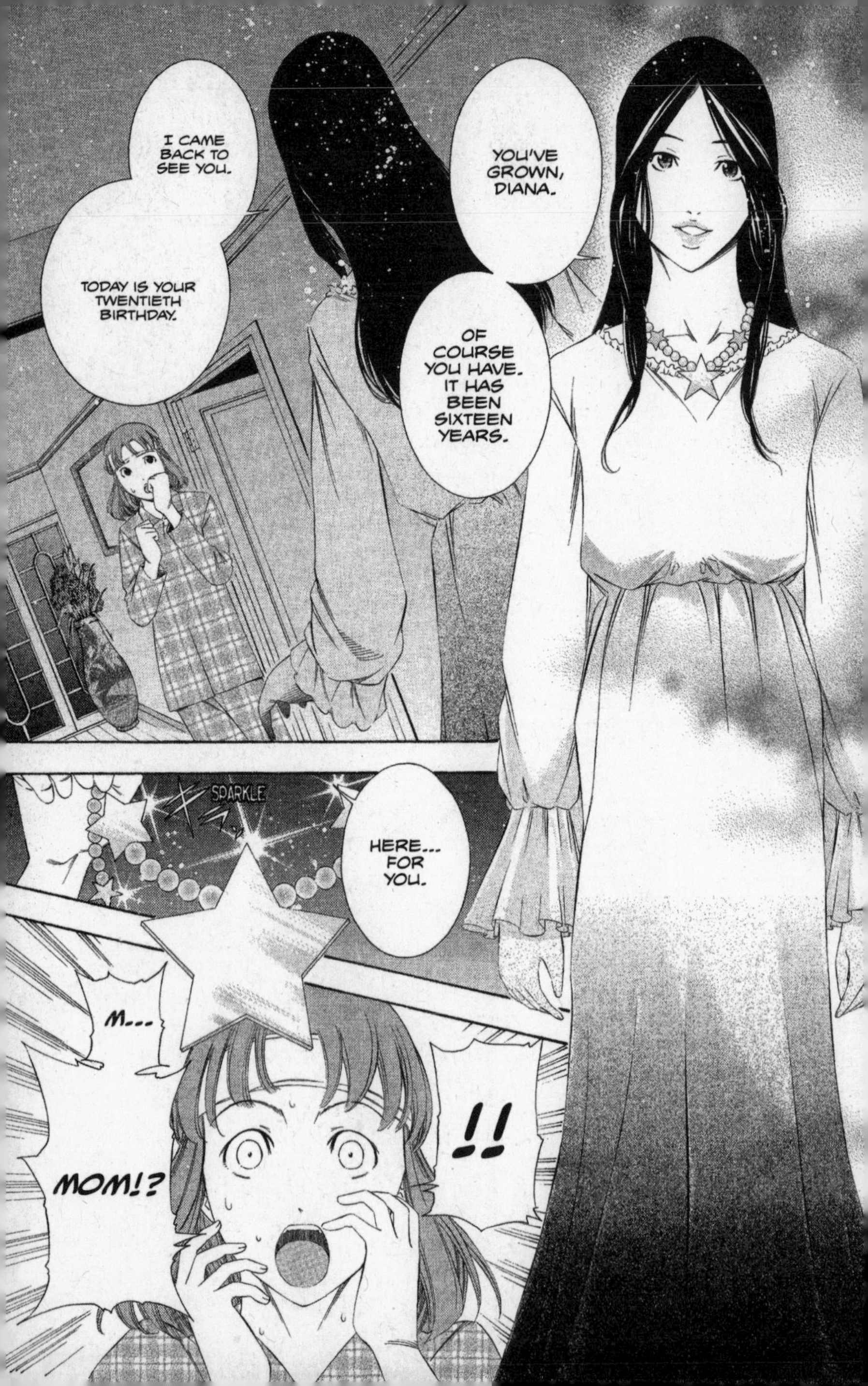
YOU'VE GROWN, DIANA.
OF COURSE YOU HAVE. IT HAS BEEN SIXTEEN YEARS.
I CAME BACK TO SEE YOU.
TODAY IS YOUR TWENTIETH BIRTHDAY.
HERE... FOR YOU.
SPARKLE
!!
M...
MOM!?

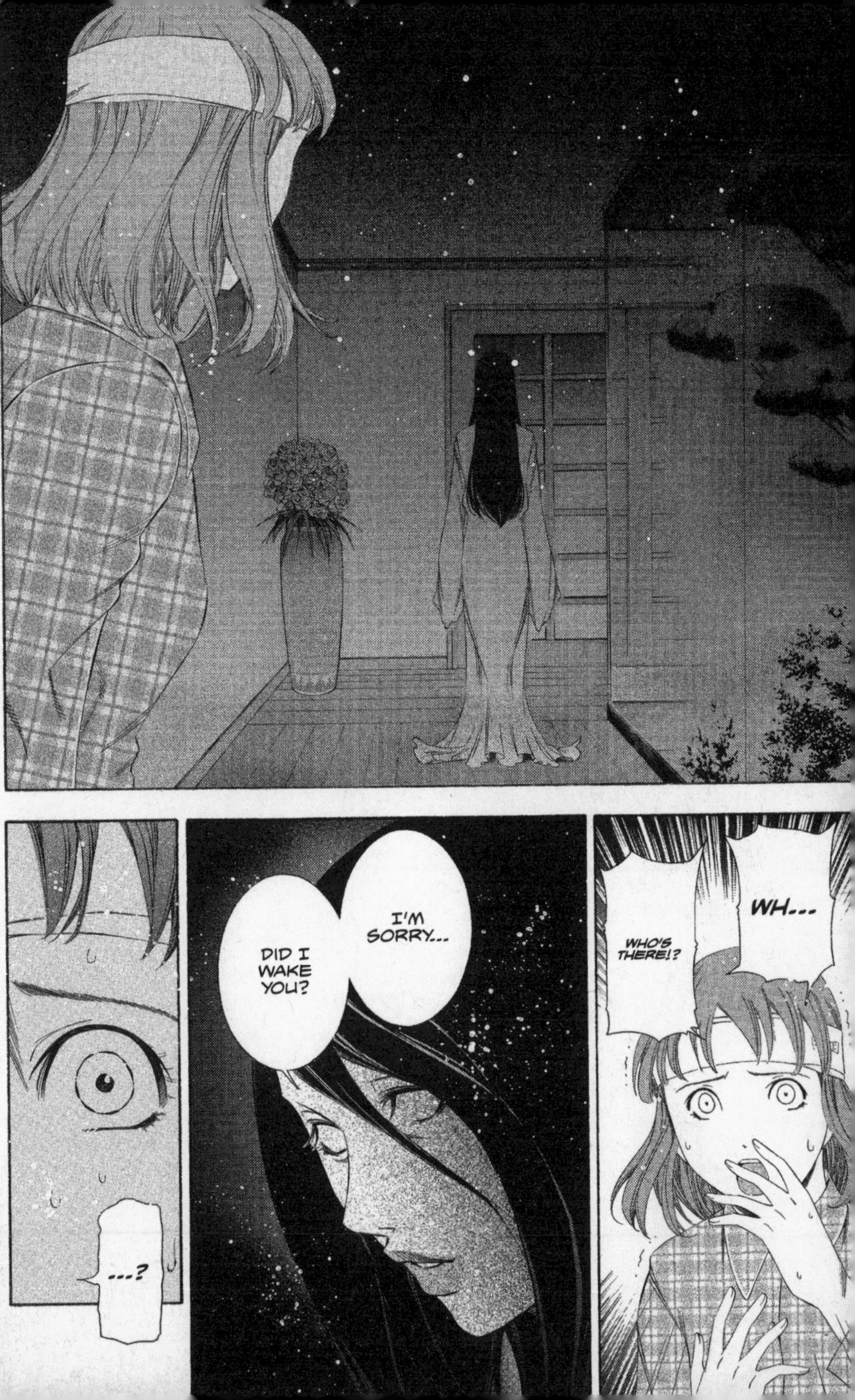
WH...
WHO'S THERE!?
I'M SORRY...
DID I WAKE YOU?
...?

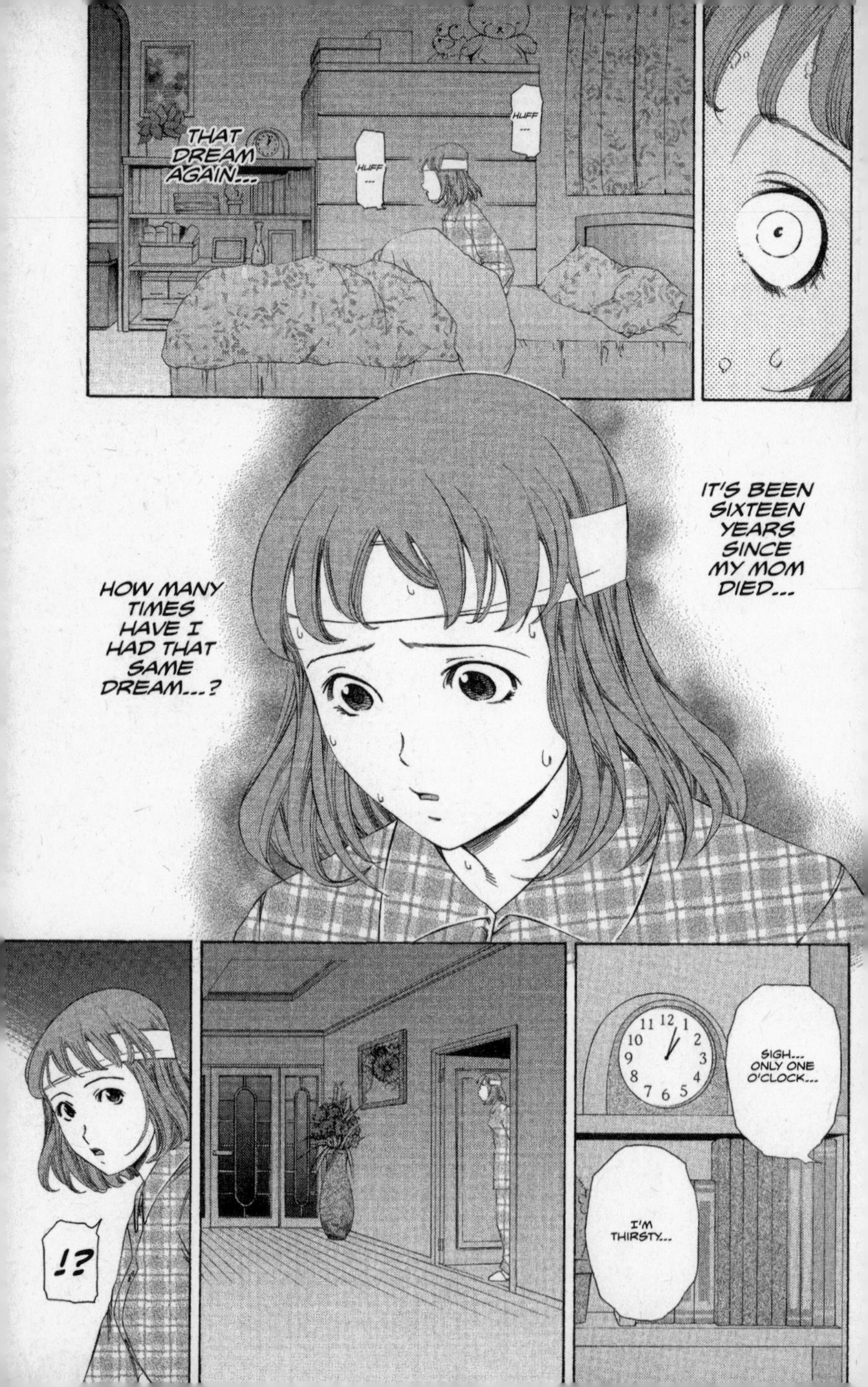
HUFF ---
HUFF ---
THAT DREAM AGAIN...
IT'S BEEN SIXTEEN YEARS SINCE MY MOM DIED...
HOW MANY TIMES HAVE I HAD THAT SAME DREAM...?
SIGH... ONLY ONE O'CLOCK...
I'M THIRSTY...
!?

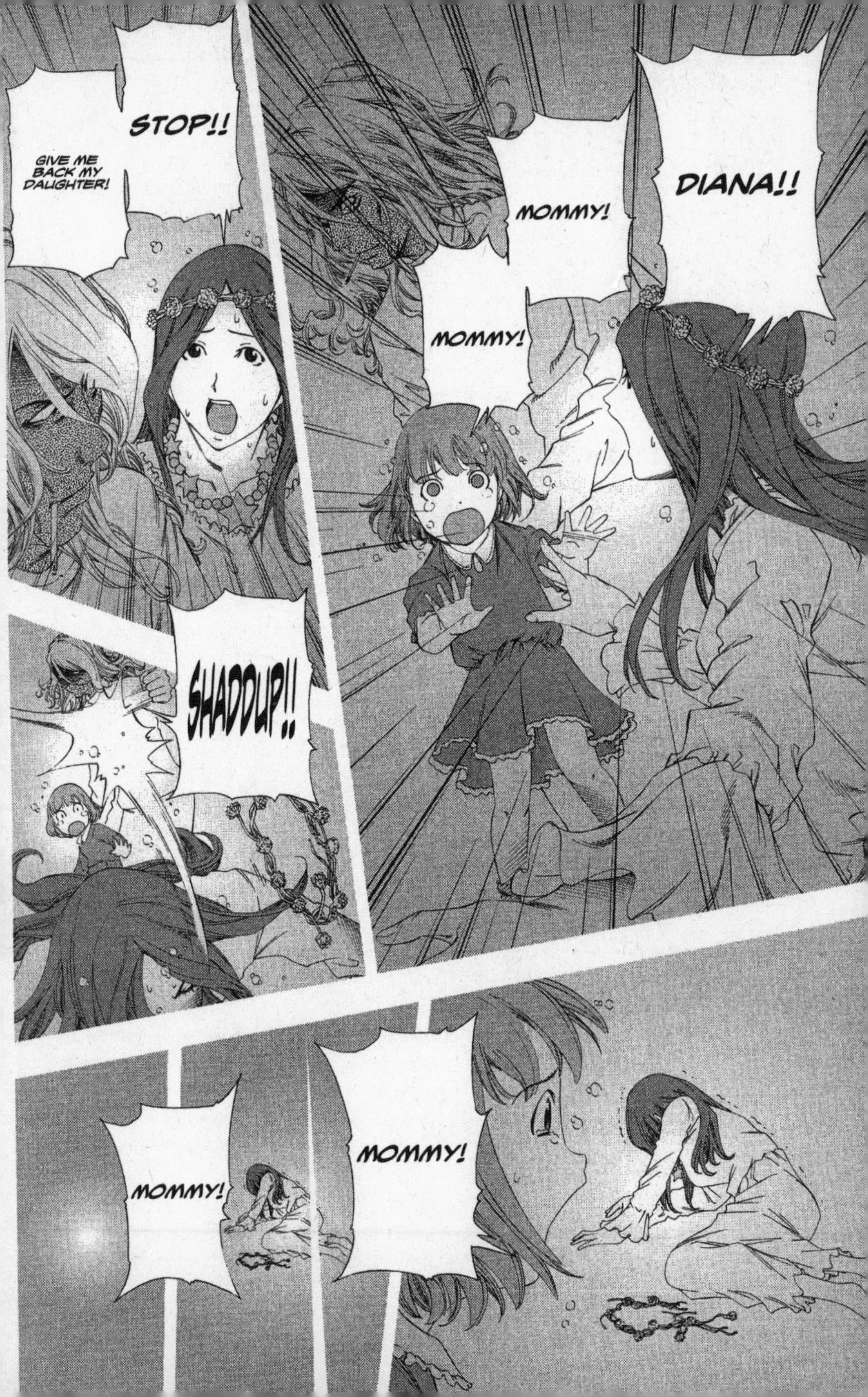
DIANA!!
MOMMY!
MOMMY!
STOP!!
GIVE ME BACK MY DAUGHTER!
SHADDUP!!
MOMMY!
MOMMY!

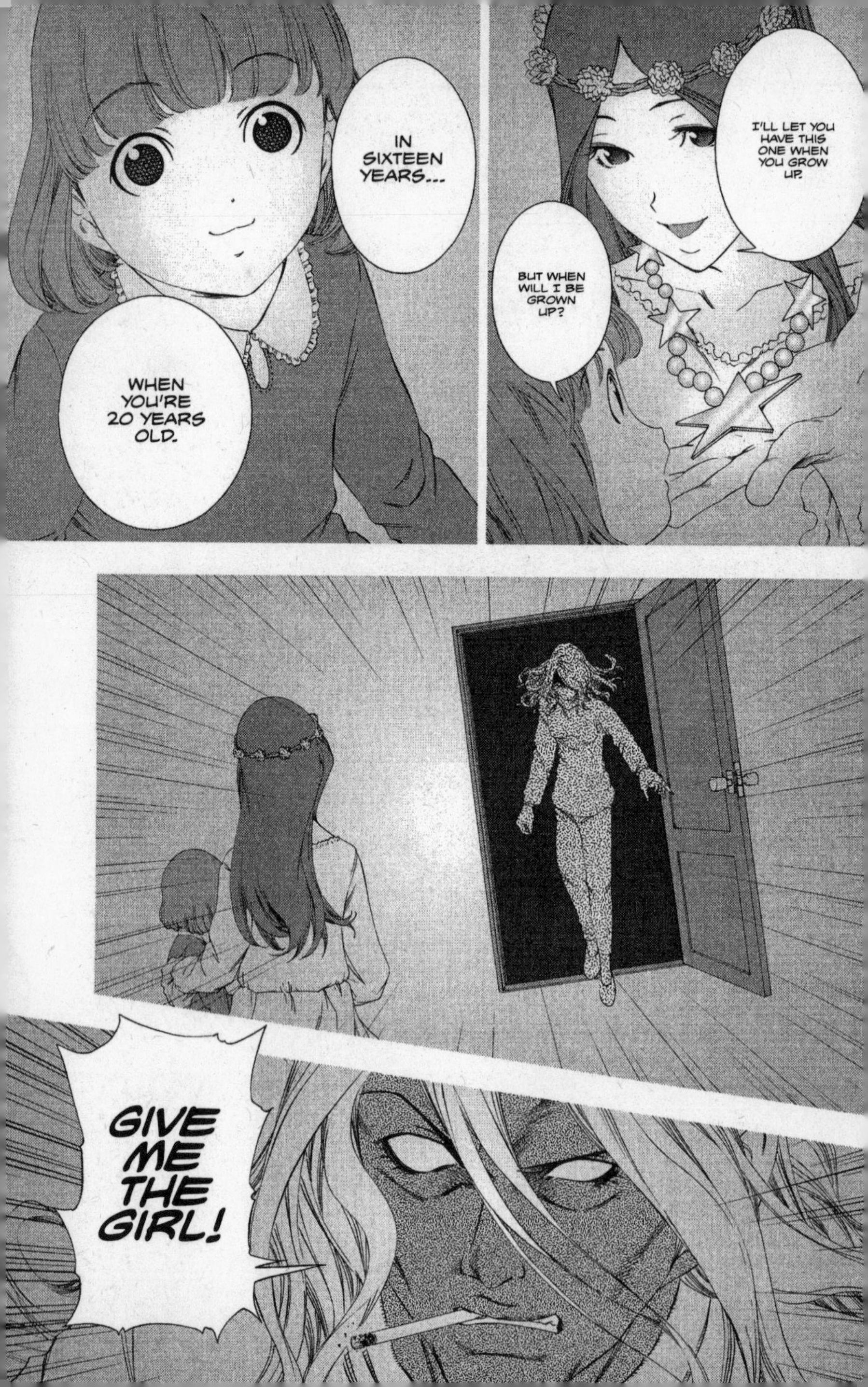
I'LL LET YOU HAVE THIS ONE WHEN YOU GROW UP.
BUT WHEN WILL I BE GROWN UP?
IN SIXTEEN YEARS...
WHEN YOU'RE 20 YEARS OLD.
GIVE ME THE GIRL!

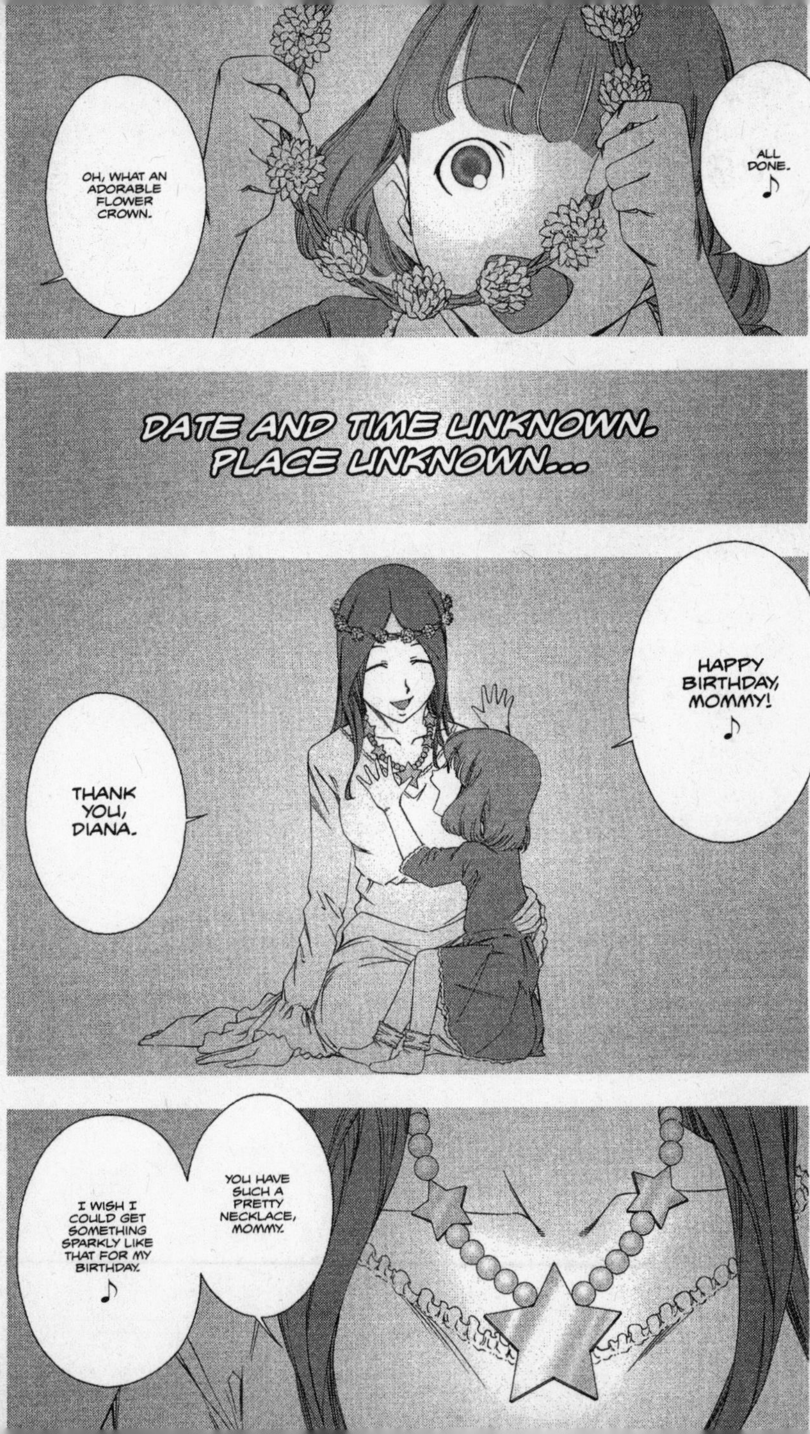
ALL DONE. ♪
OH, WHAT AN ADORABLE FLOWER CROWN.
DATE AND TIME UNKNOWN. PLACE UNKNOWN...
HAPPY BIRTHDAY, MOMMY! ♪
THANK YOU, DIANA.
YOU HAVE SUCH A PRETTY NECKLACE, MOMMY.
I WISH I COULD GET SOMETHING SPARKLY LIKE THAT FOR MY BIRTHDAY. ♪

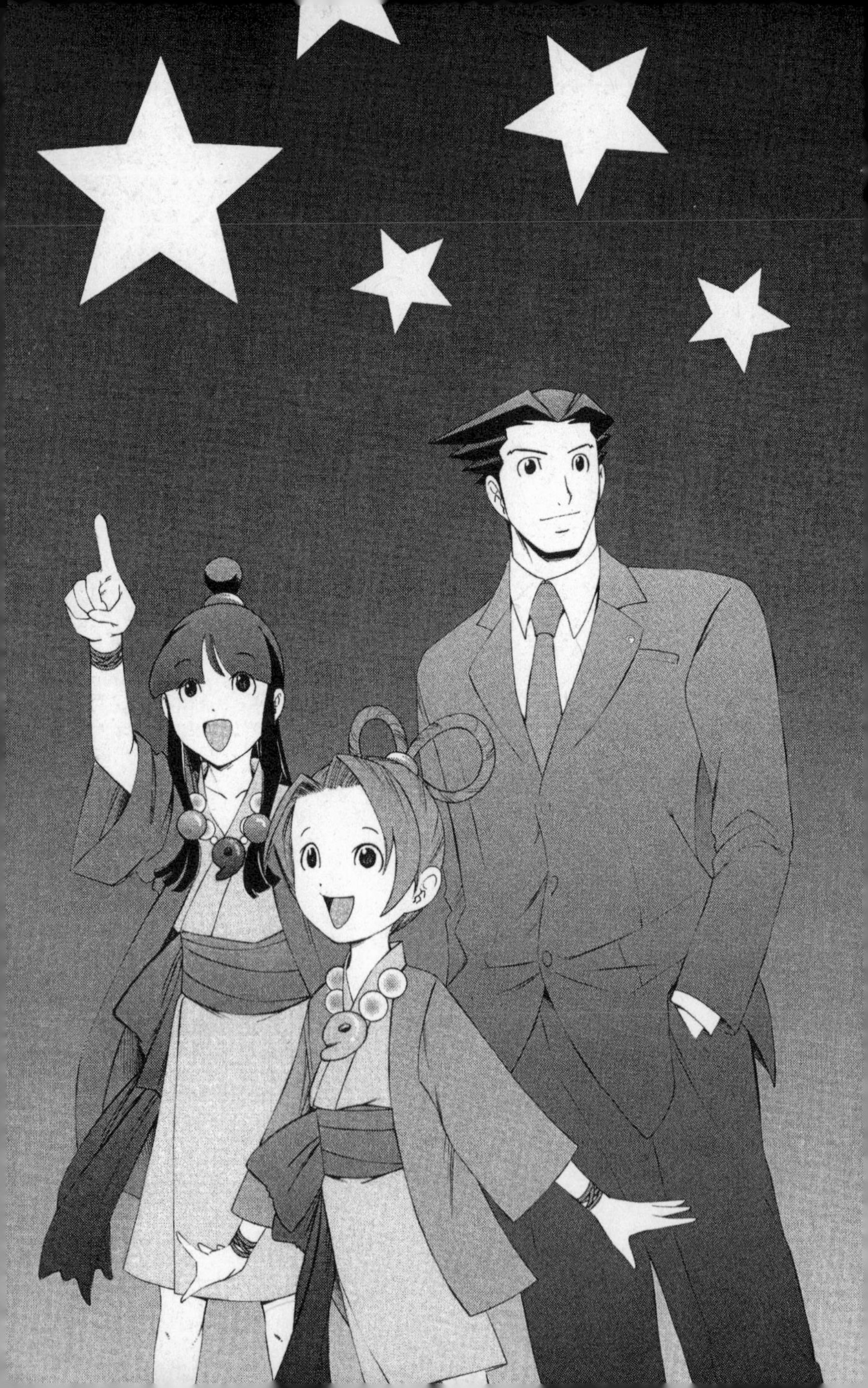

CHAPTER 10

TURNABOUT FROM HEAVEN

(PART ONE)

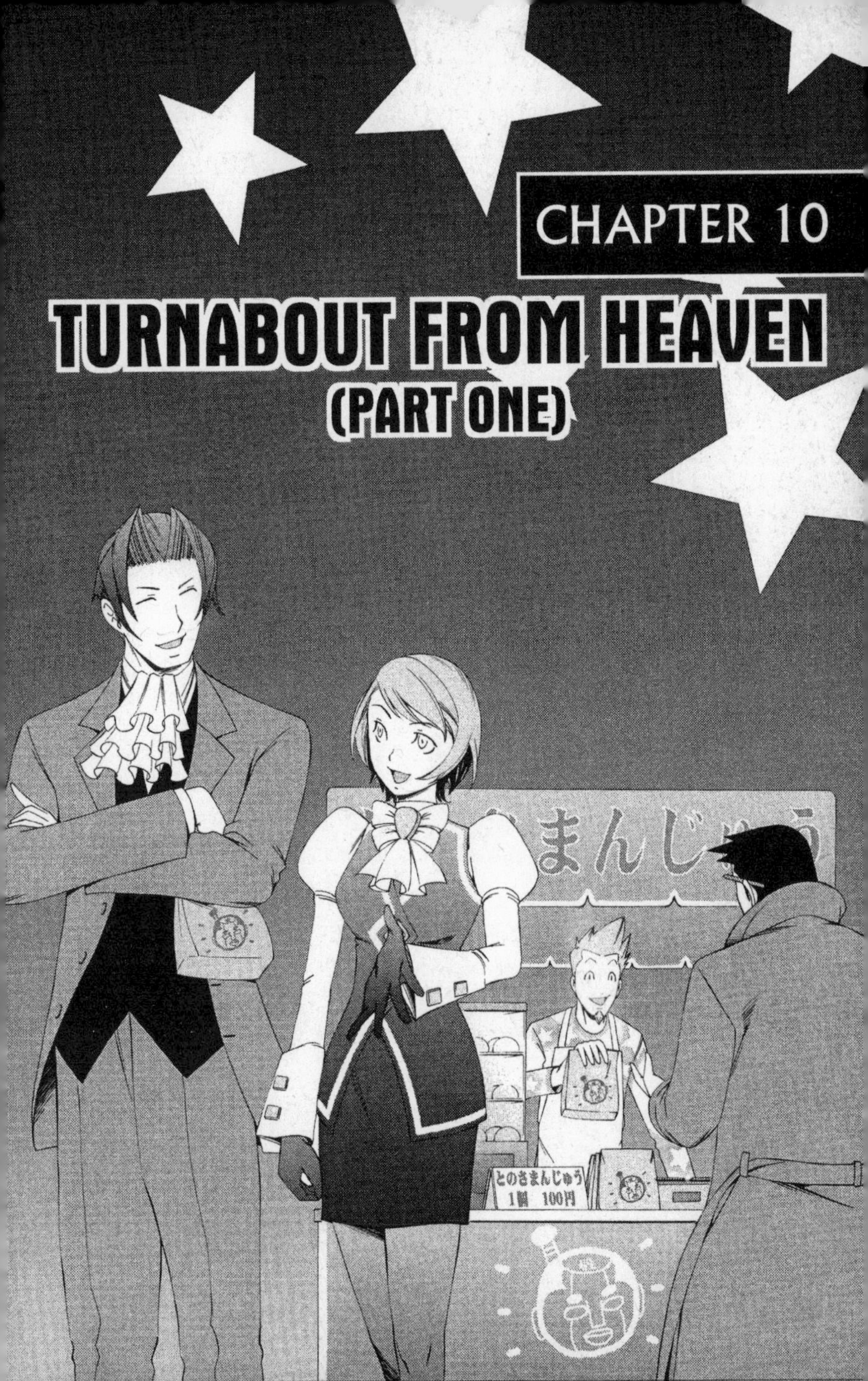
とのさまんじゅう
1個　100円

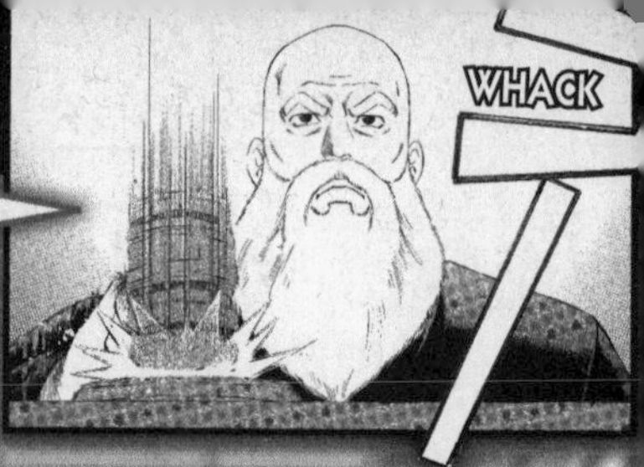
WHACK

THE JUDGE

THE COURT JUDGE, WHO LOOKS DIGNIFIED, BUT ACTUALLY IS NOT. HE HAS A HABIT OF GULLIBLY SWALLOWING EVERY SCENARIO FED TO HIM BY PHOENIX OR EDGEWORTH. HIS NAME IS UNKNOWN.

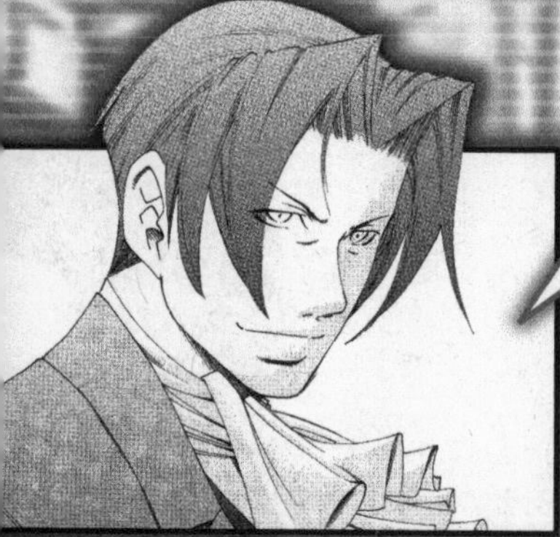

MILES EDGEWORTH

PHOENIX'S GREATES RIVAL. HE HAS BEEN KNOWN AS A GENIUS PROSECUTOR EVER SINCE HE STARTED OUT IN THE PROFESSION. IN FACT, HE AND PHOENIX KNEW EACH OTHER AS CHILDREN, AND WERE THE BEST OF FRIENDS, BOUND TOGETHER BY TRUST.

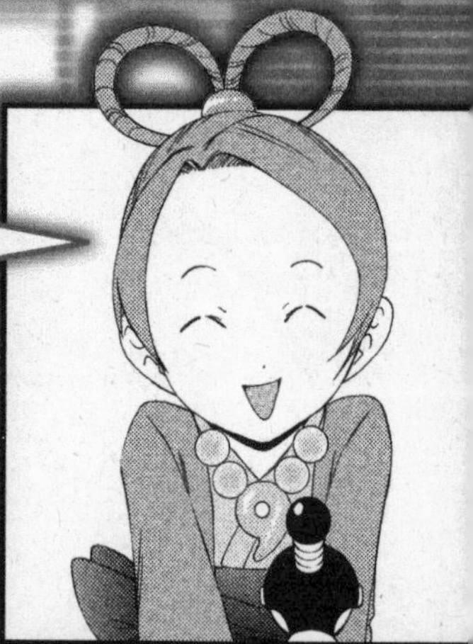

PEARL FEY

MAYA'S COUSIN. THOUGH STILL JUST A CHILD, SHE GIVES PHOENIX TROUBLE WITH HER PRECOCIOUS IDEAS. THE FEYS COME FROM A LONG LINE OF SPIRIT MEDIUMS, AND PEARL'S SPIRITUAL POWERS SURPASS THOSE OF MAYA'S. NICKNAMED PEARLS AND PEARLY.

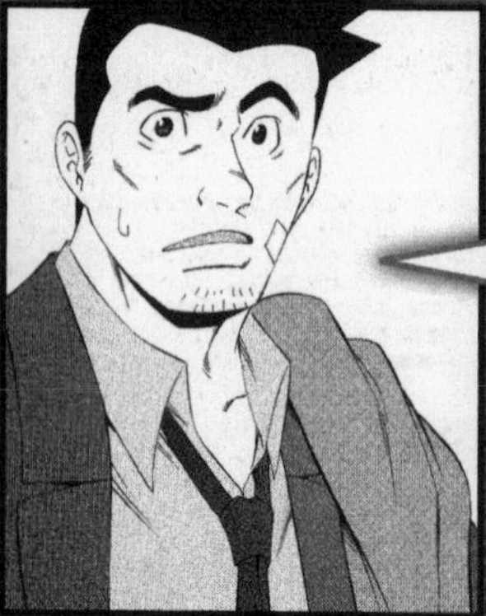

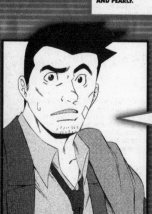

DICK GUMSHOE

A DETECTIVE IN CHARGE OF MURDER INVESTIGATIONS. HE'S A FEW CARDS SHY OF A DECK, AND SOMETIMES MISSES IMPORTANT CLUES. EVERY TIME HE DOES, HE GETS A PAYCUT, SO HIS SALARY IS VERY LOW.

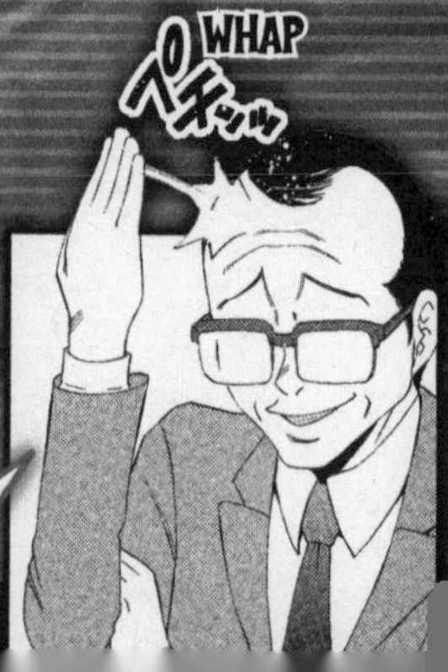
WHAP

WINSTON PAYNE

A VETERAN PROSECUTOR, BUT HE LACKS PRESENCE, AND IS COMPLETELY UNRELIABLE. STRESS HAS CAUSED HIS HAIRLINE TO RECEDE. IN A WORD, HE'S DULL.

CHARACTER INTRODUCTIONS

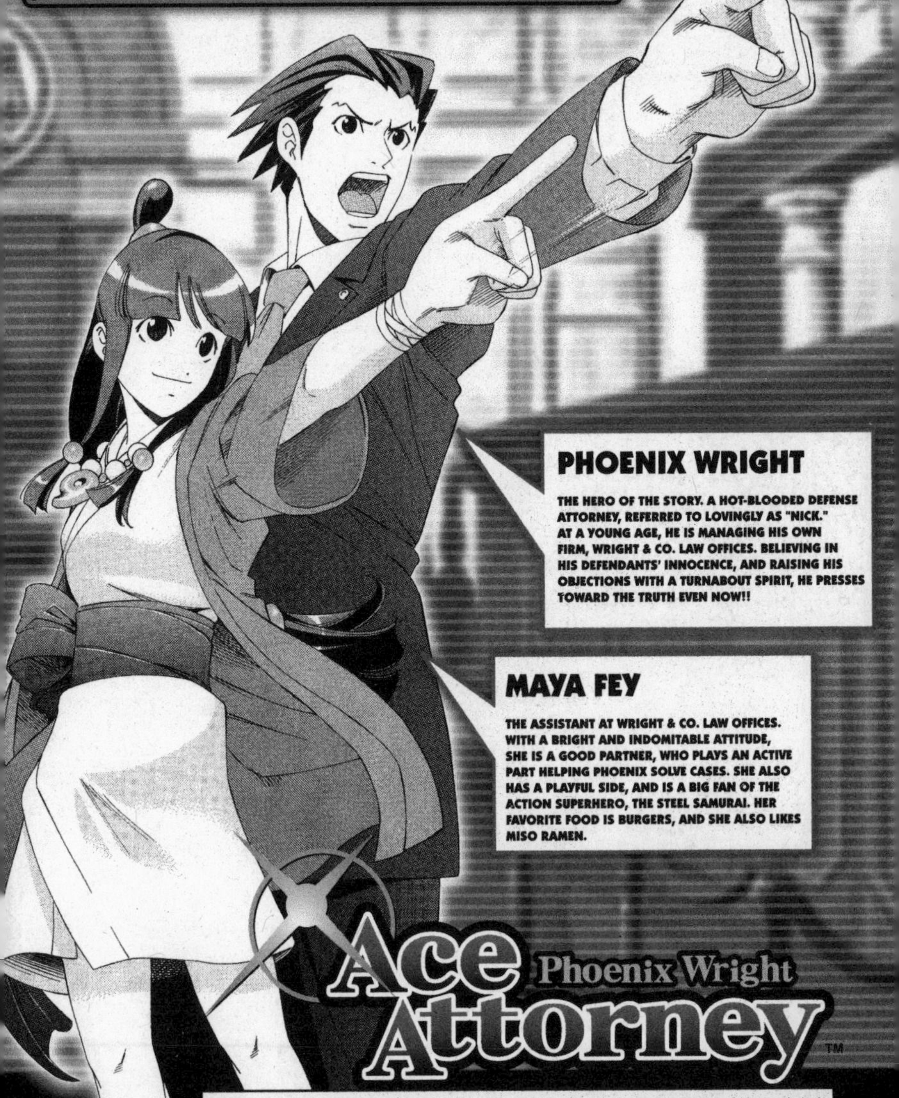
Phoenix Wright
Ace Attorney™

PHOENIX WRIGHT

THE HERO OF THE STORY. A HOT-BLOODED DEFENSE ATTORNEY, REFERRED TO LOVINGLY AS "NICK." AT A YOUNG AGE, HE IS MANAGING HIS OWN FIRM, WRIGHT & CO. LAW OFFICES. BELIEVING IN HIS DEFENDANTS' INNOCENCE, AND RAISING HIS OBJECTIONS WITH A TURNABOUT SPIRIT, HE PRESSES TOWARD THE TRUTH EVEN NOW!!

MAYA FEY

THE ASSISTANT AT WRIGHT & CO. LAW OFFICES. WITH A BRIGHT AND INDOMITABLE ATTITUDE, SHE IS A GOOD PARTNER, WHO PLAYS AN ACTIVE PART HELPING PHOENIX SOLVE CASES. SHE ALSO HAS A PLAYFUL SIDE, AND IS A BIG FAN OF THE ACTION SUPERHERO, THE STEEL SAMURAI. HER FAVORITE FOOD IS BURGERS, AND SHE ALSO LIKES MISO RAMEN.

The characters, laws and court procedures in this work are all fiction. Accordingly, the court system of this story is set in the near future, where the demand for expedited trials creates a different system than that of present-day.

Phoenix Wright Ace Attorney™

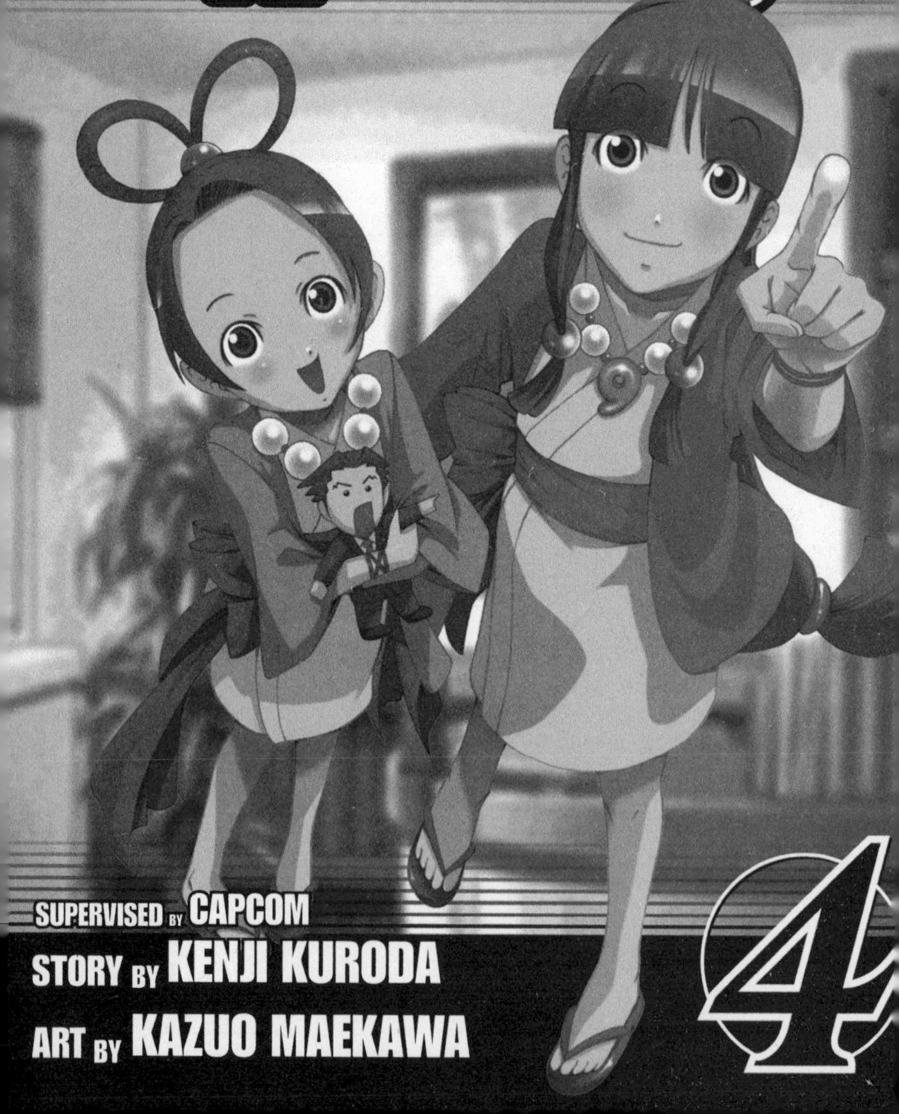

SUPERVISED BY CAPCOM

STORY BY KENJI KURODA

ART BY KAZUO MAEKAWA

4